T0330048

Bad Medicine

Bad Medicine

THE PRESCRIPTION DRUG INDUSTRY IN THE THIRD WORLD

Milton Silverman
Mia Lydecker
Philip R. Lee

STANFORD UNIVERSITY PRESS

STANFORD, CALIFORNIA 1992

Stanford University Press
Stanford, California
© 1992 by the Board of Trustees of the
Leland Stanford Junior University
Printed in the United States of America

CIP data appear at the end of the book

CONTENTS

The Problems at Hand, 235   The Matter of Quality As-
surance, 236   Essential Drugs Lists: Some Progress, 237
The Matter of Bribery, 238   Domestic Drug Industries:
Some Hard Choices, 240   External Vigilance, Unending
Consultation, 242

PREFACE

The pharmaceutical industry has long and vehemently insisted that it had the willingness, the dedication, and the ability to police itself—not necessarily to do a perfect job of policing, but to do an adequate one—to see that the majority of the public would not be unnecessarily harmed or ripped off. This was wishful thinking. Virtually no industry or professional group has ever adequately policed itself—not the Knights of the Round Table, not the medical or the legal profession, not the clergy, neither academicians nor scientists, and certainly not the media.

Where the more flagrant abuses have been exposed and corrected, major credit must probably be divided among the media that broadly publicized the situation, consumerists who applied pressure, governmental workers who took often unpopular therapeutic actions, and members of the industry itself who had the courage to face up to their social responsibilities.

Specifically, a limited number of drug companies, for a variety of reasons, have taken such responsibilities quite seriously. The record will show that a few companies—notably Syntex, Merck Sharp & Dohme, Upjohn, and SmithKline in the United States and, in recent years, Ciba-Geigy in Switzerland—have only rarely been found guilty of making unsubstantiated claims or of glossing over the hazards of their products. The most memorable explanation came from a Syntex official who once confided to us, "We have found that we can tell the truth and still make a decent profit."

As the following pages will reveal, in their promotion of drug products in developing countries, the worst offenders were originally the big multinational companies based in the United States, Europe, and, more recently, Japan. By the end of the 1980s, however, the situation had changed remarkably. More and more, it was the multinationals which had discovered that they could tell the truth and still make money. Instead, it was the local or domestic firms—many with enormous political power—that were lying to, defrauding, and endangering the lives of their fellow citizens. For many in the Third World, this was a distressing discovery. The enemy was not some faceless anonymity sitting in a board room in far-off New York or Zurich or London or Frankfurt. It was their neighbor who lived down the street.

Most of this report is devoted to areas of drug use and the pharmaceutical business which have long held our attention: the patients in the Third World and the illnesses that afflict them, the so-called prescription drugs promoted to control those illnesses, the various categories of drug companies, the constantly renewed battle against usually inexpensive generic products (spiced this time by disclosures of fraud and bribery in the U.S. Food and Drug Administration), the actions of consumerist groups, and the key role of government.

In addition, we describe a remarkable attempt in Bangladesh, one of the poorest of all the developing countries, to develop a high-quality local drug industry. We examine what has until now been a largely unexplored area, the rise in the production and use of fraudulent drugs and the role of the drug swindlers. And, as case histories, we report on three extremely important drug products or groups— the dipyrones (for control of pain and fever), high-dosage estrogen-progesterone hormone products (for use in pregnancy tests), and clioquinol or Enterovioform (for treatment of diarrhea)—all of which were or still are centers of worldwide, heated controversy.

Much of Chapter 8, "The Drug Swindlers," was taken from Silverman, Lydecker, and Lee, "The Drug Swindlers," *Int. J. Health Serv.* 20:561–72 (1990). Much of Chapter 11, "Consumer Power: The Hansson/Ciba-Geigy Connection," was taken from Silverman, M., "The Hansson/Ciba-Geigy Connection," in Hansson, O., *Inside Ciba-Geigy* (Penang, Malaysia: International Organization of Consumers Unions, 1989), pp. 194–227.

In the more than three years that were invested in this study, a small army of people played vital roles. These individuals—old friends and new—came from consumer organizations, drug companies, governmental regulatory agencies, universities and medical schools, clinics and hospitals both in big cities and in the boondocks, and research institutes. Many were former colleagues from press and radio and television, which gave us particular pleasure. Some were former students. They gave us help, support, and cooperation at interviews, medical meetings, and press conferences. They did this, we hope, not out of friendship or affection but because they, too, wanted the truth to be reported. We gratefully call the roll, as it were, country by country.

Australia: Peter Mansfield. Bangladesh: Zafrullah Chowdhury and S. H. Kabir. Brazil: Bruno Carlos de Almeida, José Augusto Cabral de Barros, Augustinho Betarello, Elizaldo Luiz Carlini, Maria des Graças Cavalcanti, Lilian Ciola, Marcio Falci, Emerson Gonzales, Friedrich Leute, Luiz Gonçalves Paulo, Leonardo Peach, Valdair Pinto, Nelson Proença, Alberto Rahde, and Antonio Carlos Zanini. Denmark: M. N. Graham and Elisabet Dukes and Inge Lunde. Egypt: Ahmed Aly Abul-Enein, Peter and Betty Dawson, Nabil Guirguis, Faisal K. Hamed, Mahmoud Hussein, Sameh Zaki Nashed, Hassanein Rifat, A. M. Sallam, and Wasif I. Wasif.

Germany: Wolfgang Bernhardt, Hans-Günther Grigoleit, and Hassan Nour-Eldin. India: Mira Shiva. Indonesia: Iwan Darmansjah, Jan Krieger, Kartono Mohamad, Eric Stadelmann, and Frans Tshai. Jamaica: Grace Allen, R. F. Kinkead, Doreen Kirkaldy, and Berwyn Miller. Japan: Hirokuni Beppu, Hiroshi and Miwako Izumi, Masami Saito, and Etsuro Totsuka. Kenya: Andrew Bulloch, Neil Butler, Colin and Margaret Forbes, Karuga Koinanga, Dorothy Kweyu-Munyakho, George Masafu, Stanley Mokaya, George Nakitare, Roy Shaffer, Peter Wanner, and Christopher Wood.

Malaysia: Kumariah Balasubramaniam, Anwar Fazal, Mohammed Idris, and Martin Khor Kok Peng. Mexico: Sylvestre Frenk, Mario Lieberman, Arturo and Lila Lomeli, Jorge Martinez, Jorge Medina, Miguel Medina, Jorge Olarte, George Rosenkrantz, Emilio Rosenstein, and Enrique Segovia. The Netherlands: Pieter van Keep. Nigeria: Segun Bamgbose, Evans Chidomere, Hammed Ayodele Ibrahim, and Ayotele Tella. Pakistan: Syed Rizwanuddin Ahmad. The Philippines: Pat Hizon, Jesus Lammatao, and Michael Tan. Senegal: Christian Chatelard, Mounirou Ciss, Fadel Diadhiolu, Samba Diallo, Adrien Diop, Lamine Diop, Issa Diop, Papa Nalla Fall, Adrien Lo, Issa Lo, and Mamadou N'Diaye. Singapore: Matthew Gwee, Gerard Hazelzet, and Lip-Chai Seet.

Switzerland: Paul Clerc, René Frey, Penny Grawel, Peter Heer, Erica Heidrich-Feldmann, André Hilfiker, Paul Hummel, Laurent Kapps, Alex Krauer, Klaus Leisinger, Henner Lappe, Gunter Lewandowski, Dana Miller, Horst Röthing, Fritz Schneiter, David Taylor, Klaus von

Grebmer, Louis von Planta, Walter von Wartburg, Allan Walker, and Walter Wenger. Thailand: Peter Kunstadter, Melvyn Leddy, Phornvit Phacharintanakul, Judith Richter, and Suphak Saphakkul. Trinidad: Edward Commissiong and Godfrey and Shirley Raj-Kumar. Turkey: Erdal and Sema (and Deniz) Akalin, Sükram Gecgil, Rifat Öktem, Tansel Tokcan, and Alev Sonat. Venezuela: Raul Fernandez Barbosa, Raul Cardona, Jacinto Convit, Manuel Guzman, Siegbert and Elly Holz, Maria del Pilar Pla, Renata Revel-Chion, Honorio Silva, and Karl von Daniken.

The United States: Alan Alemian, Alexander Bearn, Clyde Behney, Raymond Bonner, Gwynn and the late Albert Bowers, Peter Carpenter, William Corr, Susan Crowley, Paul Freiman, John Fried, Michael Hodin, Leon Jacobs, the late Jay Kingham, Larry Miike, Duffy Miller, Gerald Mossinghoff, Vicente Navarro, Nancy Noe, Mark Novitch, Esther Peterson, Linda Pfeiffer, Regina Rowan, James and Lee Russo, Natalie Shanks, Aracelia Vila, Sidney Wolfe, Judith Youngman, and Charles Ziegler. At the Palo Alto Medical Foundation: Allen Cooper, Barbara Finley, and Kathy O'Hearn. And our colleagues at the University of California, San Francisco: Eunice Chee, Ernestine Florence, Jere Goyan, Peter Lurie, and Dennis Seely. Our particular thanks go to Paula Fujiwara, whose assistance in compiling the drug labeling charts was incalculable.

The prolonged and costly travel required for this project would not have been possible without the generous support of many groups and individuals. To them, we express our gratitude: Alza Corporation, Ciba-Geigy Ltd., the Ford Foundation, Genentech, Inc., Hoechst AG (Aktiengesellschaft), Anwar Fazal of the International Organization of Consumers Unions, Merck Sharp & Dohme, Hoffmann–La Roche & Co., the Janss Foundation, the KICADIS Foundation (Kyoto International Conference Against Drug-Induced Sufferings), the Max and Anna Levinson Foundation, the Samuel Rubin Foundation, Sandoz Corporation, SmithKline Beecham, Syntex Corporation, the University of California School of Medicine in San Francisco, Upjohn Company, and Warner-Lambert Co. None of the foregoing asked for—or received—any right to censor our report. Some were invited to review the manuscript before publication but only to point out any errors in fact.

All of the funds provided for our research, made available by means of grants to the Palo Alto Medical Foundation, were used for travel and normal office expenses. Not one penny went to any of the authors in the form of salary, consultant fee, or any other compensation.

Finally, to our various children and grandchildren whose unfailing support and affection during some trying years was truly of life-and-death importance to us, we offer all our love.

Menlo Park and San Francisco   Milton Silverman
June 1991   Mia Lydecker
                                                    Philip R. Lee

A NOTE ABOUT THE AUTHORS

*M*ilton Silverman, Ph.D., born in San Francisco in 1910, was trained in biochemistry and pharmacology at Stanford University and the University of California School of Medicine.

He began his career as a newspaperman on the Palo Alto *Times* and the Monterey *Peninsula Herald* in California. From 1934 to 1959, he won national recognition as the science editor of the San Francisco *Chronicle* and as a science writer for the *Saturday Evening Post, Collier's, Reader's Digest,* and other magazines.

During this period, he also served from 1937 to 1939 as director of the Hall of Science at the San Francisco World's Fair. In 1941 and 1942, he was selected by the Western Defense Command to prepare the objective report on the exclusion of Japanese aliens and Japanese-American citizens from strategic areas of the West Coast. During most of World War II, he worked on submarine warfare research for the U.S. Navy.

He is the author of *Magic in a Bottle,* a history of drug discovery (which, translated into Spanish as *Drogas Mágicas,* played an unexpectedly strategic role in this present book), and is also author, coauthor, or editor of more than twenty other books. He has served as a foreign correspondent in Mexico, South America, Western Europe, India, Japan, mainland China, and the South Pacific. He is a past president of the National Association of Science Writers and a winner of the Lasker Award for distinguished medical reporting.

His own research has included studies on synthetic sugars, anesthetics, the pharmacology of alcoholic beverages, and cultural drinking patterns in Italy, Brazil, France, Sweden, and the United States. From 1959 to 1965, he was director of medical research for the Wine Advisory Board of the California State Department of Agriculture.

For the last twenty-five years, he has been deeply involved in research on the discovery, production, promotion, pricing, prescribing, dispensing, and use and misuse of prescription drugs. He has acted as a consultant to the U.S. Public Health Service, the Food and Drug Administration, the National Institute of Mental Health, the Social Security Administration, and the National Commission on Arthritis.

From 1966 to 1969, he served as a special assistant to Dr. Lee in Washington, D.C., and from 1969 to 1972 at the University of California, San Francisco (UCSF). Since then he has been a senior lecturer and research pharmacologist at UCSF's School of Medicine and a lecturer at the Stanford University School of Medicine.

Mia Lydecker (Mia Silverman), born in 1926 in The Hague, Holland, has been principal editor and research associate in the Institute of Health Policy Studies at UCSF. A graduate of Louvain University in Belgium in 1944, she received her licentiate at the University of Utrecht in The Netherlands in 1945 and qualified for her Master's degree, in literature and languages, at the Sorbonne in France in 1947. She studied particularly Gothic, early and middle English, and Anglo-Saxon.

She began her career as a research associate with Dr. Silverman in 1962. Beginning with investigations of cultural drinking patterns, she has worked with him during the past years in studying drug promotion and national drug insurance programs in Japan, Australia, New Zealand, Canada, nearly a dozen countries in Europe, half a dozen in Central and South America, six in Africa, and eight in Southeast Asia.

Philip R. Lee, M.D., a member of a noted California medical family, was born in San Francisco in 1924. He was trained at Stanford University, the Massachusetts Memorial Hospital, the New York University–Bellevue Medical Center, and the Mayo Clinic. He joined the staff of the Palo Alto Medical Clinic in 1956, working primarily as a family physician. From 1963 to 1965, he was director of health services in the U.S. Agency for International Development, getting his first exposure to the health needs of Third World nations, the delivery—or nondelivery—of care, and the practice of medicine in developing countries.

From 1965 to 1969, he was the Assistant Secretary for Health and Scientific Affairs in what was then the U.S. Department of Health, Education, and Welfare (now Health and Human Services). During this period, he played a major role in the implementation of Medicare, Medicaid, and other new major federal health programs.

Dr. Lee served as chancellor of the University of California at San

Francisco (UCSF) from 1969 to 1972, and since 1969 has been professor of social medicine and director of UCSF's Institute of Health Policy Studies.

He has been a member of the board of directors of numerous foundations and organizations, including the Carnegie Corporation, the Mayo Foundation, the American Foundation for AIDS Research, and the World Institute on Disability. He is a member of the Institute of Medicine and the National Academy of Sciences and a consultant to many international, federal, state, and local health agencies and legislative committees. He has served as president of the San Francisco Health Commission and currently chairs the Physician Payment Review Commission for the U.S. Congress.

His own research studies have involved such fields as the rehabilitation of cardiovascular and rheumatic patients, population control, health manpower, health care for the elderly, bioethics, health promotion and disease prevention, AIDS research and treatment policies, physician payment reform, drug regulatory policies, and government health policies in general. He has studied health care in the Soviet Union, the People's Republic of China, and many Third World countries.

During their years in Washington, Dr. Lee served as chairman and Dr. Silverman as executive secretary and staff director of the HEW Task Force on Prescription Drugs. Ms. Lydecker acted as a consultant to the Task Force. The reports of this group, published in 1968 and 1969, led to significant changes in federal drug policies and have had a continuing effect in many foreign countries. Among the most influential books published by the Silverman-Lee-Lydecker team after their return to California have been *Pills, Profits, and Politics* (1974), *The Drugging of the Americas* (1976), *Drug Coverage Under National Health Insurance* (1977), *Pills and the Public Purse* (1981), and *Prescriptions for Death: The Drugging of the Third World* (1982).

From the outset, the HEW Task Force might have been dismissed as simply one more governmental group that would investigate, write a report, perhaps testify briefly before the Congress, and then be totally forgotten. This one turned out to be different. When its first reports were issued, most top American drug experts had one verdict: From now on, the drug industry in this country will never be the same.

Bad Medicine

Chapter 1

THE PATIENTS: HEALTH FOR ALL BY—*WHEN?*

*H*alfdan Mahler served as director-general of the World Health Organization (WHO) from 1972 to 1987. In 1978 a new concept appeared and quickly electrified that distinguished group: Health for all by the year 2000. This idea was formally endorsed by all 158 WHO member nations at the Alma-Ata conference on primary health in 1981. For the remainder of his term, Mahler enthusiastically supported it.[1] Health for all by the year 2000 was no idle slogan, he declared. It apparently included not only medical care but also access to good food and clean water, and the overall social and economic development of the community. But its precise meaning was not clear. Mahler told the International Federation of Pharmaceutical Manufacturers Associations in 1982:

It does *not* mean that in the year 2000, doctors and nurses will provide medical care to everybody in the world for all their existing ailments, nor does it mean that in the year 2000, nobody will be sick or disabled. But it *does* mean that there will be an even distribution among the population of whatever health resources are available. And it *does* mean that people will use much better approaches than they do now for preventing disease and alleviating unavoidable illness and disability, and that there will be better ways of growing up, growing old, and dying gracefully. And it *does* mean that health begins at home and at the work place, because it is there, where people live and work, that health is made or broken. And it *does* mean that essential health care will be accessible to all individuals and families in an acceptable and affordable way and with their full participation.[2]

Nor was it evident whether the health-by-2000 idea was a goal with a reasonable chance of being reached by the year 2000, or whether it was simply a goal to reach sometime in the distant future.

One of the first serious doubts about health-by-2000 was expressed publicly in 1984 by one whose credentials as a strong consumerist advocate could scarcely be questioned—Charles Medawar, head of Social Audit in London and an active leader of Health Action International (HAI). In a monograph published by the International Organization of Consumers Unions, Medawar said, "'Health for all by the year 2000' is advertised as a future reality, although there is little or no rational basis for doing so."[3] He cited the authoritative 1981 Brandt Commission report on future international development, which described appalling suffering and injustice as being obvious now and warned of worse to come. The commission stated: "There is a real danger that in the year 2000, a large part of the world's population will still be living in poverty. The world may become overpopulated and will certainly be overurbanized. Mass starvation and the dangers of destruction may be growing steadily—if a major war has not already shaken the foundations of what we call world civilization."[4] The Brandt Report suggested that by the year 2000 there will still be 600 million absolute poor in the Third World. Recent projections are equally gloomy, including the warning that the number of people living in absolute poverty by the year 2000 might well number between 800 million and 1 billion.

"There is a lot to be said for optimism," Medawar noted. "But optimism in overdose is dangerous, especially in a crisis, in which the chances of success or survival are honestly low." There is the risk that if health for all has *not* been achieved by the year 2000, many people may not only be disappointed but also feel that the whole campaign had been a fraud and a hoax.

Later, a commentator observed that "some of the minimum standards and principles of drug use . . . will need to be adopted internationally—'forthwith and by acclamation'—if Health for All by the Year 2000 is not to appear a sham."[5] More recently, the Commission on Health Research for Development said, "As the close of this century approaches, the universal goal of 'Health for All by the Year 2000' is quietly slipping away."[6]

The substantial progress that had been achieved in improving world health during the 1950s, 1960s, and 1970s had slowed in many countries in the 1980s, and health status had actually declined in some. Data from such sources as WHO, UNICEF, and the World Bank, and reports from individual nations, all give a picture of gross inequities in access to essential care in most developing nations, in levels of social and economic development, and in health status.

Disaster in the 1980s

For most people of the Third World, the decade of the 1980s had been largely a catastrophe. "The decade itself has been a disaster for the world's poor people," claimed Larry Minear, of Church World Service. "Countless incidents of hunger and malnutrition, social injustice, population displacement, human rights abuses, and battlefield barbarities all have afflicted the world. . . . Poverty has risen. Excluding the People's Republic of China, the number of people with inadequate diets increased from 650 million to 730 during the 1970s—and since 1980, matters have turned from bad to worse. . . . A review of humanitarian interests during the Reagan years reveals sizeable damage for future custodians to repair."[7]

Particularly worrisome were the rising populations in developing countries and the reduced harvests. Lester Brown and his colleagues at the Worldwatch Institute reported in 1989 that, partly as a result of soil erosion, the expansion of deserts, the salting of irrigated lands, the scarcity of new cropland and fresh water, and the global warming trend, the world has now far more hungry people than it had when the 1980s began. They wrote:

A dramatic 2.6-fold increase in grain production between 1950 and 1984 raised per capita consumption by about 40 percent. But since then, growth has stopped. In each of the past two years, world grain production has fallen sharply, marking the first steep back-to-back annual declines on record. . . . In Africa, the number of "food insecure" people—defined by the World Bank as those not having enough food for normal health and physical activity—now totals more than 100 million. Some 14.7 million Ethiopians, one-third of the country's population, are undernourished. Nigeria is close behind, with 13.7 million undernourished people. In Chad, Mozambique, Somalia, and Uganda, 40 percent or more of the population is suffering from chronic food insecurity.[8]

Many developing nations had insufficient funds to cover their health needs but spent lavishly to create dams, hydroelectric plants, docks, meeting halls, presidential palaces, sports arenas, and similar big-ticket showcase items, and even completely new and ostentatious capital cities. "The government of the Philippines, in the last year of the Marcos regime," reported James Grant, executive director of UNICEF, "spent approximately five times as much on four sophisticated hospitals as on primary health care services for the whole nation."[9]

According to HAI, up to 2 billion people still have no regular access to drugs.[10] Of the total drug supply available worldwide, about 86 percent goes to the industrialized nations, with 25 percent of the world's people, whereas the Third World, with 75 percent of the population, consumes only 14 percent.[11] In Africa, an effort to improve the distribution of essential drugs was launched by UNICEF as the "Bamako Initiative."[12] Through this program, drugs are to be sold at two to three times their acquisition cost, with the proceeds used for the procurement of more drugs for the community and the support of local primary health care centers and maternal and child health services. But, consumerists have charged, the Bamako approach will do little to help the poor.

Expenditures for health in the Third World are appallingly low. In 1990 WHO officials estimated that about a half a billion people were suffering from such diseases as malaria, sleeping sickness, river blindness, and leprosy. The WHO report said that most victims of tropical diseases live in countries with average per capita incomes of less than $400 a year, and where governments spend an average of just $4 per year per person for health care.[13] About 1.5 billion in the Third World are still unable to get clean water. It was estimated that an expenditure of $4.5 to $7.5 billion each year would be necessary to provide safe water to everyone by the year 2000, but only $1.5 billion was being invested annually.[14]

Yet many if not most Third World countries were continuing to pour money into military expenditures. In Kenya, a health expert noted in 1983 that the cost of one military tank to a developing country could cover the cost of more than 2,000 protected wells with pumps. The cost of training one air force pilot could cover that of training 500 community workers able to treat all the common complaints. The cost of training, equipping, and maintaining a full-time soldier would build and maintain a dispensary, provide enough drugs, and pay the workers. The cost of a modern warplane would be sufficient to set up 40,000 village pharmacies with a range of basic medicines. A peace research group in Sweden estimated that in 1986 all public-sector development support was about $37 billion, while military expenditures of developing countries were between $60 and $80 billion. Military expenditures made in a single week during the 1980s would be sufficient to eradicate leprosy in the Third World.[15]

Things were not equally horrendous throughout the Third World. For example, whereas in southern and Southeast Asia, Bangladesh and Nepal ranked among the poorest nations in the world, other countries were clearly making progress. Four of these—South Korea, Taiwan, and notably Singapore and Hong Kong—had virtually lost their Third World status and were listed as NICs, or "newly industrializing countries." In Latin America, some progress was evident. In Africa the problems were most severe and steadily worsening. According to the World Bank, 60 percent of the people in Africa were living in poverty. By 1995, it was estimated, per capita income would continue to decline and as many as 80 percent of the people would be living in poverty.[16]

"People generally have more food to eat than they did in the early 1960s," said Jessica Tuchman Mathews, of the World Resources Institute. "Population growth is subsiding in many regions. Similar strides have been made in combating disease and illiteracy, and in providing wider economic opportunities. But, in this global move toward economic and social well-being, there is one tragic gap. Africa is odd man out." She added:

By almost any measure, Africans have less today than they did 20 years ago, as population growth continues to overtake hard-won advances in food production and economic growth. Africa, once an exporter of food, now leads the world in reliance on food imports. Its farms and fields turn barren through overuse, and millions of its people are malnourished or starving. . . . According to the UN Food and Agriculture Organization, the more than $1 billion spent on rangeland management over the past 15 years has been "largely wasted" on ill-founded projects based more on agricultural theories learned in developed countries than on the realities of the African environment.[17]

Not all of Africa's problems with inadequate food supplies can be blamed on soil problems, global warming, or other vagaries of the environment. Some must be attributed to the desperate efforts of political leaders to maintain their popularity and their political strength in the cities by freezing food prices and keeping these so low that the farmers had few incentives to grow crops.[18]

Especially disconcerting is the fact that, since the late 1950s, 1960s,

and 1970s, when most of the African countries won their independence, they have less freedom and less independence than when they
were colonies, and they have been subjected to more cruelty, torture,
and mass slayings. Bishop Desmond Tutu of South Africa, winner of
the Nobel prize for peace and a staunch enemy of apartheid, observed:
"It is sad that South Africa is noted for its vicious violation of human
rights. But it is also very sad to note that in many black African
countries today, there is less freedom than there was during that much-
maligned colonial period."[19]

An Excess of Illness

Perhaps more than any other area in the world, Africa appears to be
most threatened by a spread of Acquired Immune Deficiency Syndrome (AIDS) and other sexually transmitted infections. But serious
though the AIDS menace to world health may be, Andrew Chetley has
calculated that the total number of people who have died from AIDS
(as of 1989) is approximately equal to the number who die every month
from malaria, every week from diarrheal diseases, or every eleven days
from such vaccine-preventable infections as measles, whooping cough,
diphtheria, tetanus, tuberculosis, and polio.[20]

Even without the menace of a continent-wide outbreak of AIDS,
however, Africa is already plagued by more than its share of disease,
now with a rise in the rate of degenerative diseases like heart disease,
hypertension, and cancer—once seemingly monopolized by the industrialized countries—and the wider availability of alcohol, cigarettes,
and hard drugs.

There are several ways to consider the health problems of the Third
World. One can visit a small backcountry health clinic in a developing
country and watch five nurses and a medical officer try to provide for as
many as 300 new patients in one day.[21] Some health workers have
found it possible to cope with such a situation by giving everyone with a
headache pill no. 1, everyone with diarrhea pill no. 2, everyone with
chills and fever pill no. 3, and so on. However, supplies of the pills often
run out, and there is not enough money to buy more until the next
month or the month after, or not enough money to buy parts for the
trucks or vans that must deliver the drugs, or not enough money to buy
gasoline.

One can also look at chilling statistics, notably those that show the causes of death. James Grant, executive director of UNICEF, has put the annual number of deaths from bacterial and viral diarrheal diseases at more than 5 million every year, and the number from pneumonia at more than 3 million. "These diseases," he said, "surpass, as direct causes of mortality, all of the major parasitic diseases, including malaria, schistosomiasis, and amebiasis. The bacterial infections also cause more deaths than do noninfectious diseases, including accidents, heart and cerebrovascular diseases, and malignancies. Of most importance, the infectious diseases exert their greatest impact on young children."[22]

Although there are antibiotics and other anti-infective agents that can control most of these infections, such drugs are seldom used or used properly in Third World countries. Antibiotics obtained as over-the-counter products, commonly without a physician's prescription—or even a physician's advice—are frequently used at too low dosages and for too few days. Some of the antibiotics are "obsolete," no longer acceptable in the industrialized nations where they originated. One serious result of this widespread, inadequate treatment has been the rise of drug-resistant strains of bacteria.[23]

The chances of developing broadly effective vaccines to prevent the various types of diarrhea-causing bacteria and viruses and such tropical infections as schistosomiasis, trypanosomiasis, and filariasis do not appear to be bright. Periodically, workers attempting to develop an effective antimalaria vaccine seem to be on the verge of success, but each time victory eludes them. Biotechnology and the application of recombinant DNA might offer hope, but not soon. Unless and until some useful biological or chemical products are developed, progress will most probably come mainly through the development of safe supplies of food and water and the control of insects or other vectors that spread disease. At the same time, the short-term prospects for the poor in the developing nations give little reason for optimism. Klaus Leisinger of Ciba-Geigy and the University of Basel puts the situation this way:

Experience has shown that it is extremely difficult to obtain the participation of those affected by underdevelopment. A man emaciated and weak with hunger and illness, whose family does not always win the daily struggle for survival and who is the victim of repression and exploitation, becomes fatalistic. His feelings, stamped onto him by the living conditions of urban slums or of impoverished rural areas, are not recorded in opinion polls. The masses of the poor are mostly passive, apathetic, and without a voice. Their influence on political developments is also less, because—whatever the constitution of the particular country may say—real influence is shared amongst fewer people than is the case in industrialized countries.[24]

The conclusion seems inescapable: the chances for "health for all by the year 2000" would appear to be rather dim. But what does seem to be achievable or at least approachable by the year 2000 is something else—better health for millions more.

Chapter 2

DRUG LABELING: HOW SAFE? HOW DEADLY?

$f$or thousands of years, patients or those who looked after their health were accustomed to ward off illness or cure it by the more or less judicious use of medications, either naturally occurring or synthetic. In many instances, the benefit of such products depended on how much was known about their values and hazards, and on how well, how accurately, and how honestly this knowledge was made known. Too often, the essential knowledge was not available, or it was poorly transmitted. The result was much needless pain, crippling, and death.

Much of the promotion of drugs in undeveloped or developing nations during the late 1960s and the 1970s, as we and others have shown, was marked by the use of claims that could not be supported by scientific evidence. Great reliance was placed upon undocumented testimonials purchased or otherwise obtained from physicians, generally including some such phrase as "I could not practice medicine without it" and too often ignoring, glossing over, or concealing the known risk of serious or lethal side effects. In most instances, it seemed, the ostensible villains were multinational pharmaceutical companies, most of these based in the United States or Europe and depicted as profit-hungry monsters, exploiting the peoples of the Third World in order to satisfy their stockholders.

When serious inconsistencies, omissions, or other promotional sins in a developing nation were called to the attention of the company, spokesmen were quick to place the blame on the drug regulatory agency of that country, declaring it was this body that allowed or disallowed such a claimed indication or that required or banned disclosure of such a hazard. At the same time, the situation was further confused by demands from some critics that a drug must be, not *relatively* safe for its intended use, but *absolutely* safe. Since there is no known drug that is both effective and absolutely safe, with no known undesirable side effects, pharmaceutical companies and regulatory bodies alike were faced with an impossible situation.

The Latest Round

The volumes of information about prescribing medication that we use here are widely accepted compendia that serve as the major source of such information for health professionals. These are the books found in doctors' offices. They are often dog-eared, marked with handwritten marginal notes, sometimes torn and spattered, with key sections underlined. Above all, they are *used*.

They include *Physicians' Desk Reference*, or *PDR*, in the United States,[1] and *MIMS* or *MIMS UK* in the United Kingdom.[2] (In the British publication, *MIMS* stands for *Monthly Index of Medical Specialities*.) *PDR* is cited here, not because it represents the final word on any drug but because the information it contains is based on material that has been approved by a governmental agency of considerable standing and is accepted by many if not most physicians and drug experts.

Also included are *MIMS India* for India,[3] *IIMS*, or *Indonesia Index of Medical Specialities*,[4] *TIMS*, or *Thailand Index of Medical Specialities*,[5] *DIMS* for Malaysia/Singapore,[6] *PIMS*, or *Philippine Index of Medical Specialities*,[7] *MIMS Africa* for mostly English-speaking Africa,[8] *Guide Thérapeutique d'Afrique* for Francophone (French-speaking) Africa,[9] *MIMS Middle East* for the Middle Eastern countries,[10] *MIMS Caribbean* for the English-speaking countries in the Caribbean,[11] *Diccionario de Especialidades Farmacéuticas—Edición Mexico* for Mexico,[12] *Diccionario de Especialidades Farmacéuticas—Edición C.A.D.* for Central America and the Dominican Republic,[13] *Diccionario de Especialidades Farmacéuticas— Edición Ecuador* for Ecuador,[14] *Diccionario de Especialidades Farmacéuticas—Edición Colombia* for Colombia,[15] *Diccionario de Especialidades Farmacéuticas—Edición Peru* for Peru,[16] *INTERCON Indice de Especialidades*

Farmacéuticas[17] and *Guía de las Especialidades Farmacéuticas*[18] for Venezuela, *Dicionário de Especialidades Farmacêuticas* for Brazil,[19] and *Egyptian Index of Medical Specialities* for Egypt.[20] In most instances editions for 1987 or 1988, the years in which we conducted most of our field research, were used.

In each of our previous studies we were enabled to increase the amount of material for investigation. In our 1976 report we covered 26 single-drug entities or fixed combinations marketed as 147 products by 23 companies in the United States and Mexico and six Central American countries.[21] Our 1982 report covered 34 drug entities marketed as 515 products by 149 companies in the United States, the United Kingdom, and 26 Third World countries—6 in Latin America, 16 in English-speaking Africa, and 4 in Southeast or southern Asia.[22] Our 1986 report involved 63 drug entities marketed as 1,069 products by 303 companies in the United States, Europe, Japan, and 29 developing nations—7 in Latin America, 16 in English-speaking Africa, and 6 in Southeast or southern Asia.[23]

The present survey covers more than 40 single-drug entities or fixed combinations marketed as about 1,500 products by more than 400 companies in the United States, the United Kingdom, and 74 Third World countries—12 in Latin America, 28 in both English-speaking and French-speaking Africa, 17 in the Middle East, 11 in the Caribbean, and 6 in Southeast or southern Asia.

In the following sections "Africa" refers to the volume used in the so-called Anglophone, or English-speaking, countries: Ethiopia, the Gambia, Ghana, Kenya, Liberia, Malawi, Mauritius, Nigeria, Seychelles, Sierra Leone, Tanzania, Uganda, Zambia, and Zimbabwe.

"Francophone Africa" refers to the publication used in the main French-speaking nations: Benin, Burkina Faso, Cameroon, Congo, Gabon, Guinea, Ivory Coast, Madagascar, Mali, Niger, Senegal, Togo, and Zaire.

"Middle East" refers to the volume used in Bahrain, Cyprus, Egypt, Iran, Iraq, Jordan, Kuwait, Lebanon, Libya, Oman, Qatar, Saudi Arabia, Sudan, Syria, the People's Democratic Republic of Yemen, the United Arab Emirates, and the Yemen Arab Republic. In addition, Egypt has its own drug compendium.

"Central America" includes not only Costa Rica, El Salvador, Guatemala, Honduras, Nicaragua, and Panama but also the Dominican Republic. "Caribbean" includes the Bahamas, Barbados, Bermuda, Belize, Curaçao, Dominican Republic, Guyana, Jamaica, the Netherlands Antilles, Surinam, and Trinidad.

Not all the products analyzed here are necessarily available in each of these countries. Unless otherwise noted, only products with one active ingredient—the "single-drug entity" products—are included, and most are marketed in the oral dosage form and do not require an injection. A statement such as "see company literature" is not considered an acceptable substitute for a specific indication, contraindication, or warning; in the Third World, most physicians—especially those outside the major cities—do not have easy access to company literature. No attention is paid here to statements that a particular agent is contraindicated in patients who may be allergic or hypersensitive to that product or related substances—advice that would be as useless and irritating as a warning that "this drug should not be used by a patient who should not use it."

Some differences in the disclosure of hazards may stem from differences in editorial format and editorial decisions. In many of the *MIMS*-type publications, such as those for Southeast Asia, the products are described by therapeutic or pharmacological class; for example, one section is devoted to drugs for the relief of pain and fever, one to anti-inflammatory agents, one to digestive problems, and so on. With this kind of organization, it is possible to begin each section with what the publisher believes to be appropriate warnings. In the publications for the Latin American countries, which are usually far more informative, and for French-speaking Africa, however, the products are listed in alphabetical order, and warnings by pharmacological class are not readily available. The same problem exists in the United States, where the products are listed in *PDR* by the companies, presented in alphabetical order, that market them. (All material in *PDR* must conform to standards set by the U.S. Food and Drug Administration.) It is not clear which type of presentation is most useful to physicians and other health professionals.

In some instances the wording of the entry, and the final decision on what information is or is not included, is made not by the drug company but by the publisher of the compendium. This matter is becoming increasingly irritating to many of the more socially responsible drug companies. They have complained that their efforts to modify claims for efficacy or to present more complete warnings and contraindications have been blocked by the publishers of the *MIMS* or similar compendia. The publishers have contended that any attempts to modify their presentations represent an unacceptable interference with freedom of the press. (These same publishers rarely note that their continued existence depends mainly on money they receive from the drug companies. The fact that the companies allow the publications to continue these practices means that the drug firms are not blameless.)

In the mid-1980s many powerful pharmaceutical companies—notably those in Switzerland, West Germany, and the United States— were angrily criticizing the attitude of the publishers of the various *MIMS*-type compendia. More and more, there were threats that some major firms might pull out of the established publications and start their own compendia. The publishers of the *MIMS*-type volumes finally decided to meet with industry leaders in an attempt to find a peaceful solution.

In July 1988 the publishers of the *MIMS* compendia for Africa, the Caribbean, and the Middle East agreed that they would not publish any statements on indications, warnings, and contraindications until the companies had approved galley proofs of the material. The agreement was signed by representatives of Swiss and West German firms, but it was understood that it would apply to all drug companies. By early 1990 negotiations were under way with publishers of compendia in Southeast Asia, Mexico, Guatemala, and Venezuela. Examples of this kind of labeling and promotion are presented in the following sections.

Drugs Against Fever and Pain

Dipyrone. In the Southeast Asian and African countries included in this study, essentially all dipyrone products present a suitable warning against serious or fatal agranulocytosis. (See Table 1 in the Appendix.) This warning, however, is usually located a number of pages away. Whether every reader will take the trouble to find that possibly life-and-death information and to read it cannot be predicted.

In French-speaking Africa, the Middle East, the Caribbean, and some Latin American countries, specific warnings are contained in the label itself. Significantly, in Africa, Francophone Africa, and the Caribbean, some of the companies—most of them multinational—now provide an additional warning that advises use for control of pain *only where no other alternative is available.* The view, long expressed by many drug experts, that dipyrone should never be considered the drug of first choice, is evidently winning recognition.

In Mexico, five of thirteen products either carry no such warning against serious blood damage or present only a vague statement. In Venezuela, only two multinational firms (Winthrop and Hoechst) give an adequate warning. Eight others do not. No warnings are given for one of two products listed in Brazil. In Peru, the Hoechst label does warn of possible blood damage.

A similar situation exists for products containing dipyrone plus at least one other active ingredient. (Such products are not included in the table.) In Central America, for example, of the sixteen dipyrone combination products, two products (marketed by Hoechst and Boehringer-Ingelheim) gave adequate warnings about agranulocytosis, six offered vague statements, and eight presented none. (The heated dispute over the promotion and marketing of dipyrone products is examined in more detail in Chapter 5.) Dipyrone products are no longer listed in the United States, India, or Malaysia/Singapore. We have heard no claims by physicians in those countries that they cannot practice medicine on their hundreds of millions of patients without these products.

Aminopyrine. Once one of the most popular drugs for control of fever and pain, aminopyrine has been recognized as so dangerous as a possible cause of cancer that it has virtually disappeared from the world market. No single-entity aminopyrine products were noted in this study, and only a few combinations containing aminopyrine were found.

Phenacetin. Because of the widely recognized risk of causing serious or fatal kidney damage, phenacetin has largely but not completely disappeared. As is indicated in Table 2, six products—all containing phenacetin combined with other ingredients—were noted. Three of these were marketed by multinational companies (Robins, Roche, and Schering AG). Of the six, only the Robins product carried an adequate warning of possible kidney damage.

Benzydamine. A newer agent, benzydamine is marketed in some countries for use as a mouthwash or an ointment and in others to be taken internally. In the latter case, benzydamine products are recommended especially for the control of acute inflammatory conditions of the respiratory and urogenital tracts and blood and lymph vessels, and for the treatment of posttraumatic and postoperative pain and swelling. As is indicated in Table 3, the warnings concerning these products in those Third World nations where they are available appear to be generally meager and incomplete.

Glafenine. Although they are listed in neither the United States nor the United Kingdom, glafenine products are marketed mainly by Hoechst-Roussel and more than a dozen domestic Third World companies, for a variety of types and degrees of pain. In some nations, this is given as the treatment of mild to moderate pain, while in others it is proposed for use in all painful conditions, acute or chronic.

In most of the products promoted, usually under the name Glifanan, by Hoechst or Roussel, physicians are told to avoid use of the drug in patients with heart, liver, or kidney disease—especially if any of these conditions is severe—or who are pregnant, or who may be using alcoholic beverages. Caution is advised where children are concerned. In some cases, there are additional warnings that the drug may also cause abdominal pain, drowsiness, edema, shortness of breath, and serious or severe allergic skin reactions. (See Table 4.)

It has been reported that the possible side effects of glafenine also include life-threatening shock and respiratory failure. This has apparently been known since 1972 and supposedly resulted in removal of the drug from the market in West Germany in 1983. Spokesmen for the company have denied that use of the drug carries any significant risks. In the present study, it was noted that the label of only one product, Roussel's Glifanan, marketed in Venezuela, even mentioned the possibility of shock.

In 1990, MaLAM, an Australia-based watchdog group, questioned the promotion of Hoechst-Roussel's glafenine in the Philippines as having "outstandingly good tolerance" and noted that the drug had been charged with causing many cases of severe allergic reaction, acute kidney failure, and serious or fatal liver injury.

The labels of the glafenine products promoted by domestic companies in the developing countries are relatively and even grossly incomplete. In Indonesia, the Philippines, and Venezuela, nine of these local companies presented no warnings.

Antiarthritis Drugs

Until the years after World War II, about the only drug with substantial value in the treatment of arthritis and the various rheumatic diseases was aspirin, discovered by Bayer in Germany in 1899. A totally unrelated product, phenylbutazone, was introduced in 1949 by the Swiss firm Geigy (later Ciba-Geigy), followed shortly by oxyphenbutazone. In the early 1960s Merck Sharp & Dohme in the United States developed still another unrelated substance, indomethacin.

The two butazones, marketed originally as Butazolidin and Tandearil, and indomethacin, marketed at first as Indocin, were among the early members of the class now known as NSAIDs, or nonsteroidal anti-inflammatory drugs. Soon after their introduction, it became apparent that they could be useful in the management of arthritis, but also that they could cause serious or fatal tissue injury. Because of the attention focused on them by industry critics, notably in Sweden, Great Britain, and the United States, Ciba-Geigy's phenylbutazone and oxyphenbutazone attracted most of the criticism. Both products, it was charged, could depress the bone marrow and prevent the production of essential blood cells and therefore should be abolished.

The Butazones. Much of this attack was fueled by a confidential interoffice Ciba-Geigy memo, dated February 1983, revealing that the company was aware of 1,182 deaths caused by its butazone products. Of these, only a few hundred had been reported to government officials, as was required by law. The memo was leaked to Dr. Olle Hansson, a Swedish pediatric neurologist, who in turn leaked it to the press. In the United States, Sidney Wolfe of the Public Citizen Health Research Group wrote to Margaret Heckler, then secretary of health and human services, declaring that the 1,182 figure was far off the mark inasmuch as most butazone deaths had gone unreported. The actual number of deaths, he calculated, was probably closer to 10,000, with 3,000 of those in the United States. He petitioned that the two Ciba-Geigy products and others like them should be immediately removed from the market. His plea was refused. On the other hand, a few months after the Hansson story broke, Norway *did* ban the products.

In February 1985, after plans had been cautiously worked out by a few top Ciba-Geigy officials and several consumerist leaders, a one-day conference was held in London to discuss the situation. Hansson, seriously ill in Sweden, insisted that M.S. and M.L. attend in his place. At our strong suggestion, the conference was made open to the press. At the end, most participants seemed to agree that although phenylbutazone could not be entirely replaced by other drugs, its indications should be drastically limited in the labeling to such forms of arthritis as acute gout, ankylosing spondylitis ("stiff spine"), and a few other uncommon but serious forms in which no other drug was effective. But it should never be advocated as the drug of first choice. (In Great Britain, strict controls were already in effect: phenylbutazone products could be used only by hospital-based physicians.) Moreover, consumerists urged that oxyphenbutazone products should be abolished altogether.

In April 1985, Ciba-Geigy accepted most though not all of the conference recommendations and modified its labeling thereafter. Its phenylbutazone would be listed as indicated in only four conditions: active ankylosing spondylitis, acute gouty arthritis, active rheumatoid arthritis, and acute attacks of osteoarthritis. The restriction was not as severe as some consumerists demanded, but it was far too severe to please some Ciba-Geigy officials.

Phenylbutazone. By 1988, it was apparent (see Table 5) that most phenylbutazone products in most of the developing countries in Southeast Asia and Africa were carrying specific or at least adequate warnings of serious or fatal blood damage. In most of these countries, the Ciba-Geigy product likewise carried the statement that phenylbutazone was not the drug of first choice. (This did not satisfy some critics, who demanded that it be described as the drug of last choice.) In the Latin American countries, however, of the twelve single-entity phenylbutazone products, six—all marketed by domestic firms—carried no warning of possible serious blood dyscrasias. Some labels included such a vague piece of advice as "conduct blood studies," an unacceptable warning to the physician: it scarcely alerts him to the possibility that the drug may kill his patient.

Oxyphenbutazone. At the London conference in 1985, an even stronger protest was leveled at oxyphenbutazone, introduced originally by Ciba-Geigy under the name Tandearil or Tanderil but by then being marketed under many names by many firms. Consumer spokesmen insisted that, instead of being merely limited in its approved uses, it should be totally banished. An influential British pharmacologist, Andrew Herxheimer, declared that oxyphenbutazone and all the other butazones had outlived their usefulness and "should be given a decent burial." The proposal received enthusiastic endorsement by consumer advocates all over the world. A few months later, Ciba-Geigy accepted the recommendation and ended the marketing of all its oxyphenbutazone products for internal use. (Both phenylbutazone and oxyphenbutazone products were being used in ointments and salves for external application only, but such applications were not seriously criticized.) At the conference, some of us expressed curiosity about what action might be taken by Ciba-Geigy's competitors, who had not been invited to participate in the meeting nor subjected to consumer criticism; by 1988 the answer was evident: very little.

Oxyphenbutazone products are no longer listed in the United States or the United Kingdom (even for hospital use), or in Thailand, the Philippines, the Caribbean, or Central America. But they are still available and selling in India, Indonesia, Malaysia/Singapore, Africa, the Middle East, Mexico, Colombia, Ecuador, Peru, Venezuela, and Brazil. (See Table 6.) Of the twenty-one products noted here, nearly all marketed by domestic companies, only seven warn against serious or fatal blood damage. In India, where six companies are promoting the drug, blood dyscrasias are given as a *contraindication*, but there is no unambiguous statement that the drug can be a *cause* of the damage. Again, curiosity had been expressed about what consumer groups would do against the continuing sales of oxyphenbutazone products marketed by domestic companies. The answer: very little.

Naproxen. One of the most successful of the recent generation of nonsteroidal anti-inflammatory drugs, naproxen—prepared as naproxen itself or as its sodium salt—has been recommended for use in rheumatoid arthritis, osteoarthritis, juvenile arthritis, ankylosing spondylitis, tendinitis, bursitis, and acute attacks of gout. It is likewise indicated for the control of mild to moderate pain and for use in menstrual pain. Like virtually all other modern NSAIDs on the market, all naproxen products warn against use by patients who may be sensitive to other NSAIDs or to aspirin. Such use may be fatal. Other important warnings are shown in Table 7. In the United States, it is evident that relatively complete warnings are given for the two products marketed by Syntex, but they are less complete in Great Britain, and the risk of severe or fatal liver damage is not mentioned. In India and the Southeast Asian countries, few contraindications and warnings are given. In French-speaking Africa, where naproxen products are marketed by Laroche Navarron and Roussel, each under a Syntex license, more complete warnings are provided, as is the case also in the Middle East and the Caribbean. In the Latin American countries shown in Table 7, acceptable warnings are presented for some products but not for all.

Ibuprofen. An even more widely used NSAID, ibuprofen is not considered here; it has become available in many countries without prescription.

Tiaprofenic Acid. Marketed by only one firm, Hoechst-Roussel, under the brand name Surgam or Torpas, the NSAID tiaprofenic acid is promoted with indications and warnings that vary remarkably from one country to another. It is not listed in the United States. (See Table 8.) In some countries, it is recommended for various forms of arthritis and soft-tissue inflammation; in others it is advised for use in low back pain and in pain after surgery or trauma; in still others it is said to be indicated in all of these conditions. In Venezuela, it is listed as indicated simply for "medical and surgical inflammations."

There are similar variations in the warnings provided for the product. In some countries, caution is advised in its use in patients with heart disease, or kidney disease, or liver disease. In other countries, only kidney disease and liver disease are mentioned. In Thailand, Malaysia/Singapore, and Central America, no such warnings are included.

Piroxicam. Introduced originally by Pfizer under the name Feldene, the NSAID piroxicam has also won wide acceptance in the treatment of pain, fever, and inflammation. In the United States, Central America, Colombia, Ecuador, and Peru, the promotion for the Pfizer product includes essentially the same warnings and contraindications that apply to similar drugs. (See Table 9.) There are clear warnings that it can cause serious or even fatal gastrointestinal or liver damage. In striking contrast, there are no such clear warnings in the United Kingdom, India, Southeast Asia, Africa, the Middle East, or the Caribbean, either for Pfizer's Feldene or for the same drug marketed by other companies under other names. This failure to disclose serious hazards is particularly evident on the part of local or domestic firms. In some instances, *no* warnings are given.

Piroxicam became the center of controversy in 1986 when the Health Research Group (HRG) in Washington declared that adverse drug reactions were more frequent and more severe with Feldene than with any other NSAID. The U.S. Food and Drug Administration, HRG charged, was aware that there had already been 182 fatal and 2,621 nonfatal reactions associated with use of the drug, mostly in elderly patients. In a petition to the secretary of health and human services, Sidney Wolfe claimed that similar evidence had been obtained in Canada, the United Kingdom, Ireland, Norway, Sweden, and Belgium. He asked that the government ban use of the drug in those over the age of 60. Other experts, some in industry and others in medical centers, disputed the charges. In England, William Inman, head of the authoritative Drug Safety Research Unit at the University of Southampton, declared that piroxicam products were not altogether safe, but they were no more likely to cause damage to the gastrointestinal tract in the elderly than were other NSAIDs.[24] The HRG's petition was denied.

Antidiarrhea Agents

Everywhere in the developing nations, as was pointed out earlier, diarrhea has always been the most fearsome killer of infants. In a rural part of Bangladesh, for example, a three-year study revealed that diarrhea was responsible for more than 24 infant deaths per 1,000 live births—almost half of all infant deaths in the area.[25] In a similar study in India, diarrhea was blamed for 42 percent of all deaths in children less than three years old.[26] In many Third World nations, children suffer from this weakening, wasting ailment for many days almost every month. Even if they survive, they are generally so afflicted by loss of fluid, or dehydration, that they can scarcely function.

For at least a century, it has been known how this disease can be quickly and effectively abolished: protect all food and water from contamination. In industrialized nations, this has been dramatically demonstrated. Most food and water can be safely consumed by most healthy people. But in most parts of most developing nations, this has thus far proved to be disastrously unfeasible. Adequate food protection and refrigeration are seldom available, and protection of drinking water from sewage contamination is rarely possible.

Drug experts in research centers, especially in the pharmaceutical industry, have long sought for improved means to control diarrheal disease. Their goal was a new drug effective enough to protect travelers from industrialized nations who venture into underdeveloped lands for business or pleasure (or armies that sometimes invade them) and preferably sufficiently inexpensive to be afforded by the people who live in those countries. Some of the results have been noteworthy.

Clioquinol. Introduced many years ago as an antiseptic dusting powder for wounds, ulcers, and burns, clioquinol is a member of a chemical family known as halogenated hydroxyquinolines. It was investigated in the early 1930s at the University of California Medical School in San Francisco for the treatment of amebic dysentery.[27] In 1934 Ciba introduced the product on the market under the name Enterovioform.

In 1955 came the first reports of a new and terrifying epidemic in Japan, with thousands of victims. It was marked by paralysis, often by blindness. The damage was incurable, irreversible, and sometimes fatal. It was named SMON, for subacute-myelo-optico-neuropathy. In about 1970 the blame was finally placed on Ciba-Geigy's Enterovioform and other clioquinol products then being marketed by Takeda and Tanabe and other drug companies. Damage suits were filed against these firms, and also against the Japanese government for failing to protect its people.

The SMON damage suits had several results. The awards to victims and their families totaled close to $900 million. Probably more important, one result—after months of noisy and unproductive denunciation, threats, and confrontation—was a rethinking both by company officials and by consumerist activists and the start of quiet, productive conversation and consultation. And after the threat of a worldwide boycott and after tremendous pressure from consumerists, led notably by pediatric neurologist Olle Hansson of the University of Göteborg—and from some new individuals within the company itself—Ciba-Geigy agreed to withdraw its Enterovioform from the world market. (For an account of these negotiations, see Chapter 11.)

With Ciba-Geigy out of the clioquinol market, two key questions arose. What would other clioquinol manufacturers do? And what would consumerists do about *them*? The answer to the first question is demonstrated in Table 10. Ciba-Geigy's former competitors in the antidiarrheals business have done very well. Clioquinol products had long since been withdrawn in the United States and the United Kingdom. By 1988 they were no longer listed in Malaysia/Singapore, the Philippines, and the Caribbean. But many versions, including their chemical relatives, were being promoted successfully in India, Indonesia, Thailand, the Middle East, Egypt, Mexico, Central America, Colombia, Venezuela, and Brazil. Some were products of domestic firms, but many were being marketed by multinational companies: Britain-based May & Baker (a subsidiary of Rhône-Poulenc in France), Byk Gulden and Bayer of West Germany, Farmitalia Carlo Erba of Italy, Sandoz of Switzerland, and Carter-Wallace, Searle, Squibb, and Wyeth of the United States. (Although its clioquinol product Entox was clearly listed in the *MIMS* publications for the Middle East and Egypt, officials of Wyeth have advised that by 1988 such products were no longer being marketed in those areas.) Some of the products consisted of clioquinol alone. Others were combinations with an antibacterial compound or antibiotic.

In India, Indonesia, Thailand, Mexico, and Colombia, most of the products are promoted with information that includes a warning of possible nerve damage and cautions against prolonged use. Some actually mention the risk of SMON. But in Central America, such warnings are given for only five of nine products. In Venezuela and Brazil, they are given for none. For one Central American product, Laprin's Diyodomeb, the manufacturer attempted to convince physicians of the drug's safety by resurrecting the claim that it is relatively insoluble.

With nearly ninety different clioquinol or clioquinol-like products on the market in the countries examined in this study, the second question deserves consideration: what have consumerists done about this situation? The answer is again quite clear: very little.

Two other questions remain. First, how safe and useful are the clioquinol products? The answer may depend on the country in which the question is posed. In Brazil, for instance, Augustino Betarello of São Paulo, an internationally recognized gastroenterologist, told us that clioquinol is essential in his practice. He expressed his disappointment with the removal of Ciba-Geigy's high-quality Enterovioform from the market, for this made his patients dependent on domestic substitutes of uncertain quality. In Indonesia, clioquinol is so highly regarded as safe and effective that it is one of the main drugs imitated by fraudulent forms. In Japan, it is still viewed as a menace to public health, but in India, it is not merely accepted but listed as an *essential* drug. And in Cairo, Wasif I. Wasif, medical director of Parke-Davis for Egypt, said, "If clioquinol really injures eyesight, then half of Egypt should be blind. In my country, the charges are simply not true."

The history of clioquinol in Egypt is particularly curious. Since its introduction in the 1930s Ciba-Geigy's Enterovioform had been used widely in that country, supposedly with good effect and apparently with complete safety. In 1982 the announcement that the Swiss firm, under intense pressure from consumer groups, would remove its drug from the world market over a three-to-five-year period got an exceptionally gloomy reception in Cairo. The minister of health was so concerned that he asked a special committee of experts to investigate the situation. Members of that committee were well aware of the SMON epidemic in Japan—that outbreak had received worldwide attention in the press—and had attempted to count the number of SMON victims in Egypt. They could find none.

In December 1982 a committee of Egyptian experts—including the top pharmacologists, ophthalmologists, and neurologists at the University of Cairo Medical School—met to pool the findings for the minister. Egyptian patients, they reported, were consuming about 70 tons of Enterovioform and other clioquinol-like products each year. No matter what harmful effects these substances might have had in Japan, they had done no harm in Egypt. They were generally recognized as safe and effective—and appreciated as relatively inexpensive. The committee recommended that drugs containing clioquinol should continue to be allowed on the Egyptian market. If Ciba-Geigy intended to terminate production, Egyptian drug companies should get ready to manufacture the products themselves. A few months later, the chairman of the Egyptian government's expert committee wrote to Ciba-Geigy headquarters in Switzerland:

Enclosed please find a copy of the minutes of the meeting, held on 19.12.1982, by the committee formed to study the topic of "Clioquinol." The committee issued a resolution allowing the use of preparations containing this substance. I, therefore, would be obliged if some experts from the El Nasr Company for pharmaceutical chemicals [one of Egypt's top drug firms] would be invited by Ciba-Geigy Limited, Basle, in order to acquire production know-how of clioquinol and be trained on its local manufacturing procedure.

This leaves a final query: In view of the pallid efforts by consumerists to get rid of the other clioquinol products, should the original campaign against Enterovioform be viewed as an effort to get rid of Enterovioform—or as an effort to destroy Ciba-Geigy?

Diphenoxylate + Atropine. Promotion of the combination product diphenoxylate + atropine, marketed especially by Searle under the name Lomotil, has been severely criticized, especially because of the failure to warn against its use by young children. In recent years the labeling has been somewhat improved and is almost adequate, not only in the United States and the United Kingdom but also in India, Indonesia, Thailand, Malaysia/Singapore, and Colombia, but is sadly incomplete in the Philippines, Africa, the Middle East, the Caribbean, and Venezuela. (See Table 11.) In Mexico and Central America, the warnings for the Searle product are adequate, but those for competing products are sadly incomplete. For Lomotil, the minimum age recommended for use by children is two years in the United States and most Third World countries, four years in the United Kingdom, five years in the Middle East, and six years in India.

Loperamide. Marketed originally by Janssen under the name Imodium, loperamide is recommended in the United States only for acute or chronic diarrhea—that is, control and symptomatic relief of acute nonspecific diarrhea and of chronic diarrhea associated with inflammatory bowel disease. Similar indications are provided for eight of eleven loperamide products in Indonesia, all five products in Thailand, all three in Malaysia/Singapore, all five in the Philippines, and two of three in Mexico. In other countries—the United Kingdom, India, Africa, the Middle East, Colombia, and Venezuela—it is recommended broadly for diarrhea of any cause. (See Table 12.)

A strong warning against use in any infection in which the invading organisms may perforate the intestinal mucosa—typhoid fever, for example—is presented in the United States, and for most loperamide products in Indonesia, Thailand, the Philippines, and Brazil. No such contraindication is given in most of the other developing countries in Asia, Africa, and Latin America, and not even in the United Kingdom. In almost every case the Janssen product presents more warnings and more important warnings than does any product marketed by a domestic company in the same country.

The breakthrough: oral rehydration therapy. During the early twentieth century, there were observations that the deadly dehydration in diarrhea—the loss of water and salts—could be temporarily overcome by giving salt and water intravenously to the patients. When the intravenous treatment was stopped, however, the patients relapsed and many of them died. Treatment by mouth was hopeless, since the water and the salts were rapidly excreted. Then in 1958 E. Riklis and J. H.

Quastel, in Canada, working with segments of guinea-pig intestine, reported that the salts and water would be readily absorbed and *maintained* in the body if they were combined with just the right amount of glucose.[28] In 1960 Peter Curran in England reported that the same thing happened in rat intestine.[29] Three years later Harold Schedl and James Clifton announced in *Nature* that the same phenomenon had been demonstrated in normal humans.[30] But what would this simple salt-water-sugar combination do in patients suffering from the dehydration of diarrhea?

Oddly enough, the answers were slow in coming. In 1964 R. A. Phillips, of a U.S. Naval Medical Research Unit working during an epidemic of cholera in Taiwan, reported excellent results from the treatment.[31] A few years later an American team announced similar results during a diarrhea outbreak on an Apache reservation in Arizona.[32] Why this remarkable delay? Several reasons were apparent. People—and particularly physicians—refused to believe in the treatment. It was too simple and too inexpensive. It offered no promise of rich rewards to any drug company, nor did it fit into the glamorized picture of modern health care. It could be given in a modern hospital, of course, but it could also be applied at home. Accordingly, patients by the hundreds of millions and physicians by the thousands continued to seek for a super antidiarrhea pill or turned to the herbs and incantations of witch doctors—and infants continued to die from diarrheal disease.

Not until 1978 did WHO and UNICEF announce that they would spearhead a worldwide campaign against the diarrheal diseases—a campaign based on the use of what is now known as oral rehydration therapy, or ORT. Also in 1978 an editorial in the British journal *Lancet* declared that the discovery of the astonishing effect of combining sugar with salt and water as a treatment for diarrhea was "potentially the most important medical advance this century."[33]

The ORT campaign began in 1980. By 1985 widespread implementation of ORT programs in some countries had already reduced deaths from diarrheal diseases by 40 or 50 percent. Programs of ORT, of one type or another, had been set up, if only on paper, in countries totaling 95 percent of the Third World population. In a few countries, such as Egypt, nationwide radio and television were enlisted to spread the news of ORT, and deaths from diarrhea fell dramatically.[34] (Whether the success of the ORT program in Egypt can be sustained after termination of the substantial subsidy from the U.S. Agency for International Development, scheduled to end in September 1991, has been seriously questioned.)[35]

Health ministries and local health authorities used a vast array of devices to teach parents how to prepare and use the rehydration combination. Often these instructions gave explicit quantities of sugar, salt, and boiled water to be combined. One pediatrician in Kenya, Colin Forbes, described his own system: "I would ask the mother, 'Do you know how to make a sweet tea?' She would answer, 'Of course!' Then I would tell her, 'Put in a little salt.' She would ask, 'How much salt?' And I would say, 'Until it tastes as salty as your baby's tears.'"[36]

But the application of ORT was far from universal, and millions of children were still dying from diarrheal dehydration. The situation was frustrating to health authorities. James Grant of UNICEF declared: "Statistically, the biggest single killer of the world's children is still the dehydration caused by diarrhea. To combat that dehydration, there is now an oral therapy which is so effective that it is being used in the world's most sophisticated hospitals, so simple that it can be used by all parents in their own homes, and so inexpensive that it can be afforded by almost every family." Although ORT had been available for about ten years, millions of children had died needlessly in each of those years. Some reasons were clear, Grant said. "There is little profit to be made out of such information. The majority of the world's health professionals are still prescribing anti-diarrheal drugs—over four hundred million dollars' worth every year. Yet in almost all cases, these drugs are now known to be useless or harmful." In his opinion, resistance from the medical profession "is probably the most important obstacle to the spread of ORT."[37]

Antibacterials

Antibiotics, sulfa drugs, and other antibacterial agents are among the most widely used of all pharmaceutical agents. To many drugs experts, they are also among the most overly prescribed and overly used drugs. Each may cause serious or fatal reactions. In addition, the excessively enthusiastic use of some of them, especially to prevent rather than to treat infection, or their use against trivial or self-limiting ailments, has resulted in the appearance of dangerous or deadly drug-resistant strains of organisms.

Chloramphenicol. Effective against a wide range of microorganisms, easy to produce, and relatively inexpensive, chloramphenicol would probably be indicated for use in a long list of infectious diseases except for one unpleasant fact: in a small but significant percentage of patients, it may produce serious or fatal aplastic anemia. Accordingly, in most countries, it is recommended for use only in such life-threatening diseases as typhoid fever, *Hemophilus influenzae* meningitis, and Rocky Mountain spotted fever. (In the People's Republic of China, health officials at one time felt that the evident advantages of chloramphenicol so outweighed the risks that its widespread use was justified.)

Some industry critics declared during the 1970s that the drug was so hazardous that it should be banned completely. Others objected to such a drastic step, arguing that chloramphenicol remains probably the drug of first choice in the treatment of typhoid. Instead, they urged, all chloramphenicol products should carry three clear warnings:

• Do not use against trivial infections.
• Do not use to *prevent* infections, especially before routine surgery.
• Do not use for prolonged treatments.

It is gratifying to observe the response of most pharmaceutical firms, as is shown in Table 13. The three warnings are presented for all products marketed by multinational and domestic firms alike in the United States, the United Kingdom (with one exception), India, Indonesia, Thailand, Malaysia/Singapore, the Philippines, Africa, Francophone Africa, the Middle East, and the Caribbean. In Thailand, one domestic company, General Drugs House, provided the specific warnings but also recommended the drug for bronchitis and tonsillitis.

In Latin America, the situation is less satisfactory. Of the ten products listed for Mexico, only three—two multinationals and one domestic—provide the essential warnings. The other seven—one multinational and six domestics—do not. In Central America, Colombia, and Venezuela, only one product—Parke-Davis's Chloromycetin—provides the triple warning. It is noteworthy that in every country considered here, it is invariably the Parke-Davis product that carries the appropriate warnings.

Tetracycline. In both the United States and the United Kingdom, all products of the widely used antibiotic tetracycline carry appropriate warnings concerning its use during the last half of pregnancy and in young children, to prevent bone changes and tooth discoloration, and in the presence of kidney or liver disease. In the United States, the description in *PDR* warns that tetracycline should not be used in children below the age of eight "unless other drugs are not likely to be effective or are contraindicated."

Such warnings are provided by means of footnotes for practically all tetracycline products marketed in India, most of the Southeast Asian countries, Africa, Francophone Africa, the Middle East, and the Caribbean. Some even recommend against use in children below the age of twelve. In the Philippines, however, products marketed by Hoechst and Squibb include dosages for children of any age. But in the Latin American countries, as is shown in Table 14, adequate warnings are provided for some products but not for others.

Gentamicin. In much of the Third World, as in industrialized nations, the hazards of the useful but potentially toxic drug gentamicin have now been recognized, and physicians are warned that it may cause deafness or produce serious kidney damage. Adequate warnings are given for nearly all gentamicin products listed in the Latin American countries. Those few with seriously deficient warnings are marketed primarily by domestic companies.

Lincomycin. Introduced by Upjohn under the name Lincocin, lincomycin is listed in a dozen Third World drug compendia. (See Table 15.) In ten of these developing nations, physicians are warned that it may cause "serious or fatal colitis," or "colitis," or at least "gastrointestinal disorders." In the books for Africa, the Middle East, and Brazil, no such warning is included. Competitive products are marketed in Thailand, Mexico, Colombia, Venezuela, and Brazil. Of these, three listed in Thailand and one in Venezuela—all produced by domestic firms—carry no warnings of possible gastrointestinal injury.

In recent years, and for no apparent reason, many people in Brazil have become convinced that lincomycin is the drug of choice to treat—or even prevent—influenza and the common cold. (It is without any value in such conditions.) Accordingly, helpful neighborhood *farmacias* provide a container of lincomycin capsules on their counter, and customers may help themselves, paying the requisite number of *cruzeiros* per pill. No promotional material by any lincomycin producer can be found to account for this useless and possibly lethal misuse. In the

United States, the description of Lincocin specifically states, "It should not be used in patients with nonbacterial infections, such as most upper respiratory tract infections."

In 1988 one of the most active Third World consumer groups, the Consumers' Association of Penang (CAP), in Malaysia, demanded that lincomycin, along with a related antibiotic, clindamycin, be removed from the market.[38] The CAP demand was circulated worldwide. Upjohn in particular was charged with promoting its products for the common cold and other infections that are "minor and trivial" and was accused of covering up the risk of causing colitis and other serious gastrointestinal damage. According to CAP, Lincocin costs twelve times more than penicillin. (The significance of the comparison of Lincocin and penicillin prices is not clear. Lincomycin is designed for the treatment of bacterial strains that are resistant to penicillin or for patients who have become allergic to penicillin.) The company's promotion in Malaysia/Singapore, however, points out specifically that the drug is intended for the treatment of "serious infections" and is contraindicated in minor bacterial or viral infections. Physicians are advised to terminate treatment if persistent diarrhea or colitis appears. Drug experts are aware that colitis and other problems of the digestive tract may also be caused by such other antibiotics as penicillin, ampicillin, tobramycin, and cephalosporins.[39]

Combination antibiotics. During the past fifteen years or so, there has been increasingly heavy pressure from drug experts and consumerists to ban fixed combinations of antibiotics. In most cases, it has been charged, such combinations are highly irrational, offer little or no benefit to patients, and clearly increase hazards. Especially during the last five years, it has become clear that these combinations have lost their appeal to physicians who once prescribed them (and declared "we can't practice medicine without them") and to the companies that marketed them. In the United States and most other industrialized countries, few if any antibiotic combinations are still on the market. In the Third World, where these combinations once accounted for about one-half of all antibiotic prescriptions, they are becoming increasingly uncommon, and some developing nations have banned them completely. Of special interest are combinations of streptomycin and penicillin and of streptomycin and chloramphenicol.

Penicillin-streptomycin combinations were produced notably by

Merck Sharp & Dohme (MSD) under the name Penstrep and were recommended for urinary tract infections, peritonitis, middle ear and mastoid infections, pulmonary infections, and infected wounds. In 1983 MSD sold the rights to Penstrep to its distributor in Thailand, B. L. Hua Trading Company. In spite of considerable criticism, Hua has continued to sell Penstrep, while MSD has sought to wash its hands of the entire situation. "We have no continuing relationship with BLH as to Penstrep and no legal right to question what they do with the product," an MSD official declared in 1989. "We would not undertake activities that could be viewed as coercive of our distributor." A consumerist countered: "The honourable way would be to buy back the rights and then cease production of the product. You have the legal right and responsibility to your shareholders to have distributors who maintain your standards so as to protect your international reputation."[40]

An even more heated attack has been directed against a number of companies, some multinational and some domestic, that market combinations of streptomycin and chloramphenicol, primarily for the treatment of diarrhea, in such countries as India and the Philippines. Among these are Parke-Davis's Chlorostrep, Dey's Medical Stores' Enterostrep, Rallis's Rheofin, Boehringer-Knoll's Strepto-Paraxin, United American's Dostrol, Farmitalia Carlo Erba's Kemistrep, and Global's Marcomycin-Strep. They involve such risks, critics claim, as the nerve and kidney damage that can be caused by streptomycin, and the serious or fatal blood damage from chloramphenicol.

In India, a special governmental investigative committee recommended in 1980 that all streptomycin-chloramphenicol and a few other combination drugs were unnecessary, posed unacceptable dangers, and should be promptly "weeded out." In this case, both consumerists and the Indian Medical Association strongly supported the recommendations. After a delay of eight years, the drug controller of India—the top drug official in the country—ruled in 1988 that these products should be banned. But some of the companies—among them Dey's, Lyka Chemicals, Roussel, and Indoco—went to court and presented their case, arguing, not with scientific evidence to show that the products are safe and offer no significant risk to patients, but that the drug controller did not have the legal authority to ban them. The court ruled that execution of the ban should be stayed indefinitely. Indian consumerists reacted by urging a nationwide boycott on all drug products being marketed by the companies in India. It remained to be seen whether the boycott would have any visible effect.

Nalidixic acid. The synthetic antibacterial nalidixic acid is promoted in the United States and some other nations only for the treatment of urinary infections caused by Gram-negative organisms. In other countries, it is indicated for both urinary and intestinal infections. (See Table 16.) These inconsistencies cannot all be attributed to differing policies of national drug-regulatory agencies. In Mexico, for example, nine nalidixic acid products are promoted by various companies for use against urinary infections, while eight are advocated by different firms for both urinary and intestinal disease. Similar inconsistencies are evident among the products marketed by members of the Winthrop-Sterling group. Of the company's products, seven are said to be indicated for urinary infections, while ten are recommended for both conditions. Inadequate warnings are apparent, especially in the case of products marketed by domestic companies in Latin America.

Appetite Stimulants

Much abuse has been heaped on those drug companies that have promoted drugs for use as appetite stimulants in the Third World. Many of us have emphasized repeatedly that the major need of the poor peoples in developing countries is not for appetite stimulants, costly vitamin preparations, and other "luxury drugs," but for calories, for protein, for food. Yet it must be recognized that in the Third World, not everyone is poor and undernourished; there are also some well-to-do or even wealthy individuals. Some of these, for one reason or another, may be at least temporarily undernourished and could benefit from appetite stimulation. They are, moreover, well able to pay for such drugs.

Cyproheptadine. Introduced by Merck Sharp & Dohme (MSD) under the name Periactin, cyproheptadine is now said to be indicated in some countries for appetite stimulation, in others for control of allergies, and in still others for both purposes. As is shown in Table 17, reasonably adequate warnings are given for all MSD and competing products in the United States, the United Kingdom, India, Southeast Asia,

Africa, the Middle East, the Caribbean, and parts of Latin America. The warnings are less adequate for such products in Colombia and Venezuela.

Evidently impressed by critics who have attacked the company's promotion of Periactin as an appetite stimulant in poor countries in which the problem is not lack of appetite but lack of food, MSD officials have again emphasized that such promotion is sent only to health professionals. Regardless of such precautions, the drug is reputedly being taken by patients who cannot afford to pay for adequate food.

Pizotifen. Obvious inconsistencies are found with pizotifen products marketed by two Swiss companies, Sandoz's Sandomigran or Sanomigran and Wander's Mosegor (Table 18). (In some countries, it is also offered by either Sandoz or Wander under the name Litec.) Not listed in the United States, Sanomigran is promoted in the United Kingdom solely for the prevention of migraine attacks. Throughout the Third World, the products are said to be indicated for migraine prevention, or for appetite stimulation, or for what are described as mood changes in the elderly, or for some combination of such indications. These products were the subjects of two recent and memorable promotional campaigns in which Sandoz described its product in the Third World as "the one and only appetite stimulant," but reassured migraine patients in Great Britain that it would give only a "slight increase in body weight." The descriptions of all these Sandoz and Wander products seem to include adequate warnings. For one competitive product marketed in Thailand by a domestic firm, no warnings are presented.

Cardiovascular Agents

Clofibrate. The potent substance clofibrate is marketed under the name Atromid-S by Wyeth in the United States and by ICI in the United Kingdom and many Third World countries. (See Table 19.) It has been accepted by the Food and Drug Administration for cautious use only in the control of high levels of blood lipid, but it is not indicated in the treatment of atherosclerosis or coronary disease. In general, Wyeth and ICI have been restrained in their claims, referring only to hyperlipemia. In Mexico and Central America, however, ICI also includes atherosclerosis as an indication. In India, Cipla lists both hyperlipemia and atherosclerosis for its product Lipomid. In Indonesia, E. Merck of West Germany adds atherosclerosis to the indications for its Liposol, and a domestic firm, Pharos Chemie, adds both atherosclerosis and coronary disease for its Arterol. In Venezuela, two products marketed by domestic companies list all three conditions. With only a few exceptions, the warnings given for all of these products seem to be adequate.

Prazosin. Marketed worldwide by Pfizer under the name Minipress, prazosin has been shown to be effective in the treatment of high blood pressure (Table 20). In the United States, the description contains these words: "Contraindications—None known." But there is one critical warning. Within 30 to 90 minutes after taking the first dose, or after rapid dosage increases, physicians are cautioned, some patients will suddenly black out, or lose consciousness. A warning of this possibility is presented in the United States and the United Kingdom and in most Third World countries. It is missing, however, in Africa, the Caribbean, and Venezuela. Yet, physicians in those countries are advised to begin with a low dosage "to avoid effects of sudden response."

Cerebral Vasodilators

Grouped variously under such names as peripheral or cerebral vascular stimulants, cerebral activators, or central nervous system stimulants—or popularly but erroneously as drugs for the treatment of "senile dementia"—are a number of products that seem to have won a fair degree of acceptance, at least in developing countries. Eight of these products are considered here. Of these, only two have been accepted in the United States and three in Great Britain.

Piracetam. Under such names as Nootropil and Normabrain, piracetam is recommended specifically for cerebral vascular disturbances. In some Third World countries, piracetam is described as indicated for loss of memory, in others for lack of concentration, and in still others for intellectual deterioration. (See Table 21.) In India and Thailand, piracetam products are promoted for the treatment of mental retardation or learning problems in children. In Malaysia/Singapore, the Middle East, Mexico, and Colombia, they are recommended for the treatment of alcoholism or alcohol addiction.

In Brazil, numerous physicians were openly annoyed by a series of medical journal advertisements recommending Rhodia's Nootropil Pediátrico to alleviate emotional problems of children. In one series, the "before Nootropil" illustration showed an unhappy youngster and his vexed father examining a report card with failing grades in every subject except physical education. But in the "after Nootropil" scene, both father and son are visibly delighted with a card reporting scholastic, social, and family readjustment. No such product is listed in the United States or the United Kingdom.

Bencyclane. Marketed mainly by Organon under the name Fludilat, bencyclane is described in Indonesia and Mexico as indicated simply for peripheral vascular or cerebral vascular disturbances. In other countries, the indications are expanded to include lack of concentration, loss of memory, sleep disturbances, and intellectual deterioration (Table 22).

Buflomedil. A similar situation exists in the cases of Loftyl, marketed by Abbott, and competitive products sold under other names by domestic companies. In Thailand, the Middle East, Ecuador, and Brazil, the drug is recommended only for disturbances of the peripheral and cerebral vascular systems. In other Third World areas, Loftyl is promoted also for the inability to concentrate, failed memory, personality changes, vertigo or dizziness, poor sleep patterns, and fatigue. (See Table 23.) In a 1989 review of drug advertising in Third World countries, Abbott's promotion of buflomedil in Pakistan was described as one of the "worst examples of quackery" in the country.[41]

Cinnarzine. The agent cinnarzine, marketed primarily by Janssen as Stugeron, is listed in the United Kingdom, but only for the control of peripheral vascular disturbances. In India, it is recommended only for loss of memory, and in the Middle East and the Caribbean, only for vertigo, dizziness, or motion sickness. In the Philippines, Mexico, Central America, and Venezuela, a wide range of indications is presented. (See Table 24.)

Ergoloid mesylates. Marketed in the United States by Sandoz as Hydergine, this ergoloid product is described as of possible help in a proportion of elderly individuals who "manifest signs and symptoms of an idiopathic decline in mental capacity (i.e., cognitive and interpersonal skills, mood, self-care, apparent motivation)." In the United Kingdom, it is said to be indicated in the management of elderly patients with "mild to moderate dementia." In the Third World, the Sandoz product is recommended generally for the treatment of disturbances of both peripheral and vascular circulation and, depending on the country, for the inability to concentrate, memory loss, changes in personality, dizziness and vertigo, and intellectual disintegration. (See Table 25.) In Indonesia, Thailand, and Malaysia/Singapore, competitive ergoloid mesylates are marketed by domestic firms. These are generally described as indicated for intellectual deterioration.

Flunarizine. Introduced by Janssen as Sibelium, the compound flunarizine is presented as useful for the control of disturbances of the peripheral vascular system, or of the cerebral vascular system, or both. It is listed in neither the United States nor the United Kingdom. In Thailand and Central America, it is also proposed for the treatment of lack of concentration, failing memory, dizziness, and sleep disturbances. (See Table 26.) One consumer group criticized Janssen for making claims without adequate supporting scientific evidence, and for neglecting to warn that the drug may cause parkinsonism and depression.[42]

Pentoxifylline. In the United States and the United Kingdom, pentoxifylline under the name Trental is promoted by Hoechst-Roussel only for the treatment of peripheral vascular disturbances. In the Third World, it is recommended for both peripheral and cerebral vascular problems. In addition, in some countries, the drug is promoted as useful for confusional states, loss of social contact, sleep disturbances, vertigo and dizziness, loss of memory, and lack of concentration. (See Table 27.)

Pyritinol (pyrithioxine). Marketed by the West German firm E. Merck and several domestic companies, these pyritinol or pyrithioxine products are recommended in some Third World countries for mental retardation in children, in others for lack of concentration, memory loss, or "mental fatigue," or for treatment after brain injury, apoplectic attack, encephalitis, or intoxication. (See Table 28.) At one time, the indications for E. Merck's product in Central America included not only those mental or emotional problems associated with brain damage but one surprising other—hemorrhoids. That indication is no longer included. No pyritinol product is listed in the United States or the United Kingdom.

One experienced British physician had this to say about Merck's Encephabol and its use in developing nations:

This drug is indeed claimed to have an impressive range of indications. . . . It will surprise no one to learn that there is no scientific evidence for this drug's efficacy. I have seen this drug prescribed for children with various disabilities, including cerebral palsy, mental retardation, epilepsy, and learning and behavioural problems, in Syria, India, Sri Lanka, Malaysia, Singapore, and Indonesia. In almost all cases the drug had been prescribed by doctors, usually in private practice. Marketing is one issue, but why do doctors prescribe a drug when they have no evidence that it confers any benefit?[43]

Major Tranquilizers

Chlorpromazine. One of the earliest tranquilizers introduced for the treatment of schizophrenia and other serious mental diseases, chlorpromazine is marketed as Largactil by the French firm Rhône-Poulenc and its subsidiary May & Baker, as Thorazine by the American company SmithKline & French (now SmithKline Beecham), and under other names by other multinational or domestic organizations. It has played a major part in revolutionizing the treatment of psychotic illness, but it has limitations. In the United States, physicians are warned that it may cause brain damage—especially a condition known as tardive dyskinesia, marked by uncontrollable muscular twitching—and must be used cautiously in pregnant women, in children, and in patients with respiratory, cardiovascular, or liver disease, or epilepsy, and in those using alcohol or other central nervous system depressants.

The labeling of Thorazine in the United States and the Philippines contains reasonably complete warnings, including disclosure of the risk of tardive dyskinesia, as is apparent in Table 29. The same is true for chlorpromazine products in Indonesia, Thailand, and Malaysia/Singapore. In contrast, the labeling of chlorpromazine products by Rhône-Poulenc, May & Baker, and other companies in the United Kingdom, India, Africa, the Caribbean, Central America, Colombia, Ecuador, Venezuela, and Peru is notably deficient.

Sulpiride. Although sulpiride is not listed in the United States, sulpiride products are recommended in the United Kingdom for the control of schizophrenia, in some Latin American countries for "other mental disorders," in Venezuela mainly for the treatment of duodenal ulcer, and in Indonesia, the Middle East, and Brazil for all three conditions. It is evident from Table 30 that the important potential hazards are described in the United Kingdom but less completely in developing countries. In a 1988 British survey, it was stated, "Clear clinical evidence to support a novel effect in man is still awaited. . . . The precise role of sulpiride in psychiatry remains unclear, but current evidence does not suggest that it has a great advantage over other neuroleptics."[44] Although the sulpiride products are recommended for the treatment of duodenal ulcer in some Third World nations, it is noted in the Middle East labeling that they may *cause* gastric ulcer.

Minor Tranquilizers

Chlordiazepoxide. Introduced as Librium by Hoffmann–La Roche, chlordiazepoxide was the first of the group of minor tranquilizers known as benzodiazepines. It is intended for use primarily in the short-term management of anxiety disorders. It is not recommended to overcome the normal stresses of everyday living. In the United States, the United Kingdom, India, most Southeast Asian countries, and the Middle East, physicians are warned that prolonged use has resulted in habituation or dependency. (See Table 31.) In this table, as well as in the two that follow it, data are presented for only selected countries. In most of the others, notably in Southeast Asia, warnings are presented by means of footnote references. Caution is urged in the use of the drug during pregnancy, and by the elderly, and in patients with liver, kidney, or lung disease. Patients taking this drug should not engage in "hazardous occupations," which include driving a vehicle and working near moving machinery.

Diazepam. Brought out by Hoffmann–La Roche as Valium, diazepam became undoubtedly the most widely known of all minor tranquilizers. Physicians in the United States are warned that it should not be used to control psychotic disease. Efforts to apply a minor tranquilizer in patients with schizophrenia or severe depression have ranged from dismal to disastrous.

A large number of these warnings, as is shown in Table 32, are given for diazepam products in the United States. Generally by means of a footnote, they are given in the United Kingdom, most of the Southeast Asian countries, Africa, the Middle East, and the Caribbean. Usually, however, warnings against use in psychosis and by those in hazardous professions are omitted. In India and the Latin American countries, the warnings are far less complete. With diazepam, as with other minor tranquilizers discussed here, the risk of habituation is usually ignored in Third World countries.

Lorazepam. A somewhat similar situation exists in the case of lorazepam, marketed by Wyeth as Ativan and by many other firms under other names. The warnings for the Wyeth product are reasonably complete in the United States, and also in Mexico and Colombia. Cautions given for competitive products, usually by footnotes, are adequate in most of the Southeast Asian countries, Africa, the Middle East, and the Caribbean, but they are strikingly deficient in India and most of Latin America. (See Table 33.)

Bromazepam. Marketed by Roche as Lexotan, Lexomil, and Lexotanil, and by other companies under other names, bromazepam is not listed in the United States. Warnings are generally presented as footnotes in the United Kingdom, Southeast Asia, Africa, the Middle East, and the Caribbean, but are given specifically in Francophone Africa. In Latin America, the warnings for the Roche product are reasonably complete in Colombia and Peru, but less adequate in other countries. (See Table 34.)

Buspirone. Marketed by several American firms as Buspar, buspirone, a relatively new product, is listed at present in only a few countries. The warnings of major risks are quite complete in the United States, Mexico, and Brazil, but less so in the United Kingdom and Malaysia/Singapore. (See Table 35.) In Brazil, soon after it was introduced by Bristol, this drug became the center of a storm of protest when it was promoted to relieve tension in airport traffic controllers. Angry critics pointed out that it could not only relieve their tension but also put them to sleep. The promotion was quickly changed.

Antidepressants

Two major types of drugs are available for the treatment of severe mental depression, one known as mono-amine-oxidase inhibitors, or MAOIs, the other as tricyclic compounds. Both types may be helpful, but physicians must be warned that the two different kinds should never be used simultaneously on the same patient. The result may be a serious or fatal hypertensive crisis. Physicians are usually advised to wait for about two weeks before switching from one type of antidepressant to another.

Phenelzine. Described as a potent MAOI, phenelzine is marketed by Parke-Davis or Warner-Lambert as Nardil in the United States, the United Kingdom, Africa, and the Caribbean. In these countries, its labeling includes appropriate warnings against use in combination with tricyclics, in patients with liver disease or congestive heart failure, or in combination with such foods and beverages as pickled herring, liver, dry sausage, and broad-bean pods, all of which contain tyramine or tryptophane.

Imipramine. Introduced by the Geigy division of Ciba-Geigy as Tofranil, the tricyclic compound imipramine is now also available in many countries from domestic firms. In all the countries considered in this study, nearly all imipramine products provide appropriate warnings against use in combination with MAOIs. (See Table 36.)

Nortriptyline. In the United States, the United Kingdom, and in those Third World countries in which it is available, the labeling for all listed tricyclic nortriptyline products gives appropriate warnings against use with MAOIs and urges caution in use in patients with cardiovascular disease.

Anabolic Steroid

Anabolic steroid hormones are said to be useful in speeding the transformation of protein synthesis, controlling the bone-softening of osteoporosis, and aiding in the treatment of aplastic anemia. They recently attracted attention during the 1984 Olympic Games because they were detected in athletes who had used them in the hope of improving their athletic prowess.

Stanozolol, marketed mainly as Winstrol or Stromba by the Sterling-Winthrop group, is listed in the United States, the United Kingdom, India, Africa, and the Middle East. In the past, it drew criticism because its promotion often failed to warn that it could stunt growth in children and cause masculinization in young girls and women, and because it failed to include use by athletes as a contraindication. This situation has now changed considerably. In the United Kingdom, the warnings include the possible masculinization of females. In the other countries, there are also warnings about the stunting of growth and against its use by athletes. (See Table 37.)

Female Sex Hormones

Allyl estranol. Although it is not listed in the United States, allyl estranol, produced by Organon as Gestanon or Gestanin, is promoted in the United Kingdom for threatened or habitual abortion and in most other countries for threatened abortion or threatened premature labor. Critics have charged that there is no scientific evidence to support such claims. In India, a competitive product is listed as useful in the control of premenstrual tension. Inadequate warnings are presented for the products in the United Kingdom and India, but physicians are urged not to use the drug in patients with a history of thromboembolic disease or with breast or genital cancer, and to use caution in giving it to patients with liver disease or epilepsy. More complete warnings are presented in the Southeast Asian countries, but none are given for Francophone Africa or the Latin American countries. In Francophone Africa, it is claimed that there are no known contraindications. In Mexico and Central America, physicians are told that no warnings or precautions are applicable. (See Table 38.)

Ethyl estranol. Marketed in India by Infar as Orabolin and in Thailand and the Philippines by Organon as Orgabolin, the hormone ethyl estranol is recommended for use in debilitating disease in elderly patients in whom other measures have proved unsatisfactory. Nine specific warnings are given for the Organon product in Thailand and the Philippines, but only three for the Infar product in India. (See Table 39.)

"Sex Tonics"

A somewhat related group of products is promoted mainly in developing nations for the relief of some of mankind's most common mental, physical, and sexual problems. Each of these may contain only a single active ingredient, such as arginine or ginseng, or a combination including arginine and ginseng, along with a male sex hormone, a female sex hormone, up to a dozen different vitamins, such minerals as calcium, copper, and iron, and such other ingredients as methionine, choline, inositol, lysine, glutamic acid, procaine, caffeine, yohimbine, and strychnine. Nearly all of these appear to be products of domestic companies. (See Table 40.)

These products are promoted to relieve such conditions as the female menopause and the male climacteric, or to control physical, sexual, and psychic fatigue. One product is promoted broadly "to improve physical and mental work capacity, and prolong endurance in athletic activities . . . intensify male image or profile, and enhance sexual fulfillment." Although it is probable that few if any of these products can live up to their advance billing, they probably will do little lasting physical or mental damage and may represent merely a waste of the patient's money.

Trouble in Africa—Again

Over a number of years, it has been our growing impression that drug labeling and promotion in Latin America and Southeast Asia is far more satisfactory than it is in Africa, and that the situation in Francophone or French-speaking Africa is substantially less adequate than it is in English-speaking Africa. This latter view has now been supported by a three-year study conducted in Francophone nations— Algeria, Morocco, Tunisia, and in six in Central Africa (Burkina Faso, Congo, Ivory Coast, Mali, Senegal, and Zaire). The investigation was carried out by an unusual consortium: Medicus Mundi, the French Institute for Economic Research and Development Planning, and a number of pharmaceutical companies, and was published by a distinguished consumer group, Frères des Hommes.[45]

In those French-speaking nations, it was found, the interests of African patients are often abused by unsuitable drugs and misleading promotion. "These abuses, which are numerous enough to warrant classification, owe their perennial nature to indifference and a lack of information. . . . There are too many unsuitable drugs, too much misleading promotion, and too much laissez-faire." Where an essential drugs list policy was adopted, it was never implemented or implemented adequately.

Prices of drugs were inexplicably high. In one country, for example, the Health Ministry gave its permission for drugs to be purchased from two wholesalers at prices six to twelve times those charged by the

UNICEF–linked wholesaler. "The choice of supplier made by the Health Ministry officials was probably influenced by personal interest," it was suggested.

Prescribers in Africa often find that their sole source of pharmacological information on drugs is the companies themselves, and "the self-discipline proposed by innovative companies, like Ciba-Geigy, is far from having penetrated the whole of the industry." The study concluded that the government of France, the authorities in the African countries, and pharmaceutical companies must all share the blame.

An Evident Change

By the late 1980s it had become evident that the picture of drug promotion in the Third World had changed. With some glaring exceptions, it is apparent that *most* of the multinational firms were more willing to restrict the claims of efficacy for their products to what can be substantiated by scientific evidence. Testimonials from physicians were no longer in vogue. At the same time, *most* multinationals appeared to be more willing to disclose the major hazards of their products. We are unable to determine whether in each case this represents a change in company policy or a change in company personnel.

At the same time, it is apparent that the total *volume* of misinformation displayed to Third World physicians—exaggeration of claims and cover-up of hazards—has not changed appreciably. Now, however, as this chapter has demonstrated, the misinformation is coming mainly not from the multinational companies but from local or domestic firms. These domestic firms may be relatively small, but many of them wield enormous political power. This has already proved to be disconcerting to some consumer activists, who had comfortably assigned the role of "bad guy" to all the multinationals and of "good guy" to all the domestic companies. Now the virtue or sin of a pharmaceutical company must be judged, not by its ownership or the location of its headquarters, but by its performance.

Chapter 3

THE COMPANIES:
HEROES OR VILLAINS?

"And it came to pass that the President of the United States, the President of the Soviet Union, and the president of the pharmaceutical industry had a private audience with the Lord. Each was allowed to ask one question.

"The U.S. president asked, 'Lord, when will our unemployment problem be solved?' The Lord pondered, then said, 'The year 2020.' The President of the United States walked away, crying bitterly."

"The President of the Soviet Union asked, 'When will the first Russian be on the moon?' The Lord thought for a while, then said, 'In the year 2009.' The President of the Soviet Union walked away, crying bitterly.

"Finally the president of the pharmaceutical industry asked, 'Lord, when will the public image of our industry become favorable again?' The Lord thought for a while and then walked away, crying bitterly."[1]

Anatomy of the Drug Industry

The world's drug companies may be subdivided in several different ways. For example, there are the *multinational* companies, which operate in many countries and possibly worldwide, and there are the *local or domestic* firms, which generally do their business in only one or two countries. The firms can also be divided into the *brand-name* companies, which are responsible for most new drug development and innovation and introduce their products under patent, and the *generic* houses, with little or no research or innovation and which produce drugs only after patents have expired. This distinction is no longer important, since many of the brand-name companies have invaded the generic-drug business.

In the past, many of the firms referred to themselves as "ethical" companies, simply on the grounds that they did not advertise their prescription products to the general public. That term lost its significance when it became evident that "ethical" involves far more than public advertising. Moreover, some firms are commonly accepted as "ethical" even though they do advertise some of their prescription products to the public.

Although most Third World countries are still unable to fill their own needs for modern drugs, a few developing countries have made remarkable progress. For example, Brazil, Argentina, Mexico, India, Cuba, South Korea, and Egypt can meet a significant portion of their own drug requirements; in some cases they are exporting to other nations. A developing country may be unable to manufacture modern synthetic products but can sustain a thriving business based on native or indigenous plant and animal products.

Egypt represents a particularly intriguing case. In 1962 Abdo Mahmood Sallam—an orthopedic surgeon and close friend of President Gamal Abdel Nasser—was asked to direct the Egyptian drug industry, which had just been nationalized. It had not been much of an industry—"mostly a few people working in garages."[2] In the next six years, Sallam created Egypt's modern drug industry, incorporating those multinationals—American, British, German, and Swiss—which had elected to remain after nationalization, started new Egyptian firms, and improved quality control and distribution. In 1968 he accepted Nasser's invitation to become minister of health and served until his resignation in 1971. Later he became head of ACDIMA (Arab Company for Drug Industries and Medical Appliances).

"In 1952," one of Sallam's associates told us, "only 10 percent of our drugs were manufactured locally, and 90 percent had to be imported. Now 85 percent are manufactured locally and only 15 percent are imported. Furthermore, we are now exporting to the Arab bloc."[3] By means of government subsidies, Egypt has kept the retail price of essential drugs so low that there is little or no temptation to market fraudulent products.[4]

In most industrialized nations, it is possible to divide drugs into *prescription* products and nonprescription or *over-the-counter* (OTC) drugs. Thus, in the United States, Great Britain, and most northern European nations, a pharmacist cannot legally dispense a prescription drug unless the patient presents a physician's prescription. Throughout the Third World, the practice is essentially different. There may be a law on the books stating that a prescription is required, but with the possible exception of morphine alkaloids, antipsychotic drugs, and some tranquilizers, the law is routinely ignored by patients, pharmacists, and physicians alike. In many developing countries, the dispensing of "prescription drugs" without a prescription—or without a physician's advice—has resulted too often in irrational and ineffective therapy. It has led to the widespread misuse of antibiotics and the growing problem of resistant strains of microorganisms.

The days of glory for the drug industry were mainly the 1940s and 1950s—particularly for the big multinational pharmaceutical firms. In those years there was an almost unbelievable outpouring of remarkable new products—the sulfa drugs, penicillin and the other antibiotics, and the new steroid hormones. Profits soared to as much as 30 percent per year after taxes as based on investment. And the drug industry enjoyed unprecedented respect and admiration from the public.

End of the Glory Days

But then came the 1960s and 1970s, when the sleazy practices of some drug companies were laid bare in hearings chaired by U.S. Senators Estes Kefauver and Gaylord Nelson;[5] when the dangerously close ties between the pharmaceutical industry and organized medicine, and between the drug industry and medical journals, were revealed; when investigative reporters disclosed how American and European companies were promoting their products in the Third World, exaggerating the claims for efficacy and concealing the hazards.[6] This was the time when the industry recognized that its image had been perhaps permanently tarnished, and the time when, although drug prices rose markedly, profits dropped because the costs of doing business had skyrocketed.

A study conducted for the Pharmaceutical Manufacturers Association showed that because of tightened Food and Drug Administration (FDA) requirements, the need for more complex, more expensive, and more time-consuming tests, and the more-than-justified fears of product liability lawsuits, the cost of developing a new drug in the United States soared from an average of about $1.2 million in 1962 to $11.5 million in 1972 and to more than $230 million in 1987.[7] Moreover, it seemed to take more and more time to obtain FDA approval, five to eight years or longer, while the precious period of patent protection was slipping away. In some cases, the patent had expired even before the new product was approved.[8]

In part because of these and other problems—dwindling profits, the development of few important new drugs each year, and increasingly irksome governmental restrictions in some countries—changes began to appear in the makeup of the international pharmaceutical industry. Two giant firms, Hoechst of Germany and Roussel of France, merged in Europe. In the United States, Monsanto bought G. D. Searle, Eastman Kodak paid $5.1 billion to acquire Sterling Drug, and American Home Products took over A. H. Robins. The British firm Beecham merged with American SmithKline Beckman. Bristol-Myers merged with Squibb. Roche acquired control of Genentech. A number of American and European companies joined forces with pharmaceutical firms in Japan. Many American and European brand-name companies took over smaller generics manufacturers in the United States.

Much of this seemed reminiscent of the standard advice supposedly given to every ailing patient with a cold—*"Go home, take two aspirin tablets, and call me tomorrow."* Now, with an ailing pharmaceutical company, it was changed—*"Go out, take over two aspirin companies, and call me next week."*

At the same time, investment in the process of finding new and, it was hoped, better products was rising steadily. In 1988, for the first time ever, the amount expended for research and development by members of the Pharmaceutical Manufacturers Association (roughly $6.5 billion) surpassed the amount ($6.3 billion) spent by the U.S. National Institutes of Health, the largest medical research institution in the world. The comparable amounts estimated for 1990 were $8.1 billion for PMA member companies[9] and $7.1 billion for NIH.[10]

Industry critics were quick to point out that the investment by the drug industry represented relatively little for research but a great deal for product development, while the NIH funds were earmarked particularly for research. They noted also that neither the industry nor NIH paid much budgetary attention to the diseases that plague the Third World. Neither question can be objectively evaluated, for no hard-and-fast line separates research from development, and there is no simple way to separate the ills that afflict developing countries from those that attack industrialized nations.

Essential Drugs Lists

In a bold attempt to hold down the cost and improve the quality of health care for low-income groups, Mexico embarked in 1959 on a program to limit the drugs in its social security system to urgently needed low-cost products of proven value and maximum safety. Denounced as outrageous, a blow to proper medical care, and probably un-Mexican, it was known as the Quadro Básico (QB) program. The list now contains slightly more than 300 drugs, of which only a very small percentage involves fixed-combination products.

"The early years were difficult ones," says Mario Lieberman, head of the drugs and devices department in the Ministry of Health and one of the chief architects of the system. "Slowly, however, it became generally accepted. The industry has learned that it can live with the program, especially after we made some changes. Most physicians find no serious problems, although some of the older doctors continue to insist bitterly that the Quadrico Básico violates their right to prescribe as they alone see fit. Eventually, the program will be extended to the private sector of Mexico as well, but this can be done only very gradually, step-by-step, over many years."[11]

One of the main reasons for the acceptability of the Quadro Básico program is emphasized by Sylvestre Frenk, coordinator of research investigations in Mexico's Institute of Social Security. "Physicians and the drug companies have learned that the program is no straitjacket," he says. In the program is an "escape-hatch," a provision that enables a physician to obtain a drug not on the approved list if he can show that it is essential for his patient's welfare.[12]

In 1977 an expert panel of the World Health Organization published what has become known as the WHO essential drugs list.[13] It included 182 products that were proposed as "essential" and 32 named "complementary." Few were still under patent. Most could be purchased as generics on the world market at relatively low cost from reliable producers. There was nothing compulsory about the list; it was set forth as a guideline which could be accepted or rejected by any country, and it could be—and probably should be—modified to fit the needs and pocketbooks of each developing nation. There was no mention of banning any drug not on the list. Use of the list would not lower a country's drug expenditures, but it would help see that those expenditures were used *mainly* for those drugs most sorely needed by most people with serious or life-threatening illness.

In 1981 the essential drugs program was expanded by WHO to become the Action Program on Essential Drugs and Vaccines, or simply the Drug Action Program. The proposed list had no force of law. Nevertheless, it sent some drug companies and their trade associations into a near panic.[14]

The International Federation of Pharmaceutical Manufacturers Associations (IFPMA) warned: "An essential drugs list is, we believe, faulty in both its medical and economic reasoning. Adoption of the WHO report's recommendations . . . might well reduce health standards already attained," and in another statement: "It must be emphasized that any limited list will leave a certain part of the population's needs without adequate treatment and can thus by no means satisfy medical requirements." This argument avoided the unpleasant fact that an enormous part of the population in the Third World was *already* without adequate treatment. The list had been developed in part as an attempt to fill the gap. Predictably, the president of IFPMA attacked the concept of an essential drugs list because it was being advocated by ardent communists. He ignored the fact that it was also being advocated by ardent capitalists and even ardent middle-of-the-roaders.

In the United States, similar criticisms were voiced by the Pharmaceutical Manufacturers Association. The lists, PMA warned in 1985, would have "a very adverse impact on the practice of medicine, the level of competition in the pharmaceutical industry, the rate of pharmaceutical innovation, and the overall cost of illness in human and economic terms."[15] Although the essential drugs list was attacked by spokesmen for many American and British companies, the head of a major U.S. firm told us, "We can live with it."

The WHO essential drugs list program celebrated its tenth anniversary in 1987. As two Kenyan workers pointed out, about 80 countries—

all in the Third World—had adopted the idea. "However," they said, "this principle is not without opposition from physicians who do not want to be restricted to a list of drugs, and from pharmaceutical houses who want to maximize profit without regard to the inequalities in the consumption of their products."[16]

A WHO official, Ernst Lauridsen, noted with pleasure that development agencies and industrialized countries had donated more than $500 million in the last few years to support national essential drugs list programs. "Relations with the pharmaceutical industry are greatly improved," he claimed. "Many manufacturers have abandoned their initial condemnation of the essential drugs concept and now actively contribute on a number of fronts to international and bilateral projects, in particular to quality assurance training for staff from developing countries."[17]

Although some drug companies and a few trade associations continued to snipe at the idea of an essential drugs list and occasionally warmed up their campaign, most have acknowledged that they could live with the program and still make an acceptable profit. At the same time, a few particularly militant activists declared that the essential drugs list program had not gone far enough. Some demanded that it be introduced into the United States, Great Britain, and other industrialized nations. Some even demanded that any product not on the list should be banned. They were rarely taken seriously.

George Teeling Smith, of the British drug industry's Office of Health Economics, said in 1987:

It is worth mentioning in passing that local hospital formularies or local general practice formularies suffer none of the disadvantages of a national "limited list." Because there can still be variation between lists, no product is absolutely excluded, and the benefits of good therapeutic practice—which often comes from familiarity with the medicines actually being prescribed—can be combined with the opportunity for pharmaceutical innovation to flourish. . . .

Turning to the problems of the developing countries . . . one interesting economic argument is whether it is possible to restrict the medical services available to the rich in order to divert them to the more needy poor. Many Utopian socialists believe that this can be achieved. . . .

For the genuinely poor population there is now no dissent by anyone that a cheap "essential drug" policy should be implemented, if at all possible. However, the problem immediately arises that medicines supplied at marginal cost—or even below marginal cost—for the poor may "leak" back into the market intended for the rich. . . . Essential drug lists are now recognised to be the ideal basis for supplying medicines to the poor communities of the Third World countries. It is, however, illogical and counterproductive to extend the same principle to the advanced communities and countries in the world.[18]

In short, drug industry leaders have accepted with more or less grace the idea of using an essential drugs list approach exclusively in the public sector—public hospitals, welfare programs, and the like— but most have stubbornly resisted any application of that approach to the private sector. Of particular interest is the apparent shift in the position of the United States. At the 43rd World Health Assembly early in 1990, the U.S. delegate, Stuart Nightingale, announced that this year the United States would make its first direct contribution to the essential drugs list program.[19]

In a number of industrialized nations, installation of an essential drugs list approach has been made more or less palatable to both physicians and drug companies by a provision for a special import license. This enables a physician to obtain a special license to import an unapproved drug from another country by declaring that such a drug is essential to the appropriate treatment of a specific, named patient. Once such a provision is made into law, the record seems to indicate, it is not used very often.[20]

Patent Infringement

Many major drug companies protested bitterly against the way in which their patents were ignored or taken over in various Third World nations. To some militant consumer activists, putting patents on any- thing so important to life and health as drugs is indecent and should be abolished, and the ignoring of such patents is clearly social justice. But to the brand-name drug industry, patent infringement is clearly outrageous.

Many multinational drug companies have not always been detect- ably charitable to the people of developing nations. They have been charged with using their patents to extort money from the poor people of the Third World and with failing to invest adequately in the develop- ment of drugs to control diseases rampant in developing countries. They have set the prices as high as the market would bear. They have indulged in "transfer pricing"—setting the import prices of raw mate- rials so high that they could claim they had made no profits and hence need pay no taxes.[21] They have, at least in most cases until very recently, failed to use restraint in making claims for their products and in warning against dangerous or possibly lethal side effects.

Many multinational drug companies have been criticized for swamping physicians with too much promotion of their patented products, using small armies of detailers, company representatives ("reps"), *visitadores*, or "propas" (propagandists). Although precise figures are difficult or impossible to obtain, it is estimated that there is one detailer for about every ten or more physicians in the United States, the United Kingdom, and most of northern Europe, but roughly one for every seven physicians in India and Pakistan, one for every six in Peru, one for every four or five physicians in Guatemala, and one for every three physicians in Kenya, Colombia, and Venezuela. (In some instances, the apparent overabundance of detailers in Third World countries is required by the enormous distances some of them must travel to visit physicians and pharmacists.)

Occasionally, in some developing nations, there have been efforts by the government to reduce the intensity, improve the accuracy, and limit the overall quantity of drug promotion undertaken by multinational companies. Third World governments have sought to keep drug promotion entirely free from the bribing of physicians, pharmacists, and drug officials. In the same way, some Third World governments have protested against the interference of a foreign embassy in plans of the country to buy a low-cost generic product rather than a more expensive product obtainable from a large multinational firm. Such efforts to improve drug promotion often brought serious complaints and sometimes personal intervention by the embassies representing the multinational drug firm.

American drug companies in particular have been strongly denounced for having U.S. ambassadors lean heavily on Third World governments—as in Ceylon (now Sri Lanka) and Bangladesh—in efforts to reverse policies considered to be unfriendly to the U.S. firms.

The companies are now donating at least modest supplies of drugs without charge or are selling them at very low cost to the poorest of the Third World countries. They have sought to defend their prices by emphasizing that they need substantial profits to support their research activities. Critics, however, claimed that most of that research was aimed at controlling such ailments as cancer, hypertension, heart disease, and various diseases of the elderly—all matters of great importance in the rich industrialized countries—but very little was invested in research on tropical disease and illnesses of particular importance in developing nations.

The multinational firms complained that they were constantly subjected to irrational price controls, import restrictions, and frequent harassment by Third World governments, subjected to unending demands for bribes, and likely to be expropriated without warning at any time. (Yet, in one bizarre reversal, India—which had long been one of the most violent critics of multinational drug firms—decided to ask these companies to increase their investments in India and develop more drugs and technologies to help the Indian people.[22] Licensing, production, and pricing controls were liberalized, and a group of senior Indian officials visited New York to seek the help of such companies as Pfizer and American Cyanamid.)

During the past few years, a number of major American multinational drug companies have refused to put up with what they looked upon as harassment and have pulled out of Latin American countries. Eli Lilly gave up its investment and ended its operations in Argentina and Chile; Squibb left Chile and Brazil. SmithKline and Upjohn left Argentina; Searle left Argentina and Brazil; Merck Sharp & Dohme left Chile; Lederle left Argentina, Brazil, Colombia, Venezuela, and most Central American countries. Similar moves have been at least threatened in Southeast Asia. "In most such cases," a drug industry official explained, "the companies felt the profits they could achieve simply did not make up for the vexations and frustrations they would have to accept. They couldn't recoup their investment. Each probably asked, 'Who needs it?'"[23]

Numerous American and European pharmaceutical firms have been angered by the policy in some developing nations of refusing to allow a newly patented drug to be approved for import until a domestic company has learned how to produce it—in clear violation of patent— and get it on the market first. In some of these countries, it has been found peculiarly helpful if the head of a domestic drug company has a relative in the ministry of health, or is related to the president of the country. "Here," one Latin American observer noted, "we take pride in the fact that we have a free press. The papers can print anything they want. But it is considered indiscreet for any newspaper to criticize our president—or his girlfriend."

Most certainly, there has been patent infringement in the Third World. In Taiwan, an official of Bristol-Myers declared, violation of patents cost the company 70 percent of its sales on one product "pirated" by six infringers, and 40 percent of its sales on another drug copied by five infringers. "There is an antidote," he said. "Countries sanctioning the theft of American industry's intellectual property are our trading partners. Many, as emerging nations, enjoy privileged treatment under our trade regulations. A great deal might be accomplished if the U.S. government made it clear that only countries which respect and protect the rights of U.S. firms need come seeking favorable treatment from us."[24] Brazil and Mexico, he noted, "simply eliminated patent protection for pharmaceuticals."

In the U.S. Congress, Congressmen John Dingell, Democrat, of Michigan, and Norman Lent, Republican, of New York, noted that Brazil had amended its patent law in 1969 to deny protection for drugs, although patents on other manufactured goods were honored. They agreed that "lack of intellectual property protection is nothing less than a license for Brazilian companies to steal American research and development. . . . If the Brazilians will not play by fair rules, then they must know that the U.S. will retaliate against their exports to this country."[25]

In 1988, pressed by the American drug industry, the Congress amended the U.S. Tariff Act to require the U.S. trade representative to notify the president of countries that denied adequate and effective protection of intellectual property rights to U.S. companies that rely on patent or copyright protection. The president would then be authorized, but not required, to act "as he deemed appropriate."[26]

The White House announced in July 1988 that the president was ready to move. "President Reagan has found Brazil's refusal to provide adequate patent protection for US pharmaceutical and fine chemicals to be unfair under Section 301 of the Trade Act of 1974. In response, the President has decided to impose sanctions on certain Brazilian imports."[27]

In October Reagan ordered a 100 percent tariff on imported Brazilian paper products, consumer electronics, and certain Brazilian-made drugs. "We regret that it is necessary to take this step," U.S. trade commissioner Clayton Yeutter said. "Retaliation should be an action of last resort in any trade dispute; that has been the case here. The

Administration has made every effort to resolve this issue over the past two years. . . . We hope that it will be possible to lift these sanctions in the near future."[28]

The president of Brazil called the sanctions "absurd and unjust," and claimed that the U.S. decision was "unjustified and discriminatory."[29] There was, of course, no mention of the possibility that, if things became worse, the United States might eventually feel obliged to reexamine the import duties on Brazilian coffee.

By early 1989 President Suharto of Indonesia announced the introduction of legislation to establish his country's first patent law, including protection for drugs. South Korea had developed a compromise approach to patent protection. Canada had modified its compulsory licensing provisions for drugs. In 1990 the patent laws in Taiwan were undergoing revision.[30] But there were still serious problems with Argentina, India, and Pakistan, and Thailand and Mexico had postponed any patent protection for drugs until at least 1997.[31] The situation was not yet a happy one.

Storm over Mr. Medawar

One of the most illuminative—and at times most comical—insights into the problems of the pharmaceutical industry came in 1987, when the International Meeting of Pharmaceutical Physicians and the British Association of Pharmaceutical Physicians (BAPP) was held in Brighton, England. Denis Burley of Ciba-Geigy, vice-chairman of the BAPP, was invited to arrange the program. As a particular feature, he asked Charles Medawar to present his views, and then he invited Harry Schwartz to comment.

Medawar, director of a London consumerist group called Social Audit, was probably the most respected and certainly the most articulate consumerist in Europe. He had been closely involved with the concept of essential drugs lists—the idea that each nation should place major emphasis on the relatively few drugs, perhaps 200 or so, that were the most important for the benefit of its people. Schwartz, a former member of the *New York Times* editorial board, was writer-in-residence in Columbia University's College of Physicians and Surgeons in New York. Medawar elected to discuss the failings of the pharmaceutical industry:

I have premised the arguments in this paper on what I think to be three main points of agreement. The first is that the pharmaceutical industry does have failings; the second is that it is subject to a good deal of criticism; and the third is that the industry does not seem to be able to handle this criticism very well. . . .

The first of these questions arises in any country which lacks essential health services—but applies most of all in developing countries, especially in the light of what is still professed as a "solemn commitment" by the 160-odd member nations of the World Health Organisation to "Health for all by the year 2000." Why should these countries be expected to contribute to the future prosperity of the drug industry, when they can meet basic needs with only a few hundred essential drugs, whose research and development costs have already been paid for? . . . Because the pharmaceutical industry can expect to recover research and development costs only years after investments are made, it tends to react very sharply to criticism—perhaps because it interprets this as a foretaste of a different kind of tomorrow. The above may partly explain why the industry often seems to respond to criticism by trying to overwhelm or undermine it— rather than by acknowledging that something might have gone wrong. . . .

The point to be made here is not that the industry either is or isn't fun to have as a friend. It is to suggest that the intensity of the industry's reaction to criticism caused it to misjudge the opposition it faces and therefore to respond quite inappropriately to it.

He quoted from a statement by Kenneth Clarke, then Britain's minister of state for health:

"The reaction from the vested interests to our proposals to contain expensive and unnecessary prescribing under the health service has been close to hysterical. The pharmaceutical industry is spending hundreds of thousands of pounds on alarmist and misleading advertising opposing the scheme. They have claimed that important drugs not affected by the proposal will be banned. It is tactics of this sort which have brought the industry's promotional activities into such disrepute."

Medawar continued:

In the end, the effect of the industry's barrage was to help the Government to achieve its objective, making the industry pretty unpopular at the same time. Similarly, the industry's personal attacks on its critics—for example, questioning their sincerity or competence or political affiliations—probably work to the same general effect.

Over the past ten years, I have seen such initiatives backfire over and over again. Things may now be improving but, thinking of the immediate past, I have no doubt at all that much of the industry's response to the consumer movement has contributed greatly to that movement's credibility and rapid growth. . . . I also think it a mistake for the industry to counter what it feels is severe persecution by emphasizing its own great importance.[32]

Before he made his presentation, Medawar confided to friends that he intended to offer Harry Schwartz enough rope, in the fond expectation that the latter would hang himself with it. Afterward, Medawar told associates that Schwartz had apparently obliged.

In his account of the Brighton confrontation, Schwartz, staunch defender of the American drug industry and the American Medical Association, had this to say:

Let me discuss first the annual meeting in Chicago of the American Medical Association House of Delegates. What made this meeting unique was the attendance of the PMA executive committee. . . . It was a remarkable display of AMA-PMA amity. . . . It was an unexpectedly different scene I observed in Brighton, England. This was the meeting of the International Federation of Associations of Pharmaceutical Physicians. . . . I was there as a participant in a session, the obvious purpose of which was to have me debate Charles Medawar, the intellectual leader of anti-pharmaceutical industry Health Action International. . . . In his speech, Mr. Medawar planned his tactics well. He presented himself as a well-intentioned friend of the pharmaceutical industry. . . . Mr. Medawar is no friend of the pharmaceutical industry. If he had his way, the industry would be much reduced, and what was left would be far less prosperous than it is. He is, for example, one of the most articulate proponents of the essential-drugs policy, supporters of which now seek to have all nations, including the United States, proclaim an essential-drugs list of perhaps 200–300 items. All other drugs would be difficult or perhaps impossible to obtain.

(This last is far from the truth. The concept of an essential drugs list is aimed at giving priority to the drugs most urgently needed for most of the people in each developing country, with drastically limited budgets, but it is not aimed at banning any useful product.)

The preceding paragraphs suggest the tone and some of the content of my speech. After I finished, we all sat back for the question period. To my astonishment, most questions indicated that a majority of the audience sympathized with Mr. Medawar and disliked what I had said.

Schwartz also had some views about the editors of undoubtedly the two most authoritative medical journals in Great Britain:

In the many years that I have read *Lancet* and the *British Medical Journal*, I have seen abundant evidence of how socialist-minded the editors of those publications are, along with many of their readers whose letters they print. . . . All of this makes me worry about what will happen to the world and American pharmaceutical industries when Ronald Reagan leaves the White House and some Democrat or "soft" Republican succeeds him. It is Mr. Reagan who has frustrated the plans of Mr. Medawar and his colleagues to use WHO as an instrument with which to "tame" the pharmaceutical industry these past six or seven years. After my visit to Brighton, I can understand that, without him in the White House, the world pharmaceutical industry's situation may deteriorate drastically and quickly.[33]

After the Brighton meeting, Denis Burley, who had arranged the program, commented:

May I be accorded some right of reply to the startling article by Dr. Harry Schwartz in the September issue of *Pharmaceutical Executive*? I must say I find it rather surprising that in the late 20th century it is still believed that the views of consumer leaders such as Mr. Charles Medawar can be met by ignoring him, barring him from meetings, attaching to him political labels, or using various forms of financial, political, or journalistic muscle to subdue him. My view, and that of our Association is, if the views of the critics cannot be met by reasonable and reasoned discussion, we perhaps deserve to lose our jobs. . . . I find myself in considerable disagreement with many of Mr. Charles Medawar's views on medical and pharmaceutical matters but pay tribute to his knowledge and intelligence and the articulate and courteous way he puts forward his views. Indeed, I acknowledge that had many of us listened to him and others like him a little more carefully in the past, we might have avoided some of the embarrassing retractions and U-turns that the industry has had to endure in the past 10 years.[34]

An Alternative Voice from the Industry

During the last few years, an official of the Swiss firm Ciba-Geigy has attracted particular interest within the drug and chemical industries, both in Europe and in the United States. We met him about ten years ago, in Kenya, where he was in charge of Ciba-Geigy's pharmaceutical operations in East and Central Africa. He was engaged in defending one particular product, the antidiarrhea drug Enterovioform, which was being held responsible for the fearsome outbreak of SMON in Japan (see Chapter 11). We felt that he was browbeating a young Kenyan newspaper reporter who had written a report that criticized the drug.

Years later we met him again, in Switzerland, where he had been put in charge of Ciba-Geigy's advisory staff working on relations with Third World countries. Eventually, he became a close friend. One day we asked him, "How could you have jumped all over that poor newspaper lady in Kenya and defended Enterovioform?" "The explanation is embarrassing but really very simple," he said. "Some medical people in my home office had not told me the whole truth."

He is Klaus Leisinger; he has won the strong support of Ciba-Geigy management. To a steadily increasing number of people, he is being looked upon as the conscience of the drug industry. In February 1988 he published his first article to attract significant attention from leaders in the drug and chemical industries. It was published, not in a pharmaceutical or chemical journal, but in the *New York Times* under the heading, "Sell Solutions, Not Just Products." He said:

The special responsibilities that corporations take on in dealing with developing nations do bring trouble and expense in the short and medium term. . . . Since markets in industrialized nations are usually more attractive, why get involved in the third world at all? Because the problems of underdevelopment constitute the most pressing social issue of the 20th century. All who can contribute to solutions must do so, not only out of humanitarian motives but also in the interest of insuring long-term peace. . . . Corporations should develop policies—a kind of internal code of conduct—for sensitive areas like marketing, product quality and environmental protection. *Not everything that is legal locally is ethical.* (Italics ours.)

Other rules in our own code of conduct include having no differences between industrial and developing nations regarding quality of products and services, product safety, instructions for use and production safety. We also call for pursuing the same goals in the third world as anywhere else when it comes to environmental protection. This mostly means far exceeding local standards.[35]

For those who recalled the Ciba and Geigy firms only a few decades before, with their apparent custom of having one set of rules for the Third World and another for industrial nations, and with a habit in developing countries of "let's take the money and run," this was impressive. There was more to come.

Later in 1988 Leisinger published what he termed a "workbook" on international development. He asked M.S. to provide a foreword, which included these words:

Since the 1950s few international questions have proved to be so sensitive as the matter of how—or even if—the industrialised nations of the West should help the poor countries of the Third World to develop. A vast array of simplistic global answers has been offered by political scientists, government officials, roving journalists, and compassionate humanitarians. . . . Regrettably, says Switzerland-based Klaus Leisinger, none of these simple, obvious solutions will work, whether they come from the far capitalistic right or the far Marxist left. There is no single global program that will be appropriate for every developing nation. Simply "redistributing the wealth" would be useless. The donor nations alone cannot dictate all the decisions. Nor can the recipient countries make all the rules. . . . Dr. Leisinger proposes not a solution but a pathway to reach solutions. Involved are consultations rather than confrontations, participation by both (or many) parties, decisions based more on decency than on geopolitics, and a careful balancing of short-term and long-term goals.

In his text Leisinger said:

Today we regard it as unacceptable for high economic growth to benefit only a small social stratum in developing countries if it does not also, within a reasonable period of time, bring material advantages to the broad masses of the population. What, however, is a reasonable period of time? From the point of view of the parents concerned, and in the light of overriding humanitarian principles, no period of time is "reasonable" when children are dying of hunger or of preventable infectious diseases—and this is happening at present about 40,000 times a day, 365 days a year. Such considerations make a moral approach to the problem of the physical reality of poverty unavoidable. It becomes necessary to take a stand, because indifference or inactivity imply an acceptance of this suffering.[36]

Immediate aid programs and crisis management are essential, he claimed, but they should be carried out as well as, and at the same time as, long-term development programs. Sharing in the decision-making process must be not only those who live in absolute poverty but also the wealthier people whose perspectives may be warped in some cases by what has been called the "arrogance of the well-fed."

Leisinger also called for a reconsideration of national budgetary priorities. Too often, he noted, it is the very poorest of the Third World countries that earmarks the largest portion of its budget for weapons. He indicated how such money could be better invested:

- The cost of a modern tank would be sufficient to improve the storage of rice in order to provide a day's supply of food for 8 million people.
- The cost of a modern warplane would be enough to set up 40,000 village pharmacies with a range of basic medicines.
- Military expenditures made in a single week would be sufficient to eradicate leprosy in the Third World.

Finally, he displayed the courage to question one of the most sacred of all the environmentalists' sacred cows, Rachel Carson, whose 1962

Silent Spring became the rallying cry for all those who would preserve every animal and plant species in nature:

Thus it is that a hypothesized connection between the use of DDT and the fragility of birds' eggshells leads to a ban on its use, instead of to a restriction, which would have been sensible. People who died from malaria as a consequence of this ban are less visible and attractive to the media. "Silent spring" versus silenced children.

In the following year, Leisinger turned his attention to multinational drug companies. He stated:

Many people view pharmaceuticals for people in the Third World in a poor light. Some argue that drug manufacturers do more harm than good, marketing medicines merely for profit while side effects outweigh therapeutic benefits. There have been, undeniably, some blatant examples of entrepreneurial misconduct. Admittedly, too, the prospect of allegedly risk-free, quick and high profits will tempt some irresponsible people in the future. But such behavior is not only wrong, ethically and legally. It is also bad for business.

Internationally active companies and their management are under constant scrutiny through the media. Disclosures of misconduct damage business and demoralize employees. From my own experience, I am convinced that such cases are exceptional. They are not "the tip of the iceberg," as is often claimed. Generalized criticisms of "bitter pills" are just as misplaced as exaggerated expectations of "wonder drugs."[37]

From within its own ranks, it seems, the drug industry has found a spokesman who has drafted a pathway far different from the one followed for so many years by most leaders of the industry. Along one path designed by Klaus Leisinger lie greater social responsibility, an appreciation of decent behavior, and a higher ethical standard of behavior. Along another path, enthusiastically advocated by Harry Schwartz and many of his supporters, lie character assassination, exaggeration, and the continued pursuit of profit without regard for the clinical, social, or ethical consequences. Clearly, we should explore the ideas contained in Leisinger's work.

Another expert—also of Ciba-Geigy—Klaus von Grebmer, vice-president for public relations, with Hans-Christian Röglin, of the Institute of Applied Social Psychology in Düsseldorf, Germany, has recently focused on a somewhat related problem, which has long plagued the chemical industry in general and the pharmaceutical industry in particular.[38] This concerns the public image the industry has created for itself, which industry leaders are now vigorously striving to change.

It is clear that the public is only too well aware that the industry has been associated with unsightly, dangerous, or lethal pollution of air, soil, and water—with disastrous fires and explosions, with acid rain and the "greenhouse effect," and with drugs that are supposed to help control disease but that may cause injury or deformity or death. Some companies have sought to find a solution in "public relations," but this has been downgraded into publicity—publicity aimed at promoting public confidence and gaining trust. Those efforts have obviously failed. "He who is forever stressing that he can be trusted," Röglin and von Grebmer stated, "renders himself suspect and would do better to hold his tongue."

The industry may search for sympathetic understanding, but it should not count on receiving any. The industry cannot expect much sympathy from the public when people learn that a pill promoted with glowing praise turns out to cause blindness or the birth of deformed children. "We must therefore ask ourselves," they said, "whether the concept of public relations work designed to win trust and acceptance by seeking sympathy has not, in fact, led to the crisis."

Some chemical firms, especially some large pharmaceutical companies, have constantly complained that they are the targets of unfair criticism, that the public doesn't understand the situation. Many industrial leaders have been distressed by the communications campaigns conducted so successfully by consumer activists and public interest groups.

But, Röglin and von Grebmer noted, the lack of public understanding—not recognizing, for example, that *any* drug has the power to cause injury or death—marks the failure of industry to live up to its responsibilities. In the past, industry usually decided to say nothing in such situations in the belief that it is better to let sleeping dogs slumber. Unfortunately, they pointed out, "the dogs are generally awake." Further, they observed, consumer groups obviously like to use communications because they have learned to use them well.

Much of the present dilemma, Röglin and von Grebmer claim, stems from the fact that we live in a world in which most of us believe that big industry is competent to solve tough problems, but in which big industry cannot be trusted. In contrast, we trust the little fellow in our hometown, but we think he cannot accomplish very much. They expressed the hope that the "righteous silence" of industry will be superseded by frank consensus and openness, the seeking of discussions with the public and the media. The industry, they emphasized, must stop viewing the media as its enemy; there must be open, honest, factual discussion of the risks and benefits of every chemical product. And, they added, a company must never try to hide its mistakes. "A mistake correctly dealt with," they said, "is a company's most important asset."

Chapter 4

THE GREAT GENERICS CONTROVERSY

For many decades drug companies in the United States had been accustomed to operate under a federal law that presumably offered them patent protection or exclusivity for a period of seventeen years. After that time competitors could apply for the right to make and market the same drug. The original drug was generally known as the original brand-name or innovative product. The later versions were generic competitors. They were supposedly less expensive.

That, however, was not the whole story. In the past a company discovering a new drug would apply immediately for a patent, which usually was issued in a reasonably short time. Thereafter, as soon as the drug had been approved by the Food and Drug Administration—a process that might take a few months or a year or so—the company would be permitted to market its new product. Of the seventeen years of legal patent life, the firm still had fifteen or sixteen years remaining in which to recoup its investment. But in 1962 the law was changed to require lengthy and costly efficacy studies. In addition, the companies complained, the FDA approval process began to take an unreasonable and increasingly longer time. As new drugs became more and more complex, as more sophisticated and more time-consuming tests were introduced, as mounting pressure was exerted on FDA to keep all dangerous drugs off the market, as FDA demanded more time-consuming and more expensive tests to prove safety and efficacy, and as drug companies faced more and more lawsuits involving product liability, the approval procedures began to look like a pharmacological nightmare. Where they once could be completed easily and quickly, they now required five, eight, even ten years (although important breakthrough drugs may get faster action), with the maximum seventeen years of patent life steadily running out. Simultaneously, the price to get a new drug on the market skyrocketed to $50 or $75 million, and is now in some cases $200 million or more. Instead of having the full seventeen years of patent protection, the company would find that it had only twelve, or ten, or perhaps seven years left to recoup its investment, earn money for future research, and make a profit before generic competitors could appear and cut into their sales.

This situation brought a variety of charges and countercharges:

- The consumerists declared that the brand-name or research-intensive companies were putting extortionate charges on their patented products and were reaping indecent profits.
- The brand-name companies argued that the high prices were caused by the limited patent-protection life left to them by the long-drawn-out FDA approval process.
- In turn, some brand-name companies denounced the generic companies as inferior, unhygienic, incompetent "schlock houses," and charged that many if not most generic products were inferior, probably contaminated or impure, and represented a threat to the health or even the life of patients.
- This last attack was denounced both by consumerists and by the generic companies themselves, who insisted that *all* generic products, if they contained the same amount of the same active ingredient, were therapeutically equivalent to the brand-name product.
- Further, the brand-name firms declared, the new law would allow generic firms to enter the market and start earning profits more quickly, while any advantage for the brand-name companies would be uncertain and delayed for many years.[1]

This dispute flared with notable noise and venom, particularly during the 1960s, especially when many medical journals or medical throwaway newsletters—both financed largely by drug advertising from the brand-name industry—opened hostilities against the generic drug companies. Many of the disputes were aired during the so-called Kefauver hearings before the U.S. Senate.[2]

In the late 1960s, as members of the Department of Health, Education, and Welfare's Task Force on Prescription Drugs, we were obliged to investigate this controversial area. We spent some twenty months on our investigation and made detailed studies in such institutions as military, Veterans Administration, Public Health Service, and leading university teaching hospitals, and a variety of health insurance programs. At the end, we, our colleagues, and our consultants presented three conclusions:

- Given two drug products containing essentially the same amount of the same active ingredient, the two products may not in *all* cases produce the same clinical effects.
- But, we added, *"On the basis of available evidence, lack of clinical equivalency among chemical equivalents meeting all official standards has been grossly exaggerated as a major hazard to the public health."*
- Just as we had noted a small number of cases of nonequivalency between a generic product and its brand-name competitor, we also found a small number of differences between two batches of the same drug made by the same manufacturer.[3]

Another quarrel involved the probable savings in cost that could come with the voluntary or required use of generic products. Consumerists, noting that some generics were priced 40, 50, or 60 percent below their brand-name competitors, predicted enormous savings in the nation's drug bill. Their brand-name competitors pointed to the fact that there were very few generic products yet available for brand-name drugs, most offered only minimal savings, and accordingly, savings would be only trivial.

In the Task Force, we estimated the theoretical savings possible under a variety of approaches, most of these based on how the pharmacist would calculate his markup or dispensing fee. We concluded that the *maximum* savings on the nation's drug bill would be about 6 percent at the retail level. Under more realistic conditions, the savings might be about 2.5 to 3 percent.[4] The generics industry was distressed.

Four years later President Nixon's recently appointed secretary of health, education, and welfare, Caspar Weinberger, (who would later become Ronald Reagan's secretary of defense) testified before a senate subcommittee headed by Senator Edward Kennedy of Massachusetts and discussed the possibility of requiring the use of generics in such federally supported programs as Medicare and Medicaid. He agreed that differences in biological equivalency or availability could occur, but he added, "All the evidence to date indicates that clinically significant differences in bioavailability are not frequent." He estimated that the possible savings would be about 5 to 8 percent in overall reimbursements for prescription drugs.[5]

All during the 1970s and early 1980s, Congress heard increasing complaints from the brand-name drug companies that delays in obtaining FDA approval were cutting their supposedly seventeen years of patent protection down to eight years or less, while the generic drug companies were complaining that it was becoming needlessly difficult to get FDA approval for marketing a new generic product. In 1984 Congress passed the Drug Price Competition and Patent Term Restoration Act. This much negotiated but controversial piece of legislation was meant, on the one hand, to simplify and speed up the process of getting new generic products on the market and, on the other, to guarantee to brand-name firms that they would get, not additional patent protection, but a restoration of some of the protection—up to five years—they had lost because of government red tape.

The new act was intended to please both sides. Instead, it angered almost everybody. Consumerists were furious that brand-name companies would have additional years to charge the public with what they termed extortionate prices, and brand-name companies were equally outraged that their generic competitors would get to the market more quickly.

The Antigenerics Rumors

At about the same time, it was becoming apparent that a carefully orchestrated attack, led largely by multinational brand-name firms, was being leveled in the United States against generic drugs on the grounds that they were—or *might be*—impure, contaminated, or inadequately effective. In short, the message read, generic products simply could not be trusted.

The attacks were amazingly similar. The identity of a patient was almost never revealed, nor was the name of a physician or a hospital, which could be checked by a good reporter. It was generally "a number of doctors" were finding that "their patients were not responding properly"; or "physicians using this generic anticonvulsive drug are concerned that their epileptic patients are breaking through"; or "of course, you do what you like, but if it were my wife or my child . . . "; or "I don't know if you're worried about a malpractice suit, but . . ." Instead of hard facts, there usually were mere anecdotes.

"Such antigeneric campaigns now occur with 'predictable regularity,' " said Peter Rheinstein of the FDA's Office of Drug Standards. "Every time a brand-name drug becomes vulnerable to generic competition, the makers do whatever they can to protect their market."[6]

Three large brand-name drug companies were noticeably active in this campaign. One was Hoffmann–La Roche, of Switzerland, which was losing its patent protection on the tranquilizer Valium, one of the most profitable drugs ever discovered, and was about to face intense competition from a host of inexpensive generic diazepam products. Another was also a Swiss company, Sandoz, which was losing patent protection on its successful antidepressive Mellaril and was expecting to compete against low-cost but apparently inferior thioridazine generic competitors. The third was Ayerst Laboratories, a division of American Home Products, which was losing its patent protection on Inderal, a particularly profitable drug for the treatment of hypertension, and was facing competition from less costly propranolol generics.

These three firms, along with a number of others, apparently had the strong support of individual physicians and pharmacists who, it was suggested, spoke out, not to preserve drug company profits, but purely out of concern for their patients. The possibility that these individuals had a different reason for their attacks against generics was offered by a number of newspapers. In August 1984 the *Wall Street Journal* published an account that began:

This summer, Paul Doering is warning audiences of television and radio talk shows from Boston to San Diego that it is "dangerous" to use generic copies of prescription drugs for treating potentially life-threatening disorders such as heart disease, high blood pressure, diabetes and epilepsy. What the associate professor of pharmacy practice at the University of Florida neglects to say is that his 10-city media tour and his consulting fee are being paid for by American Home Products Corp. The company has more than a passing interest in spreading Mr. Doering's message; its single most profitable product, the heart drug Inderal, will lose its patent protection this month, and, for the first time in 17 years, it will be vulnerable to competition from less expensive generic copies.[7]

In the summer of 1985, California pharmacists received a notice headline "Generic Alert!!!!" It was sent by Pharmacists Planning Service, described as a nonprofit educational organization headed by Frederick Mayer, a Sausalito, California, pharmacist. Pharmacists were warned of lawsuits that could arise if they did not dispense "brand-name propranolol"—that is, Ayerst's Inderal. A short time later, according to *Consumer Reports*, Mayer received a $10,000 check from Ayerst "to support the educational goals of the Pharmacists Planning Service."[8]

Ayerst also supported a study at the University of Pennsylvania, which reported that the savings presumably made possible by the use of generics were of only minor significance. Based on an examination of drugs dispensed over a three-month period in 1984, it demonstrated that the savings resulting from the dispensing of generic products were far less than had been expected. The explanation seemed obvious: although all 50 states allowed or required generic substitution, in only 19 states was there a requirement that any savings must be passed on to the customer. In many states, it was found, pharmacists were adding a far higher markup on the generic products that they dispensed.[9]

Sandoz attacked the use of generic versions of Mellaril, its drug widely used to treat schizophrenia and other psychotic diseases. The company contended that generic copies of Mellaril are not equivalent and that doctors risk their patients' health if a generic is substituted. But Jerome Skelly of the FDA declared, "There is no scientific basis for Sandoz's claims." At FDA insistence, the company backed down in a "Dear Pharmacist" letter, which reversed previous Sandoz charges and acknowledged that clinical dissimilarities between generic thioridazine and Mellaril had not been demonstrated in clinical trials.[10] Hoechst-Roussel Pharmaceuticals had sent thousands of letters to doctors warning that to substitute generics for its Lasix, a drug used against high blood pressure, "could cause unanticipated clinical problems." Skelly said Hoechst's claims were untrue.

There was little or nothing that FDA could do to prevent physicians or pharmacists from putting out what the agency branded as "false and misleading statements," unsupported with scientific evidence. But, FDA announced, it could do something about a company that was paying for this kind of "disparagement." It would consider the statements to be part of the company's drug labeling and would call for whatever civil or criminal penalties seemed indicated.

In this generics warfare, neither side paid much attention to the truth. Generic companies and consumerist spokesmen frequently gave the impression that the brand-name firms could extort the high prices on their product for the full seventeen years of the patent life, ignoring the fact that eight, nine, or even more years could be used up in efforts to get FDA approval. The generics advocates insisted, not that generics were *almost always* clinically equivalent to the brand-name products, but that they were *absolutely always* equivalent. And, pointing to the fact that some generics cost only about 50 percent as much as their brand-name competitors, they suggested that virtually all generics could offer such huge savings. One consumerist group gave this account:

Generic drugs are chemically and therapeutically equivalent to name-brand counterparts but on average cost half as much. The Food and Drug Administration has never found any to be deficient in clinical use. But name-brand manufacturers continue to suggest significant differences—in, for instance, the speed with which a chemical may be absorbed by the body. Claims about such physiological rather than pharmacological attributes confuse physicians and patients.

The controversy has existed for decades. It became intense after Congress enacted compromise legislation in 1984. Name-brand manufacturers were given an extension of patent life on their discoveries from 17 to as many as 22 years—almost a quarter century in which to recover drug development costs and to profit without competition.[11]

Most of the foregoing is untrue. By definition, generic drugs must be chemically equivalent to the brand-name products. But they may or may not be clinically or therapeutically equivalent. In the past, lack of clinical equivalence has been discovered and documented—not frequently, but it has happened.[12] Moreover, the very idea that a company can market a patented drug for 22 years, or even 17, without competition is particularly nonsensical.

The brand-name supporters have likewise inflicted damage on the truth. They continued to circulate unsupported rumors of the clinical failure of generic drugs. They encouraged the belief that most generic products were made by firms that were unsanitary, incompetent, and inexperienced. (As a matter of fact, approximately 80 percent of the generic products were marketed by such brand-name firms as Abbott, Bristol-Myers, Ciba-Geigy, Lederle, Eli Lilly, Merck Sharp & Dohme, Pfizer, Robins, SmithKline, Squibb, Upjohn, and Warner-Lambert.)

Repeatedly, brand-name drug companies—the innovative firms

that are engaged in most of the new-drug development—have warned that the "unfair" competition they face from generics will sooner or later dry up their research funds and slow the discovery of new and better drugs. In spite of this gloomy forecast, however, many if not most major research-minded drug companies are now spending *more* on research than ever before.[13]

In the United States, generic products represent about one-quarter of the nation's prescription drug bill. Under constant pressure to reduce the costs of health care, hospitals, health insurance systems, and other large-scale purchasers have found the use of generics particularly appealing. These large-scale drug buyers have been singularly unimpressed by the scare tactics used against low-cost generics. It is probable that the proportion of the market taken by generics will increase as more brand-name products lose their patent protection, with the probability that they will not be rapidly replaced by important new patented discoveries.

One of the most well balanced, reasoned analyses of the nonequivalence situation was offered by one of this country's highly regarded figures in the field, Brian Strom of the University of Pennsylvania. In 1987 he presented this view:

Of the products proved to be generically equivalent by FDA standards, remarkably few have been shown to be clinically inequivalent. Certainly, unconfirmed suggestions of the possibility of inequivalence are not a sufficient basis for presuming its presence and acting on that presumption. Anecdotal reports are similarly unhelpful, since one is often unable to distinguish product failure from a natural variation in the course of the disease. Yet, ignorance about therapeutic inequivalence is no guarantee that it does not exist.[14]

The FDA's process for approving new drugs needs improvement and eventually will be improved. "In the meantime," he said, "physicians and patients can continue to consider using generic drugs, bearing in mind that their use may result in financial savings and that few generic drugs have been found to be clinically inequivalent to their brand-name counterparts."

Generics Overseas

Generic drugs have received a variety of receptions outside the United States. In the United Kingdom, for example, they are used commonly in Britain's National Health Service hospitals, but they are not generally dispensed by British retail pharmacy shops. Pharmacists have apparently little confidence in the low-cost versions. The Association of the British Pharmaceutical Industry (ABPI) was among the industry groups that warned that the hospital use of generics would be marked by the appearance of inferior or nonequivalent products and therapeutic failure. A four-year study, however, showed that nothing of the kind came to pass.[15] In West Germany, the government has placed a cap on some drug prices, holding these close to the level of low-cost generics. Many if not most major pharmaceutical brand-name firms fear that this policy may spread throughout the European Community after 1992.

In the developing countries of the Third World, generics have seldom received a warm welcome. Even with their grievous lack of foreign exchange and their shocking shortages of drugs, these countries have wasted enormous sums in buying expensive brand-name products. (See, however, Chapter 9 for an account of the attempts of Ciba-Geigy's Servipharm division and other multinationals to make low-cost, high-quality products more readily available to poor countries.)

So that Third World countries could conserve their scarce funds, the World Health Organization had long urged them to buy high-quality, low-cost generics. The problem was that few developing nations could manufacture the drugs themselves, and few if any had adequate quality-control laboratories to test the quality of drugs available on the world market. Likewise, WHO urged the smaller countries to pool their purchases in order to get the best prices. The same kind of group could join together, WHO said, to set up a regional laboratory fully equipped to carry out the more sophisticated quality-control tests. This was actually done by the Caribbean Community Secretariat, with help from the Canadian International Development Agency and the Pan American Health Organization, which established the Caribbean Regional Drug Testing Laboratory in Jamaica in 1979.[16]

"In general, generics-bashing is not as open in developing nations as it seems to be in the States," one African drugs expert informed us. "We don't see the barrage of letters to editors, or legislators, or government purchasing officials that you get in America." Rather, the attack against generics seems to be waged more through sporadic word-of-mouth campaigns, with rumors spread at various social gatherings where physicians like to relax and exchange gossip. At such meetings we have been fascinated—sometimes astounded—to learn that American physicians have seen "so many injuries and deaths caused by bad generic products that they no longer permit any generic to be administered to their patients," or that "university and teaching hospitals now ban generics and only third-rate hospitals allow generics to be used," or that American courts are "deluged by damage suits filed against generic companies," or that the U.S. FDA "no longer will approve any new generic product."

Various governmental agencies have sought to combat such vicious or ridiculous notions. Top FDA officials published this statement in the *Journal of the American Medical Association* in 1987: "Although the FDA continues to seek evidence of unequal therapeutic effects between approved generic and brand-name products in healthy or sick persons, none has yet been received. . . . We have yet to receive a documented instance of a serious problem with a generic drug."[17]

But, in many countries, physicians, pharmacists, patients, and policymakers continued to believe what they wanted to believe, and—regardless of official reassurances—many health professionals and their patients remained confused and apprehensive. In Senegal, for example, Issa Diop, head of the National Pharmacy in the Ministry of Health, told us that physicians in his country, like many in France, are not comfortable with generics. "My medical friends simply do not trust generics," he explained. "They find it impossible to believe that such products are so widely used in the United States."[18] In Indonesia, multinational drug firms are not allowed to market generics. These products are made by small local houses, and physicians do not trust these companies.[19]

The Generic Drugs Scandal

Then, beginning in 1988, there came a series of disclosures in the United States that would rock both the drug industry and the FDA. In a September 21 press release, FDA announced that a Denver generics supplier, Pharmaceutical Basics, was voluntarily recalling tens of millions of tablets of its antiepilepsy drug carbamazepine, the generic version of Ciba-Geigy's original product, Tegretol. In this case, the action was based not on rumor or anecdotal reports but on carefully controlled clinical trials. "The tablets," the agency stated, "are being recalled because they do not dissolve well and thus may not enter the bloodstream as expected. FDA has received 15 reports of problems, including some unexpected seizures."[20] The inadequacy of at least some generic products could no longer be denied.

Meanwhile, another storm was brewing. In Pittsburgh, officials of Mylan Laboratories—one of the larger generic firms in the country—felt they were being unfairly treated by FDA. "In 1985," Roy McKnight, chief executive officer, would testify later, "our employees began returning from meetings in a state of shock over the treatment they were receiving at the hands of the Generic Division Agency personnel, whose decisions are critical to our business, [and who] were repeatedly refusing to meet with representatives of our company. Our employees were regularly subjected to public abuse by these same officials." McKnight claimed he had tried to get Marvin Seife, head of FDA's generics division, to rectify the situation. "He steadfastly refused to do so and became increasingly hostile toward Mylan."[21]

Two years later Mylan officials felt they were "practically a shoo-in" to win approval for their generic product, Maxzide, for the control of hypertension, to compete against SmithKline's enormously profitable product, Dyazide. "They were understandably upset when a small firm called American Therapeutics, Inc., snared the coveted approval from the Food and Drug Administration five weeks before Mylan did."[22] Mylan quietly discussed the situation with other major generics firms that were having similar problems with FDA. All of them were unhappy, but the others feared to make the issue public, convinced they would be hit by FDA reprisals. Accordingly, Mylan decided to take action on its own. It hired its own detectives, who—among other things—dug through the garbage cans at the homes of FDA officials and turned up incontrovertible evidence that some of those officials were being bribed.[23]

Mylan decided it would be imprudent to disclose this information to anyone at FDA. Instead, the company took it to the House Subcommittee on Oversight and Investigations, chaired by Congressman John Dingell of Michigan, and to the U.S. attorney in Baltimore, Maryland, the district in which FDA headquarters were located.

The Dingell Committee Drug Hearings

The Dingell committee held its first meeting in what was called an executive session on the Generic Drug Approval Process on May 3, 1989. Dingell said:

There is substantial evidence that the irregularities are widespread. For a large number of companies submitting multiple applications for generic drug approvals, the process was rigged. . . . We hope that no more than a handful of FDA employees will ultimately prove to have been so corrupt as to merit criminal prosecution. But the acceptance of payoffs is only part of the story of a process chock-full of favoritism and inconsistency."[24]

Only the FDA review chemist Walter Kletch appeared that day. At first, he took refuge in the Fifth Amendment and refused to testify, on the grounds that his testimony might incriminate him, but later he decided to plead guilty of "accepting illegal gratuities or related crimes." Ultimately, a handful of other FDA Generics Division scientists did likewise. (Throughout, the Dingell committee worked closely with the U.S. attorney in Baltimore.)

But the star of the scandal was supervisory chemist Charles Chang. It was charged that he had accepted furniture, a computer, and a round-the-world trip as gifts from American Therapeutics of Bohemia, New York. It was at Chang's home that detectives hired by Mylan turned up incontrovertible evidence of bribery and corruption.[25] On May 9, 1989, the U.S. attorney's office in Baltimore announced that charges had been filed against Chang on two counts of "interstate travel in aid of racketeering." Each charge carried a maximum prison sentence of five years and a maximum fine of $250,000. The bribes, it was stated, were given by American Therapeutics. The Baltimore office also released Chang's affidavit, which provided additional insights into the operations of the FDA. Chang stated:

I was a supervisory chemist in the Division of Generic Drugs of the U.S. Food and Drug Administration from January 1985 to April 1989. . . . I was the supervisory chemist for Branch III, one of three chemistry review branches in the division. I was recommended for that position by Dr. Marvin Seife, the director of the division, and reported to Dr. Seife. . . . Prior to that I was a review chemist in the Division of Generic Drugs for almost nine years. . . .

Favoritism and special handling of applications were common in the Division of Generic Drugs. I was involved in this, as were many others, including the director of the division and the chief of the review support branch. Examples include numerous occasions when I was asked to take ANDAs [abbreviated new drug applications] out of turn or to approve them as soon as possible on an expedited basis. This favoritism was not necessarily the result of illegal behavior, but reflected, in part, highly personal, arbitrary, and often arrogant management. Other examples of favoritism were the result of continuous pressure put on the division, at all levels, by the industry through lobbying, conducted by executives, lawyers, consultants, and occasionally through political channels inside and outside the FDA.

Within the division there are chemists who are picky (thorough but very slow), fast (quick but not unnecessarily detailed) or lazy (those who could not be expected to do complex reviews at any speed). I believed that many of the larger and more sophisticated generic firms received special treatment, primarily through personal contacts within the division. To counteract that, I sometimes tried to help some of the smaller companies through the assignment process. When I sought to influence the order of approvals, I would assign ANDA jackets for the larger companies to the picky reviewers, while the smaller companies got the fast reviewers.

Favoritism within the division took a variety of forms, including the following: expediting lab sample review; directing chemists to review applications out of turn; making the initial branch assignment or chemist assignment; providing access or information to certain consultants; or simply holding applications by placing them in a desk drawer.[26]

The committee heard also from another important witness, Marvin Seife, who had joined FDA in 1965 and since 1972 had headed FDA's Division of Generic Drugs. This division was responsible for handling applications for the approval of generic drug products (ANDAs). Very early, Seife declared, he became aware that peculiar things were going on in the generic drugs business. One day in 1974 a large Panasonic color television set was delivered to his home, sent as a symbol of gratitude from Robert Shulman, cofounder of a major generics firm, Bolar Pharmaceuticals of Copiague, New York. "I was shocked and chagrined," he said. He returned the set immediately to Bolar, which responded with a letter of apologies. Seife added that in early February 1988 a consumer safety officer named Harvey Greenberg told him that a consultant to at least one drug firm, American Therapeutics, had dropped an envelope with many thousand dollar bills on his desk. Greenberg was quite dismayed and chased the man into the men's room and stuffed the envelope back in his pocket. Later the man, one Mohammed Azeem, phoned and apologized.[27]

It came to Seife's attention during the 1980s that an extraordinarily large number of ANDAs were being directed to one of his staff members, Charles Chang. Many of these concerned applications from such firms as Pharmaceutical Basics of Denver, American Therapeutics of Bohemia, New York, Par Pharmaceuticals of Spring Valley, New York, and a Par subsidiary, Quad Pharmaceuticals, of Indianapolis.

But Congress, the administration, and nearly everyone else (except the brand-name companies, which had problems of their own) must share the blame. They all wanted quick approval of generics.

Shortcut to Drug Approval

According to FDA regulations, a company with a newly discovered and newly patented drug is not allowed to put it on the market and begin recouping its often costly investment until it has received an approved new drug application (NDA). This involves time-consuming and expensive chemical and physical studies, animal tests, and human trials to demonstrate safety and efficacy. When the patent on such a product has expired, another company may seek to produce and market a generic version through the abbreviated new drug application (ANDA) route. This is far simpler, quicker, and less costly. It involves mainly chemical and physical studies to prove that the generic product is essentially identical to the original patented drug. Usually no animal or human trials are required unless they are needed to demonstrate acceptable absorption and bioavailability. Until 1984, however, few "newer" drugs were eligible for ANDAs. Then a law was enacted to allow virtually all products to be marketed via the ANDA route. Neither the generics industry nor FDA was ready.

In some instances, it was easy to duplicate the original product and to prove this with chemical and physical investigations; in others, it was exceedingly difficult. During recent years, one of the more intriguing cases in this area has involved a product labeled Dyazide—a combination of hydrochlorothiazide and triamterene—marketed by Smith-Kline (now SmithKline Beecham) of Philadelphia for the control of high blood pressure. For many years, until the patent expired in 1988, it represented a virtual gold mine for SmithKline, with annual sales of $300 million or more. Meanwhile, there was great competition among generic manufacturers to come up with a generic competitor for Dyazide that, at the right time, FDA would accept, but SmithKline's product was exceedingly difficult to duplicate.

Among the seemingly successful winners appeared to be Vitarine Pharmaceuticals of Springfield Gardens, New York, which had its product approved by FDA in February 1988. In July 1989, however, it was disclosed that FDA approval of the Vitarine product had involved some pharmaceutical skullduggery. Vitarine had convinced the FDA investigators by the simple expedient of taking Vitarine capsules and filling them with SmithKline Dyazide. It was obvious that the samples of the Vitarine product were chemically and physically equivalent to the SmithKline product—they *were* the SmithKline product.[28]

At a meeting of the Dingell committee on July 11, 1989, FDA commissioner Frank Young denounced the maneuver as "wholly unconscionable and intolerable."[29] He also said the agency "is making every effort to determine whether any other firms may have engaged in this practice. . . . I am deeply disturbed and, quite frankly, outraged at the conduct we have seen by some generic drug companies."

Meanwhile, the scandal continued. Only a few days later, officials of Par Pharmaceuticals and its subsidiary, Quad Pharmaceuticals, said they intended to plead guilty in federal court to charges of bribing FDA employees. Ashok Patel, senior vice-president of Par, and Dilip Shah, president of Quad, resigned from their companies. The firms faced fines of $250,000 on each of two counts.[30]

At about the same time, Charles Chang, who had been forced from his office at FDA for accepting "illegal gratuities," was sentenced to one year in prison, fined $10,000, and ordered to perform 1,000 hours of community service. Later, Shah was sentenced to jail for 60 days, fined $250,000, and ordered to spend a year of full-time community service without pay, for bribing Chang. Another defendant, Raj Matkari, a former vice-president of Pharmaceutical Basics, was fined $2,000 for giving a $2,000 bribe to Chang.[31] Pharmaceutical Basics was a member of AKZO, the powerful Dutch group that also owned Organon.

During the summer of 1989 there were constant rumors that a particularly glamorous generics company, Bolar Pharmaceuticals of Copiague, New York, was about to be hit by the generics scandal. Robert Shulman, president of the firm, vigorously denied any such calamity. The rumors were especially upsetting to Wall Street, since Bolar was the particular favorite of many stockbrokers who had watched its sensational rags-to-riches history and its position as one of the nation's largest and most reputable generics companies. The first blow fell in late August. The FDA ordered Bolar to remove its generic version of SmithKline's Dyazide from the market, on the grounds that equivalency data submitted by Bolar had been faulty. Bolar officials angrily denied any such charges.[32]

Later Bolar would endeavor to clarify the confusion by claiming that there had been no intent to commit fraud; a "clerical error" was at fault. It was not until January 1990 that attorneys for Bolar told FDA, "We have reason to believe that a number of the documents used to support our [defense of Bolar] are false."[33] (In the summer of 1990 Dingell revealed that Bolar's legal counsel had been authorized to admit that certain documents that should have been provided, including notebooks and ledgers maintained in the research and development area, were not provided to FDA, some were destroyed, and others were removed from the company's premises.[34]

There was worse to come. Bolar had also won FDA approval for a generic version of thioridazine, introduced originally by Sandoz under the brand name Mellaril and used for the control of psychoses. Sandoz objected strenuously but without success. Then, in the independent testing laboratory that was studying the Bolar tablets, some of the outer coatings began to chip, and the underlying Sandoz logo became visible. Bolar president Robert Shulman said the switch was the result of a "silly error." "This was an unfortunate, isolated incident of a manufacturing error," he said. "There was no malicious or fraudulent intent."[35]

Later FDA claimed that Bolar had obtained approval for its antibacterial nitrofurantoin by submitting samples that were actually the brand-name product, Macrodantin, made by Norwich Eaton.[36] "There can be no defense for Bolar's conduct," Congressman Dingell and Thomas Bliley, his Republican colleague, said in a letter to the company's attorney. "In the past, Bolar and its president, Robert Shulman, have attacked this Subcommittee in the press, including full-page advertisements in national newspapers. Now we find that apparently the company has also been engaged in a criminal cover-up."[37]

By early in 1990 Bolar was no longer the darling of Wall Street. Its stock had plummeted from about $30 a share to about $6, Shulman and other top officers had resigned, and the company was facing grand jury investigations.[38] In August 1990 Bolar's attorney admitted in a letter to Dingell that, in its efforts to gain FDA approval of its generic version of Dyazide, the company had indeed neglected to submit some key evidence, other evidence had been destroyed, and some had been fabricated.

A Search for the Culprit

During the entire period of the "great generics controversy," the scene was enlivened by a constant stream of denunciations and counter-denunciations. The brand-name companies greeted each disclosure of generics company malfeasance by repeating, "We told you so—the generics companies can't be trusted!" The generics companies accused the overbearing, power-hungry brand-name companies of bullying—"They're picking on us!" There was some truth in both allegations, but not much. And both sides, brand-name and generics companies alike, continued to heap abuse on FDA.

Spokesmen for FDA, headed by Commissioner Frank Young, continued to emphasize vehemently that—regardless of all its supposed incompetence, ineptness, acceptance of bribes, and inspection failures—very few people had been harmed. On November 17, 1989, Young appeared before the Dingell committee and offered a summary of what the investigations to date had revealed:

- Among the "top 30" generics drugs tested, involving more than 36,000 tests on nearly 2,500 samples, only 1.1 percent were found not to conform to product quality established by the U.S. Pharmacopeia or FDA.
- In laboratory studies of bioequivalence testing samples, of the roughly 500 sample analyses completed to date, only one case of fraud was detected.[39]

"In discussing these actions," Young said, "I must underscore the fact that none of the recalls that have occurred to date involve drugs that constitute an acute threat to public safety." Young's review was probably too little and too late. The agency's morale had been shattered. FDA's reputation had been tarnished, if not forever, at least for a long time. It was inevitable that Young had to be removed. In the time-honored tradition of Washington, he was transferred to another high-sounding position—deputy assistant secretary for health in the Department of Health and Human Services.

The evaluations of Young's years as commissioner were mixed.[40] Gerald Mossinghoff, president of the Pharmaceutical Manufacturers Association, declared, "Frank Young's achievements as FDA Commissioner were numerous and sweeping. . . . The proposals Frank championed for expedited review of AIDS and other life-threatening diseases reflected both his openness to innovation and his personal compassion." In the opinion of John Dingell, who led the investigation of generics approval at FDA, "Frank Young had the misfortune to preside at the FDA during a time when it was virtually guaranteed that knaves and rogues would prosper, and honest people would face great difficulty. . . . He was handicapped by both the budgets and attitudes of an Administration that let the agency go to seed." But Sidney Wolfe of the Health Research Group said, "Frank Young is by far the worst FDA commissioner in the past eighteen years. Over and over again, he has done what industry wants done as opposed to what medicine, science and law wants done."

In August 1990 SmithKline took an unusual and probably unprecedented step when it announced that, effective the following October, it would continue to market its Dyazide product under its brand name, for those who wanted such a product, and would simultaneously distribute a low-cost generic version through Rugby Laboratories of Rockville Center, Long Island. There could be no question about bioequivalence. Both versions would come off the same production line, under the same quality control.[41]

Two other incidents during this period attracted interest; one was somewhat humorous, the other definitely was not. In 1986 American Home Products, probably the most active and vociferous enemy of generic drug companies, entered the field itself by acquiring Quantum Pharmics. In 1989 Quantum was cited as one of the firms that had obtained special favors from FDA reviewer Charles Chang. Later investigations showed that the sins at Quantum had been committed during the period in which the firm was controlled by its previous owners.[42]

On September 11, 1989, an executive vice-president of Par Pharmaceutical told the Dingell committee that his company—already in trouble because of bribery charges and at least suspected of marketing inferior drugs—had shipped "millions of dosage units" of its products to Third World countries.[43] Some observers shuddered. As inept as some U.S. Food and Drug Administration workers had been in detecting inferior drugs, the drug regulatory agencies in most developing nations were even less effective. The generic drugs scandal was a threat not only for the United States. Many if not most developing nations were defenseless against any flood of defective generic products from an avaricious, unscrupulous drug company—whether a local firm or one based in an industrialized nation.

All through 1990 more and more unsavory evidence was disclosed. American Therapeutics pleaded guilty to making unlawful payments to FDA employees and was fined $1 million.[44] At Bolar the former research and development director pleaded guilty to charges that she had directed members of her staff to lie to FDA investigators.[45] Marvin Seife, the longtime FDA generics chief, was convicted of lying to federal investigators, sentenced to five months in federal prison, and fined $25,000.[46] In November economist David Nelson on the Dingell committee staff said, "Well over 100 generic applications have been shown to be tainted by fraud and false statements. . . . Firms producing roughly half the nation's generic drugs, exclusive of antibiotics, have either already pled guilty or are the subjects of active criminal investigations."[47]

Dingell later disclosed that employees of one generics company, Par Pharmaceutical, were so suspicious of their own company's drugs that they refused to use them, preferring to pay a higher price and get a brand-name product they could trust.[48] U.S. Attorney Breckinridge Willcox told the Dingell committee that the evidence already amassed "presents an astounding picture of corporate greed, arrogance, deceit, and reckless disregard for the health and safety of the consuming public. . . . I'm not aware of any industry as corrupt as the generic drug industry."[49]

By mid-1991 the dimensions of the generic drugs scandal were beginning to become more visible. More generics companies—among them Alra Laboratories of Gurnee, Illinois, Lyphomed of Deerfield, Illinois (a division of Fujisawa USA), and Pharmaceutical Basics of Denver—were added to the list of implicated companies.[50] In March, Bolar Pharmaceutical pleaded guilty in federal court to mislabeling and adulterating eight different drug products, falsifying records, destroying evidence, and lying to investigators, and was fined $10 million—the largest amount ever imposed in an FDA criminal case.[51]

At about the same time, Dingell reported that the generic drugs problem in some Third World nations was at least as serious as it was in the United States and sometimes far worse. As long ago as 1986, he said, members of his staff had learned that some generic products presumably made and certainly sold in Thailand contained as little as 20 percent or as much as 200 percent of the labeled amount. Dingell assailed the Thai makers of generic drugs for widespread bribes offered to physicians and pharmacists—and accepted by them. "Even worse," he charged, "is the Government Pharmaceutical Organization effort to convince the Minister of Health to rule that only generic pharmaceuticals . . . could be used in government health facilities. By a remarkable coincidence, the GPO is also the leading manufacturer of these products."[52]

In May 1991 Congressmen Dingell and Henry Waxman introduced broad new legislation aimed at establishing harsh penalties for any such slipshod practices, the giving or accepting of bribes, or concealing or falsifying evidence on the safety and efficacy of generic drugs. Among its provisions were the following:

- Mandatory or permissive debarment of a drug company from obtaining approval on any new generic drug product, with the debarment made permanent if the individual or the company had previously been convicted of a federal offense related to drug approval
- Temporary denial of generic drug approvals for periods up to 36 months if the secretary of health and human services determines that bribery, fraud, or the like has occurred
- Fines of up to $1 million for a corporation and up to $250,000 for an individual *per offense* for a variety of offenses related to generic drugs
- A "whistleblower reward" of $250,000 for anyone who tips off the government about violations of the generic drugs laws.[53]

The bill was introduced in the House of Representatives as signed by 42 of the 43 members of the House Energy and Commerce Committee as coauthors. There were some, notably generic drugs manufacturers, who asserted that its provisions were too harsh. Others claimed that they were not harsh enough and that the provisions should also apply to brand-name companies.

Throughout all these disclosures, the Pharmaceutical Manufacturers Association *Newsletter* reported on each development with much vigor and in considerable detail. Over many years most PMA officials had taken a dim view of generic products, even though many generics were actually produced and marketed by PMA members. In striking contrast during this period, most consumer activists—who had long defended low-cost generics as absolutely safe, effective, and completely acceptable substitutes for more costly brand-name products—remained remarkably silent.

The ultimate fate of the proposed legislation remains to be determined. No one could be certain of its reception in the full House, the Senate, or the White House. It seems highly probable that by the end of 1991 or early in 1992 a new and strict law will be enacted and may possibly be extended to cover all products under the supervision of FDA—all drugs, all medical devices, all foods, and all cosmetics. We dare not predict what comparable actions will be taken in the Third World.

Many observers declared that FDA itself was responsible for its woes. They pointed to its failure to put in writing the guidelines for studying, approving, or disapproving generic drugs. Some took a dim view of its notion that it should regard the drug industry as a "partner" rather than as something that needed to be regulated. Some were astounded at the way in which FDA went into a panic at the discovery that two grapes from Chile—two grapes!—had been contaminated with cyanide and rushed inspectors in from regional offices in Detroit, Chicago, Cincinnati, Kansas City, and Minneapolis to go to the docks in Philadelphia to check cartons of grapes, leaving only half of its total field force for the vital inspection of drug manufacturers, food warehouses, bakeries, and blood banks.

Perceptive observers were well aware that the troubles at FDA had been unbelievably intensified during the early years of the Reagan administration, when the agency was grievously politicized, was given vastly increased responsibilities, more work to do, more industries to inspect, a whole new industry—biotechnology—to supervise, and was under constant Administration pressure to "deregulate." And, at the same time, FDA actually had its staff sharply *cut back* by Reagan and his advisers.[54]

Some noted economists had earlier proclaimed that government regulation of industry was no longer necessary—that, under the pressures of the marketplace, industries would easily and effectively regulate themselves. In the case of the drug industry, that idea so far has proved to be a disaster.

Generics in the Philippines

In 1988 the Philippines sought to solve its prescription drugs problems—or, at least, most of them—by adopting a new national drug policy based mainly on the required use of generic products. The new legislation, signed into law by President Corazon Aquino, had teeth in it. It required that all drugs be imported, manufactured, distributed, marketed, advertised, labeled, promoted, prescribed, and dispensed by their generic names. Violations would be punished by heavy fines, loss of license, or jail sentences of up to twelve months.[55]

The new regulations were bitterly opposed, not merely by the brand-name pharmaceutical firms—many of them multinationals— but also by the Philippine Medical Association. The physicians went to court, but the supreme court ruled against them. After months of effort, led primarily by Alfredo Bergzon, the secretary of health, a longtime foe of the Marcos regime, the new program eventually won acceptance from most physicians and most drug firms. (For his leadership, the International Organization of Consumers Unions would give Bergzon its prestigious Olle Hansson award for 1989.)[56] Only a few multinationals held out—Bergzon named two of them as Wyeth and Abbott and charged both U.S. companies with "arrogance" and failure to "act in good faith."[57] Philippine officials likewise took an exceedingly unhappy view of attempts by two U.S. senators—Richard Lugar, Republican, of Indiana, and Alan Cranston, Democrat, of California— who urged President Aquino to go easy on Philippine subsidiaries of American firms.[58]

At the same time, some Philippine officials indicated that they could effectively use American military bases in the Philippines as bargaining chips to win concessions from the United States. Like many others, these officials failed to appreciate that the end of the Cold War in Europe would mean that many in the United States, instead of making concessions in order to keep the Philippine bases, now wanted to abandon these costly investments and let the Filipinos take care of their own security problems.

At the outset, it was not clear whether the main goal was to reduce drug expenditures, improve the use of drugs, limit or control the brand-name firms, or oust those companies from the Philippines. The situation remains unclear. At the very moment that consumer activists were being told that the new drug laws were only a start, and that the next steps would be the elimination of drug patents and possibly nationalization of the drug industry, President Aquino was assuring German businessmen in Bonn that drug patents would be protected.[59]

But gaining legislative and presidential approval for the new program, and winning even grudging support from most physicians and drug companies, was one thing. Getting the new program to work turned out to be something else. In January 1990, it was reported, drug companies—both domestic and multinational—were complaining about the slow processing of their applications for registration of their new products, including a number of generic products. Investigation at the Philippines Bureau of Food and Drugs revealed that, in 1989, there were some 3,000 pending applications to be processed. Because the bureau wanted to be sure that the new products were safe and effective, processing had been slow. In 1989 the bureau had approved only 89 of the some 3,000 applications.[60] The bureau stated, "The problem of processing the backlog will remain for some time."

For the drug companies, the new requirements meant much relabeling, with the generic name appearing far more prominently on the new labels. All single-ingredient products were relabeled in 1989, all two- and three-ingredient products in 1990, and all products with four or more ingredients during 1991. At the same time, government actions were delayed. By mid-1991 the number of applications awaiting government approval had finally been brought below 4,000.[61]

The long-term results of all these moves and countermoves could not yet be discerned, but—to the consternation of some who had fought for the new Philippine generic-name law—there were at least indications that the new law was bringing *higher* prices for generic-name products.[62]

Chapter 5

THE DIPYRONE AFFAIR

Few drugs would appear to be milder and more innocuous than the antipyretics and analgesics—those such as aspirin used for the control of pain and fever. With the exception of birth control agents, however, few drugs have caused more furor, dissension, and vitriolic dispute. Of this group, dipyrone, introduced in 1922, almost certainly has been the continuing center of the most bitter, vicious controversy, touching Third World countries and industrialized nations alike.

The creation of the modern agents against pain and fever, beginning in the last half of the nineteenth century, represents one of the most remarkable chapters in the history of drug development. In the early part of that century, there were only three or four important products on which physicians could depend—opium or enormous quantities of alcohol for the control of severe pain, and extracts of willow bark or costly South American cinchona bark to bring down fever. Then, in 1805, morphine was isolated from opium by a young German pharmacist, quinine was isolated from cinchona by French workers in 1820, and salicin, the first salicylic acid derivative, was isolated from willow bark in 1827.

More than half a century was to pass before there were significant developments. During the 1880s various synthetic substites for qui-

nine and for salicin were created, but all of them were either ineffective, too toxic, or both. Then, in 1883, chemist Ludwig Knorr at the
University of Würzburg created a new chemical as a possible substitute
for quinine. He sent it to Professor Wilhelm Filehne at the University
of Erlangen, who pronounced it remarkably effective in the treatment
of pain, fever, and inflammation. It was called phenazone or Antipyrine and was introduced into clinical medicine in 1884. It was the
first totally synthetic drug ever developed.

To Filehne's horror, Knorr obtained a patent on Antipyrine (in
those days such commercialization was not viewed as acceptable, but
Knorr was about to be married and needed the money) and gave the
first license to a small dyestuff manufacturer, Farbwerke Meister, Lu-
cius and Brüning, in the small town of Hoechst, near Frankfurt am
Main. Later this little company would become Farbwerke Hoechst and
eventually the immense Hoechst Aktiengesellschaft, one of the most
powerful pharmaceutical companies in the world. (It soon became
evident that the raw materials used by Germany's synthetic dye industry were also excellent raw materials for synthetic drugs, and that dye
factories could be easily transformed into drug factories.) The introduction of Antipyrine marked the beginning of Germany's half-
century monopoly of the world's supply of synthetic drugs—a monopoly that would be broken only after the development of the new sulfa
drugs in France, the United States, and Great Britain, and the outbreak
of World War II.

Two years later, in 1886, a second German drug, acetanilide or
Antifebrin, was introduced for the control of pain or fever. It was, in
fact, discovered by mistake: the pharmacist had sent the wrong drug to
the scientists for testing. In 1887 came a third product, Phenacetin. A
fourth, aminopyrine or aminophenazone, was introduced by Bayer as
Pyramidon. And in 1899 Bayer introduced acetyl salicylic acid under
the name Aspirin. (The year before, it was Heinrich Dreser of Bayer
who had introduced heroin for the treatment of morphine addiction.)
Sales of these products would yield hundreds of millions in profits and
dramatically change the practice of medicine. (Accounts of these developments have been presented by Silverman,[1] Tainter,[2] Spooner and
Harvey,[3] Brune,[4] and others.)

By 1900, before aspirin had achieved much popularity, only a few
painkillers were in wide use, but that use was exceedingly wide. Morphine and other opium derivatives were being commonly applied for

severe pain (even though a particularly nasty dispute was still raging over whether morphine was really addictive), and salicylates, amino-pyrine, acetanilide, and phenacetin—alone or in combination—were applied for such usually less severe conditions as headache, muscle cramps, arthritic pain, and menstrual pain. All of these drugs produced more or less serious side effects, which might or might not be made known to physicians and practically never in advance to patients. Eventually, especially in the United States, Great Britain, and other industrialized countries, most were taken off the market completely or limited to use only by prescription. The only important exception was aspirin, even though it was widely recognized that aspirin in excess could cause serious gastric damage. In the Third World, however, drug companies—both multinational and domestic—continued to market aminopyrine and phenacetin products into the late 1970s.[5]

The Curious Case of Paracetamol

At the turn of the century, Professor Josef von Mering of the University of Halle missed a great medical opportunity. He reported in 1890 that the surgical removal of the pancreas from a healthy animal would cause diabetes; if he had followed up that clue, he might have come upon insulin. Later, in 1903, he developed the chemical structure of a drug that might produce sleep. Unable to synthesize the compound himself, he asked the great Emil Fischer at the University of Berlin for help, and it was Fischer's group that created the first of the barbiturates. In 1893 von Mering had studied the formula of a chemical called acetaminophen and suspected that it might be useful against pain and fever.

Acetaminophen, later to be known also as paracetamol, had been synthesized in 1877, not in Germany, but at Johns Hopkins University in Baltimore. It had no evident medical value and thereafter had simply sat on a shelf for sixteen years. When von Mering tested it, he found it was indeed effective against pain and fever, but it also produced too many undesirable side effects. (Experts later suspected that he was working with impure samples.) Accordingly, paracetamol was returned to the shelf. There it would remain, unused and apparently useless, for nearly half a century until it was rescued, reintroduced, and marketed as one of the most widely known and highly regarded analgesics and antipyretics ever known. In the United States, its most popular version became known as Tylenol.

The resuscitation of paracetamol came from American research on the manner in which phenacetin, a highly effective but dangerous drug, is handled in the body. These studies revealed that phenacetin is first metabolized into two different substances. One, phenetidine, is apparently responsible for most of the unwanted toxic effects. The other, responsible for the activity against pain and fever, turned out to be paracetamol. The discovery was reported in 1949. Drug companies moved swiftly to take advantage of this finding. In 1950 the first paracetamol product—a combination of paracetamol, aspirin, and caffeine—was on the United States market under the name Triagesic.

The introduction of paracetamol was not, however, altogether smooth. In January 1951 there were reports that three users of Triagesic had been stricken with a frightening blood disease, agranulocytosis, a sudden, severe drop in the number of white blood cells and a loss of the body's ability to withstand infections. Almost immediately, Triagesic was removed from the market. Within a few years, however, it became apparent that the paracetamol had no connection with the blood damage, and by 1955 paracetamol was back on the American market, available even without prescription. In Great Britain, the work on phenacetin metabolism led the company that is now Winthrop to introduce paracetamol alone as Panadol for use only by prescription. It slowly won the acceptance of physicians and in 1963 was admitted to the British Pharmacopoeia.

A survey published in 1976 revealed that some 260 products containing paracetamol alone or in combination with other substances were on the market in the United States and the United Kingdom.[6] Among them were such widely used—and heavily advertised—products as Arthralgen, Bayer Non-Aspirin, Bromo Quinine, Bromo Seltzer, Coldene, Darvocet-N, Excedrin, Nyquil, Sinarest, Sinutab, Tylenol, and Vanquish. These vied with each other, and with such drugs as aspirin and nonsteroidal anti-inflammatory drugs (NSAIDs) like ibuprofen, for a share of a market that was of monumental proportions. (The history of the introduction of paracetamol has been reviewed by Ameer and Greenblatt,[7] and others,[8] in addition to Spooner and Harvey.)

In this warfare, waged largely on television in the United States, little attention was paid to the few but vital facts involved. Aspirin, the NSAIDs, and paracetamol are all more or less effective against various kinds of pain and fever. Aspirin and the NSAID products are also effective against the inflammation of arthritis, while paracetamol is far less useful for arthritic patients. Aspirin and the NSAIDs, especially when used in excess, can clearly be more damaging to the stomach, but paracetamol in excess can cause liver damage.[9] In addition, there is alarming evidence that aspirin given to children with fever can cause Reye's syndrome. Although many drugs can cause fetal damage when given during the *first* trimester of pregnancy, aspirin can cause such damage when given during the *third* trimester.

In the advertising onslaught, these few but vital facts have been drowned in a flood of vague but constantly repeated claims of "more effective" and "kinder to your stomach." And few television viewers wondered whether the claims that Product A or Product B was more widely used by hospitals or physicians might possibly be related to the fact that supplies of Product A or Product B had been furnished at low cost or no cost to the hospitals or physicians. Here, as has happened many times in the past, the drug industry has found that when it cannot support its claims with scientific evidence, it can successfully turn to another time-tested technique—"Double the advertising budget."

The Entrance of Dipyrone

The findings that, with the dubious exception of aspirin, virtually all of the first synthetic analgesics and antipyretics—notably phenazone, acetanilide, phenacetin, and aminopyrine—were obviously dangerous meant that eventually they had to be radically restricted in use or totally removed from the most lucrative world markets. This was a painful blow to both the pocketbooks and the reputations of the German pharmaceutical firms that had introduced them. The one important exception was Hoechst. In 1920 its scientists introduced a new product, a relative of aminopyrine, which they called dipyrone. It was marketed by Hoechst under such brand names as Novalgin, Neo-Novalgin, Baralgan or Baralgin, and Melubrin. It made a fortune for the German company. Most important, it appeared that dipyrone was not marred by *any* important side effects. Within a very short time, dipyrone products were being marketed throughout the world by Hoechst and later by other companies under a host of different names. (See also Chapter 2, on drug labeling.)

During the 1950s and 1960s, dipyrone products won increasing favor. In both industrialized and developing countries, dipyrone was used alone or in combination with vitamins, caffeine, belladonna, hyo-scine, sedatives, papaverine, and other remedies for pain and fever, and later with a variety of antihistamines, tranquilizers, anesthetics, hormones, and antibiotics. It was enthusiastically recommended for headache, toothache, neuralgia, backache, sciatica, fevers of whatever cause, lumbago, arthritis, rheumatism, menstrual pain, the common cold, influenza, and biliary, kidney, and gastrointestinal colic. It was, beyond doubt, a pharmaceutical gold mine.

This idyllic situation lasted for only about a dozen years. In the early 1930s, there came a growing stream of upsetting reports: the use of dipyrone, too, could be linked to agranulocytosis.[10] The findings were painful and undeniable but, at first, hardly disastrous. Hoechst simply declared that this serious or lethal side effect occurred only with the ut-most rarity. Consumerists—and some physicians—were not so sure.[11]

During the 1970s the use of dipyrone products was causing mount-ing alarm, especially in the United States, even though consumption was low, and in Scandinavia. In the 1973 edition of the American Medical Association's *AMA Drug Evaluations*, physicians were warned that dipyrone was being used unwisely to replace aminopyrine.

There is evidence that dipyrone, a derivative of aminopyrine that shares its potential for toxicity, unfortunately is still being misused. This is probably because it is available in injectable form and because physicians do not recog-nize its similarity to aminopyrine since it is marketed under various trade-marks. . . . Its only justifiable use is as a last resort to reduce fever when safer measures have failed. . . . Because dipyrone may produce fatal agranulocytosis and other blood dyscrasias, its use as a general analgesic, antiarthritic, or routine antipyretic cannot be condoned.[12]

In the 1977 edition of *AMA Drug Evaluations*, it was stated that the drug had become obsolete in the United States. In that same year, the authoritative *Martindale: The Extra Pharmacopoeia* in Great Britain de-clared that the use of dipyrone "is justified only in serious or life-threatening situations where no alternative antipyretic is available or suitable."[13] In Sweden, after the discovery that almost 30 percent of all victims of agranulocytosis had taken dipyrone before being admitted to the hospital, the drug was removed from the market. Essentially nothing happened, and the rate of agranulocytosis remained about the same—a finding that greatly cheered the manufacturers, who promptly declared that there was not enough evidence to link dipyrone with all cases of the blood damage. But dipyrone was removed from the market in Denmark also, and, in that country, dipyrone-induced agranulocytosis practically disappeared.[14]

In the Third World, the situation was different—and more disquieting. Many Third World nations allowed numerous dipyrone products to remain available, some of them marketed by American and European multinationals, including not only Hoechst but also E. Merck, Boehringer-Ingelheim, and Asta-Werke of what was then West Germany, Ciba-Geigy, Lagap, and Roche of Switzerland, Organon of the Netherlands, Adelco and Chropi of Greece, Medimpex of Hungary, Polfa of Poland, Takeda and Tanabe-Abadi of Japan, and Sterling-Winthrop and Carter-Wallace of the United States. Other products, especially in Latin America and Southeast Asia, were promoted by domestic firms. Often, Third World physicians were totally unaware that they were using dipyrones because the products were identified under such uninformative generic names as "metamizol," "methampyrone," or "sulpyrone"—names that seemed to be admirably designed to confuse rather than inform.

In dipyrone promotion to Third World physicians, warnings against agranulocytosis or other dangerous side effects were usually inadequate or totally absent. Patients were practically never cautioned to watch for sore throat, mouth or lip ulcers, tooth pain, rapidly increasing fever, and body aches, which may signal agranulocytosis. Further, as drug experts knew, if agranulocytosis should occur, and if the patient were treated in a modern hospital by modern clinical methods, the odds were roughly 90 to 98 in 100 that the patient could be saved. But in the Third World, where modern treatment was seldom available, the odds were up to 90 in 100 that the patient would die.

During the late 1970s and early 1980s, the dispute over dipyrone steadily became more heated. Most of the attacks were directed against Hoechst, which remained the world's largest supplier. In the United States, consumerists—church groups in particular—leveled their attacks against Sterling-Winthrop. In response, most drug companies continued to insist that dipyrone might be responsible for some cases of agranulocytosis, but that such cases were exceedingly rare.

Underlying all of these arguments were the facts that some patients developed agranulocytosis without any known exposure to dipyrone, most patients took the drug and did not develop any blood damage, it had been well established that other drugs could cause the condition, and, unhappily, there were no valid data to demonstrate the rate of dipyrone-induced agranulocytosis. Estimates ranged wildly between about 9 cases of agranulocytosis per 1,000 users and 2 cases per 10 million users.[15]

During the 1970s Hoechst officials recognized that the situation had become intolerable, and that the company's standard approaches— proclamations of complete innocence, intimidation of critics, and political pressure on governmental officials—were no longer adequate. In the case of dipyrone, Hoechst was in desperate need of hard scientific data. The company decided to set up a multination epidemiological study of the occurrence of agranulocytosis (and also aplastic anemia) among dipyrone users. The project, it was decided, would be entrusted to some of the world's most respected experts.

To direct the project, Hoechst invited Micha Levy, head of internal medicine and director of the department of clinical pharmacology at the Hadassah University Medical School in Jerusalem, who would serve as chairman, and Samuel Shapiro, head of the world-renowned drug epidemiology unit at the Boston University School of Medicine. They were empowered to select their own staff. An honorary advisory panel to supervise the investigation was appointed under the chairmanship of Richard Doll of Oxford, who had led the British study that confirmed the discovery of cigarette smoking as a cause of lung cancer. Funding of the research would be provided mainly by Hoechst— eventually to the extent of some 10 million German marks, or about $6 million—but also by the Hungarian and Bulgarian governments and the Corporation of Swedish Pharmacists.

For the research, the experts selected one country, Israel, and seven city regions: Barcelona in Spain, Ulm and West Berlin in West Germany, Milan in Italy, Budapest in Hungary, Sofia in Bulgaria, and Stockholm/Uppsala in Sweden. Data collection began in July 1980 and was completed in June 1984.

The investigators planned to take the utmost care in selecting the cases, accepting only those who developed agranulocytosis while hospitalized or who were stricken at home and then hospitalized with a diagnosis of agranulocytosis. In each case, the diagnosis had to be confirmed by one or more blood studies, and the patient had to be interviewed and hospital records reviewed in order to determine which drugs had been used during the preceding seven days. (Ordinarily, agranulocytosis occurs within a very few days after an allergic patient takes the offending drug.) Many prospective patients had to be dropped, usually because they had no clear recollection of which drugs they had been using at home, or they died before they could be interviewed.

At the end, the scientists had accepted 122 patients with agranulocytosis that had appeared while they were hospitalized, and 300 who had been stricken by the condition before they were hospitalized. For comparison, the investigators selected 1,425 controls, matched as closely as possible by age and sex, who had not used any dipyrone product. (A number of cases were excluded from the study because, Hoechst spokesmen explained, no adequate case controls for them could be found.)

After a few preliminary meetings in Europe to discuss their findings, the scientists published their first official report in October 1986 in the *Journal of the American Medical Association.*[16] The results were striking:

- In Ulm, West Berlin, and Barcelona, the risk of acquiring agranulocytosis in those taking dipyrone during the preceding week was increased twenty- to thirty-fold.
- In Israel and Budapest, the risk was not significantly affected.
- In Milan and Sofia, the risk was increased fivefold.

(No data were reported for Stockholm/Uppsala, since dipyrone products were no longer available on the Swedish market.) No significant relationships between dipyrone and aplastic anemia were found.

The immediate responses were probably predictable: "The situation is even better than we hoped," said spokesmen for Hoechst. "It's just as bad as we thought," declared some consumerists. "It's even worse than we feared," said others.

The reactions of scientists and physicians were also striking. Virtually without exception, all of them praised the investigation, known officially as the International Agranulocytosis and Aplastic Anemia Study (IAAAS), or more commonly as "the Boston Study." They described it as heroic, courageous, impressive, extraordinary, praiseworthy, welcome and important, a landmark, and "one of the most important pharmacoepidemiologic investigations carried out in the last decade"; and then—usually with great delicacy—many of the commentators proceeded to rip the report to shreds.

In an article that accompanied the original Boston Study report in *JAMA*, Gerald Faich of the U.S. Food and Drug Administration's Office of Epidemiology and Statistics said the considerable variation by region remains "unexplained and disturbing."[17] An editorial in *Lancet* stated, "These huge disparities raise some doubts about the results. . . . These findings reinforce the arguments for banishing dipyrone and where possible using paracetamol or aspirin instead."[18]

In a paper entitled, "Dipyrone: The Sadness of a Century," which marked the first hundred years since the discovery of dipyrone, a Dutch epidemiologist, Leo Offerhaus, said, "Although the investigators claimed that all the hospitals in these regions [West Berlin, Ulm, and Barcelona] were included in the study, it appeared later that some large hospitals in Berlin had never heard of the study. . . . The data collected in Israel are so contradictory and inconsistent that one may as well forget them. . . . The estimates of incidence made in the IAAAS are largely invalid."[19] Later Offerhaus stated, "The fact remains that dipyrone is a drug for which there is no obvious need (certainly not as an OTC analgesic), and for the restricted indications for which it might be useful, less dangerous alternatives are available."[20] Another Dutch epidemiologist, C. P. H. van Dijke of the Netherlands Centre for Monitoring of Adverse Reactions to Drugs, declared that the figures "are clearly unrealistic and demonstrate that the method of calculation used is unsuitable to studying this type of side effect."[21]

A. del Favero of the Institute of Clinical Medicine at the University of Perugia said:

These huge disparities raise some doubts about the results, therefore, and one should be concerned about hidden bias or some methodological problems that might have affected the reliability of the conclusions of the study. . . . Although the absolute risk is much lower than was previously thought, it is, however, by no means slight if one takes into account the size of the drug-exposed population. . . . [Hoechst's] main message that agranulocytosis had been "the problem" with dipyrone and that this problem is now "solved" is, in fact, misleading. The study confirmed that dipyrone can induce agranulocytosis. It has been found responsible for about a quarter of the drug-induced cases in the participating countries. . . . Since safer and equally effective drugs for the main indications of dipyrone exist (i.e., paracetamol and salicylates), dipyrone use should be at least restricted to patients who cannot use the above-mentioned drugs. Unfortunately the drug is still freely available over-the-counter in many developing countries and even in some countries in Europe.[22]

A team of epidemiologists from McGill University in Canada and the University of Minnesota said:

We found the IAAAS disturbing for a number of reasons. . . . The members of the investigative team have a long track record of research in this domain. Nonetheless, the study does not appear to address many of the appropriate questions. . . . We do not believe the IAAAS has shed any important new light on the risks of blood dyscrasias with analgesics, nor should its results or conclusions make an important contribution to the decisions involving the clinical use or public health regulation of these drugs. . . . We do not find the data provided by the IAAAS to add much to the existing body of scientific evidence.[23]

A quite different view was expressed by Renaud Timmers, head of international medical affairs at Hoechst. "We have not the intention to prove that the risk of agranulocytosis should be ignored," he said, "but when this risk is in a range of rarity which is definitely not worse than the risk of serious side-effects attributable to the use of alternative analgesics, we can claim to be safe with dipyrone—safe as an aspirin!"[24] One author predicted, "No doubt the drug company will be making representations for the re-registration of this therapeutically valuable product before the Drug Control Councils of the world." A Hoechst lawyer, Burkhard Sträter, stated in April 1987, "We are now in the final stages of preparing approval applications to be submitted in the US, the UK and Sweden."[25]

In Great Britain and the United States, the drug authorities were not visibly impressed or in any hurry to restore dipyrone products to good standing. In December 1987 William Jenkins, the principal medical officer of Britain's Department of Health and Social Security, replied to a query by saying, "My personal views are the same as those expressed in *Martindale, The Extra Pharmacopoeia*, 28th edition. Although arguments continue about the true incidence of serious and fatal adverse reactions to Amidopyrine and Dipyrone, I find the frequency unacceptable."[26] In the United States, Diane Walker of the Food and Drug Administration bluntly reported in March 1988, "The FDA's position on these drug products has not changed."[27]

Perhaps the most balanced view was that expressed by W. H. W. Inman, head of the internationally respected Drug Safety Unit at the University of Southampton. He said: "I do not believe anything came out of the so-called international agranulocytosis and aplastic anaemia study. The fact that an appreciable risk was measured in some countries and none in others, made me very suspicious of the method of selecting cases for study. . . . I believe the risk of serious blood dyscrasias is very small but not insignificant."[28]

The Matter of Merital

In 1976 and 1977, while Hoechst was facing mounting criticism of its dipyrone products, it introduced a new antidepressive agent, nomifensine, marketed under such brand names as Merital and Merival. The drug was accepted in West Germany, Great Britain, and other European countries, and in numerous Third World nations, but not immediately in the United States. As early as 1978, British physicians reported that Merital could cause serious blood damage. In the United States, Merital was approved only in December 1984 and put on the market in July 1985. By that time three deaths from hemolytic anemia following use of Merital had been reported in Great Britain, and British physicians were warned by the Committee on Safety of Medicines that the drug presented serious risks. At the same time, the committee revealed that it had received reports of 53 cases of liver damage, 47 cases of blood damage, and 50 influenza-like reactions with fever. There had been 4 known deaths. It was testified at a hearing in the U.S. Congress that Hoechst had withheld data on more than 50 cases of serious reactions to the drug in Europe, including some deaths. "All that time," a consumer group claimed, "Hoechst continued to maintain that there was no real problem."[29]

In its promotion in the British *MIMS UK*, Hoechst had been claiming that Merital was indicated for "depression with or without anxiety." There were no warnings about blood or liver damage. The situation in the Third World was worse. In Thailand, the drug was recommended for "mental and somatic symptoms of depressive disorders" and "senile depression." In an advertisement in the *East African Medical Journal*, the company claimed that Merital provides "more benefits for your patients. . . . Merital not only gives rapid relief from depressive symptoms—it spares your patients additional distress. . . . Highly effective . . . convenient and safe." In the Philippines, it was said to be indicated for "loss of interest, lack of drive, loss of concentration, lack of self-confidence, guilt feelings, loss of libido, lowered mood, etc." In some instances, kidney or liver disease was given as a contraindication, but rarely was there any mention of serious or fatal hemolytic anemia.

By September 1985 the situation had become so alarming that the German Federal Health Authority ordered the company to send a "Red Hand" warning to all German physicians and pharmacists. In December the British Committee on Safety of Medicines found Merital to have the highest rate of adverse drug reactions among all antidepressives and the highest rate of fatal adverse reactions. In January 1986 Hoechst announced it was taking Merital off the market worldwide "as a precautionary measure." By that time 543 reports of suspected adverse reactions, with eight deaths, had been reported in the United Kingdom alone. Hoechst wrote to all physicians, advising that patients on nomifensine should stop treatment immediately and, if necessary, be transferred to an alternative appropriate drug. All unused capsules and tablets should be destroyed. Letters recalling stock were sent to all retail and hospital pharmacists and pharmacy wholesalers.[30]

In the United States, where an estimated 100,000 prescriptions for Merital had been written, physicians, pharmacists, wholesalers, and pharmacy and medical trade publications were notified on January 21, 1986, that the drug was being removed immediately. In February a Senate committee asked the Food and Drug Administration to explain why banning the drug, which supposedly was responsible for fifteen deaths overseas and had been taken off the market in 75 countries, had not been revealed to the American public. "You have to weigh announcements against the possibility of panicking people and causing them to harm themselves," an FDA spokesman explained.[31]

The incident was another embarrassing blow to FDA, which was already suffering from a loss of confidence, in the Congress and in the public, and from a serious loss of morale and additional politicizing, the result of constant interference by the Reagan administration. In West Germany, the Merital affair was perhaps even more damaging. Physicians who had dared to speak out publicly against Hoechst's products had been subjected to intimidation and "the legal harassment to which the sponsor is apt to subject its German opponents."[32] Hoechst officials, both in Bangkok and in headquarters in Germany, flatly denied any such legal harassment by their representatives.[33]

Under these conditions, it may be understandable that many German physicians and scientists were not enthusiastic about openly opposing Hoechst on the matter of dipyrone. There were others, however, who had no such worries. The influential Medicines Commission of the German Medical Association, which had been collecting data since 1976, said, "Doctors know that in rare cases hypersensitivity reactions, including sometimes fatal anaphylactic shock, can occur. . . . They are therefore prepared, especially when giving the drug intravenously, for the possible treatment of anaphylactic shock." The German experts noted that there was a chance of serious or fatal shock in 1 per 50,000 patients when the drug was taken by mouth, but 1 per 5,000 if it was administered by injection.[34] (The case of shock with dipyrone had not been considered in the Boston Study.)

In the Federal Republic of Germany, dipyrone also became the center of a noisy battle between the Federal Health Office (the Bundesgesundheitsamt, or BGA) and the Ministry for Youth, Family, Women, and Health. In November 1986 the BGA recommended that dipyrone itself be made available only on prescription and that all dipyrone combination products be banned from the market. Curiously, the minister felt more inclined to take the advice of a committee that recommended that dipyrone should remain available without prescription. (This advisory group, generally viewed as particularly slanted toward industry, included two representatives of the drug industry, one pharmacist, one naturopath, one veterinary surgeon, and seven medical practitioners, but no representative of BGA.) After bitter and prolonged argument, the Bundesrat—the upper chamber of the Federal Parliament—stepped in and gave its overwhelming support to the BGA. The minister bowed to this pressure and announced that, effective January 1, 1987, dipyrone could be obtained only on a physician's prescription.[35] It was a distressing blow for Hoechst. (In West Germany, the 1986 order permitted the use of dipyrone on prescription and only for certain specified conditions in which no other drug was effective, but it permitted the continued use of a few dipyrone combinations. In 1990 all dipyrone combinations were banned.)[36]

Another forceful attack was launched against the company by BUKO, the German consumerist group formally known as the Federal Congress of Development Action Groups. It noted that, for reasons of safety, dipyrone had already been forced off the market in the United States, Ireland, Australia, New Zealand, Canada, Denmark, Norway, Sweden, Malaysia, and Singapore. In Japan, a government ruling had ordered Takeda to halt its manufacture of a dipyrone product in 1977, and, under heavy Japanese and Thai consumerist pressure, the company agreed to stop marketing it in Indonesia and Thailand—but only by the end of March 1989.[37]

Against this attack, Hoechst could come up with only two pallid defenses. The governmental decisions to ban dipyrone products in the various industrialized nations, the company said, were based on outdated information (actually it was Hoechst spokesmen who were using outdated arguments), and the governmental bans had been made only "for political reasons." BUKO sharply criticized the company's activities in the Third World, making these charges:

- Almost half of Hoechst's drugs marketed in developing countries are superfluous or dangerous.
- Only one-third of the preparations are really essential for health care.
- Hoechst "invents" new, unjustifiable ranges of use and conceals risks to a large extent.
- Drugs not for sale in the Federal Republic of Germany are exported by Hoechst to the Third World.[38]

Similar charges could be made—and actually had been made—against many other multinational pharmaceutical firms based in the United States, Europe, and Japan. But, to militant consumer groups, Hoechst was a particularly challenging target because it had resisted criticism with notably bitter intimidation and hostility.

The Thailand Debacle

Throughout the Third World, the drug industry—multinational and domestic firms alike—had achieved an odoriferous reputation for utilizing threats, bribes, and political influence to have its products allowed on the market, or kept there, or to permit the use of promotional materials with unsupportable claims or inadequate warnings. Hoechst had achieved noteworthy recognition for its use of heavy-handed intimidation, bullying, browbeating, and corruption to achieve its goals. It offered to provide drug officials with tens of thousands of dollars in cash, new cars, and free trips to Europe or America or to "go and see the pyramids." In Brazil, when DIMED—the division of drugs in the Ministry of Health—began investigating dipyrone, Hoechst demanded that the minister fire the DIMED director and accused him of dishonesty for having raised questions about the drug.

What was termed as undoubtedly Hoechst's most senselessly brutal attacks in the dipyrone affair came in the small Southeast Asian kingdom of Thailand, population approximately 55 million. Particularly involved were two Hoechst products, Novalgin (dipyrone alone) and Baralgan (dipyrone combined with two antispasmodic agents), along with the Thai consumerist organization, the Drug Study Group (DSG), and DSG's research and publishing branch, the Drug Information for Action Centre (DIAC). Several events marked the dispute. Hoechst distributed in Thailand a glossy new brochure extolling the virtues of Baralgan: "Saves time and trouble" . . . "No clinically relevant interactions [with other drugs]" . . . "Good gastrointestinal, renal and hepatic tolerability" . . . "High doses possible due to outstanding safety margin."[39]

The consumerists charged that there was little or no mention of the possible interactions between dipyrone and other drugs—matters that were already described in standard textbooks. The claim of "outstanding safety margin" clearly ignored the findings of the Hoechst-sponsored Boston Study, which had unequivocally confirmed the link between dipyrone and agranulocytosis. The pamphlet recommended the use of Baralgan for the control of colic, including that in menstrual pain or dysmenorrhea. It ignored the warning—required in Hoechst's home country, West Germany—against use in "trivial conditions." And it ignored the fact that, since April 1987, German authorities had already suspended the approval of dispensing dipyrone combination drugs and no longer permitted any recommendations for its use against menstrual pain.

At this very time, a West German parliamentary committee on economics arrived in Bangkok to discuss Thai-German trade and other matters. One member of the delegation was Eckhard Stratmann, a representative of the opposition party and a member of the ardent environmentalist group The Greens. Arrangements were made for Stratmann to meet with the consumerist groups and hear about the dipyrone situation. On October 21 he gave a press conference, attacked Hoechst, and announced that, when he returned to Germany, he would take the case to the German parliament and ask it to force Hoechst to discontinue Baralgan sales in Thailand.[40]

On the next day, Hoechst replied. Phornvit Phacharintanakul, the company's pharmaceutical manager in Bangkok, declared that Hoechst had voluntarily withdrawn its Baralgan sales from the German market earlier in the year "in view of the political situation in Germany at that time and not because of the adverse effects of the drug." He said that Baralgan had been available on the Thai market for more than twenty years and adverse effects had never been reported.[41] This was not particularly remarkable, since Thailand had at the time no effective system for reporting adverse effects of *any* drug product.

Phornvit vigorously disputed the claims produced by the consumerist groups, saying they were relying on outdated materials and references. What the consumerists had used as evidence was, of course, the newest data available, produced by the Boston Study, sponsored by Hoechst itself. Finally Phornvit asserted, "We have been selling Baralgan for a long time, and it has never caused us any problems." It was not entirely clear from this, however, whether *Baralgan* had caused Hoechst no problems, or whether *the agranulocytosis caused by the drug* had caused Hoechst no problems.

Although Hoechst of Thailand should have felt embarrassed, it did not moderate its promotion. It insisted that the dipyrone products could be used without risk, ignoring the results of the Boston Study and increasing particularly its advocacy of Baralgan, especially for use against menstrual pain. It handed out free samples to nurses in girls' schools, seeking to influence future users, and making totally unsupportable claims about safety. Such campaigns were bitterly assailed by such consumerist groups as DSG, which continued to point out the gaps and misstatements in Hoechst's Thailand propaganda. Hoechst did not take kindly to such opposition.

At DIAC, Judith Richter, a young German pharmacist who had come to Thailand to help in the fight for rational drug use, received special attention. She was denounced to the German embassy. Her group was described as a "puppet" of BUKO, the West German consumerist group, and closely tied to Health Action International, with highly suspicious links to Moscow. Many of the consumerists were accused of being activists, probably communists, and—in Thailand, most heinous of all—"anti-monarchists."[42]

A leading figure at DSG was Sumlee Jaidee, an associate professor of physiology at the Chulalongkorn University Faculty of Pharmaceutical Sciences. She was charged with agitating students "against the institutions of Monarchy, religion and nation." In a letter circulated allegedly by her colleagues on the faculty, it was stated that she was being investigated by the National Security Council and the Secret Police Special Security Department. The letter claimed, "There are several documents proving that she is collaborating with foreign organizations which have the goal to harm the Monarchy." Further, it was charged, "Asst. Prof. Sumlee Jaidee is in contact with Ms. Judith Richter. Ms. Richter has her residence in West Germany, but has come to Thailand for more than two years to carry out underground activities which disrupt the Institutions. Asst. Prof. Jaidee and Ms. Richter have joined hands in an evil way to participate in the dissemination of offending illegal leaflets against the Royal Family."[43] In Thailand, that crime may carry a *minimum* sentence of three years in prison. A similar letter was circulated against Suntharee Vitayanatpaisan, a lecturer at Chulalongkorn University and then head of the Drug Study Group.

It appeared to be, in the worst possible sense, a Southeast Asian witch hunt, a Thai version of the Senator Joseph McCarthy hearings in the United States during the 1950s. To representatives of American, Swiss, and British drug companies in Bangkok, the attacks against individuals have been an embarrassment to the whole drug industry. But Phornvit Phacharintanakul stated to us, "We at Hoechst-Thai had absolutely nothing to do with the attacks against the consumerist people. It is our belief that only by consulting with and working with the consumerists, and not against them, can we assure the people of Thailand of the best possible health care."[44]

Late in 1987 Hoechst in Thailand issued what was supposed to be a full clarification of the issues by producing a booklet entitled *The True Data about Spasmolytic Painkiller Combination Drugs.*[45] It repeated that it was removing its dipyrone combination products from the market in West Germany for political reasons rather than for reasons of safety. It pooh-poohed the fears about dipyrone. "In the past there were doubts about the safety of dipyrone. These doubts had been caused about 30 years ago, from the erroneous belief that dipyrone causes agranulocytosis in some people, similar to aminopyrine, which is in the same group of drugs." But the clinical evidence was all too clear. Dipyrone *does* cause agranulocytosis in some people. Company representatives likewise insisted that they had never used the term "political reasons" to explain the situation, and claimed that all the confusion had resulted from garbled translation.

Then Hoechst of Thailand sought to demonstrate its complete innocence by presenting two labels for its spasmolytic product Baralgan (or Baralgin); one was an English translation of the label being used in Thailand; the other, also translated into English, allegedly had been used in the package insert in West Germany. Hoechst spokesmen insisted that the two were identical and that therefore any accusations of using double standards were completely unfounded. But Judith Richter, who spoke German fluently, made her own translations. She revealed that the German government-required warning against use of the drug in trivial conditions had somehow not been included in what Hoechst presented as the official German package insert. Hoechst's pharmaceutical manager in Bangkok explained that the omission had resulted "by mistake."

Hoechst had made a strenuous effort to push the use of Baralgan in the control of menstrual pain, and at least strongly suggested to physicians, pharmacists, and drug regulatory officials in Thailand that women could not possibly survive menstrual pain without the product. Such a notion would undoubtedly be viewed as utter nonsense by the many hundreds of millions of women in the United States, Great Britain, Scandinavia, and other industrialized countries who had managed their menstrual periods each month quite well without any dipyrone product.

Later in 1988 the Drug Information for Action Centre and the Drug Study Group issued their own blast, *Junkyard Thailand*. This not only gave a summary of the international criticisms of the Boston dipyrone study, it also denounced Hoechst and other multinational pharmaceutical companies for dumping needlessly dangerous or useless products in developing countries and following double standards in their drug promotion.[46]

The consumer groups offered an explanation of why so few Thai physicians were willing to speak out against such practices. Many in the Thai medical community, they said, feel indebted to the pharmaceutical companies and are therefore reluctant to speak out. The Thai consumers noted: "We were confronted by influential medical academics who said, 'I won't tell you what I really think about dipyrone . . . you know, Hoechst kindly financed my medical studies in Germany,' or 'but Hoechst gave us free vaccines for our research.'"

In yet another attack, European consumerists denounced Hoechst by describing dipyrone as "a drug no one needs" and demanded that it be withdrawn completely from the world market.[47] For ammunition they cited articles published in medical journals by such critics as C. P. H. van Dijke and Leo Offerhaus, noted above, but the consumerists failed to mention that rebuttals to criticisms leveled by van Dijke, Offerhaus, and others had also been published.[48]

Late in 1989 Samuel Shapiro of the Boston Study group presented a special report at the request of Philippine drug officials. He disclosed that even though data collection for the official study had ended in mid-1984, additional data had been collected for the next year and a half. The new findings, he claimed, extended and essentially confirmed the conclusions reached in the official 1986 Boston Study report. He said:

Data from Ulm, West Berlin, and Barcelona showed a higher rate of agranulocytosis among dipyrone users than in controls. In Israel, Budapest, Sofia, and Milan, there was no perceptible increase in risk to users. Even in those regions where an association is evident, the incidence of agranulocytosis attributable to dipyrone is exceedingly small.

The reported data showing marked variability in risk rates in different population groups are all statistically significant. Marked differences in the risk of adverse effects to users of a particular drug in different population groups is not unique to dipyrone. The same phenomenon has been reported for users of an antipsychotic agent, cloxapine, and the highly publicized affair of the antidiarrheal agent, clioquinol. . . . Aspirin is known to cause life-threatening upper gastrointestinal bleeding—the average risk is about 40 per 1,000 per year.

If dipyrone were to be removed from the market, the alternative drugs would be aspirin and paracetamol [for example, Tylenol]. Aspirin is demonstrably more dangerous, and yet society deems that the risks conferred by that drug are acceptable. . . . In one regard, paracetamol is potentially more dangerous than dipyrone: accidental or deliberate overdose is usually fatal, unless appropriate treatment is given promptly.[49]

In Thailand, the Philippines, and other Third World countries, Shapiro apparently made few converts.

Top Hoechst officials in Germany had obviously been stung by the charges of intimidation and bullying leveled against them, especially in the cases of Judith Richter and her academic supporters in Bangkok. Many in top management were coming to the realization that their glowing dipyrone sales figures did not make up for Hoechst's failure to establish and maintain a lasting dialogue with consumers. But they insisted that there was absolutely no hard evidence to link Hoechst with the attacks that had been charged against the firm. "There is no evidence that Hoechst was responsible in any way for the charges of intimidation brought by Ms. Richter," says Hassan Nour-Eldin, head of the company's pharmaceutical division in Frankfurt. "If such evidence exists, and she will bring it to me, I can guarantee that Hoechst will investigate these claims—*and publish the findings.* Hoechst will never tolerate any such behavior by any of its employees."[50]

Thus, the supposedly epoch-making Boston Study, complex, costly, time-consuming, difficult for any but skilled epidemiologists to comprehend, and intended to end once and for all the bitter controversy over dipyrone, with tens or hundreds of millions of dollars a year at stake, came to an unhappy and unsatisfying end. The Boston Study was given an A+ for effort but an assortment of grades for results and clarification. One reason for the confusion was only too apparent. The Boston Study group had promised in 1986 that it would soon publish a book disclosing in full all of its data and allowing independent experts to verify the conclusions. The book was accepted for publication by the Oxford University Press and was scheduled to appear in 1991.

Not the least bizarre aspect of the entire dipyrone affair was the fact that all during the 1980s the campaign to rid the world of dipyrone had been led by highly motivated activists in Austria, Belgium, France, Germany, Holland, and Switzerland. Yet, in 1991 dipyrone in one form or another was still legally available in Austria, Belgium, Finland, France, Germany, Holland, Italy, and Switzerland.

Chapter 6

THE CASE OF THE DEADLY PREGNANCY TEST

In the early 1950s a small team of scientists at the Worcester Institute for Experimental Biology in Massachusetts began to search for a treatment to aid women who were eager to bear a child but could not become pregnant. For working materials, they turned to an assortment of so-called female sex hormones. For the first time, thanks in large part to the brilliant work of chemists at Mexico's Syntex Laboratories, these complex substances had become abundantly available at relatively low cost. Some duplicated the sex hormones occurring in nature; others were chemical relatives.

By 1955 the work at Worcester had progressed to the point at which the first human field trials could be set up, in Puerto Rico. Within a few years these and later trials had been so dramatically successful that the new products—effective when taken by mouth—had won virtually worldwide acceptance. They enabled drug companies to make remarkable profits, revolutionized a significant part of family life—and the practice of medicine—and created unprecedented social, clinical, religious, and even political controversy.

Astonishingly, the products that achieved such notable success offered no aid and comfort to women who wanted to become mothers. They had, in fact, a completely opposite effect: they could prevent pregnancy. They were the first oral contraceptives. Almost from the outset, it was evident that these contraceptives—known popularly as the Pill—were effective. Used properly, they could prevent pregnancy in nearly 100 percent of the women who used them. There was less certainty, however, about their safety. Many physicians and their patients were seriously concerned about the risk of such side effects as blood-vessel irritation, life-threatening blood clots, stroke, and even some forms of cancer. Eventually, most of these risks were apparently controlled by the use of the active materials in exceedingly small amounts.

The active ingredients in most versions of the Pill were two different hormones; one was known as an *estrogen* and was mainly responsible for the physical and emotional characteristics of females; the other was known as a *progestogen*, produced in large amounts in the ovaries during pregnancy.

Most oral contraceptives contain from about 0.03 to 0.05 milligrams of estrogen and from 0.075 to 1.000 milligrams of progestogen per tablet; these are classed as *low-dosage estrogen-progestogen* products. In marked contrast are products that contain about 0.05 milligrams of estrogen and about 10 milligrams of progestogen per tablet, to be taken several times daily; these are the *high-dosage estrogen-progestogen* products.

Since the 1950s the high-dosage forms have been recommended (or denounced) not merely for the prevention of unwanted pregnancies but also for the treatment of a variety of unpleasant menstrual and uterine problems. In essentially all industrialized nations and some developing countries, these applications are no longer of importance, since other methods of treatment have been developed, and the high-dosage forms have been taken off the market as being ineffective, too dangerous, or both.

In those Third World countries that have allowed them to remain on the market, the high-dosage products have attracted considerable interest. Two notable applications have been involved: one was to serve as a simple, inexpensive, dependable, and presumably safe pregnancy test; the other—never recommended publicly, never proved, and never effective—was to *induce* abortion. In some instances, the drugs were administered to *prevent* an impending abortion or control a variety of uterine diseases.

In the pregnancy test the high-dosage form was to be administered to the woman, either orally or by injection, every day for three to five days and then stopped abruptly. If no menstrual bleeding occurred, supposedly the woman was pregnant. Menstrual bleeding signified that the woman was *not* pregnant. Obviously, this hormone pregnancy test was simple, and it was relatively inexpensive.

Beginning in 1967 there was mounting doubt that the method was safe: preliminary reports showed that use of the test in a pregnant woman might be followed by the birth of a deformed infant. In India, where many high-dosage products were being successfully marketed— both by domestic firms and by such multinationals as Schering AG of West Germany, Roussel of France, and Organon of the Netherlands— this risk was generally ignored. Moreover, since the drugs unquestionably produced bleeding in some women, word spread from woman to woman—and from physician to physician—that the high-dosage products could easily, inexpensively, and safely cause an abortion. And since the hormones could be purchased readily, with or without a prescription, from any pharmacist, women by the millions used them to detect a pregnancy or in the hope of ending it.[1] Later, in their defense, spokesmen for the drug companies would insist that *they* had never promoted the use of these products to terminate a pregnancy. It appears also that the companies did nothing to inform either physicians or patients that, either to cause or to prevent an abortion, the drugs were worthless.

Starting in 1970, in one industrialized nation after another—Norway, Sweden, Finland, West Germany, Australia, the United States, Austria, Belgium, Italy, Ireland, the Netherlands, and Great Britain— either the high-dosage forms were withdrawn or their use for pregnancy testing was contraindicated in the package labels, supposedly being replaced by immunological tests. The World Health Organization recommended that hormone pregnancy testing be stopped.[2] Regardless of these actions, the drug companies continued to insist that the high-dosage forms were entirely safe, or that if there were any dangers, no blame could be attached to the manufacturers. The responsibility, they claimed, was that of the physician, the pharmacist, or the patient herself. In India, the situation was particularly complicated by a remarkable law—the Drugs and Cosmetics Act of 1940, enacted before the thalidomide disaster—which said that the government had the authority to ban a drug product *if it were substandard, spurious, or mislabeled, but not if it were dangerous*. Most critics—leaders of women's groups, consumer organizations, and surprisingly few obstetricians and gynecologists—were dismayed by the problem but seemed to feel that to find a solution was hopeless. One woman took a different attitude.

The Campaign Against High-Dosage Products

Mira Shiva was born in 1951 to a family of fighters. Her maternal grandfather had been a leader in the struggle to provide education for women and had died in a hunger strike demanding a women's school in his village. Her father, a forestry official, and her mother, a school systems inspector, had both been active in India's fight for independence and in social work and had written books for women and children about Mahatma Gandhi and about the value of forests and trees. Educated first in convent schools and then in the Christian Medical College at Ludhiana in the Punjab, she was awarded her medical degree in 1972. She worked in various mission hospitals in the hill country, completed a residency in psychiatry, specialized in internal medicine, and then switched to community health. In 1979 she offered her services to the Voluntary Health Association of India (VHAI). "I had no real idea of what they did, or what I could do for them, but I volunteered because our basic philosophies matched," she says. "The executive director sent me a hand-written reply. He told me, 'We're looking for people like you. Come.' I didn't know what they wanted me to do, or where to do it, or for what salary. I just showed up."[3]

Shiva became VHAI's leader in the battle to improve the supply of low-priced drugs in India and to step up the quality of drug use. She fought against the irrational use of costly vitamin combinations, especially in the treatment of children. "Malnourished children can't compensate by taking expensive high-vitamin tonics," she says. "If a poor woman with three children buys such a tonic for one child, then the other two will need to go without food." She has sought to improve the availability of low-cost vitamin A products to prevent the 40,000 cases of children blinded each year by vitamin A deficiency. She has tried to get inexpensive iodized salt, to counter the millions of cases of goiter and cretinism in India.[4] She has struggled ceaselessly against India's drug control system, a system in which the authority over drugs is split between the Ministry of Health and the Ministry of Petroleum, Chemicals and Fertilizers. "The Health Ministry is supposed to be interested in the welfare of the people," she says, "but the Chemicals Ministry seems to be more interested in the welfare of the drug industry. Also, the Health Ministry is so crippled by inadequate or ambiguous laws that it is toothless."[5]

Repeatedly, Shiva has criticized the government's differential pricing policy of trying to make essential drugs more accessible by limiting the prices that manufacturers could charge for them and then allowing the firms to set whatever prices they wanted on nonessential drugs.[6] This well-intended move proved to be a disaster. Prices on essential drugs were set so low that the companies could not make a profit on them—in fact, in many instances, they could not break even—and they simply declined to produce and market the drugs. As a result, the essential drugs may have become less costly, but they nearly disappeared from the marketplace, whereas nonessential products were expensive but available.

Shiva has called for strengthening the Indian drug-inspection program, in which there are now only about 600 inspectors for some 9,000 pharmaceutical units or companies plus untold thousands of pharmacies that have set themselves up as "manufacturing chemists." She claims, "The pharmaceutical business, even in India, cannot be treated as a cottage industry if good manufacturing practices and high quality cannot be assured." With its absurdly inadequate system of drug inspection and quality control, some observers note, India has probably the highest percentage of substandard drug products in the world.[7]

Shiva has also attacked the continuing use of antidiarrheal clioquinol products, which not only have remained on the market in India but are actually listed as "essential drugs." She has repeatedly attacked the promotion of anabolic steroid hormones for malnourished children as a substitute for a proper diet. She has branded India's present national drug policy—enthusiastically endorsed by the drug industry—as "anti-people, anti-health, and pro-industry."[8] For a number of reasons, she has not endeared herself to the drug companies. "She may appear to be a little jolly, harmless, roly-poly kind of a lady," says a Dutch drug company official in India, "but she has all the instincts of a Mafia hit-man. She goes directly to the jugular." Her major impact on the drug companies has probably come from her role in the battle against the high-dosage estrogen-progestogens.

There appeared to be an impressive amount of ammunition to use in that struggle. In 1979 in Madras, Dr. Palaniappan, professor of obstetrics and gynecology at the Kilpauk Medical College, had just reported a study on 52 babies born with harelip, cleft palate, missing or deformed limbs, or other physical or mental defects.[9] In 31 percent— 16 of the damaged babies—the mother had been exposed to female sex hormones during her pregnancy. In most of the cases, it appeared, the hormone had been administered as a pregnancy test. (Moreover, in a massive study in Singapore, the test would be shown to be unreliable.[10] In one case out of five, a positive test proved to be wrong.)

Palaniappan had presented his findings first at a medical meeting in Bombay and then had published them in 1980 in the *Journal of the Indian Medical Association*. He said: "The hormonal pregnancy test is not only ineffective in diagnosing pregnancy, but there may be added risks, especially when it is used as a pregnancy test by women who wish to continue the pregnancy. . . . As a result of this investigation, it is suggested that oestrogen-progesterone combination, in cases of missed menstruation, should be discontinued." This was upsetting to the drug companies. Even more unpalatable was a cover story on the report, published in a Bombay magazine, *Onlooker*, under the title, "Pregnancy Drugs Can Deform Babies—Ban Them."[11]

Similar disquieting reports on the fetal damage produced by sex hormones—involving not only mouth and limb defects but also cardiac, spinal, esophageal, intestinal, and kidney damage—had already been published during the 1970s. These had come from Isabel Gal and her coworkers, first at Queen Mary's Hospital for Children in Carshalton, in Surrey, and later at Queen Charlotte's Maternity Hospital in London,[12] and then from Edith Levy and her associates at Montreal Children's Hospital,[13] and particularly from James and Audrey Nora at the University of Colorado Medical Center in Denver.[14] More confirmation was provided by such investigators as Dwight Janerich and his team at the New York State Department of Health,[15] a group headed by Olli Heinonen from Boston University, Harvard, and the New York State Birth Defects Institute,[16] and Pravin Kasan and Joan Andrews at St. David's Hospital in Cardiff, Wales.[17] In the United States, most scientists seemed to agree with the conclusion reached by the Denver team: "The Food and Drug Administration has taken the position that there is no justification for using progestogen and estrogen in threatened abortion or as a pregnancy test. . . . The prudent physician would do well to adhere to the FDA guidelines."[18]

Early in 1982 pressure was brought on the Indian government to tighten the labels on the combination products and warn patients that these should not be used unless pregnancy were ruled out. The warnings had only minimal effect; usually they were printed in English, which few patients could read. But even if they had appeared in Hindi, they would have been useless because most Indian women were unable to read in any language.

Also in 1982, armed with much evidence and with strong support from women's and other consumer groups and health associations, Mira Shiva and her colleagues saw to it that the problem of the high-dosage products was given serious attention. The Drugs Control authorities were required to have the issue examined by an organization whose reputation could not be challenged—the authoritative Indian Council for Medical Research. A special committee selected by the council undertook an investigation and then recommended to the Indian drugs controller—the top governmental drug official—that he ban the high-dosage forms. It was just what the consumerists had wanted. "We emphasized as strongly as we could that we had nothing against the *low-dosage* forms," Shiva says. "They were acceptable. They were reasonably safe, and we needed them as oral contraceptives for those Indian women who preferred them to sterilization and IUDs [intrauterine devices]. It was the *high-dosage* forms we had to get rid of."[19]

On June 21, 1982, the drugs controller, S. S. Gothoskar, accepted the recommendation and announced the ban: all manufacture of the high-dosage products was to be halted by December 31, 1982, and all sales by June 30, 1983.[20] The apparent triumph for the consumer groups would put India on the same side as most industrialized nations. In England, for example, physicians were cautioned that oral contraceptives were never to be used unless pregnancy had first been ruled out. In the United States, the package inserts for even low-dosage estrogen-progestogens all carried a warning against use in pregnancy. In the United States and most of Europe, the high-dosage products could no longer be found. They had been replaced as a pregnancy test by readily available tests on urine.

But in India, the health and consumer groups were far from victory. The proposed ban ordered by the drugs controller was immediately opposed by the Federation of Associations of Obstetricians and Gynaecologists (the very doctors who presumably were looking out for the interests of pregnant women), by the Organization of Pharmaceutical

Producers of India (the association representing the multinational drug companies), and by the three major companies still involved—Nicholas Laboratories of Australia, Unichem Laboratories of India, and Organon of the Netherlands, operating in India under the name Infar (India) Ltd. (Such European firms as Ciba-Geigy, Roussel, and Schering AG had already withdrawn their high-dosage products from the market.) Nicholas would soon pull out of the controversy by withdrawing its product.

Organon, a remarkable pharmaceutical enterprise, is part of the AKZO group (Algemene Koninklijke Zout Organon), created in 1969 with the merger of a chemical and salt-mining organization, an artificial-silk company, and a firm to produce hormones. Organon itself was begun in 1923 to produce insulin and other hormones derived from animal glands. It started, quite logically, in two small rooms connected to a slaughterhouse in the Dutch village Oss and was the first firm on the European continent to supply insulin for the treatment of diabetes. It grew with amazing speed, especially after the 1950s, when it took a prominent role in the development and production of cortisone, steroid sex hormones, and other corticosteroids, pituitary hormones, and vitamins.[21]

The drug companies took their case to the Bombay and Calcutta supreme courts and asked that the ban against the high-dosage products be stayed until a legal decision could be reached. To the consternation of the consumers, the court ordered that the ban be stayed for two years.[22] In spite of repeated efforts by the health and consumer groups to get the stay order revoked, the stay was continued for four years while the matter was taken up by the Supreme Court of India. Then, in 1986, instead of taking a stand and ruling one way or another, the court said that there should be public hearings to determine whether or not *all* estrogen-progestogen products, low-dosage oral contraceptives as well as high-dosage versions, should be allowed on the market.[23]

The supreme court ruling undoubtedly delighted the drug companies. The four-year delay had already given them four more years to continue their profitable sales. Now, extending the dispute to include the low-dosage forms would grievously complicate the issue. Nobody wanted to get rid of the low-dosage products, since they were vital as oral contraceptives. The consumer and women's groups had never asked that they be abolished. Physicians would never stand for a ban on them. Including them in the proposed hearings would lead only to confusion—which, it appeared, was precisely what the drug company lawyers had in mind.

The Public Hearings

The first of what would eventually be four public hearings was set for February 5, 1987, in Madras. No official information was sent to the consumer groups. Mira Shiva was alerted only after a consumerist stumbled on the official announcement—a few lines buried in columns of routine governmental notices published in a Bombay newspaper, the *Indian Express*. The notice appeared on January 24 and stated that all documentary evidence and testimony must be written and submitted in advance—with thirty copies—by January 27.[24] "It was difficult for us in so short a time to make so many copies of so much material," Shiva said. "We did the best we could. Then, when a few of us appeared in the Madras hearing, we knew we were in trouble."[25] Somehow the drug companies had been well prepared. They had neatly printed copies of their affidavits and testimonials. They had at least a dozen attorneys and perhaps a score of physicians willing to testify as experts. The press had also been tipped off.

At the hearing, chaired by the new drugs controller, Prem Gupta himself, the two sides presented their basic arguments, which would be echoed time after time. The industry representatives and their physician friends declared that the high-dosage forms were harmless, that they were essential, and that no other country had banned them. Their medical experts insisted that "we could not practice without them," that there were no suitable substitutes available, and that they personally had *never* seen any birth defects caused by them. If any of these products had ever done harm, the company attorneys added, such a sad development had *never* been brought to their attention.[26]

On their side, Shiva and her few associates claimed that the high-dosage forms were harmful and had caused injury, that there was no clinical need for them, and that they had already been ousted from many countries, and that the Indian Council for Medical Research and the Indian drugs controller agreed that they should be withdrawn. A newspaper account in the *Times of India* afterward described the hearing as "farcical," with a handful of consumer representatives pitted against a powerful and determined opponent, the drug manufacturers who were seeking to block the ban.[27]

The second hearing came on April 10, in Delhi. Again, Prem Gupta was in the chair. This time he had personally notified Mira Shiva well in advance. "We had about six physicians with us to testify," she says, "but they had many more—perhaps fifty or sixty—and many of these were specialists in obstetrics and gynecology. But our submission document included chapters from the latest gynecology and pharmacology textbooks, views of experts from all over the world, a review of the world literature, and evidence that the companies themselves were aware of at least some of the hazards of their high-dosage products."[28] Shiva challenged some of the claims of the industry physicians and asked why the companies were apparently less concerned about shortages of essential drugs in India than about getting a banned drug unbanned. A few of the industry physicians became so enraged that they went to Chairman Gupta and demanded that Shiva apologize publicly for insulting the entire gynecological profession. The drugs controller tactfully suggested that they forget it.

On her part, Shiva asked Organon/Infar to explain how it was that, if its high-dosage estrogen-progestogen products were so essential, it was not permitted to market them in the Netherlands. No explanation was forthcoming. (Later an Organon official in the Netherlands did offer an explanation: "Menstrogen Forte—Organon's high-dosage product—is licensed in the Netherlands," he said, "but is not marketed there for commercial reasons.")[29] She noted that the standard obstetrical and gynecological textbooks in the United States and Great Britain routinely included warnings against the use of high-dosage estrogen-progestogen products. Similar warnings were contained in Indian textbooks.[30] The deputy drugs controller of India, however, waved a red-covered volume, which he described as "the standard Oxford University textbook," and which, he proclaimed, "highly recommends the use of these medicines." "Unfortunately," Shiva says, "none of us was allowed to get close enough to identify the red book."[31]

Particularly confusing were the results of a "questionnaire" submitted by the drugs controller to selected Indian physicians, asking them if estrogen-progestogen combinations were needed in medical practice. Industry spokesmen gleefully reported that the doctors had almost unanimously voted yes. But the questionnaire was not submitted to any physician who had endorsed the ban on the high-dosage products.

Furthermore, the survey was so phrased that the physicians could not know whether it was referring to low-dosage oral contraceptives, to high-dosage forms, or to both.[32]

In building their major defense of the use of the high-dosage versions, the industry experts emphasized their need especially in the treatment of a variety of conditions lumped together under the name secondary amenorrhea—that is, failure of menstruation for any reason other than pregnancy. Some Indian gynecologists testified that it was totally impossible for any doctor to treat secondary amenorrhea without the high-dosage products. "If you take away these drugs," one of them declared, "you are punishing our patients."

The health and consumerist group experts dismissed such an argument as nonsense, and pointed out that their medical colleagues in Europe and the United States were treating their secondary amenorrhea patients without the high-dosage combination forms, largely because American and European physicians had access to sophisticated diagnostic methods that were generally not available in India, and their patients did quite well. Furthermore, they said, most of the secondary amenorrhea cases in India resulted not from hormone deficiencies but from such conditions as malnutrition, anemia, tuberculosis, and stress, where there was no call for hormone therapy.[33] And, they added, if hormones were indicated, the physician should use progestogens alone, estrogen-progestins cyclically, or low-dosage combination products.

Shiva had also called on leading British experts for consultation and included their replies as part of her testimony. For instance, H. S. Jacobs, professor of reproductive endocrinology at Middlesex Hospital Medical School in London and a member of Britain's Committee on the Safety of Medicines, told her: "These drugs would be unacceptable in the United Kingdom. . . . It is unethical to attempt to introduce them. . . . I am shocked at the irresponsibility of the companies trying to profit from such second-rate preparations."[34]

Stephen Franks, senior lecturer in reproductive endocrinology at St. Mary's Hospital Medical School in London, said: "I feel strongly that there is no justification for the use of these drugs in amenorrhea, menstrual irregularities and other 'gynaecological disorders.' . . . I think it would be irresponsible and dangerous to encourage the use of high-dose estrogen-progestogen combinations in management of these gynaecological symptoms."[35]

From the University of Newcastle-upon-Tyne, M. D. Rawlins, professor of clinical pharmacology, commented: "I am, frankly, dismayed that the Indian pharmaceutical industry should wish to seek to maintain their market in high dose estrogen-progestogen products. There is no scientific or clinical justification for the continued use of these products and I would hope that the companies concerned, even at this late hour, would voluntarily withdraw these products from the Indian market."[36]

After the session, the Bombay *Indian Post* reported: "So stage managed was the hearing that even such obvious slips were ignored as the one on the part of the representative of a medical profession who admitted that she prescribed the drug for pregnancy testing, although four years ago the Drug Controller obliged the manufacturer to add a warning that the drugs should not be used for pregnancy testing."[37] (Organon and its Indian subsidiary Infar continued to get more unfriendly comment from Europe. In the Netherlands, Organon's home base, its promotion of the high-dosage products was drawing bitter attacks from WEMOS, the highly active Dutch consumerist organization.)

During the first two hearings, the Unichem and Organon/Infar representatives had repeatedly insisted that their high-dosage products were safe because (1) they could not be obtained without a physician's prescription; (2) modern physicians would no longer prescribe such drugs for pregnancy testing; and (3) the drugs were clearly labeled with a warning against their use in pregnancy. If the drugs were improperly used, the companies claimed, it was only because they were being handed out by quacks and other unqualified individuals— which, of course, was against the law, and in such cases no blame could be directed toward the manufacturers.

The health and consumer groups had collected evidence from different parts of India where the high-dosage forms continued to be used for pregnancy testing and for indications not generally included in medical textbooks. Included in the material they collected was an article by a young British physician, Trisha Greenhalgh, who had spent four months in India during 1984 observing the manner in which physicians actually managed their patients. She reported in *Lancet* in 1986:

I introduced myself as "a foreign doctor interested in diseases in this area," and followed 2,400 patients through medical consultations. . . . High-dose oestrogen-progesterone combination preparations have repeatedly been shown to be teratogenic [fetus-damaging]; in India they are allowed to be sold specifically for dysfunctional uterine bleeding. Yet they continue to be pre-scribed as the cheapest and most widely available pregnancy test in the country (I never saw it prescribed for anything else).[38]

Early in 1987 she added:

No instructions were given to these patients by the GP or the pharmacist. The package insert for the drug gave clear warning of its possible teratogenicity but in no case was this insert passed on to the patient. . . . In all cases the aluminum wrapper for the drug had a warning that it should only be dispensed on the prescription of a doctor.[39]

Hearing number three was scheduled for July 10 in Calcutta. Even by the day before, the drug companies realized they might be facing new difficulties. The Federation of Medical Representatives Associa-tions of India—the association of 10,000 drug company detailers and salesmen—threw its support to the consumerists. So also did an asso-ciation of Organon/Infar's own employees and the governmental As-sociation of Health Service Doctors. On the evening before the hear-ing, these and other groups staged a noisy demonstration before the Organon offices. The Calcutta hearing was chaired, not by the drugs controller, Prem Gupta, who was out of the country, but by Das Gupta (no relation), his deputy. The company representatives and their sup-porters were allowed to present their case first. They spoke effusively, lengthily, and often to resounding applause.

When Mira Shiva and the drug activists were given their turn, they were prepared. They had nearly forty experts with them, including ex-perienced obstetricians and gynecologists, representatives of women's groups and health associations, leaders of local medical societies, and even the secretary of the Indian Medical Association. The chairman decided that different rules would now apply. "The chairman was very firm with us," Shiva recalls. "He let us have not more than three min-utes for each of our speakers. If there was any applause, he stopped it immediately. But not all of our speakers were allowed to talk. For the industry speakers, though, he let them have six, or seven, or even eight minutes apiece. He permitted applause from the audience."[40]

At a critical moment, and against massive protests, one Organon speaker was given permission to speak for a second time. An angry consumerist pulled the microphone away from him, and the Organon man shouted, "So, you have brought your goons!" The consumerist re-torted, "Goons? I will show you goons!" Fists began to fly, one speaker was hit on the nose by a news photographer's camera, and the police were called. A newspaper reported:

The police were summoned at the Central Drugs Laboratory here this afternoon when doctors became restive during a public hearing under orders of the Supreme Court over the fate of hormonal combination of estrogen and progestogen. At one stage, the situation turned so violent that the meeting had to be adjourned for about two and a half hours. During the melee that followed, some of the participants, including representatives of the drug industry and eminent physicians, had an exchange of blows and fisticuffs. Slogans were raised and invectives hurled.[41]

The fourth and final hearing came on July 15 in Bombay. Prem Gupta, the drugs controller, had returned to India and was back in the chair. He would allow no disturbances. The police, although in plain clothes, were very much in evidence. This time, both the drug companies and the consumerists had their expert obstetricians and gynecologists ready to testify. In addition, Shiva and her allies found they now had support from another group of medical experts, the child specialists. Pediatricians testified that use of the high-dosage products for pregnancy tests was "a cause of great concern" to them.[42] These were the physicians who would have to provide care for the defective babies after they were born.

Representatives of many women's groups spoke and presented evidence showing that—regardless of industry claims about the adequacy of warnings on the labels—in India, the high-dosage products were in fact being used unsafely. Another touchy issue was raised when a representative of Unichem workers testified, "If these products are banned, many of us will lose our jobs." A dignified elderly lady replied, "If you are holding your job now by crippling other people's children, then you should lose it."

Perhaps the fundamental dispute came down to this interchange: One top Indian gynecologist said, "Show me one study in India that proves that these substances are dangerous." Whereupon an equally eminent Indian gynecologist retorted, "Show me one study in India that proves they are safe."[43]

The Party Lines

All during the hearings, there was a curious unwillingness of the two sides to debate the same issue.

To the consumerists, the issue was simple: *the high-dosage estrogen-progestogen products may be harmful to unborn children; there is no clinical need for them; and therefore they should be banned in India.*

To the drug companies, the issue was equally simple—but different: *the low-dosage estrogen-progestogens, when not used during pregnancy, are safe; the high-dosage products are needed in a variety of menstrual disorders; they have not been banned elsewhere as unsafe; and therefore they should not be banned in India.*[44]

Part of this remarkably confused situation could be attributed to the failure of the Indian drugs controller to rule that the public hearings would cover not the low-dosage forms (on which there had been no dispute) but only high-dosage forms (on which the dispute was all too apparent). Part could be charged to some of India's most honored obstetricians and gynecologists, who had somehow been persuaded to testify in direct opposition to the world's scientific literature—and even in opposition to what they themselves had said, published, and taught only a few years before.[45] But much could be directed toward the legalistic maneuvering of the industry attorneys, whose efforts to confuse could not be mistaken. Pieter van Keep, Organon's international medical director, took strong exception to this opinion. "The gynecologists mentioned did not condone the use of estrogen-progestogen drugs in pregnancy," he said, "but their use in gynecological practice and this is *not* in direct opposition to the world scientific literature."[46]

In the debates, the safety of the low-dosage forms—those used as oral contraceptives—was accepted on all sides. The safety of the high-dosage forms was something else.[47] The testimony presented to the chair went something like this:

INDUSTRY SPOKESMEN: There is no published evidence that, even when used during pregnancy, the high-dosage products are harmful or are being misused.

CONSUMER SPOKESMEN: How can you say that? Reports and warnings have already appeared in such authoritative scientific and medical journals as *Nature*, *Lancet*, the *British Medical Journal*, the *British Journal of Obstetrics and Gynaecology*, and the *International Journal of Gynaecology and Obstetrics* in Great Britain, the *Medical Journal of Australia*, and the *New England Journal of Medicine*, the *American Journal of Epidemiology*, the *Archives of Environmental Health*, and the *Journal of the American Medical Association* in the United States. They are all internationally recognized publications. And they all show that these products are dangerous.

INDUSTRY SPOKESMEN: Ah, but there are no such reports in *Indian* medical journals.

CONSUMER SPOKESMEN: But what about the big report from Professor Palaniappan? That was published in the *Journal of the Indian Medical Association*.

INDUSTRY SPOKESMAN: We think it was not a very scientific study.

A similar failure to face up to the issues came in the matter of expert witnesses. The drug companies produced a number of obstetricians and gynecologists who testified that the high-dosage forms were absolutely vital for the treatment of such disorders as secondary amenorrhea. Arguments like these were presented:

INDUSTRY SPOKESMEN: Our eminent authorities agree—the high-dosage products are indispensable. Our physicians cannot practice without them.

CONSUMER SPOKESMEN: But other experts, both in England and in India, say the high-dosage forms are not needed.

INDUSTRY SPOKESMEN: Our experts are eminent authorities. Your experts don't matter. Their views are merely the personal views of a few well-meaning doctors.[48]

CONSUMER SPOKESMEN: How is it, then, that British and American physicians treat their patients successfully without the high-dosage drugs?

INDUSTRY SPOKESMEN: But, you must admit, they are not treating *Indian* patients.

The company representatives brought forth still other defenses:

• These drugs have been used for twenty years or more, and no injuries have been reported to the manufacturers. Accordingly, it is unlikely that they are unsafe.

• Any drug can be misused. Picking on the estrogen-progestogen products is irrational, arbitrary, and discriminatory.

• The drug cannot [be] and is not misused. If it is misused, it is not the responsibility of the manufacturer.

• The estrogen-progestogen drugs are not misused because . . . such drugs are sold [only] by retail through prescription.

• If the drugs are sold without a physician's prescription, that is the responsibility of the physician or the pharmacist, and not of the manufacturer.

• The high-dosage products have never been *banned* in Great Britain, as the consumerists have claimed. (True, but they have been *withdrawn* in the U.K. and virtually every other industrialized country in the world, which practically comes to the same thing.)

- Any decision to ban the products in India would be in contravention of the principles of natural justice and fair play.
- There were cases of fetal damage before the high-dosage products came into use. Probably they were all caused by the intermarriage of cousins or other too closely related persons.

Pieter van Keep of Organon disputed the views of consumerist leaders. He stated:

Whoever summarized the testimony presented to the chair did not realize that the whole argument is beside the point. The use of these drugs during pregnancy is not the issue: *no one* is in favor of this. The issue is the use in nonpregnant women or *abuse* during pregnancy. The evidence for teratogenicity if used during pregnancy is lacking, [a claim that is strongly disclaimed] but so is the evidence for complete safety. The real question is: is there a place for such products in gynecology in nonpregnant women? The industry's view is that there is a place for them, but this is rapidly decreasing in importance with increasing availability of modern diagnostic tools—including echography, biopsies, and laboratory tests. The consumerists are against the abuse and refuse to listen to arguments in favor of use in nonpregnant women. The industry has perhaps also been insufficiently able to make its point. The whole conflict has been a *dialogue des sourds*, a dialogue between deaf mutes.[49]

Finally, the Verdict

The final public hearing came to a close on July 15, 1987. It was expected that, in such a disputed affair, the drugs controller might need to take several weeks—perhaps a month or two—to consider the problem. All through the rest of the year, however, the drugs control authorities remained silent. The drug companies did not seem particularly alarmed by the delay—some of them, it was reported, had put their factories on a three-shift schedule to build up an enormous stockpile of the drugs—but the consumerists kept pressing for a decision. On June 1, 1988, Mira Shiva wrote again to the drugs controller:

We have waited anxiously for your verdict on high dose EP [estrogen-progestogen] drugs since last July end, by when you were to take your decision. . . . Now the public hearings are over and you must have definitely tallied the arguments for and against the ban to help you in your verdict. Specially since ICMR [the Indian Council for Medical Research] has again recommended the drug to be banned and since the Drug Technical Advisory Board too recommended its ban, your verdict should not be further delayed. Since this case will undoubtedly set a precedent, we expect you to ensure not only immediate banning of the product but withdrawal of these products from the market and destruction of the stock.[50]

On June 15, 1988, the drugs controller finally handed down his decision, although it was not publicly announced for another two weeks: The ban on the high-dose products was to go into effect.[51] As a matter of fact, in March 1987 Organon had taken all oral dosage forms of the high-dosage product off the market in all countries except India, where the matter was still before the court. In India, the Organon product was withdrawn in January 1988. At least one company, however, indicated that it would continue its legal battle to get the Indian ban overturned.[52] Organon's injectable product had been ordered off the market in January 1988.[53] "To appreciate all this," commented one observer, "you must understand that all of India is a jungle. We have tigers in our forests. We have tigers also in our law courts."

Even before the drugs controller handed down his more-or-less final decision, the International Organization of Consumers Unions had given Mira Shiva its new, prestigious Olle Hansson Award, named for the late Swedish pediatric neurologist who had led the worldwide fight against clioquinol and other irrational drugs, and against socially irresponsible drug companies. "I knew Dr. Hansson," Shiva says. "He was a very brave, courageous person." True. We, too, knew Olle Hansson well. To him, Mira Shiva was even braver and more courageous. "To understand Mira Shiva," he once told us, "you must realize that there is one thing she simply does not know: she does not know that she might ever fail."

Chapter 7

BANGLADESH AND THE NOBLE EXPERIMENT

India finally won its independence from the British Empire in 1947. Two nations were created out of British India: Pakistan, a Muslim state, and India, a secular state. Pakistan was divided into two sections, East and West. In 1971, after a bloody nine-months civil war, the two Pakistans separated and the eastern portion became Bangladesh.

Today Bangladesh might seem to be an almost inconsequential Third World nation. With its population of approximately 112 million and an area of only 56,000 square miles, it represents barely three-tenths of one percent of the land mass of Asia. It is, however, a crowded land: Whereas the population density is roughly 66 persons per square mile in the United States, 284 in the People's Republic of China, 334 in Pakistan, and 612 in India, it is estimated to be 2,000 per square mile in Bangladesh—much as if one-fourth of the population of the United States were jammed into a state the size of Wisconsin.

Bangladesh is predominantly a flat tableland, only a little above sea level. It is bordered on the west and the north by several Indian states, on the east by a small stretch of Burma (now Myanmar), and on the south by the Indian Ocean. Three river systems—the Meghna, the Ganges flowing out of India, and the Brahmaputra coming out of Tibet and Assam—make possible an enormous network of water transportation, and also the spread of waterborne diseases. They are vital to the country's production of jute, rice, coffee, tea, tobacco, and sugar cane. "During the dry season, water covers perhaps 15 percent of my country," says a Bangladesh official. "During the rainy monsoon season, it feels as though there is water over 115 percent."

For centuries the territory now called Bangladesh has been hit by floods, droughts, famine, cyclones, hurricanes, plagues, and unending poverty. Life expectancy for both men and women is in the mid-fifties. Infant mortality now runs about 115 per 1,000 live births. The various diarrheal diseases are so prevalent that the International Centre for Diarrhoeal Disease Research was established in the capital city, Dhaka (formerly Dacca). The literacy rate is only about 25 percent. Squalor is visible everywhere. Visitors arriving at the international airport in Dhaka are greeted by hordes of beggars, many of them holding out their starving children, many of them crippled, deformed, grotesquely disfigured by leprosy, who press in on foreigners and clutch at their clothes, pleading for money.

Those Bangladeshi who can afford it (and there *is* an elite in the nation) usually go for their medical care to India, the United States, the United Kingdom, or Thailand. There are six universities and ten medical schools, which have turned out about 16,000 physicians, of whom an estimated 10,500 are located in the cities. Unfortunately, most of the people live in some 68,000 villages out in the country, which have few if any trained physicians or pharmacists.

Traditionally, the diagnosis and treatment of disease is handled as part of the religious life of the villages. Local healers provide most medications for the people, and many of these products are supposedly prepared and administered according to the old ayurvedic or unani systems. Based on the ancient Vedas, or religious texts of India, ayurveda has been practiced for thousands of years. Unani is described as a Moslem system based on that of the ancient Greeks.

One observer, Francis Rolt of the British group War on Want, wrote in 1985:

The ayurvedic and unani systems have become big business in Bangladesh, wide open to unethical practices and abuse. It is now rare to find an ayurvedic practitioner who prepares his own medicine. . . . The commercial drive of several big companies . . . has transformed ayurveda in Bangladesh from an holistic system in which the doctor knew and treated the whole patient with medicines he prepared himself, into a system in which the doctor merely prescribes, or the patient self-prescribes, a pre-prepared and commercially packaged "medicine" made in a factory by a large company.

The companies marketing these "traditional" remedies, Rolt claims, use techniques that are crude but effective, relying on ignorance and fear.

They stress impotence, venereal diseases, and other "diseases" described variously as "nocturnal emission," "thinness of semen," "loss of vital fluid," etc. . . . One preparation is said to be a great boon to the unfit to revive his lost manhood. It bestows strength, stamina, and energy in a man who is prematurely grown old due to youthful excesses. It is a sovereign remedy for sexual debility, impotency, and in cases of general debility and lowered vitality.

Many of these "traditional" medicines contain 40 percent or more of ethyl alcohol. More than a dozen of the several hundred ayurvedic and unani companies are also licensed as distilleries. One of the more memorable products is known as Mrito Sanjhi Boni ("Bring the Dead Back to Life").

Regular use of it makes up for all wastes of flesh, blood, marrow, and semen, and restores the failing memory. . . . In Spermatorrhoea and Impotency it is nectar like, in Typhoid and in collapsing stages of Cholera, its effects are electrifying, and in chronic indigestion, loss of appetite and colic pain, it is . . . prepared out of purely indigenous drugs, is absolutely free from recalcitrant effects and safely guarantees permanent cure.[1]

Other high-alcohol tonics were promoted for the prevention or cure of jaundice, uterine infections, heart disease, leprosy, dropsy, diabetes, and gonorrhea.

Of the three largest pharmaceutical-distillery firms, one was described as owned outright by a brother of the secretary of health, while another was owned in considerable part by the secretary himself. According to Rolt, the secretary was not totally committed to traditional medicine. At the same time, he was a government representative on the board of directors of the Bangladesh subsidiary of the giant German drug company Hoechst, and also a board member of the subsidiary of the British firm Fisons.[2]

The situation involving nontraditional or Western drugs was not substantially better, and in the early 1980s the pharmaceutical situation in Bangladesh was described as an absolute shambles. Some experts declared that nearly one-third of the country's expenditures for drugs was wasted on "unnecessary and useless" medicines: vitamin mixtures, tonics, alkalizers, cough mixtures, digestive enzymes, "pallia-tives," "gripe water" for bowel complaints, and scores of other unessen-tial drugs. One authority claimed that one-third of the brand-name products registered in the country were "useless, unnecessary, and at times harmful."

A British firm, Glaxo, was charged with marketing 56 products, nearly half of which were needless and costly vitamins and tonics, and of those only 3 were approved for sale in Great Britain.[3] Several firms, both domestic and multinational, were producing high-dosage female sex hormones, which were often prescribed for use in a fetus-damaging pregnancy test and were sometimes used in an attempt to cause abortion.[4] The Dutch company Organon was severely criticized for promoting its anabolic hormone Orabolin for undernourished children, and Hoechst was attacked for pushing costly vitamin-mineral combinations for children who could not get enough food.[5] An Ameri-can firm, Bristol-Myers, was denounced for its advertisement in the *Bangladesh Times* advising the public, "We are pleased to announce that our life-saving anti-cancer drug 'CeeNu Capsules' are now available in Dhaka with all important chemists and druggists."[6] The advertisement ignored the fact that, in the United States, the company was required to label its drug BiCNU, or carmustine, with the strong warning that it could be used only by specially trained physicians and only as a pallia-tive for a relatively few uncommon malignancies. One Bristol-Myers executive replied to the criticism in Bangladesh by saying that "it was a little more aggressive than what we normally print."

Both physicians and pharmacists, it was reported, were being "easily persuaded to prescribe or sell useless and even dangerous drugs by glib company representatives, heavy promotion, and gifts." According to an account in the *Dhaka Courier*, "A practising doctor in Faridpur was presented with a television set by one company so he would prescribe its products. . . . Another was presented with a refrigerator. . . . 'What can I say,' asks a lady doctor in Dhaka, pointing at an expensive gold necklace. 'They offer gifts like this. I'm obliged to help, aren't I?'"[7]

Who was responsible for dumping all this pharmaceutical rubbish in Bangladesh? Some of the blame could unquestionably be laid on the nearly 200 domestic companies working in the country. Much could be attributed to the multinationals. Eight of these had substantial produc-tion and marketing operations: three were British firms, Fisons, Glaxo, and Imperial Chemical (ICI); one, May & Baker (M&B) was a subsidiary of a French company; two, Pfizer and Squibb, were American; one, Hoechst, was German; and one, Organon, was Dutch. Together they accounted for some 75 percent of the Bangladesh market. If there were to be any reforms, they would be the most likely targets.

The Experiment Is Launched

The first years in Bangladesh were turbulent. In addition to the normal complement of floods, hurricanes, and other natural disasters, there was frequent political upheaval—periodic coups and attempted coups, more or less bloody, with or without assassinations. In a relatively bloodless coup in late March 1982 the army chief of staff, Lt. Gen. Hossain Mohammad Ershad, took over power as chief martial law administrator. Scarcely a month later, on April 27, his Ministry of Health and Population Control announced the appointment of an eight-member expert committee, six physicians and two pharmacists, to recommend how to improve the country's miserably inadequate drug supply and develop a new national drug policy. Among other matters, they were also to investigate the state of the pharmaceutical industry in Bangladesh. Named as chairman was Nurul Islam, director of the Institute of Postgraduate Medicine and Research in Dhaka. "Professor Islam had been extremely close to the previous administration," says a Dhaka newspaperman, "but as undoubtedly the most well-known doctor in the country, he simply couldn't be left out."

Conspicuously absent from the committee were any invited representatives from the Bangladesh Medical Association. But, it was noted, the president of the medical association was an official of Pfizer's Bangladesh subsidiary and owned stock in at least three other drug firms, while the general secretary of the BMA was medical director of Pfizer. At the same time, there was criticism of the inclusion of a physician, Zafrullah Chowdhury, who had recently created a new pharmaceutical company specializing in generic-name products and thus competing with the brand-name multinationals.

The expert committee had been asked to submit its report on May 10, after barely two weeks of work. The report was actually turned in on May 11. In that time, the members had completed their study of more than 4,100 products licensed in the country. Islam said it had been "a herculean job." "Of course," Zafrullah explained later, "we didn't do all that work in two weeks. Many of us had been thinking about the problem for many months. We'd been studying the WHO guidelines on essential drugs. We knew what had to be done, which American and European textbooks could best serve as guides. We'd been thinking and talking about which drugs were the ones the country really required and which were duplicative, or relatively unnecessary, or excessively dangerous."[8]

In general, the drugs nominated for ouster were these:

- Most combination products, including antibiotics, painkillers, vitamins, and minerals, unless there was no single-entity product available to give an acceptable result
- Multiple-ingredient cough mixtures, throat lozenges, gripe waters, and antacids
- "Me-too" products having "only trivial differences from older and less expensive products"
- Tonics, most enzyme products, and "so-called restorative products whose sale flourishes on consumers' ignorance"
- Products whose therapeutic value is "doubtful, trivial, or absent," or which are apparently harmful or likely to be misused
- Most products not listed in such internationally recognized volumes as the *British Pharmacopoeia* or the *U.S. Pharmacopeia*.[9]

The expert committee expressed appreciation to the multinational companies for providing valuable medicines to Bangladesh, but added that the job of producing antacids, vitamins, and other simple preparations in the future "will lie solely with the national companies, leaving the multinationals free to concentrate their efforts and resources on those items not so easily produced by smaller national companies."

There would be no royalty agreements with overseas firms on most products unless the company had a factory in Bangladesh, and raw materials would be purchased only on the basis of competitive world prices. There would be no more "transfer pricing." All products would be made under acceptable quality controls. Using these criteria, the committee then proposed a phased withdrawal program to get rid of 1,707 of the roughly 4,100 products then on the market:

- In Category I would be 305 products described as harmful. They should no longer be imported or manufactured, and existing stocks should be withdrawn from sale and destroyed within one month.

- In Category II would be 134 products listed as irrational combinations or needlessly expensive drugs. They were to be given six months for the sale of existing stocks or, in some instances, reformulation into acceptable combinations.
- In Category III were 1,268 products labeled as either useless and unnecessary, or "famous brand name products" made under license. They would have to be withdrawn within nine months.

The committee members were in general agreement that they had performed a difficult but necessary task, and the results of their labors would then be judged calmly and dispassionately by all interested parties. It was not a very realistic hope.

The Experiment Explodes

Within a few days, it was reported, the new policy had attracted unprecedented worldwide attention.[10] Letters of support and enthusiastic approval flooded into Dhaka from such consumer groups as Health Action International, War on Want, OXFAM, women's associations, and religious groups. A government press release said, "A large number of local as well as foreign publications have paid glowing tribute to the authorities for their foresight in adopting the policy." A spokesman for HAI said, "Bangladesh has done what any health-conscious nation should do."[11] A report in the *Guardian* observed:

The military government of Bangladesh has at a stroke done something that no other developing country—or developed one for that matter—has dared to do: it has enacted, almost in its entirety, the World Health Assembly's resolution on essential drugs. . . . This draconian act has been interpreted as a massive assault on the multinational companies that dominate the country's drug market. In fact, it should mean that many more Bangladeshis will get the drugs they really need at a price the country can afford. . . . What concerns the multinationals most of all is that the Bangladesh idea will catch on, as both War on Want and Health Action International hope it will. The stakes world wide are enormous.[12]

The *Washington Post* noted that more than 70 percent of the products proposed for withdrawal had already been described by the U.S. Food and Drug Administration and its British counterpart as "therapeutically worthless."[13] In London, the Royal Society of Medicine's distinguished journal, *Tropical Doctor*, declared in an editorial: "If the

Bangladesh government can make a success of this venture, the benefits in terms of reduced expenditure and increased availability of medicine to those in need will be prodigious. As an example to other nations, its effects could be well-nigh incalculable."[14]

In the other nations, the significance of the Bangladesh experiment was forcefully brought to the attention of the authorities:

The widespread publicity attracted by the drug policy, combined with the belief among some consumer organizations and interest groups that other Third World countries should adopt similar strategies, has placed the Bangladeshi policy beyond the realm of a purely domestic matter. National drug regulatory authorities in several countries have been inundated with publications praising the positive effects of the Bangladeshi policy. Several resolutions have been adopted in regional and international forums calling upon other Third World countries to follow the Bangladeshi experiment.[15]

The Bangladesh government at least implied that the new program was an unqualified success. A government press release stated that the new policy "has been acclaimed the world over as an epoch-making step."[16]

The government in Dhaka, at that very same time, was also inundated by vigorous protests, objections, and denunciations. On the day after the expert committee submitted its report to the Ershad government, most major newspapers mentioned it in only a two-line account. At the *Bangladesh Times*, however, one reporter and his editors recognized the significance of the event and gave it full coverage. That afternoon, the reporter was picked up by the police and taken to army headquarters for questioning. When his fellow reporters learned of this development, they warned that unless he were released by midnight, they would all print the story in full. He was promptly released.[17]

On the following day, Jane Coon, the American ambassador, called—without making an appointment—on General Ershad and Shamsul Huq, the minister of health. She had been instructed by Washington, she said, to make the United States position clear. She strongly urged that the new program be called off, softened, or at least delayed until there could be meetings between the Bangladesh government and the U.S. drug industry. She mentioned that American drug companies might be tempted to pull out of Bangladesh or cut back on plant expansion, and that the policy could interfere with new American investments in the country. She suggested that further action be held off until a neutral expert review committee could come to Bangladesh.

In Washington, a spokesman for the State Department admitted that the U.S. Pharmaceutical Manufacturers Association (PMA) had asked it to bring pressure on Bangladesh. "The State Department," it was said, "has a statutory responsibility for assisting American interests abroad. In this particular case, the U.S. Government is also concerned that these regulations may inhibit further investment in Bangladesh."[18] The British government took a similar position. Douglas Hurd, minister of state, said:

We are keen that the Bangladesh Government should use its scarce resources wisely. We are also keen that they should succeed in their policy of encouraging foreign investment to help with the development of an industrial economy. We, in common with other Western governments, have explained this to the Bangladesh Government through our High Commission in Dhaka. It is important that in trying to achieve the aims of the pharmaceutical policy they do not discriminate against foreign owned manufacturing companies in Bangladesh and do not frighten off prospective foreign investors.[19]

In an interview, the West German ambassador, W. von Marschall, presented almost the identical picture and warned that the new policy would most probably interfere with future German investments.[20]

The pressure put on Bangladesh by the U.S. State Department, at the instigation of the U.S. drug industry, drew a scorching attack from Sidney Wolfe of the Public Citizen Health Research Group in Washington. In a letter to George Shultz, secretary of state, he assailed the action as "unconscionable." He voiced his dismay that the U.S. government had let itself be used by the powerful multinational pharmaceutical companies "to promote and protect their exploitation of the impoverished citizens of undeveloped countries."[21] "Perhaps you are unaware," Wolfe told the secretary, "that many of the U.S.-based multinational drug companies are foisting on innocent people in the developing countries drugs which our own medical authorities consider worthless and unnecessary."

In its analysis of the Bangladesh affair, War on Want recalled an American attempt in the 1970s to browbeat a small Third World country:

The US had demonstrated previously just how far it will go to prevent sovereign governments from adopting similar policies. In Sri Lanka [then Ceylon], when Pfizer was asked to produce more in accordance with the needs of the country . . . [and provide desperately needed supplies of Pfizer tetracycline to fight a frightening outbreak of cholera] and also cut the manufacture of unnecessary drugs from 40 to 25 percent, the US government threatened to stop all food aid.[22]

Ambassador Coon's efforts to halt the Bangladesh program did not succeed. She did, however, arrange to have the Dhaka authorities meet with a "neutral expert committee." The neutrality of the group could have been questioned. It consisted of four members, representing three American drug companies—SmithKline, Squibb, and Wyeth—and the PMA.[23] They flew to Dhaka, spent a week consulting with Bangladesh authorities, flew home, and wrote a report. The report was never made public.

The discovery that applying pressure through diplomatic channels had apparently been ineffective did not stop the multinational companies. In full-page advertisements in major Bangladesh newspapers, they warned that the new policy would only harm the provision of health care to the people of the country, keep the sick from obtaining necessary medicines, and allow low-quality drugs to flood the market.[24] They portrayed the whole experiment as an international plot engineered by OXFAM, War on Want, and Zafrullah Chowdhury, and as a Christian plot aimed against Moslems.[25]

Multinational drug company representatives pointed out that, of the 1,707 products scheduled for withdrawal, only 174 were being manufactured by their firms; all the rest were products of the small domestic companies. Thus, these domestic firms would be the most seriously affected.[26] (This ignored the fact that although the number of the multinational products was small, their sales were relatively enormous.) It was likewise emphasized that a major stockholder in the big subsidiaries of the multinational firms was the Bangladesh government itself.[27] In addition, the multinationals commented, it was curious that while the new policy would wreak havoc with modern or Western drugs, it would leave unscathed the hundreds of "traditional" ayurvedic or unani remedies, which could be ineffective, dangerous, mislabeled, or adulterated—and which, in some instances, contained as much as 45 percent alcohol.[28]

Almost from the outset, the multinationals found that they had strong support from Bangladesh's physicians and pharmacists. Pharmacists declared they would be forced out of business, and physicians in general "grew apoplectic" at what they saw as a restriction on their right to prescribe as they—and they alone—saw fit.[29] Some officials of the Bangladesh Medical Association proposed that the new program be scrapped and be replaced by a rigidly enforced law providing that by-prescription-only drugs could be dispensed only with a physician's prescription. There were no suggestions on how this could be managed with an average of one physician for about each 6,000 inhabitants.

Perhaps the most extraordinary aspect of this whole affair was the performance of a weekly publication called *The Pulse*. Labeling itself "A Medical Journal," it was owned by Anwarul (Bobby) Islam, who was also the executive editor of the *Bangladesh Observer* group of newspapers owned by his uncle.[30] *The Pulse* was apparently financed at least in considerable part by the multinational drug companies with paid advertising and with copies purchased and distributed free of charge to thousands of physicians, pharmacists, and other health professionals. Its editorial policies were not too difficult to detect:

On May 9, 1982, *The Pulse* commented on the appointment of Zafrullah Chowdhury to the expert committee and called for his resignation "in view of the fact that he is a manufacturer of drugs." On December 12, 1983, the headline read: "Drug Policy Needs to Be Reviewed: Banning of Most Drugs Has Resulted in Large Number of Cholera Deaths." On January 2, 1984: "Drug Policy Comes Under Heavy Fire." On February 6, 1984, while some Bangladesh newspapers were declaring that the new policy was being acclaimed the world over, *The Pulse* charged: "Policy Total Failure." On March 5, 1984: "Shortage of Medicines Spread Cholera, Other Diseases." In this article, *The Pulse* claimed that the lack of anticholera antibiotics resulting from the new government policy had resulted in a shocking number of cholera deaths.[31]

The journal tried to support this view by quoting an interview with William Greenough, the eminent director of the International Centre for Diarrhoeal Disease Research in Dhaka.[32] Greenough stated that the article was at best ill-informed and at worst criminal. No effective anticholera antibiotics had been banned. There had been no notable increase in the number of cholera deaths. Further, he said, not only had he not been misquoted; he had never even been interviewed.

It was apparent that Ershad's government had been overawed by the enormous reactions to the new policy. Some officials wondered how there could be a spontaneous, international outpouring of praise and a simultaneous, spontaneous, international outpouring of bitter invective. The explanation: there was nothing spontaneous about either reaction; each was the result of a carefully planned, well-orchestrated approach.

On the one hand, the multinational companies had turned for support to their traditional allies: physicians, pharmacists, and their professional organizations, and the publishers of newspapers or magazines that depended on drug advertising. On the other, the consumerists turned to *their* traditional partners: health associations, women's groups, and religious and charitable organizations. They were able to have a flood of commendatory letters and telegrams arrive in Dhaka by simply writing or telephoning to their friends all over the world and asking for help. As one activist put it, "We really beat the bushes on this one."

The Experiment Pays Off

Under other circumstances, the Bangladesh experiment might have been viewed as a small but fascinating project conducted in a small, unhappy country, of great interest to ivory-tower socioclinical researchers and perhaps of some value to the people of Bangladesh. But this was not to be. For a variety of reasons, outside forces magnified the matter totally out of proportion and made it the subject of headlines in New Delhi, Hong Kong, New York, Washington, Berlin, and London.

In the first place, a number of powerful multinational drug companies looked upon the noble experiment as a major threat to their worldwide profit system, their long-range research ambitions, and their entire capitalist structure. Before it could spread and contaminate other countries, it must be destroyed once and for all. In contrast, to consumer activists, the experiment seemed to represent a heaven-sent opportunity to put into effect some of their most cherished dreams. If the approach worked in Bangladesh, as surely it must, they believed it would spread quickly to other developing nations. And, some of them suggested, it would logically then extend at last to the industrialized world, and victory over the feared multinational drug firms would be complete.

But, as the experiment proceeded, it was seen that there could be no complete victory for either side. Compromises would be inevitable. It was realized almost immediately that the deadlines originally set for withdrawal of the three categories of drugs—put at one, six, and nine months, respectively—would need to be extended to six, nine, and twelve months. Another compromise resulted in the removal of 60 products from the withdrawal list. Although all supplies of some 300 "harmful" or "dangerous" products were to be collected and destroyed, such firms as ICI, May & Baker, and Organon managed to obtain export licenses and ship the rescued materials to Yemen and other countries in the Middle East and Africa.[33]

One celebrated case concerned a combination of vitamins, iron and other minerals, and folic acid known as Heptuna Plus, marketed by Pfizer and promoted especially for women during pregnancy. The expert committee—with the support of clinical pharmacologists in England—classified it as just another costly mixture of multivitamins and iron, and placed it in Category II as an irrational and needlessly expensive combination product. Immediately, there were protests, not only from the company and the American embassy, but also from Professor Feroza Begum, described as the country's most fashionable gynecologist, a past president of the Bangladesh Medical Association, and a major Pfizer stockholder and member of the Pfizer board of directors. Instead of a direct reply from Pfizer the drug administrator received instructions from "the highest authority" in the government not to bother the company any more. Soon thereafter, Ershad and some of his fellow generals flew off to confer with President Reagan and then tour U.S. military bases in Southeast Asia. Finally, nearly two years after the action began, Pfizer decided on its own to withdraw Heptuna Plus.[34]

Shortly after the new policy was put into effect, there were alarming rumors of drug shortages. If such shortages did occur, and if they were substantial, these were not documented. An obvious explanation for any lack of shortages is that the banned drugs continued to appear on pharmacy shelves—or under them. It was obvious that many patients would continue to demand their favorite gripe water, restorative, or other remedy, illegal or not, and that many physicians were either unaware of the new policy or not particularly impressed by it.

One British observer wrote: "Self-treatment is common. So the demand for banned drugs has taken time to decline. . . . The Ordinance has been resented by some doctors as curtailing what they see as their freedom to prescribe in the patient's best interest. . . . There has been some continued prescription of banned drugs."[35] Another wrote: "Within a few months of the implementation of the drug policy, drugs that had been banned became available in Dhaka, as well as in other parts of the country. The majority of these illegal imports are of Indian and Pakistani origin, but the origins of others are unknown. The banned drugs cost several times more than they did when their sales were not illegal in the country. Seizures have been few and far between. The demand for banned drugs continues."[36]

Though most of the banned products being smuggled over the borders were supposedly produced in adjacent India—or in Pakistan, where strong family business ties still existed—others carried labels presumably indicating manufacture in Hong Kong, Japan, Great Britain, Belgium, West Germany, Switzerland, Yugoslavia, or the United States. Many of them sold at a profit from 100 to 500 percent higher than when they were legal. The higher prices, it was suggested, were enough to cover "payments to government officials so they will ignore the smuggling operations."[37] One precaution was scrupulously observed: "No banned drug is to be sold to a foreigner or to anyone who speaks a language other than Bangladeshi."[38]

In most cases, it seemed that these smuggled products were at least correctly labeled. If the label stated that the container held X tablets of Y drug, each with Z milligrams of the active ingredient, the odds were good that this was the case. In contrast were the so-called fraudulent or spurious products, either made locally in Bangladesh or smuggled from abroad, with the pills colored, shaped, flavored, and marked to mimic the original product. Often, the fraudulent tablet contained but a portion—perhaps only a minute portion—of the active ingredient, and often it was not actually the ingredient listed on the label. Instead of being an antibiotic, as shown by the label, it might be merely colored flour. "Attempts to trace the manufacturers of spurious products have been unsuccessful because they do not have any permanent business address," it was stated. "Though the sale of spurious products is an offense, very few have been arrested."[39]

Another vexing problem concerned products that were not on the banned list but were simply of poor quality. In 1984 the report of a WHO-sponsored survey gave an evaluation of "good" to the 8 large multinational companies in Bangladesh. Of 25 medium-sized domestic firms, a few were said to maintain good quality-control systems, 15 had "fairly satisfactory" programs, while between 5 and 10 had "poor systems." Most distressing was the picture of 130 small-sized firms. "It has been estimated that some 20 percent of these companies have only poor quality-control laboratories, and the remaining 80 percent have nothing worth mentioning."[40] The best defense a Bangladesh official could produce was, "Perhaps our system is not good, but India's is worse."

One of the most significant aspects of the Bangladesh experiment was provided by Zafrullah Chowdhury, the member of the expert committee whose appointment had so infuriated *The Pulse* and the multinational pharmaceutical companies. The son of a policeman, Zafrullah was born in Chittagong, now Bangladesh's second city, studied at the Dhaka Medical School, and won his medical degree in 1964. He spent the next seven years in England, taking postgraduate training in Leeds, London, and Dedham, and specializing in vascular surgery. In 1971 he returned home to join the Freedom Fighters in their struggle to win independence for Bangladesh. When peace came, he found no suitable openings for a skilled, British-trained vascular surgeon. "If I wanted to survive," he said, "I discovered that I had to do bread-and-butter surgery for the next ten years."[41]

Zafrullah recognized that his country's awesome health problems could never be solved simply by curative medicine practiced by a few qualified physicians. "Prevention would be much more useful than curative medicine, and certainly less expensive. And, at least so far in the future as we could see, paramedics would probably be more important than physicians." In the villages there were few licensed doctors—perhaps 1 for each 30,000 of the population. There were plenty of villagers, but turning them into paramedics presented difficulties. "Less than 2 percent of the women and 8 percent of the men were literate," he says. Even with such a handicap, he commenced a training program. In a few years he was allowing some of his young paramedics to do minor surgery, setting broken bones and performing abortions. "This made the medical mafia very nervous," he recalls. "The minister of health—he knew me, he had been one of my teachers—told me, 'Stop this or we must send you to jail!' I said to him, 'I would very much love to see you try to do this.'" In 1976 he was actually taken to court and charged with allowing a woman to do surgery. "I will take the responsibility," he told the judge. "If anything goes wrong, you can put me in jail."

Nothing went wrong. In fact, Zafrullah was winning international recognition for his work. In 1976 he and his wife, Susanne, also a physician, reported on 600 women given a tubectomy—the tying off and removal of a small section of each Fallopian tube to prevent pregnancy. In developing countries, this had long been considered a highly desirable procedure, but its use had been limited by the lack of trained physicians. In the Bangladesh series, 234 of the operations had been performed by licensed physicians. The other 366 operations were performed in village health centers by young female paraprofessionals. (Each had undergone at least six months of basic in-service training and about two months of part-time training in tubectomy surgery. Each had been required to assist in several tubectomies before being allowed to work by herself. Thereafter, a qualified physician was always on call.)

In the tubectomies done by physicians, the infection rate was 6.4 percent. In those done by the paramedics, it was only 5.5 percent. There were a few complications, the Chowdhurys reported. "The uterus was perforated in 4 cases (3 times by a physician, once by a paramedic)." They sent a report on their study to one of Britain's top medical journals, *Lancet*. The editors of *Lancet* were so impressed that they not only accepted the manuscript but published it as their lead article.[42]

In the next few years, Zafrullah increasingly appreciated the need to provide the people of Bangladesh with the drugs they really required—not costly brand-name drugs of dubious quality, but low-cost, high-quality generic products. None of the existing pharmaceutical firms, multinational or domestic, displayed much interest in meeting that need. "They offered me a job to keep me quiet," he says. "I didn't want their job. I was ready to sue them. Instead, my friends and I decided to do something on our own."

With start-up funds provided from the United Kingdom and the Netherlands, they established a limited-profit trust and then acquired land at Savar, a small village about 25 miles from Dhaka—equivalent to a drive of one to three and a half hours or more, depending on whether the highway was under water or on how many bullocks, goats, camels, and other livestock were dozing on the road. There they built what is now the Gonoshasthaya Kendra (People's Health Center) and Gonoshasthaya Pharmaceuticals Ltd (GPL). In June 1981, the year before the Ershad coup, they were producing their first two drugs, the antibiotic ampicillin and paracetamol to control pain. By 1988 they were offering about 40 different products, all listed as essential by WHO, and at prices from 33 to 60 percent less than their competitors. A WHO investigation rated their quality-control operations as excellent. GPL probably ranked tenth among all drug companies in sales and sixth in volume of product.[43] Under the trust agreement, net profits were limited to 15 percent; of this, one-half went to plant expansion and improved living conditions for its workers, and one-half to other social development programs in Bangladesh.

Gonoshasthaya Kendra seemed to be a combination of health center, training school, integrated community, and factory. Inside its guarded walls were garden plots for fruits and vegetables, yards filled with flocks of chickens and ducks, and pools that were used as rice paddies in the dry seasons and as fish farms in the wet months.

The GPL plant now employs about 320 workers, including 20 pharmaceutical experts. A remarkable proportion—about 70 percent—are women. At first, this situation was disconcerting to some of Zafrullah's associates. In most Moslem villages, it was routinely accepted that women are not suitable for schooling. "When we decided to establish the factory," he said, "the next thing we decided was that we were going to help the poor people—and among the poor, the most deprived and the most oppressed are the poor women. If you want to have development, you have to involve them. Unfortunately, poor women don't have a skill that is marketable in an industry, so we started a special school for them."[44]

His managers complained. "Women? Women cannot do this. This is a sophisticated white-collar industry." Zafrullah insisted, "Then we will teach them." His colleagues were still not satisfied. "But women will get pregnant!" "Of course they will, but probably not all at the same time."

At GPL the women were taught not only the methods of drug manufacture but also how to grow the best food crops, cook nutritious meals, and take care of their children, and how not to become pregnant every year. They were even provided with showers—almost unheard of in a Bangladesh village—so they could bathe themselves when they came to work and after they finished. And GPL also arranged to train workers not only for itself but also for other drug companies.

To Zafrullah, the Bangladesh experiment has been of tremendous value to his country. "Certainly," he says, "it has not been an unqualified success. There is still much to be done—the quality of Bangladesh drugs is not yet what it should be. It has been an uphill struggle, but success is in sight."[45] Should the Bangladesh approach be tried elsewhere? Perhaps in other developing countries, he says, with modifications to meet their individual requirements. Should it be applied in industrialized countries like Britain or the United States? Not unless you intend to wipe out their research.

In 1985 and 1986 three different investigators presented their assessments of the project. First, in 1985, was Francis Rolt, whose account was published by War on Want under the title *Pills, Policies, and Profits*, a name somewhat reminiscent of our earlier *Pills, Profits, and Politics*.[46] A year later *The Public Health and Economic Dimensions of the New Drug Policy of Bangladesh*, by D. C. Jayasuriya, was produced by the U.S. Pharmaceutical Manufacturers Association and the International Federation of Pharmaceutical Manufacturers Associations. The author was a Sri Lankan attorney who had been involved in studies of family-planning programs and had served as a consultant to the WHO essential drugs program. Third was *The Bangladesh Example: Four Years On*, by D. J. Tiranti, published in 1986 by the International Organization of Consumers Unions in Penang, Malaysia. The author was described as a founder and coeditor of the *New Internationalist*. To hardly anyone's surprise, there was not total agreement among them. By and large, Rolt and Tiranti approved of the Bangladesh experiment; Jayasuriya did not.

In his report, Jayasuriya found that there had been no significant savings in drug prices. "The Bangladeshi government and others have reported that drug prices have fallen since the new policy was introduced," he said.[47] "Several comprehensive surveys indicate, however, that price reductions are rare and that most drugs have increased in price." For some banned drugs, he found, no substitutes were available. "Even if a substitute is available, the practitioners may not have confidence in it. . . . Some practitioners were frank enough to admit that they openly advocate the purchase of banned drugs, if available, at whatever cost. . . . Some doctors said that patients resist when substitutes are prescribed." A 1985 survey disclosed that more than 250 different banned products were still present in wholesalers' warehouses and retail shops.[48] Alarmingly, there had been a dramatic increase in the number of establishments manufacturing traditional ayurvedic and unani medications, which were essentially beyond the reach of the new program.[49]

The losses suffered by the eight multinational drug companies were put in the millions of dollars. "The effects on foreign drug companies . . . have left indelible scars on the country's image as the basis for an attractive, safe, and reliable business community."[50] The drug policy and the various measures taken since the establishment of the program, Jayasuriya claimed, had not made "even the slightest dent" in the problem of improving access to essential drugs. Further, he insisted, the Bangladesh program is not at all "a replica" of the WHO essential drugs policy.[51] "A conspicuous and disturbing feature of most of the publications dealing with the new drug policy," he said, "is the implication that the program has been an unqualified success. . . . It is not an unqualified success."[52]

Rolt and Tiranti each claimed that drug prices, both wholesale and retail, had fallen.[53] There had been fewer imports of dangerous drugs, and the black market in banned drugs seemed to have declined. There had been fewer imports of needless products.[54] Tiranti cited a statement by Nurul Islam, chairman of the expert committee, to show that physicians' prescribing habits had been improved, to the benefit of patients:

Now that luxury or harmful drugs are no longer available [Professor Islam was quoted as saying], prescriptions by doctors have greatly changed: before the Ordinance there would be six to eight items in a prescription and the recipe would include a "digestive enzyme," tonics and irrational combinations of vitamins and minerals. Now these products are banned, the number of items per prescription has fallen, and unqualified practitioners are changing their prescribing habits too.[55]

(Soon afterwards, Nurul Islam gave up his post on the expert drug committee. Honored as the first chairman of the group, he had afterward been attacked as dictatorial, unable to accept criticism, and despotic. He now has his own profitable drug company, Jana Sheba [Public Service Pharmaceuticals].) Tiranti added:

With dangerous drugs prohibited and with industry switching to producing more essential drugs, it is justifiable to talk of progress. . . . Most of the manufacturers, after initial opposition, have responded well to the challenge of the changed market. They have been adaptable, switching from the manufacture of prohibited drugs to those more relevant to the country's health needs. And, from the partial figures that are available, there is no evidence of any major slump in company sales.[56]

To Francis Rolt, with the program as brilliantly successful as it appeared to be, it seemed incredible that it had not been widely adopted elsewhere. "Given the very clear successes of the Bangladesh initiative," he said, "it is surprising that other countries haven't followed its lead."[57] An experienced American scientist working at Dhaka's International Centre for Diarrhoeal Disease Research may have offered at least a partial explanation: "Before, we had bad drugs, badly used. Now, it's somewhat better drugs, but still badly used. The next step is to insure that good drugs are used 'goodly.' "[58]

One reason for the glaring disagreements over the Bangladesh project was the unavailability of reliable statistics on Bangladesh, and especially statistics on drug sales. Few could be obtained from either government or industry sources, and those that could be found were usually suspect. Reliable figures on how well or how poorly the multinationals had been hit were similarly hard to come by. The information such companies were willing to release on their Bangladesh operations was neither complete nor widely believed.

Without doubt, the multinationals had been hurt. It is currently accepted that the share of sales held by the multinational drug firms in Bangladesh had been slashed from more than 75 percent in 1981 or 1982 to about 40 percent in 1988. "They're still making money," says a pharmaceutical expert in Dhaka, "but now they have to work for it. They have lost the easy life." An informal survey in mid-1988 of American drug companies showed that the firms with Bangladesh subsidiaries were far from happy. One revealed that it is "just hanging on" and "a candidate for close." Another said, "Under no circumstances would we consider an operation in that country if we were not already there." And yet, another firm, Ciba-Geigy of Switzerland, started substantial operations in its new Bangladesh plant late in 1989.

By 1991 the big multinationals in Bangladesh that had threatened to close down their operations and pull out of the country were still operating. Bangladesh physicians were still practicing medicine, and Bangladesh pharmacists had not been forced out of business. And by early 1991 the noble experiment in Bangladesh—so widely acclaimed, so applauded, so enthusiastically depicted as the forerunner of similar programs destined to sweep throughout the Third World—had not yet been picked up by another country. The end of the chapter is yet to be written.

Chapter 8

THE DRUG SWINDLERS

*T*he multinational drug industry has been roundly attacked in virtually every developing nation—sometimes with justification, sometimes without—for robbing the poor, exploiting the sick, charging exorbitant prices, using its patents and trademarks to make obscene profits, killing innocent victims with experimental drugs, and generally behaving in a most indecent manner. These and similar charges began in the early 1960s and grew in clamor during the 1970s and 1980s. The attacks have continued even though many of the multinationals have now obviously decided to mend their ways. (Some multinationals, it must be recognized, have yet to accept their social responsibilities and to improve their behavior.)

In one aspect, the problem has become more severe. This involves the manufacture and marketing of products that are spurious, fraudulent, or counterfeit:

- The capsules or tablets have been shaped, colored, flavored, marked, and packaged to mimic the real product.
- They may contain, for example, a life-saving antibiotic like penicillin or chloramphenicol, as indicated on the label, or they may consist only of worthless flour or starch.
- They may contain the actual ingredient as labeled, but it has

been so "cut" that the capsules or tablets hold perhaps only 80 percent, or 50 percent, or 10 percent, or none of the labeled quantity.
- They may be priced the same as the real product or possibly at an apparently bargain level.
- At best, they are worthless. At the worst, they can kill.

The multinationals have generally stayed out of such operations. Most of those who make and market the low-quality or worthless fraudulent products are robbing and endangering or killing their neighbors. In many if not most Third World countries, it has been found difficult or impossible to control the operators of the fraudulent drug business. In some countries, they are on the increase.

Deceit in Indonesia

Indonesia consists of a long arc of more than 13,000 islands—all of them tropical and green, some with volcanoes, several of breathtaking beauty, about half of them occupied—that loop gracefully along the equator roughly from Singapore to Australia. They extend for about 3,500 miles, somewhat equal to the distance from Los Angeles to Bermuda or from New York to London. With its population nearing 180 million, Indonesia is the second most populous nation in Southeast Asia, ranking second only to India, and the fifth most highly populated in the world. In the wealth of its natural resources—petroleum, natural gas, tin, bauxite, rice, tea, maize, tapioca, peanuts, sugar, spices, and valuable woods—it surpasses India, Japan, Korea, and Taiwan.

Under Dutch control since the early seventeenth century, Indonesia declared its independence in 1945 and achieved it in 1949 after years of fighting. An American correspondent describes its recent political history in these words: "Their country has had to absorb more jolts in fifty years than the United States has in two hundred: occupation by the Japanese during the Second World War; a revolution to throw off colonial rule; several secessionist efforts; and religious wars. . . . It has the largest population of Moslems of any country in the world, yet it fears Islamic fundamentalism. It fears communism. It is wary of Western liberal democracy."[1]

Since 1965, when its Moscow-leaning first president, Sukarno, was ousted by the new president, Suharto, Indonesia has operated under what is termed the New Order. It is, by definition, a democracy. Much of its technical modernization has been brought about by a group of young Indonesians, many of whom were educated under Ford Foundation scholarships at the University of California in Berkeley and hence are known as the Berkeley Mafia.

The Dutch during their three centuries of control had done practically nothing to train the Indonesians for self-government, but the people have advanced significantly under the New Order. Infant mortality dropped from more than 100 to about 80 per 1,000 live births. Life expectancy rose from 47 years in 1970 to 56 years by 1985. Literacy has risen above 70 percent. Poverty is still widespread, but Indonesia "does not have the absolute poverty of such South Asian countries as India, Bangladesh, and Pakistan."

Family Business. Much of the credit for Indonesia's progress has been attributed to President Suharto, who seems to be viewed as a benevolent father or a kindly uncle. This respect, however, has not carried over to his wife, his sons and daughters and in-laws, and his close business associates, who are all linked in a shadow operation referred to vaguely as the Family Business. By grabbing exclusive import licenses and trade monopolies, taking advantage of new protectionist laws and regulations, moving without invitation into profitable businesses, and similar ploys, key players of the Family Business have acquired major shares or total control of such industries as plastics, tinplate, timber, construction, telecommunications, cotton, sugar, cement, milk-powder manufacture, tea plantations, oil trading, machinery parts, cooking oils, insurance, baby food, airplane chartering, shipping, and the operation of sports and recreation facilities.

The voraciousness of the Family Business had long been suspected, but it was not until remarkably full documentation was published by the *Sydney Morning Herald* of Australia in April 1986, and in later accounts in the *Asian Wall Street Journal*,[2] that the extent was appreciated. The Indonesian government lashed out immediately by turning back approaching ships and planes loaded with Australian tourists and ordering Australian journalists to leave the country. President Suharto drew little censure after the disclosures, but his children, other relatives, and business associates were treated less kindly. "Rapacious seems to be the most common term applied to them," it was reported.

If the Family Business has moved to any significant degree into the drug industry, that has not yet been revealed. Regardless of who controls it, however, the Indonesian pharmaceutical business already has serious problems. The University of Indonesia's internationally recognized pharmacologist, Iwan Darmansjah, stated in 1988:

The situation has somewhat improved since 1983. We finally managed to get rid of all combination antibiotics. But more than half of all drugs on the market even today are combination products. Many if not most are marketed as sales gimmicks, without any scientific evidence of their advantages over single-ingredient products—and they're needlessly expensive. Most of the combinations that remain are irrational or harmful—combinations of steroids and antirheumatic agents, steroids plus antiasthmatics, combination antidiarrheals, and combination "anti-influenza" cures, most of which contain an analgesic, a sympathomimetic, a cough suppressant, an antihistamine, and a couple of vitamins. Any pharmacologist—any physician who knows his business—is fully aware that none of those ingredients alone or all of them together can cure influenza.[3]

Counterfeit drugs: the Tempo exposé. But even more alarming to many experts has been the rapidly expanding growth of counterfeit drugs. More and more, patients were receiving "painkillers" that did nothing for pain, "anesthetics" that did not produce anesthesia, "antibiotics" that did not control infections. "For perhaps three or four years," said Iwan Darmansjah, "everybody knew about it, but we were all afraid to talk. We knew it was becoming worse. Yet nobody dared to speak up. I kept my mouth shut. Then, in 1988, after a change in the president's cabinet, I thought the time was right." He agreed to meet with the editors of *Tempo*, Indonesia's most influential weekly news magazine. The editors might have paid no attention to a less eminent source, fearing to offend some member of the Family Business or some other politically powerful individual, but Professor Iwan could not be readily ignored. They assigned a top-notch team of investigators to the job. On May 21 they broke the story, naming names, dates, and places.[4]

Revealing that the output of fraudulent products may have risen to the point at which it involved 30 percent of all drugs in circulation, the magazine made these disclosures:

• In an army hospital in the capital city, Jakarta, investigators found boxes of what was supposedly Organon's Oradexon, a powerful and sometimes lifesaving steroid indicated for use in cerebral edema caused by a brain tumor or abscess, in septic or anaphylactic shock, or in severe asthmatic attacks. The counterfeit drug was inactive. The wholesaler who distributed the drug to the hospital denied any responsibility or any knowledge of its source. Later, a detective agency hired by Organon found similar false Oradexon in two local pharmacies, which had acquired the product from an unlicensed wholesaler who simply could not recall where he had purchased it.

- In North Jakarta, national police raided the home of an enterprising man who was manufacturing an "antiarthritis" drug out of flour. He was caught red-handed, taken to court, and received a jail sentence of four months.
- In Semarang, another counterfeiter was caught with an enormous stock of fraudulent drugs held in an underground cache. He drew a jail sentence of six months.
- In Purwakarta, police seized approximately one ton of fraudulent drugs in a single pharmacy.
- One man, long suspected to be a "brain of the drug counterfeiters," was arrested and charged with both manufacturing and distributing fraudulent drugs. His lawyer insisted that his client was an innocent merchant who never would make counterfeit drugs and was only holding the supply for a friend.
- Another Jakarta pill-maker, also reputed to be a master counterfeiter, was defended by his attorney, who declared that his client was innocent for three reasons: "He has been inactive for five years," "He has gone bankrupt," and "He has disappeared and I don't know where he is."

More than 30 different drugs, some over-the-counter products and some requiring a prescription, were involved in the massive counterfeiting. Among them were a number of minor cough-and-cold remedies; analgesics and antipyretics for the relief of headache, menstrual pain, and fever; and medications for rheumatism, which were designed to mimic products made by local Indonesian firms. Also included were copies of such drugs as Parke-Davis's anesthetic Ketalar and its analgesic Ponstan, Hoffmann–La Roche's tranquilizer Lexotan and its sedative Mogadon, Sandoz's analgesic Optalidon, and Ciba-Geigy's antidiarrheal Enterovioform. (In previous years, Enterovioform had won such popularity that it was known simply as Pil Ciba—the "Ciba pill." In the early 1980s Ciba officials were already complaining that a bogus product was being marketed in Indonesia and cutting into their sales.

Then, in 1985 Ciba responded to a powerful drive by consumerists and withdrew its Enterovioform from the market worldwide. [See Chapter 11.] This did not bother the makers of the fraudulent drug—which has no activity at all—and they were still selling Pil Ciba throughout Indonesia in mid-1988.)

In Jakarta, *Tempo* reporters located three centers that police admitted were "unofficial wholesalers" or "the illegal drug market," but that seemed to be violating no laws. Prices there were often astonishingly low. "A pharmacy that does not take advantage of this channel and buy at these bargain prices," a reporter was told, "practically cannot survive." Among the products offered at such attractive prices was one labeled Penbritin 250, Beecham's ampicillin, produced in capsules each containing 250 milligrams of the active antibiotic. The real drug was recommended to Indonesian physicians for use (usually 8 to 16 capsules per day) in infections of the respiratory, genitourinary, and gastrointestinal tracts, septicemia, and peritonitis. On the black market in Jakarta, it was being labeled and promoted in the same way, but it was marketed in capsules each actually holding only about 80 milligrams of ampicillin. To get its possibly lifesaving effect, the patient would need to take from 25 to 50 capsules each day—but neither the physician nor the patient, by merely reading the label, could know that.

But how to punish? Finding the counterfeiters seemed to pose no great problem for the authorities. Imposing more than a minimal penalty or closing them down was another matter. Brig. Gen. Koesparmono Irsan, head of the national detective police force, told *Tempo*, "In the end, it gives you a headache because the results are never adequate. The punishment handed out to drug counterfeiters is generally only three to four months."

It is not clear whether the authorities did not have the appropriate laws on the books or whether they had not yet learned how to apply such laws. According to Kartono Mohamad, then president of the Indonesian Medical Association, "These fraudulent drugs are mostly manufactured by local firms. Some may be produced by presumably reputable, registered drug houses. Some undoubtedly come from unregistered, illegal, fly-by-night companies. Others seem to be turned out on a part-time basis by a used-car dealer, an architect, a real estate dealer. They are very elusive. The punishment they receive is not very severe—not enough to keep them from going back into the same business. It could be that they have political friends."[5]

An official of a European drug company commented, "Of course they have excellent political connections. Even if they are arrested, they serve only for a month or two, then get out and go back to their old operation or start a new one. One of those fellows has been caught and sentenced to prison seven times, but he's out now and still in business." The rewards apparently justify the risk. A successful venture with only one bogus drug can earn the swindler a hundred thousand dollars or more. To some professional drug-industry castigators, it has been disconcerting to find that the guilty party in this kind of drug swindle is not some money-hungry corporation in Europe or the United States. In most of these cases the villain is the fellow who lives next door.

Incident in India

The government-run Sir Jamsetjee Jejeebhoy Hospital—popularly known as the J.J.—is one of the oldest and most revered hospitals in Bombay. Early in 1986 it experienced a rash of tragedies. On January 15 a patient named Bapu Thombre was admitted after suffering a head injury and was sent to the neurosurgery ward. Five days later his kidneys suddenly stopped working. On January 23 he was dead. From then until February 7 thirteen others died with the same kind of kidney failure. They ranged in age from 10 to 76. Four of the total of fourteen had brain tumors, three were being treated for head injury, one had suffered a stroke, three had glaucoma, two had cataracts, and one had a corneal graft. Two of them seemed well on the road to recovery. At autopsy, all showed vast, irreversible kidney destruction.

All fourteen victims had been given the same four drugs during their hospitalization: acetazolamide, mannitol, gentamicin, and glycerine. The use of all four was eventually halted. To R. D. Kulkarni, the professor of pharmacology, glycerine was the most likely suspect; glycerine, he knew, may sometimes be contaminated with glycols, and glycols can cause fatal kidney damage.

The glycerine swindle. Laboratory analysis of the hospital's most recent supply of glycerine showed that it was not hospital grade but "industrial grade" and consisted of 9 percent glycerine, 21 percent water, and about 70 percent glycols. "To call such a concoction glycerine is a mistake," an investigator commented afterwards. "It can more correctly be described as diethylene glycol with a dash of glycerine." Hospital glycerine then cost about 54 rupees (about $4.15) per kilogram; the industrial grade could be bought for 30 rupees (about $2.30).

Questions arose quickly: How did the dangerous fluid get purchased by the hospital? Why was it accepted? Why was its use not stopped more promptly? Where had everybody been? Apparently neither the dean, R. S. Chandrikapure, nor the hospital superintendent, V. G. Deshmukh, took steps to withdraw the suspected drugs. "For two vital days," it was noted, "the dean enjoyed his holidays and did nothing." The superintendent argued that "every death that takes place is no signal for him to rush to the hospital, and that there was nothing he could do about the deaths which had already taken place."[6]

The Lentin hearings. Efforts were made, especially by the medical community, to hush up the matter, but newspaper pressure eventually brought an official inquiry. A retired judge of the Bombay high court, the Honorable Mr. Justice B. Lentin, was asked to serve as a one-man investigative commission. The hearings, which Justice Lentin insisted be open to the public and the press, were no whitewashing procedure. They lasted 301 days. The report, submitted on November 30, 1987, demonstrated that Justice Lentin was one exceedingly tough jurist. At the end, he said of the victims:

They did not ask to be born; they did not choose to die. They died. They died as they had lived, quietly, and in poverty.
Little could they know that by their deaths they would arouse an outcry of public indignation which would lay bare lack of probity in public life, malaise and corruption in places high and low indulged in contempt of the laws of God and man. . . . It is time to pause and forage into the murky water of lies, deceit, intrigue, ineptitude and corruption to salvage the truth about what led to this ghastly and tragical episode.[7]

No blame could be placed on the doctors, the nurses, the paramedics, and the rest of the personnel on the ward, Justice Lentin said. "But . . . the Dean, Dr. Chandrikapure, and the Superintendent, Dr. Deshmukh, are guilty of negligence and dereliction of duty." Both the dean and the superintendent, Justice Lentin concluded, were unfit to hold any post with responsibility.

Justice Lentin could find no evidence that any of the wholesalers or distributors involved in the deal had warned the hospital that the glycerine was industrial grade. Pharmacology professor Kulkarni was identified as the person who had actively intervened to have the glycerine supply contract awarded to a particular firm. Analytical laboratory reports had proved to be "false and misleading," and had provided "imaginary and incomplete reports." Justice Lentin came down heavily on the hospital purchase committee, which "functioned in a slaphappy manner, followed totally unsatisfactory procedures, and purchased medicines, including life-saving drugs, indifferently or as guided by corrupt members or interfering ministers." He found few kind words for the regional Food and Drug Administration, which supposedly had investigated the tragedy. "The entire structure of FDA has been corroded by rampant and unabashed corruption, deleterious indiscipline, naked favouritism, crude nepotism, and gross ministerial interference at every stage and a sense of non-accountability all round."

"Unfit to hold ministerial post." Justice Lentin did not overlook the Ministry of Health. "Bhai Sawant as Health Minister was, for the FDA and the general public, a disaster of the first magnitude. He has not set an example either of efficiency or rectitude. . . . He is guilty of gross ministerial interference and favouritism for extraneous consideration and misuse of power and authority . . . coupled with dereliction of statutory duties. . . . He is unfit to hold a ministerial post."

After it appeared that the report might be kept from the public, newspaper pressure was exerted again, and the government promised to release the document on March 30, 1988. On March 10 the health minister, Bhai Sawant, resigned. The government endorsed practically all the points made by the justice. It suspended the dean, the superintendent, and two others from the J. J. Hospital, and three FDA officials, including one of the commissioners. Some members of the Maharashtra state legislature tried to defend the indicted health minister and proposed action against Justice Lentin. Both national and state medical associations elected to maintain a discreet but embarrassed silence. A governmental housecleaning came only after eight former J. J. Hospital physicians spoke out publicly to confirm "the rot in the institution" and pleaded for the appointment of competent and responsible senior staff with the power to run the institution without the need to bow before bureaucrats and ministers.

Drug Fraud Brasileiro Style

Perhaps more than the people of any other nation in Latin America, the population of Brazil has been particularly plagued by counterfeit or fraudulent drugs. The explanation, says a Brazilian drug expert who serves as professor of pharmacology in the University of São Paulo Medical School and a consultant to the World Health Organization, is "a combination of ingenuity, incompetence, corruption, stupidity, and possibly the world's most ridiculous drug inspection system."[8] Estimates generally agree that the fraudulent products represent at least 20 percent of the products sold in Brazil's nonhospital pharmacies. (Pharmacies in hospitals apparently maintain a tighter control, buy only from reputable wholesalers, and check on the quality of the products they accept.) During the past few years, such products as these have shown up:

- A drug labeled as Lilly's anticancer vincristine intended for intravenous administration was found to contain less than 30 percent of the amount stated on the label.
- Capsules of the antiepileptic phenytoin contained barely 25 percent of the labeled amount, far too little to control convulsions.
- Fake penicillin and tetracycline products contained only a small portion of the labeled amount of the antibiotic, or none at all.
- Psychoactive drugs such as Valium and Librium were deliberately spiked, not by the manufacturer but by enterprising pharmacists, with a substance such as atropine in the mistaken belief that this, by causing dry mouth, would prevent drug abuse—and possibly help evade the laws covering treatment of drug addicts. "Unfortunately," says Luiz Gonçalves Paulo of the Federal University of Rio de Janeiro, "too many of the patients came too close to dying from atropine poisoning."[9]
- A supposedly remarkable new antibiotic was so highly praised that it was purchased by the welfare system. It was found to contain only an inert substance, fubá flour. It was promptly renamed Fubacicline and then thrown out.

Nelson Proença, a distinguished São Paulo dermatologist and president of the Brazilian Medical Association, agrees with his colleagues that the problem of counterfeit drugs is already bad, is becoming worse, and represents a serious threat to Brazil. "If they buy a worthless drug to help something trivial—perhaps the common cold, which will go away anyhow—they only waste a little of their money. But if they use a worthless antibiotic on a very sick child with a serious infection, and the child dies, that is unforgivable."[10] The foreign, multinational drug companies operating in Brazil do not appear to be implicated in the counterfeit drug business. According to Proença, "It is the small, domestic operations which are doing all this damage."

Marcio Falci, an official of the German firm Boehringer-Ingelheim in São Paulo, described the operators as "mostly small, clandestine laboratories, selling directly to second- or third-rate pharmacies. Their products may be terrible, but their fraudulent labels are beautifully printed. Their so-called scientific data is nonsense. They're not registered. They can't get government contracts. They avoid price controls. They carefully avoid government inspection. They simply pollute the pharmaceutical industry."[11] Another expert, Leonardo Peach, professor of pharmacy at the University of São Paulo, suggests, "It is very hard to understand these people. I don't think they're dishonest. They're simply stupid."[12]

How in the world could a country as sophisticated and civilized as Brazil allow such wasteful, useless, or deadly fraudulent drugs to remain on the market? "This is a matter," Antonio Zanini told us, "which I think I am in a position to explain to you. At the outset, you must realize that, under Brazilian law, a pharmacy inspector is paid about $115 each month. Yet, on this insignificant stipend, he manages to live very well indeed. Once you comprehend this, everything else falls into place."[13]

Antonio Carlos Zanini is in an excellent position to know the ins and outs of drug fraud. Born in 1938 to a well-to-do São Paulo family, he obtained his medical degree from the University of São Paolo, specialized in clinical pharmacology and neurology, took postgraduate training in the United States, worked briefly as a medical specialist for Pfizer and Ciba-Geigy, and then planned to settle down and practice medicine. He achieved a good deal of attention, however, as the author of one of the most widely known pharmacology textbooks in Brazil and as a drug consultant to the World Health Organization. In 1980 his friend the minister of health urged him to join the ministry as director of health surveillance. Said Zanini: "This was one very big responsibility. I was in charge of all foods, drugs, cosmetics, and hygienic supplies, and of health inspections at all of Brazil's ports, airports, and borders."

The inspectors. When he looked at the system for inspecting drugs Zanini realized he might have some troubles.

There were only a couple of federal drug inspectors. They were not authorized to inspect pharmacies. They could inspect only drug factories, and nobody had taught them exactly how to inspect a factory. In addition, they could go in and inspect any factory they wanted at any time—providing that they could first arrange a formal invitation from the company.

In contrast, the job of inspecting pharmacies was entrusted to a small army of state inspectors—the people who were, on the average, paid about $115 a month.

What does the state inspector inspect? Well, he is supposed to see that there is actually a licensed pharmacist there, at all times, as the law requires. Now, many a pharmacist is willing—for a modest payment—to lend his name to the pharmacy owner, and then come around perhaps once a month to collect his salary. If it's inconvenient to come in person, they can probably mail a check to him. Meanwhile, the pharmacy owner hires some young, untrained person at a minimum wage to advise customers and dispense the drugs.

If the pharmacist is ambitious, he may lend his name to many pharmacies and collect many fees. Of course, this is also against the law, but if the state pharmacy inspector collects a small bribe, who will tell the authorities?

But there is more. Many of these state inspectors are married. They have children. They have a nice house, and a car, and other necessities. They are not satisfied with their state salary and their bribe from each of the pharmacy owners in their assigned territories. They moonlight—they serve as unofficial salesmen for the illegal factories that manufacture counterfeit drugs. It is very easy for them. If the pharmacy owner does not want to buy the fraudulent product, the inspector will suddenly realize that the owner has no licensed pharmacist on the premises, or some of his drugs are mislabeled, or the labels have become loose and fallen off, or the floors are dirty, and he will hit the owner with a big fine or put him out of business.

The drug inspectors may also participate in tax evasion, allowing the pharmacy owner to report and pay the tax on only a small order of drugs, and to neglect to report and pay tax on the large quantity he actually bought. For overlooking this variety of larceny, the inspectors again believe they are entitled to further compensation.

Who inspects the inspectors? Appropriately bribed, the inspectors can look the other way when a pharmacist gives illegal injections to a patient or slips an illegal kickback to a prescribing physician. Zanini claims:

It is a dirty system. The inspectors who know they are peddling fraudulent drugs certainly know also they are bad products. The pharmacists who are forced to buy them also know it. These inspectors—they investigate drug dispensing, make their decisions, apply the penalty, and make no reports. There is no way to audit them. If there is bribery, dispensing bad products, tax evasion, kickbacks to physicians, there is no way to detect it. The problem is right in front of you: Nobody inspects the inspectors.

Ironically, some ethical pharmacists have refused to go along with this kind of corruption; most of them have been forced out of business.

Zanini repeatedly urged the government to set up a control system that would stop at least some of the fraud, save government money, and almost certainly save lives. High officials blocked the idea. "What is so shocking to a lot of us is that many of the professors in the pharmacy school know about this, but they just keep quiet. The pharmacy association knows this. The consumers association knows this. But they do nothing. Why? Because there's so much politics at stake." The drug industry, he emphasized, cannot be blamed for this kind of inspection corruption. "It is the pharmacy owner who bribes the inspectors," he says. "But the industry, by keeping its political friends in power in the legislature, has prevented anybody from cleaning up the inspection mess."

To Elizaldo Luiz Carlini, professor of psychobiology at the Paulista School of Medicine in São Paulo, this is precisely the kind of situation that should be expected in Brazil. "Unfortunately, corruption is among our oldest traditions. You must remember that the very first letter sent from Brazil almost five centuries ago by the great explorer, Admiral Cabral, to the Emperor of Portugal, contained a request for a bribe— an appointment for Cabral's nephew."[14]

Governmental changes. In 1985, as part of a governmental shake-up, the conservative minister of health was ousted, along with Antonio Zanini and his deputy, Luiz Gonçalves Paulo. "They had to let me go," Zanini said. "I owned a farm. I was a capitalist." All three were replaced by leftists. Carlos Sant'Ana became minister of health, Moreira Lima took Zanini's place, and Paulo was replaced by Suely Rozenfeld. For the next two years the management of drugs in Brazil became an area of total catastrophe.

The first national formulary of all Brazilian drugs, giving the active ingredient, all other ingredients, therapeutic classification, generic and brand names, dosage form, registration number, and names of all manufacturers—an invaluable mine of information that Zanini and his colleagues had put together in four years of work—was essentially sabotaged. Moreira Lima and Rozenfeld, deciding that Brazil already had enough drugs, blocked approval of some 2,000 new drug applications or the updating of indications, contraindications, and warnings.

The Interferon affair. One of the more memorable incidents in the history of Brazilian drug control occurred during this period.[15] Earlier, in 1981, Paulo had said to Zanini, "We have a peculiar situation here. A small Brazilian company has somehow got a license for an ointment, Inter-IF, for use in virus infections of the eye. It's supposed to contain interferon—the compound that may be so important for cancer treatment, and that's so rare that it costs a fortune for each milligram. No other country has a product like that. What do you think?" Zanini told him, "Let's ask our laboratory people to see how much interferon this stuff really contains."

The Brazilian analytical laboratories said they did not have the technical facilities to measure interferon content. A request was then forwarded to the Pan American Health Organization, the American arm of the World Health Organization, whose officials said regretfully that they, too, had no facilities to test for interferon and suggested sending the material to the National Institutes of Health in Bethesda, Maryland, probably the greatest medical research institution in the world. The NIH agreed to undertake the analysis, and in due time NIH scientists reported that they could detect absolutely no interferon in the Brazilian ointment.

The Brazilian license to market Inter-IF was promptly canceled, but the company went to court and claimed that the NIH test had not been performed in Brazil and therefore had no validity. The judges ruled for the company. Paulo then sent inspectors to the plant, found it was not fit to manufacture any drug, and ordered it closed. The company went into bankruptcy, but it sold its brand name and license for the so-called interferon ointment to another company. Thereafter, *that* license expired, but Rozenfeld—for reasons she did not disclose—ordered it renewed. Since 1988 there have been other governmental shuffles, with leftists replacing conservatives and conservatives replacing leftists. Meanwhile Brazil's problems with drug regulation, and especially with drug swindlers, continue to plague the country.

Of course, Indonesia, India, and Brazil are not the only nations that are threatened by fraudulent drugs; problems have occurred in such countries as Nigeria, Colombia, Pakistan, Bangladesh—and the United States. These products have appeared before in practically every country, industrialized or not, but this has not been widely publicized. "It was feared," a drug official in one developing country explained, "that patients would be needlessly alarmed."

Our first printed account of the drug swindlers appeared in the *International Journal of Health Services* in October 1990.[16] In November, the story was reported in the *Newsletter* of the Pharmaceutical Manufacturers Association,[17] and received international coverage in the news magazine *Newsweek*.[18] The bogus products, the magazine disclosed, are threatening Third World countries and industrialized nations alike.

The drug swindlers have not been abolished forever. They can appear again, at any time. All that is needed is a person with a small laboratory at his disposal, a total disregard for human beings, and a touch of larceny in his heart. The only safeguard is eternal vigilance—and a national distaste for corruption.

Chapter 9

SO SHINES A GOOD DEED . . .

*I*n the wealthier, industrialized countries of the world, there are periodic efforts by one or more of the nations themselves, or by charitable organizations, or by one or more industries, to provide aid and assistance to the poor, sick, and hungry peoples of the Third World. All of these efforts have undoubtedly been well intended. For one reason or another, many of them have been failures. Some have been disastrous.

In his thoughtful consideration of this situation, Klaus Leisinger of Ciba-Geigy has noted the often heartrending difficulties involved in deciding whether international aid should go to a project that will give the best long-term results or to one that will help victims who are suffering *now*. High economic growth is often considered a primary goal, he said, but such growth must bring material advantages to the broad masses of the population within a "reasonable" period of time.[1]

In the planning of international development projects, Leisinger emphasized, the donor alone cannot make all the decisions. Neither can the recipient country make all the rules. He said, "To achieve a real dialogue, all the parties involved must abandon all claims to a monopoly on the 'truth,' and must try to avoid adopting a superior attitude in which their own 'truth' is unquestioningly held to be better than any other."

The role of multinational drug companies deserves special examination. Certainly in the past, at least until the early 1970s, most major firms received only harsh criticism for their failure to respond to the problems of the Third World and their unwillingness to make any significant investments in research on tropical diseases—those of particular concern to developing countries. If they did create and market a successful drug for use in a developing nation—and this did happen once in a while—they were accused of profiting off the poor and the sick. In turn, the drug companies responded by claiming that, in consideration of their stockholders, they could not afford to squander money in developing new drugs for people too poor to pay for them. Unless people had been willing to invest their money and become stockholders in a corporation, the company could never have done any research in the first place.[2]

By the mid-1980s the situation had undergone some changes. A Swiss report indicated that international research investment in drugs for tropical diseases had tripled from about $30 million a year in 1975 to between $90 and $100 million by 1984. Of that latter amount, roughly $25 million came from the United States and private American foundations, $25 million from European countries, $25 million from research-based multinational drug companies, and between $15 and $25 million from socialist countries and the developing nations themselves.[3] These research investments and other contributions to appropriate drug use included the following:

- In the United States, Sterling had developed an important new drug for the treatment of malaria.
- SmithKline was working on an oral vaccine to protect children against a killing form of diarrhea, and also on an antimalaria drug and an antimalaria vaccine.
- Pfizer was helping Brazil develop a campaign against the widely prevalent parasitic infection, schistosomiasis.
- In Switzerland, Hoffmann–La Roche was developing yet another antimalaria drug.
- Johnson & Johnson of the United States, Organon of the Netherlands, Hoechst of West Germany, and Ciba-Geigy and Hoffmann–La Roche of Switzerland had each set up research institutes to concentrate on tropical diseases.
- In France, the Syndicat National de l'Industrie Pharmaceutique (SNIP) had organized training courses to help establish quality-control laboratories in a number of West African nations.[4]

Several other projects seem to deserve special attention. Nearly all of them are focused on Third World countries in Africa, for good reason. Leisinger has pointed out:

Whichever indicator is used for measurement, Africa south of the Sahara is the least developed area of the world. Between 1960 and 1982, while the per capita incomes of even the poorest countries of Asia and Latin America were rising, they fell in the lowest-income countries of Africa by 0.1% per year. . . . Other important indicators confirm the plight of black Africa. Nowhere is infant mortality higher (104 per 1,000 live births), life expectancy shorter (50 years), or the literacy rate lower (on average, 27%). . . . While food production per head has risen significantly everywhere else in the Third World, in Africa south of the Sahara, it has steadily fallen (by about 20%) since the middle of the 1960s.

As many observers have recognized, however, there is another facet to this problem in Africa:

The squandering of money on all manner of prestige projects, while serving to enrich a few individuals, has sometimes resulted in public funds that are needed for essential and more urgent projects becoming even more meagre. . . . With these problems in mind, it is also worth pointing out that in 1981, Africa south of the Sahara spent twice as much on military equipment as on "health."[5]

A Better Drug Chain

Early in 1981 a few American drug company leaders agreed that they were not doing enough—or enough of the right things—to assist the sick, impoverished people in the Third World. Donating funds or free drugs—"throwing money at the problem"—did not seem to be the answer. It was all too well known that the drugs that actually reached a Third World nation were too often administered to the wrong patients for the wrong diagnosis, in the wrong quantities, and often for too few or too many days. They were allowed to spoil in unrefrigerated storage facilities. Most peculiarly, they seemed to vanish mysteriously from warehouses and pharmacy and hospital stockrooms and appear in the hands of street sellers.

The drug company leaders met first with a number of private charitable organizations, each of which would be delighted to get donations of free pharmaceuticals from the industry, but none of which could guarantee that the medicines would reach their proper destination in the proper condition. At length, the company officials called on C. Payne Lucas, a pioneer in U.S. Peace Corps activities, one-time director of the Africa region for the corps, and then executive director of Africare. Founded in 1971, Washington-based Africare was a private, nonprofit group developed to improve the quality of life in rural Africa. It was primarily an organization of blacks in the United States, devoted to helping blacks in Africa. Lucas told them: "I don't think we should consider shipping free drug products. Let's get together with a government and health ministry in Africa committed to tackling the problem and see if we can set up an efficient drug delivery system."

In a remarkably few months, a joint project was arranged to include the Pharmaceutical Manufacturers Association (PMA), Africare, and the government of the Gambia, the smallest of all the African nations.[6] Wedged like a narrow splinter of land into the much larger country of Senegal in West Africa, the Gambia has an area of approximately 4,000 square miles—twice the size of the state of Delaware, four times that of Luxembourg—and a population of about 700,000. The Gambia was in sore need of help. Life expectancy was then about 32 years for men and 34 for women. Infant mortality was estimated to be about 215 per 1,000 live births. The mortality rate for children under five years was put at 45 to 50 percent, the highest in Africa. Health conditions in the cities were bad; those in the rural areas were worse.

Thirteen member firms of PMA agreed to participate in the demonstration project: Abbott, Bristol-Myers, Eli Lilly, Johnson & Johnson, Merck Sharp & Dohme, Pfizer, Schering-Plough, Searle, SmithKline, Sterling, Syntex, Upjohn, and Wyeth. Some contributed cash, some gave supplies of free drugs, and some gave both. Their contributions totaled more than $260,000. "But it quickly became apparent," said Alan Alemian, who headed the program for Africare, "that the drug industry—on such short notice—could not provide us with the essential personnel having the needed skills. We therefore explored the possibility of working out some kind of collaboration and support from the U.S. Public Health Service's Indian Health Service."[7] The Indian Health Service provided three pharmacy experts, to be paid by the project, from reservations in New Mexico, Oklahoma, and Arizona. They agreed to work in the Gambia for three months apiece. In addition, the Canadian government supplied a university expert to serve for two years as chief pharmacist while Gambians were trained to replace him.

In Banjul, the capital city, the Gambia's medical director committed his staff, with the support of the Africare team, to a systematic analysis of the pharmaceutical delivery system. What they found was distressing. No one seemed to have any real knowledge of how much of each drug was needed in each health center, how much of which drugs had been ordered, and from whom, which had been delivered, how much and where the supply for each product was actually stored, which were still fit for use, and why they had been ordered in the first place. Often, they found, regardless of what information was or was not available, rural health centers simply ran out of drugs.

Several months of determined efforts by the Gambians and the visiting experts were required to design, install, test, and demonstrate the new system and train the people to run it. The Africare team left on July 7, 1982. By August 1983 the system had been in place for a full year, and year-end evaluations were held at Central Medical Stores and the Royal Victoria Hospital in Banjul, at the Regional Medical Stores in Mansakonko, and a dozen up-country health centers and dispensaries. An effective inventory system had been installed, tested, and verified. A simple but adequate filing system was working. Necessary office equipment had been installed, warehousing had been improved, and cold storage facilities were in operation. A rational system for drug ordering had been developed. Key personnel—Gambian nationals— had been trained to take over the program eventually. "The system," Alemian reported, "was viewed as getting more drugs out to the patient-care level in a more equitable fashion, and generally preventing clinics from completely running out of stocks. In addition, at least some of the health ministry people were convinced that lives had been saved."

The project assisted by Africare/PMA in the Gambia had hardly been completed when a second and more extensive program was undertaken 400 miles to the southeast, in Sierra Leone. For this country, with its population of about three million, PMA companies—this time also including American Cyanamid and Norwich Eaton—agreed to supply substantial support representing about $333,000. Help was also provided by the World Bank, the World Health Organization, UNICEF, the U.S. Peace Corps, the U.S. Agency for International Development, the German Technical Aid Agency, and other groups. As in the Gambia, Africare furnished some technical and material assistance, but the Sierra Leone Ministry of Health directed, administered, and staffed the project from the outset.[8]

Since then, Africare has provided similar technical assistance to a project in Nigeria and is planning to support the national program in Ghana. There could be little doubt that the improved drug distribution system could succeed in Africa and probably elsewhere, operated by Third World people themselves, if only two nonpharmaceutical problems could be overcome—inadequate transportation (which usually meant not enough fuel or truck parts) and the lack of foreign exchange.

The Essential Generics War

After months of deliberations, a panel of highly competent drug experts working as a special World Health Organization committee published in 1977 its first version of what has become known as the WHO essential drugs list.[9] It consisted originally of 214 products, of which 182 were classified as "essential" and 32 as "complementary." These would be of the greatest use in treating the most serious illnesses afflicting the most people in developing countries. The majority were no longer under patent and could be bought on the world market as generics and at relatively low cost. The list was proposed as suggested guidelines, which could and probably should be modified by each nation to fit its own medical and economic situation.

The essential drugs list was variously interpreted. Some saw it as the list of the *only* pharmaceutical products that could be allowed in any Third World country. Some considered it to be mainly a guideline, indicating those products that should be given top priorities while permitting the use of other products. Others viewed it as applicable only to developing countries, while still others were convinced that it was equally applicable in the United States, the United Kingdom, and all of western Europe. It was declared to be a victory for generic-name drugs, a defeat for brand-name products, or neither of these.

The response of most multinational drug companies was clear and almost instantaneous. The International Federation of Pharmaceutical Manufacturers Associations (IFPMA) warned: "An essential drugs list is, we believe, faulty in both its medical and economic reasoning. Adoption of the WHO report's recommendations . . . might well reduce health standards already attained."[10] The Association of the British Pharmaceutical Industry said such a restricted prescribing list would "disastrously inhibit the development of future pharmaceutical innovation."

Another IFPMA statement declared, "It must be emphasized that any limited list will leave a certain part of the population's needs without adequate treatment and can thus by no means satisfy medical requirements." But, as we noted earlier,[11] that argument neatly skirted the unpleasant fact that an enormous part of the population in the Third World was *already* without adequate treatment. The list had been developed as an attempt to fill the gap, by earmarking most of whatever funds were available for the most critically needed products. In yet another denunciation, the then president of the IFPMA claimed that the concept was being strongly advocated by left-wing radicals in the industrialized nations.[12] That much was undoubtedly true. But the concept was also being advocated by right-wingers and those in the middle of the road.

Even while most major multinational drug companies were noisily opposing the concept of the WHO list, one Swiss firm determined that it could live with the idea. Without specifically giving its corporate blessing to the essential drugs list, Ciba-Geigy announced it was already setting up a special division to market many of the listed essential drugs. In 1977 it created its Servipharm subsidiary to market the first thirty products at bargain prices, but only to Third World countries, and primarily through sales to governmental health agencies. Of most importance, the company assured, these would not only be low-priced drugs, they would also carry Ciba-Geigy's world-recognized guarantee of high quality.[13] Just as most multinational drug firms had attacked the basic idea of the essential drugs list, they now directed their denunciations against Ciba-Geigy for treachery and for providing what they saw as aid and comfort to the enemy.

Like other Swiss firms, to whom international trade is as mother's milk, Ciba-Geigy has claimed a century-long interest in the welfare of what are now termed the Third World countries.[14] It—or its predecessor companies—had long been marketing useful drugs for the treatment of leprosy, amebiasis, malaria, cholera, and other tropical infections. In 1963 it became the first private organization to set up a medical research center in southern Asia when it established its own research laboratory at Goregaon in India. In 1974 it was one of the first companies to formulate a corporate policy specifically acknowledging its responsibility to meet the special needs of developing countries. Of particularly strategic importance, it had already in place a distributing network that covered practically every important Third World country and that had remarkably close ties, professional and personal, to health ministry officials, medical educators, leading physicians, and professional health societies.

The announcement of the WHO essential drugs list could not have come at a more appropriate time for the Swiss company. For at least three years it had been using special committees to study the drug supply problems of the Third World. A year after the WHO list appeared, Ciba-Geigy's new Servipharm division was in business. The Servipharm products were technically generics on which the patents had expired. But they were what have become known as "branded generics"—behind them was the reputation of Ciba-Geigy for producing high-quality drugs. Furthermore, it was emphasized, the bargain prices did not represent products that had stayed too long in storage and whose shelf life was about to expire. While the company's competitors assailed the new venture or attempted to ignore it, some outside observers hailed it. In 1982 the conservative *Business International* had this to say:

Ciba is the first known major drug company to establish a specific corporate policy acknowledging an ethical responsibility to meet the "special needs" of developing countries. The commitment is more than a matter of words. Ciba has established a subsidiary, Servipharm Limited, that concentrates exclusively on the needs of institutional customers—who may choose from a broad range of 60 essential and nonessential drugs and receive in return a guarantee of Ciba-Geigy quality at cheaper generic prices. The subsidiary also employs Ciba-Geigy's packaging and distributional savvy for the benefit of isolated rural customers who are often overlooked by conventional suppliers. Servipharm now operates in 45 developing countries and represents the largest single effort by private industry to date to square the profit motive with development objectives.[15]

Other observers took a more critical view. A briefing paper for a 1982 Health Action International meeting in Penang decried any attempt by multinationals to offer low-cost, high-quality products to the Third World. Such an offer, it was said, "will inhibit the development of local pharmaceutical industry. This risks lasting dependence for the countries concerned. It could conflict with one of the fundamental aims of the WHO's Action Programme on Essential Drugs, which calls for 'development of local or regional production of the most commonly-used essential drugs on a step-by-step basis.'"[16]

The provision of drug products represented only one part of the Servipharm program; another involved service projects to the Third World. In this phase, Servipharm experts assisted in such operations as a feasibility study of creating a drug quality control laboratory in Dubai, helped in a cholera control program in Zanzibar, and worked with several African and Latin American health ministries to support oral rehydration therapy (ORT) campaigns against diarrhea.

Ironically, Ciba-Geigy's efforts to support ORT antidiarrhea campaigns came even while the company was under fiery attack from consumers for its embroilment in the affair of clioquinol, marketed originally by the Swiss firm as Enterovioform and Mexaform. (See Chapters 1, 2, and 11.) This was the antidiarrhea product that was linked to the outbreak of SMON, striking some ten thousand victims in Japan alone, and that caused Ciba-Geigy hundreds of millions of dollars in damages, worldwide harm to its good name, and grievous internal dissension.

Although a few other brand-name drug companies gingerly began to follow Ciba-Geigy's lead, most held back and continued to oppose the Servipharm concept. Typical of the disagreement was the pharmaceutical showdown that affected the Dominican Republic in the West Indies during the mid-1980s.[17] Earlier, in 1979, the small country had been nearly devastated by hurricane David and tropical storm Frederick. It was brutally hit by skyrocketing gasoline prices. At about the same time, Dominican sugar—the country's major export crop—was battered by plunging prices and a shrinking market.

Health care, which had never been adequate, began to disintegrate. Physicians and nurses threatened to go on strike. Hospitals were turning away patients. The costs of medicines had increased by 250 percent, and pharmacies in at least three major cities threatened to close. At the same time, the government was helping hospitals use scarce health funds to purchase highly sophisticated and expensive equipment. The president of the Dominican Medical Association declared that a "national hysteria" had been aroused.

At this point, the minister of health called on the member firms of the Asociación de Representantes y Agentes de Productos Farmacéuticos (ARAPF) to officially lower their profit margins. The ARAPF members—about 90 percent of them U.S. and European firms—refused. The minister then asked them to reduce their profits on only 300 essential products; the ARAPF refused again. Recognizing that this trade group had enormous political power, the minister seemed powerless. But there was one multinational firm—Ciba-Geigy—that was *not* a member of the ARAPF. Through its Servipharm division, the Swiss company offered to supply essential products at low prices to the government.

For a short time, the ministry wrestled with its decision. Most Dominican physicians, it was generally accepted, had been brainwashed by the multinational firms. They had been convinced that all generic products were suspect and could not be trusted. This view was accepted as the gospel in the Dominican Republic, even though generics were being used safely, economically, and ever more widely throughout the United States. These Servipharm products, however, were not simply generics—they were generics with Ciba-Geigy's reputation for quality behind them.

The health ministry decided to take a chance. It arranged for the formation of an agency known as PROMESE, which could buy drugs at preferential rates and supply them to the poorest sectors of the population through public hospitals, rural clinics, and more than 500 "people's drugstores." "Servipharm," an American observer said, "was the alternative between cheap but undependable generics and expensive ethical drugs. . . . In short, Servipharm constituted the difference between a poor medicine and a medicine for the poor."

By the end of 1988 the pharmaceutical scene in the Third World had definitely changed. Servipharm reported that its products had been used by nearly a billion patients in more than 80 countries.[18] At the same time, it had become apparent that the International Federation of Pharmaceutical Manufacturers Associations and most (though not all) multinational firms had learned they could live profitably if not happily with the WHO essential drugs list idea. They stressed, however, that the list should be used only for public health programs, government hospitals, and other elements of the tax-supported public sector, but should not apply to the private sector.

At about the same time, it was reported, some 60 multinational companies had offered to provide about 250 different medicines and vaccines—including most of those on the WHO essential drugs list—at reduced prices to the least developed nations.[19] These 60 companies had quietly stopped their warfare against generic products; they were now marketing them. And Ciba-Geigy could no longer be charged with giving aid and comfort to the enemy.

The Tropicare Project

Warner-Lambert, a large and well-established American pharmaceutical firm—Parke-Davis is one of its chief components—has been producing drugs in its own African factories since the 1970s. It began with plants in two onetime British colonies, Kenya and Nigeria. In the early 1980s officials began looking at the idea of adding a plant in Senegal, part of French-speaking West Africa. "Our friends in WHO had been stressing to us the need for social cooperation in these Third World nations," a Parke-Davis official recalled. "This was all very well for some of our European competitors. The British companies still had close connections with the former British colonies. They kept effective entrée into government circles. They knew the top people in medicine. The French companies had similar links to key government and business and medical people in the former French colonies. But we didn't have any such mother-country ties. We were the new kid on the block."

Parke-Davis opened its new $3.5 million plant in Dakar, the capital city of Senegal, in May 1983. It claimed to be "the first U.S. drug firm to establish a manufacturing presence in French-speaking West Africa." Late in that same year it approved a three-year plan to invest $1 million in a new program to provide education and training for paraprofessionals. That program became Tropicare.[20] Michael Ogrizek, Warner-Lambert's medical director for Africa, said: "Our goal is not to replace existing education programs and training networks run by schools or hospitals. We are seeking new audiences, which is why most of [our material] is geared to health care providers in the bush, at the farthest reaches of the health care chain."

By 1988 Tropicare was operating in six African countries: Cameroon, Ivory Coast, Kenya, Nigeria, Senegal, and Zaire. At the heart of the program is a series of about two dozen 30-minute slide presentations with audio cassettes, each covering a specific tropical disease, childhood illness, or issue of health care management. Throughout, every possible emphasis is placed on prevention.

"We mention drugs when drugs are indicated," Christian Chatelard of Parke-Davis Afrique de l'Ouest told us in Senegal, "but there is not one bit of promotion on any Parke-Davis product. Our company has financed and supervised the preparation of the materials. Each of our company representatives—you would call them detailers—is required to spend one day each week in the field in putting on these demonstrations. Far out in the bush, where there is no electricity, we have equipped our people with projectors that can operate off the outlet of an automobile cigarette lighter. More than 200,000 paramedics have already seen our programs. There is no sales connection. However, it is possible we have made a few friends in the neighborhood."[21] Senegalese health experts concur.[22] We can testify to the reception accorded some of the presentations. A 30-minute showing to a packed audience of nurses, students, and paramedics—entertained only with a free cola drink—was saluted with tumultuous applause and followed by a barrage of questions and discussion.

According to Aracelia Vila, who has coordinated the entire Tropicare operation from corporate headquarters in New Jersey, the "centerpiece" of the program is a Joint Therapeutic Commission established in each country concerned. Each commission is composed of top governmental policymakers, independent medical experts, deans of local teaching hospitals, representatives of nursing and midwife associations, pharmacists, community health workers, and even military physicians. They have seen to it that each program is medically correct and socially acceptable.[23]

"We emphasize preventive self-help," she said. "We insist on local management and local participation. We conform wherever possible to international standards set by such bodies as WHO and UNICEF. Tropicare is not simply another charity. It represents a long-term commitment to improve living standards. At the same time, of course, it can create more healthy and affluent customers who may one day buy Warner-Lambert products." To Warner-Lambert, Tropicare will eventually attain two goals: it will meet humanitarian needs, and it will achieve commercial dividends.

A separate series has been developed in cooperation with the U.S. Overseas Private Investment Corporation (OPIC). For this, the material has been prepared not only in French and English but also in six native languages—Hausa, Igbo, Lingala, Pidgin, Swahili, and Yoruba. Warner-Lambert has shared copies of the programs with a host of nongovernmental organizations, public hospitals, and universities outside of the host country. The International Red Cross has used Tropicare to help train its personnel. By early 1989 plans were under way to extend the Tropicare program to Latin America. It is now operating in Colombia, where it has been adapted to the local conditions and infrastructure. Applauded by WHO and by the health authorities of every country in which Tropicare was at work, the new kid had achieved acceptability on the block.

The Damn Fly and Its Worms

Stretching across tropical Africa is a vast area that parasitologists recognize as the land of onchocerciasis, the disease more familiarly known as river blindness. Its vector, or carrier, is the blackfly called *Simulium damnosum*.[24] That zone runs from Senegal and Guinea in the west through Mali, Ivory Coast, Liberia, Ghana, Nigeria, and Cameroon to Zaire and Angola in the south, and Sudan and Ethiopia in the east. Across the Red Sea, it has appeared in Yemen. In the Americas, there are centers of infection in Mexico, Guatemala, Colombia, Ecuador, Venezuela, and Brazil.

The infection is caused by a microscopic, threadlike worm, which is transmitted through the bite of the female blackfly. When an infected fly bites a human being, the parasites generally set up headquarters in the skin, where they may cause unsightly nodules and itching that can last for as long as ten years. Worse, the microfilariae—the microscopic embryos of the parasites—can invade the eyes, where they may produce total and permanent blindness.

The bloodsucking blackfly female lays her eggs in only one place—a fast-flowing stream. The eggs have an adhesive coating that lets them cling to submerged rocks, weeds, or tree branches. Usually the eggs hatch in 36 to 48 hours and become larvae, which, after about a week, go through a pupal stage, and after two to four days or more, emerge as flying insects.

Because of the breeding preferences of *Simulium damnosum*, onchocerciasis occurs mostly near river rapids and other fast-moving water, and accordingly acquired the name river blindness. In addition to the clinical damage and suffering it causes, the disease has had a devastating socioeconomic effect—it has forced millions of people, especially in Africa, to abandon some of the most fertile, easily irrigatable land and leave it unfarmed.

How widespread is onchocerciasis? World Health Organization figures put the number of victims at 20 to 30 million, with about 18 million seriously affected. Others put the number as high as 40 million. An additional 85 million are said to be at risk of getting the infection. In some villages in Africa, it has been claimed, more than 15 percent have been blinded by the disease. In some, it has been reported, 60 percent of those over the age of 55 are partially or completely blind. Invasion of the eye and blindness is apparently related to how frequently and how many times the victim has been bitten.

Two drugs have been used against the disease, either alone or in combination. Diethylcarbamazine (DEC) can kill only the microfilaria form of the parasites, and Suramin (sometimes known as Bayer 205 or Germanin) is active against only the adult form. Unfortunately, DEC must be administered daily for seven to ten days under medical supervision, and may cause dizziness, nausea, and mild to severe allergic reactions. Some physicians recommend that the patient be hospitalized for the treatment. Suramin, widely applied for the treatment of African sleeping sickness, or trypanosomiasis, must be given intravenously once a week for at least five weeks, is highly toxic, and can cause serious side effects and sometimes death. "Neither," a WHO statement warned, "is appropriate for large-scale curative or preventative use."[25]

In 1974, on the basis of many years of field studies, a group of African nations, international development banks, and United Nations agencies embarked on a program of aerial spraying of watercourses in the Volta River basin, in Upper Volta and Ghana. The Onchocerciasis Control Program was to use larvacides that might kill one of the development stages of the blackfly. The plan was to cover eventually an area across Africa of more than 500,000 square miles, with some 26 million inhabitants.[26] The total cost would be enormous.

In the following year, in Rahway, New Jersey, scientists at the Merck Sharp & Dohme research laboratories turned up a new antiparasite drug named ivermectin, which seemed to have promise in the control of a number of parasitic infections of farm animals. By 1981 there were already reports that it could be used against a host of roundworm, insect, tick, mite, and other infestations. In 1983 a Merck team reported: "Data obtained in many trials and many countries indicate that ivermectin possesses exceptional potency against an unprecedented array of nematodes and arthropod parasites. . . . It is now in commercial use in various countries for the treatment and control of parasites in cattle, horses, and sheep, and is expected to become available for use in swine and dogs."[27] Even more exciting, ivermectin was also effective against the onchocerciasis wormlike organisms that cause river blindness. And, at least in experimental animals, it appeared to be strikingly free of side effects.

The human studies on ivermectin were placed under the direction of Mohammed Aziz of Merck. Born in 1929 in what is now Bangladesh, he received his medical degree from the University of Dhaka in 1954 and took his residency training at St. Joseph's Hospital in St. Paul and the University of Minnesota Hospital in Minneapolis. Clearly more interested in medical research than in medical practice, he moved in turn to Johns Hopkins, the University of Maryland, and then to the London School of Hygiene and Tropical Medicine, where his fascination with parasitology became evident. Late in 1976 he was recruited by Merck Sharp & Dohme to become director of domestic clinical research. Three years later he became head of international clinical research and inherited full responsibility for the human trials with ivermectin.

In 1982 Mohammed Aziz and a group of coworkers from the University of Dakar in Senegal and the University of Paris published their first findings on a group of 32 Senegalese men. These patients had early onchocerciasis infections, which so far attacked only the skin and had not yet proceeded to eye involvement. The new drug, the scientists reported, dramatically controlled the infection. A single tablet, taken by mouth, stopped the worms for a month or more. All subjects tolerated the drug well. It had only "minimal" side effects. They added: "Further studies with heavily infected patients and patients who have eye involvement should be carried out in different parts of the world to evaluate the full extent of therapeutic efficacy of ivermectin in onchocerciasis. . . . If further clinical investigation with larger numbers of patients supports the findings of this study, ivermectin may prove to be a major advance in the treatment and/or eradication of one of the major parasitic diseases of our time."[28] To public health workers, the new drug was perhaps most remarkable because it could be taken by mouth—the services of a skilled physician were not necessary—and because the treatment was effective for months after a single dose. Now, for the first time, it was possible to think realistically of laying out a full-scale public health campaign.

By 1986 Aziz and his coworkers could state that more than a thousand patients had been treated successfully in Senegal, Ghana, Liberia,

Togo, Mali, Ivory Coast, Guatemala, and France. (Most of the patients treated in France had come from West Africa.) "Perhaps," Aziz wrote, "the administration of a single dose every six to twelve months will suffice to keep microfilariae at a low level in the skin and the eye and thus to prevent damage."[29] Ivermectin could not repair eyes that were already destroyed. But it apparently could protect undamaged eyes from harm. When he published these findings, Aziz knew that he himself was dying from cancer; he died the following year at the age of 58.

In October 1987, just before Aziz's death, P. Roy Vagelos, the chief executive officer of Merck, announced at simultaneous press conferences in Washington, D.C., and Paris that ivermectin, now under its brand name Mectizan, had been approved by the French drug authorities and was ready for broad application, at least throughout French-speaking West Africa. But Vagelos had more to say:

Since it became apparent that people in need were unable to purchase it, Merck decided to make "Mectizan" available at no charge to public health programs. We feel that this is the best way to assure that the drug will be made available in the most effective and expeditious manner. We are taking these unprecedented steps because of the exceptional circumstances surrounding this disease. The areas where this disease is endemic are usually extremely poor and often remote, requiring major public health initiatives.[30]

Plans had already been arranged through the World Health Organization to set up an international panel that would oversee the trials and assure that the public health program in each involved country was appropriate. Merck was able to report in 1988 that the programs in the first eleven countries had begun.

The few examples cited here could not possibly cover all the contributions made to developing nations by drug companies, alone or in groups. Other firms have done their bit. But it must be understood and accepted that some companies have done little more than make and market their products at a profit, and some have probably done more harm than good. What seems important is the evidence that one company, or a few working in concert, can make a difference. Shakespeare touched on this matter. In the final scene of his *Merchant of Venice*, Portia declares: "How far that little candle throws his beams! / So shines a good deed in a naughty world."

Chapter 10

AMMUNITION FOR THE CONSUMERS

In the past, especially in industrialized societies, the physician was expected to dictate all the details of health care: to decide all the details of drug therapy, which dietary regimen was indicated, and whether and what kind of surgery was needed. The consumer—in this case, the patient—had only two responsibilities: to pay the bill and to be grateful. Fortunately or not, those days of "father knows best" are beginning to vanish in the United States and perhaps in other developed nations. Even in the Third World, a few patients are beginning to ask *why* one drug rather than another is being prescribed, *why* a surgical operation is to be performed, *why* a patient is being hospitalized. More and more, it is becoming evident that patients do not always agree that father knows best.

Any questioning of the concept "father knows best" should not be misread as "father knows nothing." A well-trained, experienced, up-to-date physician knows a great deal. Such a person, if blessed with compassion and understanding, can play a vital role in the prevention and treatment of illness. This is as true now as it was in the reputedly good old days, though it may not be as popularly believed. We remember those days and the friendly doctor who made house calls. Graham Dukes has written:

What the family doctor of fifty years ago did, he did very largely with his own head, eyes, and hands, and, with simple, understandable tools, as many doctors in developing countries (and not only there) do today; he had the time to do his work well, and if he indeed did it caringly and skilfully, the result was often an evident matter, and a cause for his own rejoicing, as well as that of his patient. . . . This sort of memory is stirred by the type of paperback which, from time to time, sets out hysterically to alert and alarm the public as to the wickedness of doctors. Having put the medical profession on a quite unnecessary pedestal for several generations, the population is now periodically urged to cast it down and spit upon it. That is uncomfortable, unproductive, and generally undeserved. There is surely no reason to think that doctors care any less about patients than once they did.[1]

This questioning attitude on the part of consumers has become notably apparent in the matter of which drugs should be allowed on the market. The revelation that the evidence of some physicians was purchased by drug companies has been healthy. The testimony of physicians that "I can't practice my profession without it" has been exposed as no adequate substitute for scientific data and subjected to the ridicule it deserves. Much of this dispute, however, required factual data to become believable. Such information was not readily available until the late 1960s. Consumer activists had scant material to support their claims.

The Task Force Reports

In 1967 the secretary of the U.S. Department of Health, Education, and Welfare (now Health and Human Services), acting on a request from the Lyndon Johnson White House, directed us to investigate the problem of adding coverage of out-of-hospital prescription drugs for the elderly to the new Medicare program. Until then—and, in fact, with few exceptions until now—Medicare provided coverage for prescription drugs only for hospitalized patients. Accordingly, the secretary set up the HEW Task Force on Prescription Drugs. (One of us, P.R.L., acted as Task Force chairman, M.S. as director of the Task Force staff, and M.L. as a consultant.) One of the Task Force's first decisions was to arrange for two nationwide surveys to be conducted by the U.S. Public Health Service. The studies were to determine which out-of-hospital drugs were purchased by the elderly, how much they paid for them, and where they obtained the funds for the purchase. Then, as an afterthought, to these questions we added two more: Why was the drug prescribed? What was the diagnosis or the intended therapeutic effect?

When the data came in, we were astounded. In practice physicians were not prescribing in the way they had been taught in medical school. They were calling for irrational combinations of drugs, drugs that were too risky for the trivial conditions for which they were recommended, products that were all too likely to react adversely with each other. When we presented our first unofficial report, one professor of clinical pharmacology in Los Angeles said we were fabricating our data. On our invitation she examined our complete reports, then commented, "If this is the way that American physicians prescribe, then God help American patients!"

Those findings led us to examine drug promotion by drug companies, drug company budgets, drug company profits, the ties between the drug industry and organized medicine and those between the industry and medical journals supported by drug advertising, the role of pharmacists (who often knew more about drugs than did most of the physicians whose prescriptions they filled), the drug insurance programs already in operation in this and other countries, and the key elements of any program to be proposed for this country.

In 1968 and 1969 the Task Force published its reports.[2] Although these seemed to impress many physicians, pharmacists, patients, lawmakers, and drug company officials and their stockholders, we were somewhat dissatisfied. In our research we had collected much additional information which we did not print, since it did not apply strictly to providing out-of-hospital drugs for the elderly under Medicare. We were also dismayed by what the new administration under Richard Nixon was intending to do to our various health programs. We returned to California, where all three of us joined the faculty of the University of California in San Francisco. There we reorganized and updated the material for publication. We added more evidence on the misdeeds of the companies, much of it obtained from old friends, former students, or former classmates who had gone to work for drug companies and who were horrified by what their own firms were doing.

Our manuscript was rejected by university presses, on the grounds that it might offend drug companies that were supporting drug research in the schools, and by general publishers, with the explanation that the firms were publishing medical journals that carried much drug advertising. The University of California Press eventually published the book in 1974 as *Pills, Profits, and Politics*.[3] For practically the first time, consumers now had a wealth of ammunition to use in their struggle for better, safer, and less costly drugs.

The "Drugging" Books

Another phase of our investigations into the drug industry had already begun. On the urging of a young physician who was practicing in a California town close to the Mexican border, M.S and M.L. went to Mexico to observe and document the activities of the drug companies. With support from a Ford Foundation grant, we examined the situation not only in Mexico but also in Guatemala, Costa Rica, Colombia, and Ecuador. With the aid of old friends and colleagues, we obtained priceless information on Argentina and Brazil. We worked with clinical pharmacologists, epidemiologists, endocrinologists, cardiologists, the drug regulatory experts in the Ministry of Health, industry leaders, and pathologists—the specialists who really knew what was happening. In some countries, we were able to work with former newspaper colleagues.

It became obvious that in Latin America there were two types of medical care. Some physicians had been trained in excellent medical schools, kept up with the medical literature in their field, attended scientific meetings, consulted frequently with their colleagues, spurned the advice of drug company *visitadores*, and practiced a type of medical care that was as good as the best available in New York, Boston, or San Francisco. Others had been graduated from second- or third-rate medical schools, had never studied a medical book since they obtained their license to practice, devoted no time to scientific journals, attended no medical meetings, consulted with their colleagues only to arrange a golf match or a bridge game, allowed their prescribing patterns to be dictated by drug salesmen, and practiced a type of medicine equal to the worst in New York, Boston, or San Francisco.

We were able to compare the claims of effectiveness and the warnings and contraindications made for the same drug by the same drug company—American, French, Swiss, or West German—in the United States and in one or more Latin American nations. In a shocking number of cases, we found, the company vastly exaggerated the claims of usefulness by including material that could not be supported by scientific evidence, or by glossing over or totally ignoring serious or possibly lethal side effects.

Early workers in this field, such as Michael Dunne and Andrew Herxheimer in England, Sanjaya Lall in India, Wilfred Lionel in Sri Lanka, Wolfgang Haworka in Malaysia, John Yudkin in Tanzania and Mozambique, and Robert Ledogar in the United States, had already exposed some of the unsavory promotion of a few drugs in a few developing nations. But they did not have the facilities and the financing needed to conduct extended surveys in numerous countries.

Our findings were published in 1976 by the University of California Press as *The Drugging of the Americas*.[4] The impact of this book could scarcely be ignored. Publication was followed by two days of committee hearings in the U.S. Senate, chaired by Gaylord Nelson of Wisconsin. Our report was carried on the wires of United Press International, the Associated Press, Reuters, and other international news services. It was given prominent attention in newspapers, radio, and television throughout Latin America and in Canada and the United States. It was featured in the international edition of *Time* magazine. It became part of an hour-long TV documentary on PBS, the Public Broadcasting Service. Latin American embassies in Washington, D.C., telephoned us or sent representatives to request additional data.

The reaction of the drug industry was somewhat unexpected. At one emergency meeting of leaders of the U.S. Pharmaceutical Manufacturers Association (PMA), several urged that some steps be taken to disprove our report. One official, however, is reported to have said, "I've been telling you fellows for more than ten years to cut it out or you'd be caught. Well, they've caught you. You can't disprove a damn thing." In another session, a drug company president asked, "Is there some way you can stop Silverman and Lee from saying all those rotten things about the way we do things?" And the PMA president is said to have replied, "Sure, stop the rotten way you do things."

The Marketing Codes

The American drug industry took a significant step soon after the Nelson hearings when the PMA quickly set up a code of marketing behavior. In 1981 a similar code was adopted by the International Federation of Pharmaceutical Manufacturing Associations (IFPMA). It called upon all its members to conduct all their dealings with government agencies, health professionals, and the public with "complete candor." Drug companies were urged to limit their claims to what could be supported by scientific fact and to disclose important risks. Entertainment at drug company seminars or other meetings should be restrained and conducted with dignity in keeping with the scientific nature of the occasion. Free samples to physicians should be limited— but the door was left open to give a physician whatever he requested. (It was not clear whether the "whatever" included more drug samples, more dollars or pesos or rupees, a European or American vacation for physician and wife, or an education at a European or American university for the physician's children. There was ample evidence that some drug companies were willing to offer such bribes and that some physicians were more than willing to accept them.)[5]

If the IFPMA code had been presented simply as a guide for behavior, it might have been welcomed. Instead, it was depicted as a solution. It was said that since the code disapproved of certain practices, those practices no longer existed. The code had one fatal flaw: It had no mechanism for surveillance or enforcement. Some industry critics termed the IFPMA code a farce. One described it as "vague, incomplete, amateurish rubbish, done just to clean up their image, designed to impress and not to work."[6] One industry leader admitted that it carried all the threat of the Boy Scout oath. It was called a paper tiger—a paper pussycat would be more accurate.

In 1979 we were asked to participate in an international conference on SMON and clioquinol (see Chapter 11) in Kyoto, Japan, and to present a report on our Latin American studies. There we first met Olle Hansson. There also enthusiastic consumerists from Africa and Southeast Asia urged us to do for them what we had already done in Latin America. This led to a series of visits to numerous developing countries and, in 1982, to the publication of *Prescriptions for Death*.[7]

We learned again that there were differences not only in the quality of training of physicians. Too often, there were far too few physicians to treat the number of patients who needed them. "If you see there are perhaps five hundred patients waiting in line to see the doctor," an Egyptian drug expert explained to us, "you don't bother to wait. You go directly to a pharmacy and get the prescription drug without a prescription."[8]

In some countries, such as Mexico, Venezuela, and Brazil, governments permitted too many new medical schools to be put into operation. "In some instances," a Mexican observer noted, "there are so many new schools that we can't find adequate teachers for them, and so they turn out poorly trained students." In some Third World nations, this flood of new doctors could be used to treat patients, but there are not sufficient funds to pay them for practicing medicine. Accordingly, many of them—perhaps as many as 30 percent—are forced to work as taxi drivers, salesmen, and waiters.[9]

How well many of these physicians prescribe has been seriously questioned. Jorge Olarte, of the Laboratory of Intestinal Bacteriology in Mexico City's famed Children's Hospital, puts it this way: "Many physicians prescribe antibiotics admirably. They know I may be watching them. But in the afternoons, they work in private practice. They are subject to patient pressure—patients demand an antibiotic for any fever, any discomfort, any intestinal problem. So they prescribe chloramphenicol [a drug apt to cause serious or fatal blood destruction] for any fever, any diarrhea, for upper respiratory infections, for urinary infections, for the common cold—and we still see aplastic anemia."[10]

In other developing nations—Venezuela and Indonesia, for example—some domestic or local companies expect to pay a physician for each prescription of their products that he writes. "We pay a small fee, not as a bribe but as a commission," a company official explained. "We pay money to facilitate—to get what we're entitled to get legally, but get it faster." In Indonesia, pharmacologist Iwan Darmansjah said, "Some companies still use 'contract physicians.' They pay these people a kickback—perhaps 15 percent—on every prescription for their own products that they write, and use them to write testimonial papers. Who is being bribed? Practicing physicians, especially those in positions of authority. Government officials, and not only minor officials. Here, it is almost universally believed that corruption reaches the highest level of government."[11]

In other Third World nations, a still different type of practitioner is evident. Pediatrician Colin Forbes in Kenya told us of watching a demonstration by a famous healer in Zimbabwe: "Swathed in snake skins and monkey fur, he went through his impressive performance and seemingly did much good for his patients. Then he retired to another building, removed his snake skins and monkey fur, put on a tie, shirt, and handsome two-piece suit, and went off in his chauffeur-driven Cadillac."[12]

The Consumerist Campaigns

During the late 1970s and particularly the 1980s, a number of non-governmental groups became more and more active in efforts to increase the supply of needed drugs in the Third World and to improve the quality of drug use. They sought to ban ineffective, needlessly expensive, dangerous, or needless products from the market. They urged countries to refuse acceptance of a new product unless it was demonstrably safer, more effective, or less costly than products that were already available. Some—including particularly active members of Health Action International—suggested or demanded that the essential drugs list program be used not as a guideline for priorities but as a step to get rid of all "nonessential" products, not only in developing nations but in industrialized countries as well. Their main targets—in some cases, their only targets—were the large, powerful, and generally profitable multinational drug companies in the United States, Europe, and Japan. Local or domestic firms, even though *their* actions might be irresponsible and their products unacceptable, generally escaped unscathed.

Among the most active and effective consumer groups have been these:

- The Health Research Group, headed by Sidney Wolfe and closely allied to Ralph Nader's Public Citizen, and the Interfaith Center on Corporate Responsibility, involving a large number of Roman Catholic and Protestant groups, based in the United States. Wolfe has frequently criticized not only the drug industry but also the U.S. Food and Drug Administration for what he felt were irrational decisions.
- In Great Britain, War on Want, OXFAM, Social Audit (headed by Charles Medawar), and Andrew Chetley, working in both the U.K. and the Netherlands, Andrew Herxheimer and his *Drug and Therapeutics Bulletin*, Dianna Melrose, and Philippa Saunders.
- In West Germany, BUKO (Bundeskongress entwicklungs-

politischer Aktionsgruppen), which has kept a particularly watchful eye on such German drug companies as Bayer, Hoechst-Roussel, and E. Merck, and Ulrich Moebius and his *Arzneimittel-Telegramm*, a prescribing guide for physicians. Moebius has often attacked the industry. He has also often acted as a consultant to drug companies.

- In the Netherlands, WEMOS (Werkgroep Medische Ontwikke-lings Samenwerking (Work Group for Medical Development Co-operation), which has constantly scrutinized the activities of the Dutch firm Organon.
- In Japan, ICADIS, a spin-off from the group that played a prominent part in the SMON lawsuits involving Enterovioform.
- In India, the Voluntary Health Association of India (VHAI) and the All India Drug Action Network (AIDAN), which have vigorously—but not always successfully—attempted to ban ex-cessively dangerous drug products.
- In Pakistan, Syed Ahmed and his coworkers.
- In the Philippines, the Health Action Information Network.
- In Korea, the Citizen's Alliance for Consumer Protection.
- In Australia, the Australian Consumer's Organisation and nota-bly MaLAM, the Medical Lobby for Appropriate Marketing, Australia-based but operating internationally.

In 1982, during his final year in medical school, Peter Mansfield, an Australian, spent two months working in the People's Health Center near Dhaka, Bangladesh. He was shocked by the poverty and disease. He was also shocked to discover that many health problems were being made worse by the manner in which major pharmaceutical companies were marketing their products. Too often, he learned, drugs were being promoted in the Third World with claims that were misleading, inaccurate, or untrue. The following year, while he was a hospital intern, he started MaLAM. Mansfield designed MaLAM by taking ideas from Amnesty International, *The Medical Letter* in the United States, and Charles Medawar's Social Audit publications in England. He is now a family doctor and runs MaLAM in his spare time, assisted by health professionals in Australia, the United Kingdom, West Germany, France, and Canada.

The MaLAM team produces a "MaLAM Letter" every month, ad-dressed to the heads of the offending drug companies. These letters simply point out the promotional claim in question and ask the company for whatever scientific evidence it can provide to support that claim. Copies of each letter are signed by hundreds of MaLAM subscribers—nearly all of them prescribing physicians—from all over the world. "MaLAM is not designed to attack drug companies," Mansfield has said, "but rather to encourage improvements to specific marketing practices. The hope was that many marketing practices might cease as soon as top executives were informed of them. Failing that, executives might decide to stop abuses in small markets to protect their company's corporate image in the larger markets."[13]

Strictly speaking, since nearly all of the organization's subscribers are physicians, MaLAM is not actually a consumer group. Its goals, however, are essentially those of such groups because MaLAM seeks a better break for consumers. Certainly its work has been effective. It has politely reprimanded more than two dozen major pharmaceutical companies in the United States, Great Britain, West Germany, the Netherlands, Belgium, France, Switzerland, Italy, Hungary, and Japan. In a few instances, the company responded by taking the product completely off the market or deleting the unsupported (or unsupportable) claim. In most cases, the company toned down the statement so that it was no longer offensive to physicians. Occasionally, a company refused to respond to Mansfield, usually a painful mistake for the firm because the Australian physician would report that fact in a journal like *Lancet*, which was read by physicians all over the world. "Doctors have a greater potential than governments to alter international marketing behavior," he and his colleagues said, "because prescribing patterns influence drug company profits."[14]

In the same way, although none is technically a consumer operation, other publications have had a major influence on the prescribing practices of physicians and thus on the health care of patients. Among these are *The Medical Letter* in the United States, Andrew Herxheimer's *Drug and Therapeutics Bulletin* in Great Britain, and Hirokuni Beppu's *The Informed Prescriber* in Japan.

Finally, the two organizations that have had probably the greatest impact on drug company activities are the International Organization of Consumers Unions (IOCU) and its related Health Action International (HAI), both with their drug-related work based in the same two cities, Penang, Malaysia, and first The Hague and now Amsterdam in the Netherlands. IOCU has been able to work quietly but effectively with various elements of the drug industry, governments, physicians, pharmacists, and the media. Perhaps its most influential action was to develop the boycott against Nestlé's and the WHO marketing code for breast milk substitutes. (Although it has been hailed as a complete triumph for consumerists, the milk substitute code has been far from totally effective. It has minimized undesirable practices but not eliminated them. "The WHO code of marketing expressly forbids the direct promotion of infant formulas to the public and to health workers," it was disclosed in 1987, "but the International Baby Food Action Network has recorded hundreds of examples of companies deliberately breaking the code.")[15]

The HAI Proposals

Organized in Geneva in 1981, HAI is smaller but far more militant. In recent years it has been especially active at meetings of the World Health Organization and the World Health Assembly. It has repeatedly expressed its contempt for the IFPMA drug marketing code. Some leaders of HAI have also indicated the need for a drug code, perhaps the establishment of an international version of the U.S. Food and Drug Administration under the World Health Organization. WHO leaders have not warmed to the idea, preferring to continue their role in the setting of guidelines. Other activists have called for a new and official international code. One of the most vocal advocates of the code approach has been Dr. Kumariah Balasubramaniam, known familiarly as Dr. Bala. He has worked with both IOCU and HAI. His proposals have included these:

- Third World countries should not permit the importation or use of any expensive drug product under a brand name when the same drug is available at high quality under its generic name at low cost.
- Third World countries should not permit the importation or use of any drug which has no proven therapeutic effect, which is excessively dangerous, which has been banned by industrialized nations, which has not been approved by the country in which it is manufactured, or which has passed its shelf-life expiration date.
- No new product should be approved unless there is a demonstrable need for it—that is, there must be evidence that it is more

effective, or safer, or less costly than competitive products already on the market.

- As a compromise measure, the essential drugs list should be expanded from about 250 drugs to 600 or 650 and made applicable to both public and private sectors.
- The number of company representatives or detailers in each country who promote a company's products to physicians or pharmacists should be drastically limited.
- Arrangements should be made for pool purchase of drugs in large quantities in order to obtain the best market prices on the world market.
- The brand-name firms in industrialized countries should be induced to conduct more research on tropical diseases.
- Regional quality-control laboratories should be established.
- Drug research laboratories in Third World nations should be established to develop new drugs.
- Where necessary, government price controls should be placed on drugs.
- All patents on drug products in developing nations should be abolished or patent protection should be drastically limited.

"It seems clear," he said, "that two alternatives are open to Third World countries regarding pharmaceutical patents: (a) exclude both pharmaceutical products and processes from patent protection, [or] (b) exclude pharmaceutical products from patent [protection] and grant protection for pharmaceutical processes but provide adequate safeguards aimed at ensuring satisfactory working of the patented invention."[16] Not all of these ideas have been endorsed by all consumer leaders. Most have been vigorously opposed by the brand-name industry. In WHO and other United Nations agencies, early enthusiasm for the code cooled when it appeared that no one could figure how to get it adopted and then enforced.

Some critics of the industry have claimed that drug company research could be easily and speedily replaced by research in government or university laboratories. The record says otherwise. In the past forty or fifty years—since the discovery of the first antibiotics—most important new drugs have come from the profit-oriented brand-name industry. It is also noteworthy that in those nations in which profit-making was frowned upon by Marxist dictates—in particular, the Soviet Union, the People's Republic of China, and Cuba—the discovery of important new drugs has been almost a total failure.

In recent years the drug industry has tried to dismiss the consumer organizations as merely special-interest pressure groups—which, of course, they are. But the drug industry—like the tobacco industry, the alcoholic beverage industry, the petroleum industry, and the National Football League—is also a special-interest pressure group. It is obvious that groups like these devote considerable time to convincing the public that they have only the public's interest at heart, while they make substantial amounts of money. Moreover the drug industry has maintained some potent friends.

Several years ago, Jeane Kirkpatrick, former U.S. ambassador to the United Nations, told members of the Pharmaceutical Manufacturers Association that the attacks against the drug industry within the United Nations system are all part of a broad attack on all multinationals. She denounced especially the essential drugs list, the war against patents and trademarks, and the proposed international drug-marketing code. She said: "In confronting efforts aimed specifically at the pharmaceutical industry, you are confronting a very highly developed, full-blown effort to render multinational operations in the world impossible. . . . There is a very powerful ideology which sees you as the enemy. It is not only being promoted by UN agencies everywhere and by UN bureaucrats everywhere, but in U.S. colleges and universities. We must think about it, inform ourselves about it, and act."[17]

An international conference was scheduled in 1986 to be held in the United States to review antibiotic use around the world. It was organized jointly by WHO and the National Institutes of Health. Among the topics for discussion were to be costly overuse, reckless prescribing, and the development of antibiotic resistance in some strains of bacteria. The speakers would include antibiotics experts from all over the world. Then drug industry leaders learned that the speakers would also include at least four people who were viewed as no friends of the drug industry: Charles Medawar of Social Audit, Andrew Herxheimer of "the UK consumer organization," Sidney Wolfe of the Health Research Group, and M. N. G. Dukes of WHO. This information was sent by Thomas Christie, a vice-president of Wyeth, in a letter to the assistant secretary for health in the U.S. Department of Health and Human Services. "I cannot recall ever hearing or reading of one of them speaking in admiring terms of the United States pharmaceutical industry," Christie wrote.

It quickly became apparent that WHO needed the financial backing of the U.S. National Institutes of Health, that NIH needed the backing of the Reagan White House, and that the White House had said No. The meeting was canceled.[18] It was replaced later by a drastically scaled-down version, which attracted little worldwide attention.

The industry's marketing code may be ignored or dismissed as weak and ineffective. The same cannot be said about the industry.

Chapter 11

CONSUMER POWER: THE HANSSON/CIBA-GEIGY CONNECTION

*T*wo Swedish physicians were asked in 1962 to examine a four-year-old boy afflicted almost from birth with an uncommon disease attacking his skin and digestive tract; the diagnosis was acrodermatitis enteropathica. From the time he was six months old, he had been treated with a drug known variously as clioquinol, chinoform, oxyquinoline, vioform, and Enterovioform. After fourteen months of therapy, the boy had mysteriously developed atrophy of both optic nerves. His vision had been virtually destroyed.

To the two doctors, ophthalmologist Lennart Berggren and young pediatric neurologist Olle Hansson of the University of Uppsala, there were two immediate explanations: The blindness might be a previously unknown aspect of the disease. Or it might have been caused by the drug. In a brief note to the British journal *Lancet* early in 1966, they reported their suspicions that the drug was to blame.[1] Their report brought prompt and vigorous protests from the manufacturer of the product, Ciba Ltd., in Basel, Switzerland.[2] (In 1970 Ciba would merge with another large Swiss firm, J. R. Geigy AG, to form Ciba-Geigy Ltd.)[3] The drug, company spokesmen insisted, could not be responsible. Nothing like this had ever happened before. And, they said, their clioquinol products were so insoluble that, when given by mouth, they could not conceivably be absorbed out of the digestive tract. If they could not be absorbed from the stomach and intestines, there was obviously no way they could reach and injure the optic nerves or any other sensitive structures.

The argument was evidently convincing to Ciba, but not to Berggren and Hansson. They reported in 1968 that ten hours after they and other subjects had swallowed clioquinol, it could be detected in their urine.[4] The conclusion was inescapable: the drug could not reach their kidneys unless it had first been absorbed from the digestive tract.

To Ciba this was a matter of grave concern. The sales of Enterovioform, its major clioquinol product, for the treatment of acrodermatitis enteropathica were trivial, but the company's clioquinol products were being sold in enormous amounts—enormously profitable amounts—for both the prevention and the treatment of diarrhea. Annual sales, mainly in the tropics, where diarrhea was an ever-present problem because of contaminated food and water, were estimated to be more than 100 million Swiss francs, or roughly $50 million.[5] Any criticism threatening to disrupt sales of such magnitude would obviously be viewed with alarm. At stake here, however, was not merely the future of one relatively unimportant drug but the reputation, the integrity, and eventually the corporate policies of one of the largest and most influential pharmaceutical companies in the world. Eventually, too, the issue would also involve one of the most eloquent demonstrations of the power of consumer pressure.

Enterovioform had been developed in the early 1930s, not in Switzerland but in the United States, for the treatment of amebic dysentery. (See also Chapter 2.) In the early 1930s, at the University of California Medical School in San Francisco, it came to the attention of a group of tropical-disease researchers and pharmacologists who were trying to find an improved treatment for amebic dysentery, the relatively uncommon but particularly serious type that can attack not only the intestinal tract but also the liver and other internal organs. In 1931 the California group, headed by pharmacologists Hamilton Anderson, Dorothy Koch, and Norman David, reported that the compound was remarkably effective against amebic dysentery in monkeys.[6] David, along with Herbert Johnstone, A. C. Reed, and Chauncey Leake, reported in the *Journal of the American Medical Association* in 1933 that it was effective in man.[7] (M.S. joined the University of California pharmacology group the following year to undertake his doctoral research. He had nothing to do with the antidysentery product himself except—largely because of superstition—to carry a pocketful of tablets whenever he went to a tropical country.)

The investigation in San Francisco had been financed by a small grant from the Swiss research firm Ciba, later to become Ciba-Geigy. Ciba introduced the product on the market in 1934 under the name Enterovioform. In its promotion, the company soon recommended the drug not only for treatment but also for prevention, and not only for use against amebic dysentery but also to ward off or treat bacillary dysentery, "traveler's diarrhea," "summer diarrhea," and a host of other more or less related disorders. The company gave assurances of safety because, it constantly emphasized, the substance was so insoluble in water that it could not possibly pass through stomach or intestinal walls and harm other parts of the body. (When they learned of this claim, the University of California workers in San Francisco were stunned. They knew—and had so reported in their scientific publications—that the drug most certainly could escape from the intestinal tract and affect other parts of the body.) The California scientists were aware that the drug was *relatively* insoluble in body fluids, but it was not *completely* insoluble; it could be absorbed out of the digestive tract in experimental animals, it could produce liver damage, and it could cause death.

The first signs of trouble came in 1935. Two Argentine physicians reported that they had given Enterovioform to patients and that each had observed a patient who developed signs of serious nerve damage.[8] Their findings were reported to Ciba. This was the beginning of what would later be termed the SMON scandal, one of the worst drug disasters in history. A Swiss veterinarian, Paul Hangartner, told Ciba in 1965 that dogs treated with the drug had developed severe convulsions and epileptic-like attacks.[9] (Later investigations disclosed that Ciba scientists had made similar discoveries as early as 1939.) "The reports of animal experiments proving that oxyquinolines are absorbed from the intestinal tract into the body," Olle Hansson said afterward, "did not provoke the drug companies to investigate whether this also happened to humans. They simply denied it."[10] How had the Ciba scientists missed such a vital fact? Years later they admitted that they had used the wrong analytic method to test urine.[11]

The Appearance of SMON

Some 5,000 miles from Sweden the Berggren-Hansson announcement had an unexpected effect. In Japan, beginning in about 1955, thousands had been stricken by a puzzling but devastating illness marked first by loss of sensation and then by paralysis of both legs, often violent gastrointestinal upsets, and visual disturbances sometimes leading to total blindness. Many of these changes were irreversible, incurable, and permanent. Some victims died.[12]

The disease was named SMON, for subacute-myelo-optico-neuropathy. By 1970 about 10,000 cases had been documented in Japan alone. Hospitals were jammed with victims of the epidemic, and new wards had to be built to accommodate them. In some cases an extraordinary number of the patients were inhabitants of the same village. In others, they had been patients of the same physician.[13] Although patients with SMON were relatively rare outside of Japan, cases were reported from the United States, the United Kingdom, Sweden, Norway, Denmark, the Netherlands, France, West Germany, Indonesia, Switzerland, Australia, India, and other nations.[14]

Blame for this horror was placed by various investigators on vitamin deficiencies, metabolic disorders, agricultural pesticides and insecticides, contamination of drinking water by industrial wastes, and a hypothetical "SMON virus." It was noted that many of the Japanese victims had been regularly using Enterovioform, Mexaform, or other forms of clioquinol—often in large doses, for prolonged periods—to control diarrhea. In Japan, many people were accustomed to using the drug regularly as a "digestive stabilizer," or a benevolent "vitamin" for the digestive tract. Accordingly, clioquinol was proposed as a possible cause of SMON, but Ciba and other companies then marketing clioquinol products belligerently leaped to its defense; clioquinol, they continued to insist, was so insoluble that it could not be absorbed from the digestive tract. Japanese physicians continued to be informed by company representatives or company literature that the drug is harmless:

- It is a safe and effective product.
- It is hardly absorbed from the intestines.
- It has no side effects, or if there is a side effect, it is only temporary, so the prescription need not be discontinued.
- It is even safe for children.[15]

Even earlier, Norman David—one member of the San Francisco team that originally developed the drug for treatment of amebic dysentery—warned that the use of clioquinol products in prevention "must be rigidly controlled and should not be carried out as extensively or as freely as is done in the prophylaxis of malaria with quinine."[16] Some investigators reported that the clioquinol products were essentially worthless for the prevention of "traveler's diarrhea" or "summer diarrhea."[17]

When Berggren and Hansson published their findings in 1968, demonstrating without a doubt that clioquinol *is* able to pass through the intestinal wall, most Japanese scientists paid little attention. Then, in 1970, Tadao Tsubaki and his coworkers at Niigata University concluded that clioquinol was the major cause of SMON.[18] In that same year—at the insistence of Reisako Kono and the other members of the governmental SMON commission, and over the most strenuous objections from Ciba-Geigy—the drug was banned from the Japanese market.

The evidence was not complete. There were some victims of SMON who declared they had never taken any clioquinol product, or who could not remember, or whose medical records were confusing or missing. (Medical historians have long been aware that such gaps often occur in attempts to pin down the cause of an outbreak.) Some Ciba-Geigy spokesmen argued that since Enterovioform could not be blamed in *every* case, it could not be blamed in *any* case. Such arguments did not prevail. Within a short time after clioquinol was taken off the market, the Japanese SMON epidemic came to an end.

Start of the Damage Suits

A deluge of damage suits began in 1971 against Ciba (by then Ciba-Geigy), along with the Japanese firms Tanabe and Takeda, which had likewise been marketing clioquinol products, and also against the Japanese government. The government was included as a defendant on the grounds that it was supposed to protect the health of the Japanese people and had failed to do so. (The next year Ciba-Geigy was induced to remove Enterovioform voluntarily from the market in the United States. In Great Britain, the drug was never formally banned. Instead, it was made available only on a physician's prescription. It was omitted from the British *MIMS*, and British physicians simply stopped prescribing it.)

While the litigation was getting started, a small Japanese delegation met with Lennart Berggren and Olle Hansson in Sweden. "They told us about SMON—at that time, in 1975, I knew practically nothing about it—and asked for help," Hansson recalled. "They told us that the Ciba people claimed Enterovioform was absolutely safe—that it was never absorbed into the body. Well, I knew that was a damn lie, and I said, 'Sure, I'll help you.' "[19] For Hansson, who was then 39, his answer would plunge him into a new career—at first a virtual one-man crusade against Ciba-Geigy, and then the leadership of a worldwide consumer campaign against this powerful multinational corporation. He soon took steps to have Enterovioform removed from the market in Sweden. Then he moved his battle into the courts.

The company did not bow down before the legal onslaught. It stubbornly resisted the suits that were brought first in Japan and later in other countries where SMON victims had appeared; it continued its vigorous promotion of Enterovioform for use in practically every variety of diarrhea, insisting that the drug was remarkably safe, had been used by millions of patients without trouble, and could be taken without hesitation for either treatment or prevention. The outbreak of SMON was dismissed by company spokesmen as a "Japanese disease," probably the result of some deficiency in the Japanese genetic pool; there had been relatively few cases in other countries. When Hansson made his first visit to Japan, in 1976, he saw victims of SMON. "There were maybe thirty of them, waiting for me at the Tokyo airport," he said later. "My God! I'll never forget it. Many of them were in wheelchairs, paralyzed. Many came to me, and put out their hands, and wanted to touch me. They were blind. I tell you, that made some impression on me."

Hansson and other experts made an obvious impression in the courtroom. Attorney Etsuro Totsuka and neurologist Hirokuni Beppu of Tokyo described Hansson's testimony in particular as absolutely crucial. In case after case, the patients were victorious, and the defendants were forced to pay damages, but Ciba-Geigy continued to promote and sell clioquinol outside Japan.

By 1979, when Hansson had moved from Uppsala to the University of Göteborg, it became possible to arrange a five-day international SMON conference in Kyoto.[20] This meeting brought together for the first time the top Japanese experts who had been working on the SMON problem, along with experts on adverse drug reactions from the United States, Great Britain, and other countries in Europe. The friendships forged at that meeting among scientists, lawyers, and the press would play key roles in campaigns to achieve honest, accurate drug promotion and labeling.

The months that followed saw several important developments. The damages awarded in the Japanese SMON cases had already exceeded $400 million, with many suits still to be decided. Ciba-Geigy representatives in Third World countries vigorously denied that the payments made by the company to SMON patients represented any admission of guilt. One said, "The payment is an admission that some SMON patients had clioquinol side effects. . . . We do not admit that clioquinol causes SMON." Ciba-Geigy paid, he said, because it *felt* responsible. The fact was that the company paid because the courts *found* the company responsible. A few years later this same Ciba-Geigy man had been promoted to company headquarters in Switzerland. "When I claimed that Enterovioform could not be proved to be responsible for SMON, I was wrong," he told us. "The explanation is simple but painful. The people in our medical department had not told us the whole truth."

The Tanabe and Takeda Apologies

At least as significant in Japanese tradition were the formal apologies presented to the SMON victims or their representatives. On May 16, 1979, Ichiro Matsubara, the president of Tanabe, apologized in court. He said, "Our company makes a start today for the resolution of SMON problem which we have longed to realize. Now, in the settlement which will be achieved between plaintiffs and us, we deeply apologize to the plaintiffs, patients and their families for their grave and miserable sufferings caused by the SMON disease. Furthermore, we regret deeply that we delayed to make a start until now, owing to various circumstances."[21]

Shinbei Konishi, then the chief executive officer and later board chairman of Takeda, apologized on June 11 to a small delegation that had come to his office. It was unofficial, and no record was kept of his remarks; nevertheless, it was an apology and was accepted as such.[22] On September 15, at a brief ceremony, representatives of Tanabe, Takeda, and Ciba-Geigy (Japan) each made a short statement—the so-called one-sentence apology—which was promptly dismissed as nonsense by the SMON leaders.

The top officials of Ciba-Geigy in Switzerland still refused to follow the long-standing Japanese tradition. They declined to offer a formal apology by the head man of the company. Instead, in 1979 an apology was offered by the Japanese subsidiary of the company. A spokesman for Ciba-Geigy (Japan) transmitted the following statement through the courts:

Since the beginning of this lawsuit, the plaintiffs and their representatives have told the court of many sufferings caused by the SMON disease. It has been repeatedly stressed that only a SMON patient can truly understand his fellow patients' sufferings. We believe that we must solemnly accept their grievances. We who manufactured and sold clioquinol drugs deeply sympathize with the plaintiffs and their families in their continuing unbelievable agony; there are no words to adequately express our sorrow. In view of the fact that medical products manufactured and sold by us have been responsible for the occurrence of the tragedy in Japan, we extend our apologies, frankly and without reservation to the plaintiffs and their families.[23]

But Ciba-Geigy (Japan) failed to abide by the centuries-old Japanese tradition: the apology was not presented by the head man of Ciba-Geigy. The Japanese remained unappeased.

On April 30, 1980, Ciba-Geigy made another unfortunate decision. A delegation of SMON victims and their supporters came to headquarters in Basel and asked to meet with the company heads in order to present their grievances. No appropriate officials could be found. One company spokesman declared a few months later, "We didn't know they were coming. It was a holiday anyhow, and all our top people were away."[24] Louis von Planta, chairman of the board, gave a different explanation to Hansson afterward. "We had been advised by our own legal department and by our Japanese associates at Tanabe and Takeda that it would not be proper to meet with the delegation. Such a meeting might weaken our position in the lawsuits." Whatever the reason, the results were unpleasant. Hiroshi Izumi, one of the leading attorneys in the SMON suits and head of the delegation to Basel, was blunt: "This means war against the Japanese people."

Hansson was infuriated by what he considered to be Ciba-Geigy's insulting attitude. He had already published his book, *Arzneimittel-Multis und der SMON Skandal*. He had organized a boycott among Swedish physicians against all Ciba-Geigy products, which was spreading to Norway and Denmark. Reinforced by ammunition in four new books—first, two by our California group on shocking drug promotion in Latin America, Africa, and Asia,[25] quickly followed by similar publications by Dianna Melrose[26] in Great Britain and Mike Muller[27] in Mozambique—he broadened his attack to strike at other drugs and other companies. His main target, however, remained Enterovioform and the other clioquinol products. He was outraged when, regardless of events in Japan, Ciba-Geigy continued to promote and sell Enterovioform and to reap rich profits. He wrote to von Planta and demanded that Enterovioform be taken off the market.[28]

In October 1982 the company finally offered a placating gesture and announced that, because of "other developments" in the treatment of diarrheal disease, Enterovioform and Mexaform would be removed from the market worldwide—but this would be performed gradually, over a period of three to five years.[29] Hansson was furious. He told us of his intention to level a new attack against two of Ciba-Geigy's highly profitable antiarthritis drugs. "What I have to tell you," he said, "is that I now have friends in the enemy camp. How do you call such people? Moles? I have moles inside Ciba. They are ashamed of their own company. They are sending me copies of secret internal memos." (We never knew the identity of the moles; they were always referred to only as "It.")

In May 1983 Hansson wrote to us about the antiarthritis drugs Butazolidin and Tanderil (or Tandearil). "It," he said, had turned up some "terrible material." A month later, he told us that Ciba-Geigy was aware that some of its secrets were being leaked—"They know there are traitors." He wrote to von Planta, urging him to stop the sale of the two products, claiming they were too toxic and no longer needed, especially since safer substitutes had been developed. His plea was rejected.

Hansson and the Press

Failing to change the company's position, Hansson turned to his constant allies, the Scandinavian and the British press. In late November and early December, the *Sunday Times* in London, *Dagens Nyheter* in Stockholm, and other newspapers disclosed a confidential Ciba-Geigy memo showing that company scientists themselves were concerned about the safety of the arthritis drugs. "In the presence of many newer, equally effective NSAIDs [nonsteroidal anti-inflammatory drugs] now available on the market, with comparatively less toxicity, it is reasonable and necessary that the risk and benefit for Butazolidin and Tanderil should be carefully reassessed." The Ciba-Geigy experts questioned whether "promotion of the drugs was justified for arthritis." More alarming, the "liberated documents" revealed, Ciba-Geigy was aware of 1,182 deaths caused by the two drugs up to 1982, but less than 200 of these had been reported to official drug regulatory agencies. "These drugs should be taken off the market immediately," Hansson told a Swedish reporter. "Warning voices have been raised, but have been effectively quelled by Ciba-Geigy's marketing strategy."

Early in 1984, he confided to us that he was seriously ill with cancer. An operation had not been successful, and he was scheduled to undergo radiation and chemotherapy. In late September he felt he was well enough to attend a meeting of the Swedish branch of Health Action International in Lund. Just before the meeting began, he dropped what he described as "a few little bombs." He talked to reporters about Enterovioform and Ciba-Geigy's stubborn refusal to bring a speedy end to its sale. Then he talked about the company's cover-up of the Butazolidin and Tanderil deaths and its refusal to halt their marketing. For good measure, he dropped "a new little bomb"—Ciba-Geigy had just introduced a remarkable new antiarthritis agent, Voltaren, and had disclosed its dangers in Germany and Great Britain but apparently failed to do so in Sweden. At the same time, the Swedish press reopened another Ciba-Geigy scandal, the affair of the potent pesticide Galecron.

In 1976 the company had tested Galecron in Egypt. "They hired five or six children, asked them to stand in a field, and an airplane sprayed them with Galecron," he told us. "Then they collected the urine and analyzed how much was absorbed, and so forth. The kids got nauseated and did not feel good. The story came out a few years later. It made a big scandal. It was an old story, but now it had its second life here in Sweden. Believe me, I had nothing to do with this secondcoming, but it happened at just the crucial time."

Threat of a Boycott

The Swedish papers used large headlines, and they editorialized about a possible worldwide boycott against Ciba-Geigy, perhaps one like the boycott used a few years earlier against Nestlé for the promotion of its infant formula in developing countries. But this journalistic onslaught occurred not only in Sweden: it spread over Europe, notably to Switzerland and to Swiss television, and it caused what "It" described to Hansson as "total paranoid panic" in Ciba-Geigy.

Company officials in Basel took the boycott threat with utmost seriousness.[30] They had seen their neighbors at Nestlé virtually brought to their knees by the infant-formula campaign. They were aware that many of the same consumer activists who had run the Nestlé boycott were now closely associated with Hansson. Ciba-Geigy was aware, too, that serious trouble was also brewing in the World Health Organization, where some activists were calling for an international WHO drug-marketing code to regulate all drug promotion, labeling, and advertising. Hansson broke with many of his activist friends on this matter of a code, feeling strongly—as we felt—that in the short run it might be a benefit for the developing nations of the Third World, but in the long run would be an unmitigated disaster.

One consultant, Ulrich Moebius, publisher of the German medical newsletter *Arzneimittel-Telegramm*, proposed a simple solution to Ciba-Geigy's problems: "The consumer people—the International Organization of Consumers Unions—will meet this December in Bangkok. It is then that a boycott may be voted. If you want to avoid trouble, you must talk to Hansson first. I can talk to him and try to arrange things."[31]

Hansson was willing to meet with Ciba-Geigy—but only at the top level, with the chairman of the board. Louis von Planta, as chairman of the board, had been blamed for many of the costly blunders that had marred the Enterovioform controversy. But he had also shown courage and compassion in refusing to sanction time-consuming appeals and other legal delays and in promptly paying the damages in the suits lost in Japan.[32] On the urging of Klaus von Grebmer, head of Ciba-Geigy's public affairs division, and Walter Wenger, a von Planta aide, von Planta agreed to meet with Hansson.

The Ciba-Geigy Meetings

To prepare and plan for such a confrontation, Moebius and von Grebmer flew to Göteborg on November 11, 1984, and met with Hansson at the airport restaurant. Hansson had not yet worked out all the matters to be discussed. He related later that he told von Grebmer that in his opinion the people in the Ciba-Geigy medical department were professional liars and had been arrogant toward consumers for twenty years. He said that he believed that top management was not informed of what was going on in the medical department. The only thing the consumerists needed and insisted on from the company, he said, was correct information about its drugs.

Von Grebmer assured Hansson that Ciba really wanted to work in the public interest and would take very seriously the points raised. An effort should be made to find a common ground for future constructive dialogue. Hansson assured von Grebmer that he had "no intention of hitting Ciba over the head." But, he emphasized, there was a serious danger that there would be a Ciba-Geigy boycott voted at the IOCU congress in Bangkok. "The Japanese," Hansson said, "are the most aggressive in the consumer movement now, and they are mad like hell at Ciba." He recommended that Ciba-Geigy provide complete information on all its drugs, especially the antiarthritic drugs Butazolidin and Tanderil. He cited the speedy withdrawal of the company's clioquinol products as being the main issue. Back in Basel, von Grebmer reported to von Planta, Alfred Bodmer, chief executive officer, and Walter Wenger and told them it had been a mistake not to have had an exchange of views with Hansson in years past.

A second agenda meeting was held on November 17 in London. Moebius, von Grebmer, and Wenger participated. Hansson offered to act as an unpaid consultant in the field. His first advice to Ciba-Geigy was to withdraw its clioquinol products immediately if they wanted peace and reconciliation with Japan and the consumer front. He also explained the absolute necessity for the head of the company, Dr. von Planta, himself, to go to Japan, meet the SMON patients, and make a personal apology for himself and his company. Japanese culture required such an apology because Ciba-Geigy and its drug Enterovioform had caused one of the biggest drug disasters in medical history.

Hansson then laid out his other points. Tanderil should be removed from the world market completely, and the indications for Butazolidin should be radically limited. Ciba-Geigy should provide more fair compensation to the SMON victims outside Japan, and it should make a concerted effort to locate all such patients. It should provide an efficient channel whereby consumer complaints could reach top management. (Hansson was then unaware that Ciba-Geigy had instituted such a program only a few months before.) From its profits on Enterovioform—which he called "criminal profits"—Ciba-Geigy should establish some kind of foundation to support and enhance consumer protection. Wenger expressed his gratitude for the meeting and his regret that such a meeting had not taken place years before.

Until then, Hansson did not know that one of his demands was already being met in Basel. The pharmaceutical division at Ciba-Geigy had already reported to von Planta that, if he insisted, the company could speed up the withdrawal of Enterovioform. "I am a practical man," he said. "I dislike needless controversy. If the pharmaceutical people are now willing to do away with a point which has become a critical point, a source of criticism, why not do it and do away with criticism."[33]

Hansson's meeting with von Planta was scheduled for November 20 in either Geneva or Stockholm. Because Hansson was too ill to travel, the meeting took place on November 22 at Göteborg's Europa Hotel and included von Grebmer and Wenger from Basel and Moebius from Berlin. Von Planta announced that the company had found it possible to move more quickly in ending the production and marketing of Enterovioform and would withdraw it in about four months. The drug would not be sold anywhere by Ciba-Geigy after March 31, 1985, he said. Hansson was gratified.

Other issues from the London meeting were handled quickly when von Planta guaranteed that he would reinvestigate the matter of more equitable payment to SMON patients in Sweden and other countries and make whatever adjustments seemed indicated. Hansson then asked to meet with von Planta alone. He first explained why von Planta, as chairman of the board, must go to Japan and make personal apologies to the Japanese patients. Von Planta said that he was willing to do whatever the heads of Takeda and Tanabe had done, and that to his knowledge they had not apologized. When Hansson told him that the company in Japan had misinformed him and that there had been apologies, one in the courtroom, one during a sit-in in the Takeda company, von Planta agreed to look into the matter further and to do whatever the other heads had done.

Agreement on two issues proved to be impossible. On the matter of using some of the Enterovioform profits (Hansson suggested 100 million Swiss francs) to establish a foundation that would sponsor "projects that are important for human health and welfare," von Planta listened, took some notes, and commented that such a foundation might be part of the company's new consumer protection policy, but that this would require careful consideration.

Then Hansson called for amnesty for whichever of his moles might be at work. Swiss law had long held that leaking industrial secrets was almost as serious an offense as leaking military secrets. Hansson argued that medical information was not the same as industrial information, and that publication of data on drug toxicity and adverse side effects could not conceivably threaten Switzerland's security. Von Planta said he felt powerless to correct the situation but would examine the problem further. At the end of the three-hour session, the two men agreed that they had held not a confrontation but a conversation. The company executive promised to have more answers within a week. Hansson urged a reply by December 2, to give him time to influence any call for a boycott at Bangkok at the IOCU congress a week later.

On November 30 Wenger, von Grebmer, and Moebius brought disappointing news to Göteborg. Ciba-Geigy had not found any way to support a foundation, although it would give 10 million Swiss francs (about $4 million) to WHO to support the Oral Rehydration Project to combat diarrhea in Third World countries. And the company continued to balk at removing its Butazolidin and Tanderil products from the market, claiming that the decision should be made by the drug regulatory agencies in each country. And there appeared to be no way in which Hansson could protect his moles.

Short of temper, Hansson wired von Planta, "This terminates our dialogue." "It was my impression," von Planta replied, "that mutual understanding had on the major issues been established and agreement reached on most of these issues. It would be a great disappointment to now learn from you that the dialogue has already come to an end." He asked for further consultation. Hansson was moved. "I was impressed by your civil courage concerning the possible meeting with the Japanese SMON victims," he wrote. "Accordingly, in the hope that your difficulties to convince your staff about the new policy [are] just a matter of time, I have advised my friends in the consumer movement to show patience."[34]

The IOCU congress in Bangkok opened on December 9. No Ciba-Geigy boycott was voted. Six days earlier, the disastrous leak of deadly methyl isocyanate gas had occurred at the Bhopal, India, plant of Union Carbide, killing more than 2,000 and injuring 50,000, and made headlines around the world. For at least a time, the IOCU delegates were more interested in Union Carbide than in Ciba-Geigy.

In mid-December we (M.S. and M.L.) visited Hansson in Göteborg. During the week before Christmas several hours each day were devoted to our taping his detailed account of his battles with Ciba-Geigy. In particular, he described his current campaign against Ciba-Geigy's arthritis drugs and asked for our help. A meeting had been arranged between some of the company's top experts and knowledgeable consumer experts and rheumatologists. Although Hansson had done much of the work of organization, he was not well enough to participate. He asked us to represent the United States and, since he could not do so, to represent Japan also, who, he said, trusted us.

The Butazone Confrontation

Attending the meeting in London on February 6, 1985, were about a dozen representatives of Ciba-Geigy, headed by Walter von Wartburg and Klaus von Grebmer, perhaps a dozen representatives of consumer groups, and the press. The consumerists demanded that Tanderil be taken off the market, and that the uses of Butazolidin—once including the treatment of almost every variety of arthritis and rheumatic disease—should be limited to such conditions as acute episodes of gout and the treatment of ankylosing spondylitis, or "stiff spine." "Safer alternatives for both drugs have existed for years," it was claimed. "For all except a very few patients, they have outlived their usefulness. It's time to give them a decent burial."

The Ciba-Geigy delegation paid careful attention to the presentations. They did not scoff or argue or offer any defense, such as "the company knows best." Von Wartburg promised that his group would study the situation and give an answer in a few weeks.

Early in April von Grebmer and von Wartburg visited us in California with the news that Ciba-Geigy had decided to remove Tanderil from the market and to drastically minimize the indications for Butazolidin. For three days, while we taped the discussion, they told of their dealings with Olle Hansson. Their account differed only in minor details from Hansson's. On the second day they asked us to attempt to negotiate a solution to Ciba-Geigy's unhappy situation in Japan. They felt that we were trusted by Hansson and by the Japanese, and they knew, they said, that we had many friends in drug research. Our friends—Hansson, Andrew Herxheimer in London, Anwar Fazal at IOCU in Malaysia, Philip Lee, and the others—said we had no choice. At this very time a letter arrived unexpectedly from Hiroshi Izumi in Tokyo also asking us to undertake negotiations.

We reached Hansson in his hospital room in Sweden on May 19 and told him we had agreed to undertake the negotiations. We would charge Ciba-Geigy and the Japanese for any necessary transportation and business expenses, but we would take no salary, consultation fee, or any other compensation. Hansson expressed his gratitude. He died the following week; he was 49 years old.

Beginning in June 1985 and continuing for the next year or so, the two of us seemed to be on a continuing commute between California, Tokyo, Basel, and Penang, Malaysia, the headquarters of Anwar Fazal, then the international head of the International Organization of Consumers Unions, along with meetings in New York, Washington, London, Amsterdam, Oslo, Jakarta, Singapore, and Anchorage, Alaska, to confer with various Ciba-Geigy officials or consumerist leaders. In addition, Ciba-Geigy people and consumerists visited us in California in a steady stream.

In our first meetings in Basel, Penang, and Tokyo, we began to realize the true nature of our assignment. At Basel, we found that some of the senior Ciba officials felt that, in his meetings with Olle Hansson, Louis von Planta had offered to give away too much. According to Hansson, von Planta had promised without any qualifications to apologize to the SMON victims, as Japanese tradition dictated. According to the Ciba-Geigy people, von Planta promised to do only whatever the heads of the Japanese companies—notably Tanabe and Takeda—had done. And, the Swiss assured us, the presidents of those companies never did apologize.[35] The Ciba-Geigy people were stunned when we told them that we had the text of the formal apology by Matsubara of Tanabe and that two of our lawyer friends heard the informal apology by Konishi of Takeda.

Consumer activists thought that Hansson had not demanded enough. Some of them wanted to see von Planta publicly humiliated. One insisted that the Ciba-Geigy board chairman not only should apologize, he should apologize publicly before hundreds of SMON victims and their representatives, with full coverage by newspapers, radio, and television, and should be required to give a press conference. We balked. Hansson and von Planta had reached substantial agreement on what Ciba-Geigy should yield and what the consumerists should demand. We felt that the company should not be pressed to make further concessions, nor should it be allowed to escape with fewer.

Problems with Mr. Knop

In Tokyo we devoted two weeks to negotiations. We drafted texts of the proposed apology to be delivered by von Planta and of the proposed response to be given by Hiroshi Izumi. We cleared these with both sides, by telephone and telex. By early July we all felt that we were close to agreement and were contemplating an early September date for the ceremony. At this point Ciba-Geigy asked us to meet with Dutch-born Henk Knop, former president and then chairman of the board of Ciba-Geigy (Japan). Knop had headed the Japanese subsidiary during the court battles over SMON and Enterovioform, and he took the court decisions as a personal affront. He said that no apology was needed. We reminded him that von Planta had agreed to apologize. He said that the commitment was not necessary; the guilt of clioquinol was never established.

What about the mountains of scientific evidence proving beyond question the toxicity of clioquinol? What about the court decisions that, in Japan alone, had brought settlements of some 194 billion yen ($776 million)? What about the unchallenged record of Ciba-Geigy's deceit, lies, and clumsy attempts at cover-up, and its insistence on continuing Third World clioquinol sales until 1985? Knop pooh-poohed such comments. And what about the apologies made by the heads of Tanabe and Takeda? Knop insisted that neither had ever apologized. Izumi and the other SMON leaders expressed astonishment at Knop's views. Even some of the top people in Basel seemed dismayed. We felt that we could make no further progress and returned to California.

During the next four months there was a constant interchange of letters, telex messages, and telephone calls between us and Basel, Tokyo, and Penang. Von Grebmer and von Wartburg came to see us several times. We went to Switzerland in January 1986. They urged us to return to Tokyo and renew the negotiations.

It seemed time for us to talk to Dr. von Planta. He telephoned us in February and reconfirmed what he said to Hansson in Göteborg—that Ciba-Geigy would follow any steps undertaken by the Japanese companies Takeda and Tanabe. He made a straightforward pledge, with no qualifications, to do what the others did as soon as he received confirmation of that. We agreed to exchange recording tapes and typed transcripts of the telephone calls to avoid misunderstandings. By the end of that month we were assured by Basel that "beyond any question" Matsubara of Tanabe had made a formal apology. Konishi of Takeda admitted that he had apologized informally, but he had apologized.

Ciba-Geigy called for another round of meetings in mid-March. On our way to Japan we met with von Grebmer in Honolulu. He presented us with new complications, most of them evidently originating in Ciba-Geigy's Japanese affiliate. He suggested that if Mr. Izumi would go to Basel, perhaps Dr. von Planta could apologize to him there. Or Dr. von Planta might go to Tokyo and make his apology—without the presence of the press. Both suggestions were unacceptable.

In Tokyo we met with Hiroshi Izumi, who was deeply offended by Ciba-Geigy's proposals. We met also with Henk Knop, who called the affair a finished business. Later, von Planta invited us to meet with him, Walter Wenger, and Klaus von Grebmer at Ciba-Geigy's corporate headquarters at Ardsley, New York. We accepted, but only if Henk Knop would participate and voice his opinions openly. Von Planta finally agreed that the heads of Takeda and Tanabe had actually apologized to the SMON victims. We agreed on November 10 for the ceremony, or as soon thereafter as Mr. Izumi could make arrangements, and discussed time and place, size and nature of the audience, and media coverage.

When we telephoned to Hiroshi Izumi the news of Ciba-Geigy's changed attitude, to our dismay Izumi outlined new preconditions and made new demands, most of which Ciba-Geigy would not accept. After two weeks of cautious discussions, some of Izumi's colleagues induced him to withdraw his new demands.

Again we seemed to be close to success. Then Walter Wenger telephoned in October to say that Ciba-Geigy could not proceed with the ceremony because the other companies in Japan were opposed to it. The company was also having great problems with the Ministry of Health and Welfare. We found that the ministry had no objections to the proposed apology. Wenger admitted to us that Ciba-Geigy officials had not talked to people in the ministry but had talked to a trusted consultant who had been close to the ministry. He had, he said, a letter from the consultant. But he would neither send us a copy of the letter nor give us the name of the consultant.

Many of the details of Hansson's campaign against the drug company were included in his *Inside Ciba-Geigy*, edited by a committee of his colleagues and published in 1989.[36] It was a bitter, detailed indictment of the company's operations, but unfortunately did not include any mention of the respect which had developed between Hansson and von Planta. It also included in considerable detail an account of our efforts to bring agreement between the company and the SMON group.

Failed Mission, But—

At the end, it appeared that our efforts—and an important part of Olle Hansson's work—had come to nothing. After more than eighteen months of nerve-racking negotiations, exhausting travel, and long days and nights of walking-on-eggs mediation, we had been unable to find an acceptable solution. Ciba-Geigy had not achieved the peace it sought, and it remained a tempting target for vengeful consumer action. Its promises appeared to be worth very little. Certainly, the reputation of its Japanese affiliate remained soiled and tarnished. The Japanese SMON victims and their representatives did not get the full apology to which they had long felt entitled. Both sides had to share in the responsibility for the failure.

Yet that was not the whole story. In Basel, although Ciba-Geigy had made a final judgment, which was ridiculed by consumerists, a few courageous company officials had demonstrated that they could talk openly and effectively with consumers, not merely confront them. Further, at least some consumer leaders had found that they could talk quietly and usefully with drug industry representatives. They had learned that it was more productive to seek to improve the industry rather than to punish or humiliate it. Here and there, the reasons for mutual fear and distrust were beginning to crumble.

Chapter 12

THE ESSENTIAL ROLE OF GOVERNMENT

In practically every country in the world, industrialized or developing, it has apparently been agreed that, at different times, probably for different reasons, and certainly to different degrees, the use of drugs is too important to be entrusted to physicians, pharmacists, or the drug industry. Particularly irritating to physicians, pharmacists, and industry officials has been the discovery that the regulation of drugs in most nations has been taken over by government officials—and, most galling, by government *bureaucrats* (those who are appointed, not elected, to their posts). The fact that some drug regulatory officials may be physicians or pharmacists, and may be among the most knowledgeable drug experts in a country, has not protected them from constant verbal abuse.

Regulation in the United States

In most industrialized nations, the drug regulatory system was developed over periods of many decades, or even a century or two. In the United States, the important moves have included the following three.

Passage of the Pure Food and Drugs Act in 1906. Designed more to control the promotion and marketing of bad foods than to affect bad drugs, the Pure Food and Drugs Act came after newspaper and magazine exposés and the publication of Upton Sinclair's *The Jungle*, which disclosed the appalling unsanitary conditions in the Chicago stockyards.[1]

Passage of the 1938 Amendment. In 1937 the fame of sulfanilamide had spread around the world, and tablets by the millions were being used each year. An ingenious Tennessee-based firm decided to put the remarkable antibacterial on the market in liquid form, dissolved in di-ethylene glycol. It was introduced under the name Elixir Sulfanilamide. In the body, di-ethylene glycol—sometimes known as antifreeze—destroys the kidneys. Elixir Sulfanilamide destroyed the kidneys and killed more than a hundred people, most of them children. (The chemist who devised the concoction soon committed suicide.) Congress acted quickly and enacted the 1938 Food, Drug, and Cosmetic Act. This legislation required the manufacturer of any new drug to present convincing evidence to the Food and Drug Administration that the product was relatively safe for use *before* it was put on the market.[2]

Thalidomide and passage of the Kefauver-Harris Amendment in 1962. Introduced in 1958 by a German firm, thalidomide won quick favor as an extraordinarily safe sedative. With the exception of only a very few countries—notably France and the United States—it was quickly accepted everywhere. Then, starting in Germany in 1959, there came the first reports of children born with phocomelia, a strange deformity marked by seal-like flippers in place of arms and legs. In 1961 a German pediatrician found that at least 50 percent of the mothers had taken thalidomide during their pregnancies. Before the product could be removed from the market, an estimated 10,000 phocomelia-deformed babies had been born in at least twenty different countries. In the United States, where the drug had never been approved but was available in some cases as physician samples, the tragedy induced Congress to pass the controversial 1962 Kefauver-Harris Amendment. This tightened safety requirements and also required the manufacturers to provide FDA with evidence that the drug was both safe and effective for its intended clinical purpose.[3] This proof-of-efficacy requirement would drastically increase the time and cost of getting FDA approval for a new drug; it would delay, often by many years, the time at which a drug company could market a new product and begin to recoup on its investment. The situation would assuredly outrage elements of the powerful drug industry and their supporters.

The Dreadful Drug Lag

The period between 1938 and 1962, especially in the United States, was marked by a flood of new drugs, especially new antibiotics, new tranquilizers and other psychoactive agents, and many combination products that today are considered to be irrational. It was a time that brought great satisfaction to drug companies and their stockholders. But after 1962, company spokesmen pointed out, there was a dramatic decrease in the number of new pharmaceutical products introduced each year. The result came to be known as the drug lag. In one case after another, it was found, a new drug was approved for use in Great Britain, West Germany, Italy, Switzerland, Canada, Australia, or the Scandinavian countries before it reached the American market. The inference was clear: American patients were being prevented by their government from gaining access to important new drugs; the cause was clearly the 1962 Kefauver legislation, which should therefore be repealed.

The argument, which—fueled by the drug industry—raged for a quarter of a century, was largely nonsense. The dramatic increase in new products introduced in the period 1938–1962 was matched by a slight improvement in medical care, but the improvement was scarcely dramatic. The falloff in the introduction of new drugs did not begin *after* enactment of the 1962 legislation: it was already evident in the late 1950s.[4]

One of the most memorable disputes during those years involved an early beta-blocker, propranolol, introduced by Wyeth-Ayerst under the brand name Inderal. It was approved relatively quickly in the United States for the treatment of cardiac arrhythmias, but FDA held up its approval for the control of two other conditions—angina pectoris and hypertension—for about six years. In an emotional denunciation, one European drug industry spokesman accordingly assailed FDA for being responsible for killing 250,000 Americans. He spoke of the "mass murder activities of regulatory authorities" and claimed that the FDA delay had lasted for eleven years.[5]

As Graham Dukes, head of drug studies in WHO's office for Europe in Copenhagen, has pointed out in his authoritative *The Effects of Drug Regulation*, the charges leveled against FDA for its propranolol actions were ridiculous. Even though it was approved at first only for the treatment of arrhythmias, the drug was freely available in the United States, and American physicians were legally allowed to prescribe it for any condition in which they thought it might benefit the patient. Many of them, in fact, *did* prescribe it for angina and high blood pressure. Furthermore, even without propranolol, American physicians had available to them alternative forms of medication "with comparable life-saving potential." There had been no 250,000 preventable deaths; there had been no FDA mass-murder. But the accusation of FDA had become part of the literature, and—even though it had been totally debunked—it was still being cited as gospel.[6]

Careful studies in the United States and Western Europe have demonstrated that there is a drug lag of one variety or degree in essentially every industrialized nation. In some instances, for example, a new drug may be marketed in Sweden or the Netherlands before it becomes available to Americans. In others, it may be introduced in the United States before it appears in Sweden or Holland. "Although a 'drug lag' can be demonstrated," it has been noted, "it varies from drug to drug and country to country, and many factors other than drug regulatory decisions appear to affect it. . . . The central question which has been raised with respect to drug lag is therefore whether or not a 'drug lag' created by regulatory controls actually benefits or harms the public health. No agreement has been reached on this issue."[7]

Part of the problem lies in the fact that there is no simple way to weigh the negative effect of a regulatory provision that delays the approval of a good drug against the positive effect of a provision that delays or prevents the approval of a bad drug. In any case, Dukes has concluded, "there is no conclusive evidence of a deleterious effect on the flow of innovative products."[8] In many if not most industrialized countries, the furious debate over the "drug lag" has been largely defused by new regulations whereby the consideration of *important* new drugs can be placed on a fast-track schedule. Such products, possibly of major or lifesaving importance, are given consideration many months or even years ahead of time. Dukes has stated:

It is not generally true that regulatory agencies have a large backlog of applications relating to products representing *major therapeutic advances*. Formally or informally, the agencies the records of which have so far been amenable to study seem to be able to ensure that, even where there is an accumulation of unfinished work, the (apparently very few) products which represent real breakthroughs will be dealt with promptly and efficiently.[9]

In some developed nations, additional regulatory controls have been introduced. Some countries require that certain products be used only on hospitalized patients or prescribed only by certain classes of physicians. In a number of developed countries, notably those in Scandinavia, a new product cannot gain approval unless it can be shown to be safer, more effective, or less costly than older products, or otherwise "medically needed." Increasing consideration is being given to required postmarketing surveillance.[10]

No matter how tight these new regulations have become, and no matter how irritating they may have been to drug companies, they have not been tight enough to keep all excessively dangerous products off the market.[11]

- In 1980 the antihypertensive drug Selacryn was withdrawn by SmithKline & French after significant liver toxicity became apparent.
- In 1982 Eli Lilly withdrew the anti-inflammatory agent Oraflex, but not until the drug had been implicated in nearly 100 deaths. Criminal charges were brought successfully against Eli Lilly executives for withholding from FDA damaging information on this drug.
- In 1983 Johnson and Johnson withdrew Zomax, a nonsteroidal anti-inflammatory agent, after five fatal anaphylactoid reactions occurred in patients who had used the drug.
- In 1983 Merck Sharp & Dohme withdrew Osmosin, another antiarthritis medication, which had been associated with twelve deaths.

In such nations as Great Britain, to which FDA critics often pointed as examples of how swiftly, informally, and pleasantly the drug approval process could be conducted, the record of withdrawals was even worse. More products had to be withdrawn from the British market because of previously unsuspected dangerous or lethal side effects.[12]

Regulation by Persuasion

Key individuals have appeared occasionally and, at least for a time, have done more to affect drug regulation by their personality, their powers of persuasion, and their willingness to do battle than all the laws and regulations on the books. Americans were exposed to such a person when a longtime government employee, George Larrick, retired as FDA commissioner in January 1966 and was succeeded by James Goddard. During the Larrick regime, which had started in 1954, FDA had reputedly worked with at least modest success and practically no fanfare. Only when Senator Estes Kefauver began his investigations was it seriously charged that, at least under Larrick's administration, FDA had worked without fanfare because it had not been doing much work at all—certainly in the case of drugs—and that the regulators had become entirely too friendly with the industry to be regulated.[13]

Soon after James Goddard, a career Public Health Service physician, succeeded Larrick, he addressed a Pharmaceutical Manufacturers Association convention and told the drug company leaders that his agency had been investigating complaints involving nearly one-third of the PMA members. "Some advertising cases have been quite abusive of regulations," he said. "They have trumpeted results of favorable research and have not mentioned unfavorable research; they have puffed up what was insignificant clinical evidence; they have substituted emotional appeals for scientific ones." He denounced the drug industry as suffering from a long-standing case of irresponsibility. He called some companies to task for their slovenly research and misleading promotion.

Under Goddard's leadership, FDA installed the new Investigational New Drug (IND) and New Drug Approval (NDA) programs. The use of "Dear Doctor" letters was intensified. In this approach, a company found to be making false, misleading, or unsupportable claims would be obliged either to face a costly seizure and court case or to amend its advertising claims and send a letter to that effect to every practicing physician in the United States. Goddard told industry leaders:

Now, I will admit that government employees do not have a corner on all wisdom. I will admit that there are grey areas in the IND situation. But the conscious withholding of unfavorable animal or clinical data is not a grey-area matter.

The deliberate choice of clinical investigators known to be more concerned about industry friendships than in developing good data is not a grey-area matter.

The planting in journals of articles that begin to commercialize what's still an investigational new drug is not a grey-area matter.

These actions run counter to the law and the ethics governing the drug industry.[14]

In the memory of most of his audience, it was the first time in decades that anyone had used the words "ethics" and "drug industry" in the same sentence.

Goddard was soon charged with instituting new procedures that were far too complex, too time-consuming, and too expensive. "What they really were objecting to," the commissioner said, "was that it made them do their homework a little more carefully." He himself was vilified for pointing out the dangers of LSD and other potent psychedelic drugs, for declaring that marijuana was far less dangerous to society than alcohol, and for suggesting that the current laws against marijuana use were too harsh and impractical.

Within a few months after Goddard embarked on this multifaceted campaign, there were the first demands that John Gardner, then secretary of Health, Education, and Welfare, should fire him. Some of these demands came from industry leaders. Some came from members of Congress who were furious that anyone would say anything good about marijuana or anything bad about alcohol. Month after month, these demands became more insistent, but the secretary stood behind Goddard. "I'd rather have a man I have to slow down once in a while," he said, "than a man I have to wake up."[15] Essentially all of the programs that Goddard rammed into existence—programs which some industry spokesmen declared the industry could not possibly survive— remain very much alive. The industry likewise survived and remains prosperous.

An equally impressive program was instituted even earlier in Latin America. In the late 1940s or early 1950s, we began hearing about a remarkable drug regulatory program in Venezuela, which was said to be the best in Latin America and could serve as a model for all Latin American countries. The Venezuelan program was said to be directed by a onetime German physician, Siegbert Holz, who ran it with ruthless Prussian efficiency. He was described variously as a despot, a tyrant, and a dictator. Depending on which account one wanted to believe, he was either Nazi-like or an ex-Nazi.

In 1987, when two of us (M.L. and M.S.) were in Caracas to interview Venezuelan drug officials, physicians, pharmacologists, and pharmacists, we asked about Dr. Holz and were advised that Holz and his wife were living in retirement in Caracas.

"I think we should call on him," M.L. said. "Here, I've found his telephone number in the directory."

"No way," M.S. replied. "I'm not going to waste any time with some old Nazi."

M.L. insisted. We called and reached Frau Holz. Frau Holz, she said, did not have English, but she did speak both Spanish and German.

"*You* speak German," we said to M.L. "*You* do this."

M.L. put on her smoothest, most sugary approach. She addressed Frau Holz as *Gnädige Frau*, and practically groveled. At the end, she said, "Well, we're not welcome, but they will see us. But she says we must bring our papers to prove that we are who we say we are."

We discussed the situation with our friend Honorio Silva, president of the Venezuelan Pharmacology Society. "I know where the Holzes live," he said. "I'll drive you there." What happens next deserves telling.

Later that afternoon, we arrived at the Holz home. We were equipped with passports and identity cards. We were ushered into a sitting room and offered glasses of lukewarm water. Ice was not needed; the atmosphere was chilly enough without it. M.L. and Elly Holz engaged in some German conversation. Siegbert Holz said nothing but kept staring at me. At length, he disappeared from the room and returned in a few minutes with a pile of books wrapped in a dusty cloth. From the pile, he extracted one and put it on the table.

"Do you recognize this?" he asked—in quite acceptable English.

"Of course. That's *Drogas Mágicas*. It's the first Spanish translation of my *Magic in a Bottle*. It was published, I think, in 1942 or 1943. I can't tell you much about it. But, if you like, I can tell you what I said in the foreword about my young daughter."

"You are *that* Silverman?"

"Naturally."

"*Lieber Gott!*" he declared. "We thought you might be Nazi agents."

"But when you talked to me by telephone earlier today," Elly Holz told M.L., "your German was so perfect that I was positive you must be one of the many Nazis who are still operating in South America."

"That is so easy to explain!" M.L. told her. "When I was growing up, I was living in Nazi-occupied Holland. We all had to learn German. But I was part of the Dutch underground, and I had to learn to speak perfect German."

"But you?" we said. "We were told that you two are Nazi refugees."

The Holzes exploded in laughter. *"Nazi* refugees? We were *Jewish* refugees!"

Out went the lukewarm water. In came the coffee, the tea, the beer, the wine, the *schnapps*, the cognac, the plates of cookies and sandwiches. In came the friends, the neighbors, the colleagues, even Raul Cardona, the current head of Venezuela's FDA. There was much talk and laughter and handshaking and embracing. It was one hell of a memorable afternoon.

When Hitler came to power, Siegbert and Elly—they had not yet married—were fellow medical students at the University of Berlin. They fled to Italy, where they completed their medical studies, earned their doctor's degrees, did get married, and emigrated to Venezuela, where Siegbert's parents had moved even earlier.[16] When the young Holzes arrived in Venezuela in 1939, they both got jobs in a small port city. Siegbert worked part-time in a poorly paid government job and part-time trying to set up his own medical practice. In 1945 they moved to the capital city of Caracas. Siegbert started teaching and doing research in pharmacology at the University of Caracas. "This was truly pioneering work," he told us. "At that time, there was no pharmacology in Caracas." He also began to work in the Ministry of Health, becoming increasingly involved in drug regulation.

"The situation was not very good," he recalled. "Of course, there must be communications between the drug industry and government. Without good communications, there will be little progress. But in the 1940s, here in Venezuela, industry and government were very close— too close—and the communications were all in one direction. The industry seemed to be doing all the talking and the government did all the listening."

Slowly, quietly, but effectively, Holz set up what was called a wall between industry and government. Soon industry leaders found that the government was no longer to be dominated, and government officials no longer had to take orders from industry leaders and their friends in politically powerful families. In those early years, Holz was bitterly attacked by the pharmaceutical industry. He was assailed for demanding that the industry must produce scientific evidence that their products were safe and effective. If such proof was not forthcoming, they learned, the products were simply not approved for marketing in Venezuela. Holz was constantly attacked and denounced. "But there was one thing about the man," an industry official explained to us. "He was one very tough person, but he was fair. Furthermore, he saw to it that while drug disasters occurred in other countries, they did not happen in Venezuela."

Siegbert and Elly, who had served alongside him as a key pharmacological adviser, retired in 1981. The policies they had established, however, did not change. The officials who succeeded them were the young pharmacologists they had trained and whom the Holzes view as their own children. Throughout Venezuela the Holzes are regarded with universal respect and admiration. "In this job," Siegbert Holz emphasized to us, "a knowledge of pharmacology is important. But at least as important is an understanding of ethics—of what is ethically right and what is ethically wrong—and a desire to help people."

The drug regulatory system in Venezuela is considered to be good—perhaps the best in Latin America—but it is not accepted as perfect. One problem involves price controls on drugs. As other countries have learned, price controls if too rigid may have an unintended effect. The control system in Venezuela, for example, was set up to make drugs inexpensive and easily accessible to the public, but the prices were put so low that the situation proved irresistible to smugglers. Low-cost Venezuelan products were smuggled—usually by the "mule people," mostly women wearing voluminous skirts ideally suited for concealing packages of drugs—across the border to adjoining Colombia, where drug prices were uncontrolled. As a result, Venezuela had its low drug prices but it also had drug shortages.[17]

Another problem lies in the fact that Venezuela, like many other Third World countries, does not recognize drug patents. A representative of a Swiss firm explained it to us: "If a new product is proposed for registration by a multinational company, the authorities may hold up approval until a domestic company is prepared to make an imitation. In some cases, a new drug is actually introduced first by the imitator, then later by the innovator."

The Nairobi Nonconfrontation

On a proposal by the Scandinavian countries, the so-called Nordic Bloc, WHO agreed to hold a special conference of experts on making the use of drugs more rational throughout the world. Participants would be limited to selected representatives from consumer groups, the drug industry, and governmental agencies. The public and the press would be excluded. A five-day conference was set for November 1985 in Nairobi, the capital of Kenya. In many circles, it was agreed that the Nairobi meeting would be an Event, one of the major turning points in the development of drug regulation.

Many consumerists were overjoyed. They intended to work toward adoption of a WHO international drug-marketing code—perhaps along the lines of the WHO infant formula code—to replace whatever codes might have been previously established by individual nations. They wanted all countries to approve new drugs only on the basis of medical need—that is, only if the products could be shown to be safer, more effective, or less costly than older drugs. They wanted WHO to become an international drug regulatory body. To many consumer activists, their strategy in obtaining the infant formula code could be utilized with equal success in obtaining a drug code. Industry representatives were apprehensive. They, too, had learned from the battle over infant-formula marketing. And they, too, had an objective—prevent the consumerists from attaining *their* objectives.

Even before the Nairobi meeting began, it was only too evident that Halfdan Mahler and most other WHO leaders had little appetite for any WHO international drug-marketing code. It would be difficult if not impossible to win approval for any such program without virtually destroying WHO itself. The move would almost certainly be opposed by the United States. If the code were adopted over American objections, the United States would probably leave WHO, taking along its annual financial support, which represented about 25 percent of the total WHO budget. The United States had already reacted in this fashion when it withdrew from UNESCO in a protest against the scandalously irresponsible conduct of its leaders. It was probable that Japan and West Germany, which together accounted for nearly 20 percent of the WHO budget, would also withdraw. And there was a good possibility that other major drug-producing nations—France, Great Britain, Italy, Switzerland, and the Netherlands—would take similar action, slashing the WHO budget by another 10 percent or so. Furthermore, one WHO leader admitted, even if a code should be adopted, there was no conceivable way in which it could be enforced.

At the end of the conference, Halfdan Mahler, the director-general, issued an hour-long summation. He said, in part:

This Conference has had the effect of stimulating dialogue between experts with widely differing viewpoints and bringing home to you the importance of cooperation rather than confrontation. . . . The experts agreed that the prime responsibility for rational drug use rested with governments, which should nevertheless be able to call upon the support of WHO—taking a leadership role—and of all the other disciplines represented at the Conference. . . . It was generally felt that the pharmaceutical industry has major responsibility for complying with established norms [in drug promotion] and avoiding different standards in different countries. . . . There was unanimous agreement that there was no place for supranational drug regulation by WHO. . . . In conclusion, the experts were unanimous in expressing their satisfaction at the proceedings and at the hope that the Conference inspired for solving the world's drug problems through collaboration in a new spirit—the "spirit of Nairobi."[18]

At the end of the conference, it was agreed that the subject might be considered further at the next World Health Assembly, to be held in Geneva in May 1986.

The consumerists and industry spokesmen displayed somewhat different reactions. Virginia Beardshaw of HAI had this to say:

The Nairobi meeting is only one step on the long road to rational drug use worldwide. Nevertheless, the meeting's outcome represents a real success for the network. Through the new strategy, WHO's essential drugs concept will be supported by the legislative and regulatory guidelines which countries need to create effective drugs policies. Of course, we will have to work hard against entrenched opposition to ensure that they are the right guidelines. . . . We can be pleased.[19]

Gerald Mossinghoff, president of the Pharmaceutical Manufacturers Association in the United States, presented this view to his board of directors:

The international health activists got a lot less out of the conference than they had hoped for or anticipated.

They wanted an endorsement by the conference to take to the 1986 World Health Assembly of an International Marketing Code along the lines of the Infant Formula Code. They did not get that.

They wanted an endorsement by the conference of a so-called "Medical Needs" test—under which even safe and effective drugs would be kept off the market if they did not satisfy a bureaucratic judgment that they would be better than or cheaper than existing drugs. They did not get that.

They wanted WHO to assume the role of an international regulatory body. Dr. Mahler, the Director General of WHO, made it clear time and again throughout the conference that WHO should not become a supranational regulatory body and that all of the decisions in these matters are national decisions to be made by national governmental authorities. He did go further than we would have hoped in seeing a leadership role for WHO in advising government in these matters.[20]

In short, Mossinghoff told his industry colleagues, the industry had not been damaged in Nairobi as much as it feared.

In May 1986 the World Health Assembly met as scheduled in Geneva and considered, among other matters, the results of the Nairobi conference. Nothing of much significance happened in Geneva, either. One somewhat cynical British commentator observed, "The mountain had labored and brought forth a mouse. A very small mouse." There had been, however, one important development: the two sides had sat down together and talked.

Export of Unapproved Drugs

During most of the twentieth century, American drug companies watched with poorly concealed envy the way their European competitors raked in rich profits by selling to foreign countries products that had never been approved in their own countries, or even had been once approved and then forced off the market as being ineffective or unacceptably dangerous. Many of these sales were made to Third World nations that had drug regulatory systems unable either to judge which drugs could safely be imported or to control unacceptable promotion. In the United States, any such activity was banned. The exportation of drugs not approved by the Food and Drug Administration was forbidden by federal law.

In 1981 consumerists in the United States sought to curtail the dumping of unsafe products in Third World countries by at least notifying those countries of products that had been removed from the U.S. market or put under restrictions because of their lack of safety. On January 15, 1981, only a few days before he would leave office, President Jimmy Carter signed an executive order calling for notification of other nations when products were restricted or taken off the market because of undue risks and banning the export of those products that clearly represented a serious hazard to health or the environment. Carter said:

The central idea of the policy I am announcing today is full disclosure of information to our trading partners. A number of laws already require that we notify foreign countries when substances banned or significantly restricted for use at home are exported. My order improves these notifications. It will clarify for other countries the reasons why the substances in question are banned or strictly controlled in the United States and will help them judge for themselves whether they wish to allow the substances to enter and be used in their countries.[21]

Even before it was issued, the presidential directive was opposed by such members of President-elect Ronald Reagan's transfer team as Edwin Meese and David Stockman, who were already working with the White House staff. When the directive was signed, it was savagely attacked by the American drug industry. Lewis Engman, president of the Pharmaceutical Manufacturers Association, described it as an "eleventh hour act of arrogance, which attempts to thwart the express will of Congress [and] will have no effect on those it purports to protect. It can only result in the loss of American jobs." He said that the order would only ensure that sales go to foreign firms or to those U.S. firms who shift production overseas, and added, "It is quite appropriate to provide an importing country full information about any medicine it wishes to purchase; it is something else entirely to tell it what it can and can't buy." Engman was tampering with the truth. The Carter directive had little if anything to do with what drugs a foreign country could or could not buy. It was concerned with what drugs a U.S. firm could or could not export. On February 17, Reagan was securely installed in the White House. He rescinded the Carter directive.[22] He had begun to pay off his political debts to drug industry friends.

For American firms, there were three possible solutions to the problem of dumping unapproved drugs in the Third World. One, which would provide maximum protection to the life and welfare of people in other nations—notably people in developing countries—would be to induce European and Japanese pharmaceutical companies to follow the lead of the United States and decline to export unapproved drugs. It was quickly apparent that any such approach had no great appeal to the European and Japanese companies.

The second approach, which was actually adopted by many U.S. companies, was what we termed the South Slobovian method. It involved finding a suitable foreign country—it might be called South Slobovia—where the drug regulatory agency was already friendly to the United States, or could be induced in one way or another to become friendly, and would approve the product not approved by FDA. Once this was accomplished, the U.S. firm would build a factory in South Slobovia and proceed to ship its Slobovian-approved product all over the world. The method worked, but it was not very efficient, and it meant the loss of jobs that were filled by foreign workers.

The third option was an attempt to remove or radically weaken the American law. This approach would infuriate consumerists worldwide and cause the greatest blow to those who were concerned with the health and well-being of people in the developing nations. This was the road the American drug industry and its friends in Congress elected to travel.

Three members of Congress eventually became closely involved in this matter: Senator Orrin Hatch, Republican, of Utah, and Senator Edward Kennedy, Democrat, of Massachusetts, both on the Senate Labor and Human Resources Committee; and Congressman Henry Waxman, Democrat, of California, chairman of the House Subcommittee on Health. Over many years, we had worked closely with them, especially with Kennedy and Waxman and members of their staffs. They were accustomed to call on us frequently for advice, counsel, and background information from our own research. We had become good friends. Now, in the matter of exporting unapproved drugs, they wanted not only advice but also our blessings. We found we could not provide the latter.

In numerous telephone calls, confidential correspondence, meetings, and public testimony before the respective congressional committees, we gave our view that the amendments to the Food, Drug, and Cosmetic Act proposed in 1983 were badly flawed. They would undoubtedly improve the competitive position of the American drug companies, but they would also pose a serious risk to the health of people living in underdeveloped or developing countries.

The battle lines were quickly drawn. We were supported by Sidney Wolfe of the Health Research Group, the International Organization of Consumers Unions, Health Action International, and other consumer groups, and opposed by most American drug companies. We were supported at first by the Carter administration and then opposed by the Reagan administration. The drug industry declared that the United States had no divine right to tell other countries what drug products they could or could not import. "We cannot play nanny to the rest of the world," we were told.

We had the editorial support of the *New York Times*, which stated:

If F.D.A.'s standards are too high, let them be revised, not circumvented. American Cyanamid, a leading exporter of drugs, has told Congress the bill would create 50,000 new jobs in the United States. But the International Chemical Workers Union, the industry's largest, strongly opposes the bill and calls its potential effect on jobs "greatly exaggerated." . . . The Food and Drug Administration's tighter rules may be a regrettable handicap in vying with foreign competitors. But extra safety is not a bad selling point.[23]

In mid-1985 Gerald Mossinghoff of the U.S. Pharmaceutical Manufacturers Association testified that removing the ban on exporting unapproved drugs would result in the creation of 8,300 to 10,400 new jobs in the United States and Puerto Rico and increase annual drug exports by $400 to $500 million within five years.[24]

At one Senate hearing, FDA Commissioner Frank Young insisted, "Each sovereign government has the chief responsibility to determine the types of drugs that can be imported from abroad."[25] In short, he suggested, it was arrogant for the United States to attempt to dictate drug policy to any developing nation. This view scarcely jibed with the record. Too often, if a Third World country acted to *block* the importation or marketing of a U.S. drug product for whatever reason, the result was a visit from the American ambassador, who would deliver various more or less thinly veiled threats to the offending country.

All through 1984 and 1985 and most of 1986, we worked constantly with our friends in Congress, with drug industry attorneys, and with consumerists, trying to find some formula on which we could reach a satisfactory agreement. Should the revised policy be set up for any drug product or for only those new biotechnology products created by genetic engineering and requiring factories far too expensive to be duplicated overseas? There were endless arguments over whether antibiotics should be included, which countries could be said to have "medically sophisticated" or acceptable drug regulatory agencies, how to prevent transshipment, or how to keep a drug from being reexported to an unacceptable nation. One drug company official said the transshipment problem could be readily solved simply by making any such shipment illegal. But we were concerned because all our laws and regulations had not stopped nuclear secrets or components of secret weapons from leaking into the hands of Communist nations. If we could not prevent weapons transshipments, how could we prevent drugs transshipments?

The proposed amendment, as part of an omnibus health bill, was supposed to face action in both houses of Congress late in 1986. For some reason, consumer activists—flushed with their victory over Nestlé in the infant-formula battle—were convinced that they could easily mobilize enough consumer power to defeat the drug-export legislation. A few hours before adjournment, both houses passed the amendment, which was signed into law by Reagan on November 14.[26] The consumerists had discovered that mounting a boycott of the U.S. Congress—although the idea was accorded some merit in certain circles— was not as easy as staging a boycott of the Nestlé company.

The new amendment was not a good bill, but it was not the disaster that it might have been. It would mean bigger sales and larger profits for some American drug firms. How much damage it would do to the health of the Third World remains to be seen. Among its extremely complicated provisions were these:

- Twenty-one developed nations (Australia, New Zealand, Canada, Japan, and 17 in Western Europe) were specified as approved countries to which unapproved drugs could be exported.
- The exported product must be approved in advance by the importing country.
- The drug must already be partway through the approval process at the U.S. Food and Drug Administration, and the sponsor of the drug must be actively pursuing approval of the pharmaceutical in the United States.
- The drug had not previously been taken off the American market because of ineffectiveness or lack of safety, and an application for approval had not been *denied* by the United States.
- An unapproved drug intended for the treatment of a tropical disease could be exported to a country not on the approved list with the approval of the U.S. secretary of health and human services.

American observers were fascinated to note that the action of the U.S. Congress on the export of unapproved drugs was bitterly denounced—"treachery" was one of the milder epithets—by international and national consumer groups, notably in Great Britain, the Netherlands, West Germany, France, and Switzerland. But it is perhaps worthy of note that in *not one* of those countries had consumer groups succeeded in stopping the exportation of unapproved drugs from their own countries.

For these and other European nations, however, the time for important decisions was still to come. The European Economic Community (EEC) was scheduled to commence operations in 1992. How the various involved groups—consumerists, government officials, and drug companies—would handle the sensitive matter of exporting unapproved drugs was yet to be determined.[27] Numerous options were apparent:

- Make no effort to set up a unified EEC export plan for unapproved drugs and thereby avoid much difficult and time-consuming debate.
- Ban the export of any drug unless it had been approved by one (or two, or three, or four) European countries.
- Ban the export of any unapproved product unless it was included in one version or another of a WHO essential drugs list.
- Permit the export of any drug approved for domestic use by *any* member of the EEC.
- Forbid the export of any product banned by three, four, or more members of the EEC. (This approach had been tentatively approved by the European Parliament, but was rejected by the more powerful policy-making European Commission.)

The outcome of this battle was yet to be decided. It appeared, however, that victory would eventually go—not as easily or as swiftly as they had hoped—to the consumers.

One result of the furore over the exportation of unapproved drugs was a request from several congressional committees to the Office of Technology Assessment—often called the research arm of the U.S. Congress—to survey the promotion and labeling of drug products in the Third World. It was never made clear how much this request stemmed from an actual congressional interest in drug labeling and how much from an attempt to mollify consumerists and other industry critics who were still seething over passage of the 1986 Drug Export Act.

The design of the OTA survey was markedly different from that of our own research. It would be limited to a study of only those products marketed by U.S.-based companies or their subsidiaries. No product would be identified by its own name or the name of its manufacturer. In any labeling found to be deficient, the precise deficiency would not be disclosed. The conduct of the survey was entrusted to an experienced and extremely competent staff. The research was concentrated on four countries—Kenya, Thailand, Brazil, and Panama. Publication of the OTA findings was scheduled for early 1992.[28]

For numerous reasons, particularly the fact that the two studies were looking at different "universes"—different Third World countries, certainly different companies, and probably different drug products— any attempt to compare the results of the two investigations would be unreasonable. (We had been urged by colleagues in OTA, friends in the Congress, and some industry leaders to join forces with the OTA group but respectfully declined. We were convinced that we could operate more easily and effectively without any official ties to the U.S. government, especially in those Third World countries in which we already had close friendships of long standing.)

Chapter 13

HARD CHOICES

For two decades we have been examining the performance of the pharmaceutical industry in the Third World, in particular the manner in which it promotes and labels its products. We feel that there is now a worldwide crisis involving pharmaceuticals, and we know few of those concerned with drug products—physicians, pharmacists, administrators of health programs, patients, and the industry itself—who would challenge that view. Among those groups, however, there is little if any agreement on the exact nature of the crisis.

To the drug industry, there is already an intolerable degree of regulation and a serious threat to innovation. If aspirin were to be discovered today, some industry spokesmen have suggested, it would never be approved by the U.S. Food and Drug Administration. Companies can no longer look forward to receiving a decent return on investment, and the future looks still more forbidding. Many industry leaders are uncomfortable with the need to engage in public dialogues, to face public accountability.

To government, in industrialized and developing countries alike, drugs account for a large part—perhaps too large a part—of skyrocketing health costs.

To administrators of health programs, both public and private, and to such critics as clinical pharmacologists, experts on infectious diseases, and epidemiologists, there is far too much irrational prescribing—the wrong drug, for the wrong patient, at the wrong time, and in the wrong amounts, with no consideration of costs.

To some physicians, pharmacists, and other health professionals, there is far too much interference in what has been traditionally their private territory. One incensed physician exclaimed, "People are daring to criticize the way physicians prescribe and pharmacists dispense!" And when patients are asked, "Isn't your health worth *any* price?" some have answered, "No!"

And to consumers, the price tag on drugs is getting too high and the magic of these "magic bullets" is becoming tarnished. The tax funds and out-of-pocket expenditures for drugs no longer look like such a bargain. In the United States and many other industrialized nations, doctor and hospital bills for many if not most people are covered by some kind of health insurance or government program, whereas many people have to make out-of-pocket payments for out-of-hospital drugs. In the Third World, some patients may be able to obtain prescription drugs at little or no cost through a government system or a philanthropic group program.

In poor countries, provision of out-of-hospital drugs may seem in theory to be efficient, but the actual situation is often less assuring. A patient may be able to pay for only a two- or three-day supply of an antibiotic, whereas a seven-day treatment is considered to be the absolute minimum. The product dispensed to the patient may have been so cut that it contains only a pitifully small fraction of the labeled amount. In tropical countries, the drug may have been stored so long without essential refrigeration that it has become worthless or even toxic. Or, too often in the Third World, the patient is told that supplies of the drug have been exhausted, and no new supplies are scheduled to arrive for three months, or six months, or more. In six months, or three, or less, the patient may be dead.

In recent years, patients are becoming increasingly aware that any drug may cause a more or less serious adverse reaction. These hazards are no longer of interest solely to pharmacologists—they are of interest to patients; they alarm patients; they interest lawyers. And when these events occur, whether they involve a thalidomide, or Chloromycetin, or Enterovioform, or Oraflex, they damage the name not only of the manufacturer alone—most patients do not remember who makes which drug—these adverse reactions blacken the name of the whole industry.

The drug industry in general and the multinational firms in particular have long sought to justify their actions and their profits on the grounds that the pharmaceutical industry is a particularly high-risk business, that many hundreds or thousands of new agents must be tested for each one that gets to the market, and that high profits are essential to pay for that vital research. Such arguments have become singularly unimpressive. Of the thousands of new products that are tested, the great majority are quickly dropped from consideration after the first and inexpensive stages of testing. Moreover, it is obvious that the profits are what is left over *after* all the costs for research, production, marketing, promotion, and taxes have been paid.

Problems Related to the Crisis

A number of specific problems are associated with the pharmaceutical crisis. Critics charge that an inordinate amount of industry money and effort goes into the development and promotion of unneeded "me-too" drugs—drugs that are no better, no more effective, no safer, and no less costly than older products, but are merely sufficiently different to win a patent. The fact that many of these me-too products have been widely accepted in some countries and have achieved financial success is no evidence of their clinical value.

Consumerists charge that not enough research is directed toward the development of drugs needed to control such Third World diseases as malaria, leprosy, trypanosomiasis, bilharzia, schistosomiasis, and a host of bacterial and viral infections that cause diarrhea. Multinational firms have countered that investing large amounts of money in the development of drugs for countries which, at least in the near future, will be unable to pay for them, is little less than economic suicide. Further, some of these large research-minded firms have noted, they are already investing hundreds of millions in the development of drugs and vaccines for use against diseases particularly afflicting the Third World. Some consumer activists maintain that multinational drug companies have an inescapable moral or social responsibility to develop drug products to be provided to poor countries at low or no cost. In response, spokesmen for pharmaceutical firms have noted that such companies as British Petroleum, General Electric, Westinghouse, Volkswagen, Toyota, Mitsubishi, Dior, Yves St. Laurent, Heineken, and Fiat have shown no particular feeling of social responsibility to provide their products at little or no cost in the Third World.

Much of the industry, both multinational and domestic, has been accused in the past—and in many cases found guilty—of using inadequate and even deceitful promotion. Over the years, however, some drug companies have promoted most of their products, most of the time, with honesty, dignity, and restraint.

Partly because of some unhappy aspects of drug promotion, much of the public has become convinced that there must be a pill for every ill. Some segments of the industry have come to believe their own propaganda. So have many prescribers.

Too often, patients continue to injure themselves by a lack of compliance—by a failure to follow a physician's instructions, or even to read the label. In many developing countries, most patients are unable to read the label.

There is a popular belief, fostered in large part by the pharmaceutical industry, that the more drugs on the market, the greater the opportunities for a physician to select the best drug for a patient. That would seem to be obvious. But, beyond a certain point, the number of available products has little to do with the delivery of good health care—the availability of more products usually means simply more confusion. At least partly because of this superabundance of products, the industrialized countries—the rich nations—are generally held to be over-drugged. Yet in spite of the superabundance, the Third World countries—the poor ones—are woefully underdrugged.

For the drug industry, the Third World has a fascinating significance. The industry cannot look to the industrialized nations—the United States, Europe, Canada, Australia, New Zealand, and Japan, now being joined by Singapore, South Korea, and Taiwan—for much dramatic growth in the near future. Naturally, as drugs are developed to control diseases that are now largely uncontrollable—the common cold, for example, or AIDS, or many forms of cancer—some companies will benefit handsomely. By and large, there will be mainly a jockeying for position in a reasonably limited market. As one company gains ground another will lose it. But in the Third World, only the merest fraction of the market has been touched. For reasons that in most cases are painfully clear, most Third World people in most places at most times cannot get the drug products they need.

The Silverman, Lydecker, and Lee Studies

Since the early 1970s we have focused on the international activities of the pharmaceutical industry, beginning in Latin America. In 1976, in *The Drugging of the Americas*, we presented our first findings: "It is abundantly clear that there are glaring differences in the ways in which the same multinational pharmaceutical companies describe essentially the same drug products to physicians in the United States and to their medical colleagues in Latin America. This holds true not only for global corporations headquartered in the United States. It is true also for such companies based in Switzerland, France, West Germany, and other nations."[1] We revealed that many of the pharmaceutical firms were making claims of efficacy that could not be supported by scientific evidence. Many were glossing over, minimizing, or totally ignoring serious or potentially lethal side effects.

Our views were quickly and strongly attacked by the drug companies, who insisted that they were breaking no Latin American laws. (In some instances, we were able to demonstrate that they actually *were* violating such laws.) But, we insisted, that was not the critical issue. "Whether or not a drug company failing to make full disclosure of risks is meeting legal requirements is only of secondary importance. The primary issue is whether or not the company is meeting ethical requirements. Laws and regulations do not establish the ethical obligation: instead they merely specify it."[2] The reactions of the media, consumer groups, various governmental agencies in both the United States and Latin America, and the pharmaceutical industry were unexpected and dramatic.[3] As one result, we felt we should devote much of the next fifteen years to further studies of drug promotion and labeling in developing countries.[4]

Our present study was initiated in 1987, beginning with the mobilization of friends and colleagues throughout the world who had aided us in our earlier research and the collection, organization, and often translation of essential updated printed material. The survey covered more than 40 single-drug entities or fixed combinations marketed as about 1,500 products by more than 400 companies in the Third World and also, where they had been approved, in the United States and

Great Britain. Two of us (M.S. and M.L.) conducted on-site studies in three countries in Latin America (Mexico, Venezuela, and Brazil), three in Africa (Senegal, Kenya, and Egypt), and eight in southern and Southeast Asia (Turkey, India, Nepal, Bangladesh, Thailand, Malaysia, Singapore, and Indonesia). We worked with knowledgeable experts, including clinical pharmacologists, hematologists, epidemiologists, experts on infectious disease, endocrinologists, cardiologists, rheumatologists, gastroenterologists, and pathologists. Many were friends of long standing. We consulted also with consumerist leaders, government officials at many levels, medical educators, and industry representatives. (Earlier, we conducted similar on-site studies in Costa Rica, Guatemala, Colombia, and Ecuador in Latin America; Nigeria, Zambia, and Tanzania in Africa; and Sri Lanka, Hong Kong, South Korea, Taiwan, and the Philippines in Asia. Many of the relationships we had established during those earlier surveys offered us invaluable assistance during the present investigation.)

We found that although the problem of faulty and inadequate drug promotion and labeling had not gone away, it had changed remarkably. The chief offenders were no longer the big and presumably evil multinational drug companies of the United States, Europe, and Japan. Of the firms we investigated, most were making claims for efficacy that could be supported with scientific evidence. Most were more willing to disclose the potential hazards of their products. With a few glaring exceptions, most of the multinationals had evidently reached the conclusion that they could tell the truth and still make a decent profit. (We are unable to tell in each case whether this welcome change represents a change in company policy, or a change in the behavior of company personnel, or indeed a change in personnel.)

In contrast, and to the dismay of many consumerists, we found that most of the misinformation was coming mainly from local or domestic firms, usually small in sales volume but equipped with astounding political influence. (See Chapter 2.) It had long been the contention of many consumer activists that, unlike multinational firms, small domestic companies would be far more likely to tell the truth.

During the past few years, a number of multinational firms have responded to severe criticism of some of the ineffective or needlessly dangerous products they were selling and removed them from the market. Too often this merely left a vacuum, which was quickly filled by domestic firms that introduced the same product under the same or a different name. The risk to the public remained unchanged. But it was unusual, we noted, for a domestic company engaging in such a practice to receive much criticism.

The Work of Many

The changes and accomplishments described in the foregoing chapters represent only a small beginning, but they represent the thoughts, the efforts, and the courage of many groups and of hundreds or thousands of individuals.

- Key roles have been played by WHO, UNICEF, and other international organizations; consumer groups like the International Organization of Consumers Unions and Health Action International; groups, such as International Medical Services for Health (INMED) in the United States, that help poor countries find dependable suppliers of high-quality, low-cost products; and religious and other nongovernmental organizations, which provide as much as 40 percent of the health care in some developing countries.
- Credit belongs to the International Federation of Pharmaceutical Manufacturing Associations and its national members for softening their former rigid opposition to essential drugs lists and for beginning to enforce their own code of marketing ethics.
- A few pharmaceutical firms deserve particular recognition for undertaking research on diseases that afflict poor countries, and credit belongs to firms such as Servipharm in Switzerland for providing high-quality drugs at remarkably low prices to the poorest of the Third World nations.
- Great praise must be awarded to individuals in many industrialized countries who have expended much time, thought, and effort—sometimes at their own peril—to develop rational drug use in the Third World, and to those scientific organizations that are now beginning to study the problems and propose solutions.

At the same time, it must be recognized that the medical and pharmacy professions and their professional schools both in industrialized and in Third World nations have, with a few notable exceptions, thus far shown little interest in these matters.

The Problems at Hand

Although many of the major multinational firms have dramatically modified their promotion and labeling standards, there are still serious difficulties in developing countries.

- Grossly exaggerated claims are still being made for some drug products.
- Known hazards are not adequately disclosed to physicians, pharmacists, and patients.
- Drug companies are still producing and excessively promoting expensive "luxury drugs"—for example, multivitamins alone or in combination with minerals, combination antibiotics, or combinations of an antibiotic with an antibacterial.
- Injectable forms of vitamins, minerals, amino acids, and other agents are produced and promoted even though the drugs could be equally effective, safer, and less costly when taken by mouth.

Similarly, there are serious and potentially lethal problems associated with the dispensing of drugs.

- Pharmacists (or others) regularly dispense a "prescription drug" without a physician's prescription, even though this may be both illegal and unsafe.
- Expensive brand-name products are often dispensed when generic products that are equally appropriate and far less costly are available.
- Drugs kept too long in pharmacies (or other storage facilities) disintegrate rapidly, with the resultant loss of potency or even the formation of toxic breakdown products.
- In some instances, a bottle of drugs may be accidentally or fraudulently mislabeled, so that the container does not hold the drug indicated on the label.
- The pharmacist may dispense the drug listed on the label, but it has been so "cut" that each tablet or capsule contains as little as 10 percent of the labeled amount of the active ingredient, or the active ingredient may have been replaced entirely with an inactive substance such as flour or starch.

• Injections are often offered on the premises and may be given by an untrained attendant on a patient's demand for vitamins, calcium, glucose, and other drugs.

The Matter of Quality Assurance

One of the most serious problems afflicting most if not all developing countries is the difficulty or the impossibility of assuring the quality of drugs, through access to national or regional testing laboratories. In the case of a product manufactured by a reliable multinational firm, which presumably uses the same standards of quality in making drugs for export as it does in making those for home use, a Third World buyer may have some confidence in the quality of the products. This confidence may be strengthened if the exported product is certified under the WHO Certification Scheme on the Quality of Pharmaceutical Products Moving in International Commerce.[5] Such certification, of course, does not apply to drugs manufactured by a local or domestic company. (It is not enough to assure quality control only in the manufacturing process; it must also be assured throughout the entire distribution chain.)[6]

We would put a very high priority on sound programs of drug-quality assurance in developing countries. Such programs could be vital for the detection and rejection of inferior products offered—possibly at apparent "bargain rates"—by foreign drug firms; in the evaluation of the quality of products made by domestic companies; and in the detection of mislabeled, spurious, or fraudulent drugs. (See Chapter 8.) They could be invaluable in checking the quality of low-cost generics and could play a strategic role in evaluating imported drugs not approved in the country that exports them.

In theory, it would be ideal to have the appropriate testing facility in each country. In the Third World, however, regional laboratories working for groups of countries could be entirely adequate and far less costly. Several sources of assistance are available: WHO, multinational pharmaceutical corporations, strong regulatory agencies like FDA in industrialized countries, academically based groups for technical aid, and the World Bank and such national foreign aid agencies as the U.S. Agency for International Development for financial and managerial assistance.

Unless governments can assure their people that drugs on the market meet high standards of quality, it will be impossible to implement an effective national drug policy. The health of the public may be compromised, consumers will be cheated on the drugs they buy, and governments and other purchasing agencies will be defrauded.

Essential Drugs Lists: Some Progress

The concept of essential drugs lists, to be modified to suit each country's needs, has been accepted by virtually all countries in the Third World. The International Federation of Pharmaceutical Manufacturing Associations has withdrawn its bitter opposition and accepted the idea, at least for programs in the public sector.[7]

In 1990, to the amazement of many, the United States dropped its vigorous and long-standing opposition. Stuart Nightingale, associate commissioner of FDA, described the new U.S. position: "The United States fully supports the goals and objectives of the Revised Drug Strategy, including, of course, the Action Program in Essential Drugs." He went on to note: "In addition, I am pleased to state that for the first time, my Agency is making a modest contribution directly to the Action Program on Essential Drugs. We have to continue to participate financially as well as to continue to offer technical cooperation, especially in assisting in quality assurance, good manufacturing practices, and strengthening of drug regulation authorities in developing countries."[8]

There is need for agreement on the significance of an essential drugs list. Should it be treated primarily as a guide, to indicate priorities in making drug purchases? Or should it be treated as if it were carved in granite, with absolutely no variations permitted and no unlisted drug to be allowed on the market? The latter policy would be endorsed by some consumer activists, but it would be opposed by many drug companies and would be a strong temptation to set up smuggling operations and a black market in prescription drugs. Unquestionably, it would infuriate many physicians wanting to provide the best possible care for their patients.

But approving the idea of essential drugs lists is only the beginning. The Third World nations have yet to implement the concept with adequate vigor. In most developing nations, the drug regulatory agency is without sufficient authority, trained personnel, funds, or political will to get ineffective or needlessly dangerous products off the market. Too often, such an agency can be swayed by industry or political pressure or outright bribery.

The Matter of Bribery

Throughout the Third World, bribery and corruption have always been an accepted way of life. These practices have helped government regulatory officials decide whether to accept or reject a proposed new drug, or to approve or turn down proposed labeling. They have influenced inspectors to clear an import shipment quickly or only after weeks or months of delay. In fact, declared Malcolm Baldrige, secretary of commerce in the Reagan cabinet, small payments to foreign officials are not really bribes. "That's something called 'grease.' It's sometimes called facilitating payments, but it means you are not trying to bribe anybody to do anything outside of the law, or changing the payment, or buying your product."[9]

In some cases, as when poorly paid government workers are concerned, the "grease" may involve only a few hundred rupees or cruzeiros or pesos. But if the inducement goes to a high-ranking government official, or an influential physician, it might mean the gift of a color television set, a new car, a new house, a new wing on a hospital, a free trip for self and wife to Europe or America, or a prepaid college education in a topnotch European or American university for the physician's children. We wrote in 1982: "Wiping out bribery of physicians and government officials, or even reducing corruption by any substantial degree, will probably not be readily accomplished. The mere enactment of new laws or regulations in the Third World cannot have any value unless they can be enforced. Unfortunately, enforcement is itself an expensive maneuver; regulators and inspectors would have to be employed, and—with the small salaries paid to government workers in developing countries—the inspectors themselves could be easily bribed."[10]

Lee Kuan Yew, the prime minister of Singapore, recently observed, "In most countries, men who go into politics are officially very poorly paid. They get their rewards in other ways, like commissions, kickbacks, patronage and perks."[11] A country that underpays its politicians (and, we would add, its civil servants), the prime minister observed, invites "a lot of hypocrisy, fiddling, and eventually dishonesty and corruption."

Until only a few years ago, most people in the industrialized world consoled themselves by smugly deciding that bribery and corruption flourished only in the poor countries of the Third World. This idea was rudely shattered in 1981, when a four-man Austrian investigative team reported that essentially the same kinds of bribery and corruption were going on in such scarcely underdeveloped countries as Austria, Switzerland, and Germany. The drug companies involved included Bayer in Germany, Sandoz in Switzerland, and Aesca, an Austrian representative of U.S.–based Schering.[12]

Then, commencing in 1989, came a series of shocking disclosures that bribery had been found in that temple of propriety, the U.S. Food and Drug Administration itself. (See Chapter 4.) The investigation, conducted mainly by a congressional committee and the U.S. attorney's office in Baltimore, involved particularly the division responsible for regulating generic drug products. But instead of being shrugged off as an unimportant though possibly amusing little affair, as would probably have happened in a Third World nation, this one resulted in the levying of heavy fines—some in the hundreds of thousands or even millions of dollars—and jail sentences. Significantly, the penalties hit not only the bribe takers but also the bribe givers. Although he was not personally implicated in the bribe scandal, the commissioner of FDA was moved out of his position.

Less dramatic but potentially far more damaging to patients is the routine, continual bribing of physicians by pharmaceutical companies in the United States and other industrialized countries. It is not called bribing—it is more tactfully listed as one variety of promotion. In the United States, this has meant free vacations, tickets to a sporting event, expensive gifts, all-expense trips to medical conventions held on a glamorous island in the Caribbean or the South Seas, "research grants" to support inconsequential and useless tests of a new "me-too" product, and other gifts from overzealous promotion departments. Too often, these and similar manipulations have induced physicians to prescribe an unneeded drug or a drug that is less effective, less safe, or more costly than others. Such groups as the American Medical Association, the American College of Physicians, and the Pharmaceutical Manufacturers Association have all adopted "guidelines" to cover relations between drug companies and physicians. The value of such guidelines has been doubted.[13]

"There's definitely a conflict in the pharmaceutical companies between the marketers and the scientists," said Charles van der Horst, professor of medicine at the University of North Carolina. "The scientists are out to better humanity, and the marketers want to make money." In defense, Mark Grayson of the PMA claimed, "The pharmaceutical companies are marketing in a very responsible way. In any industry, you can find isolated abuses, but damning a whole industry just isn't justified."

But Sidney Wolfe of the Health Research Group has shown that the problem cannot be so lightly dismissed. Existing laws need to be enforced and new laws must be enacted. "For the FDA not to have criminally prosecuted a drug company for advertising and promotional violations for 20 years in the face of a massive amount of violative activities, is an invitation to continued lawbreaking," he declared. "Even if the FDA was to do a perfect job in deciding which drugs are safe and effective enough for which diseases to merit marketing, the current criminal, unethical, and immoral marketing practices of many drug companies seriously undermine this aspect of FDA regulation."

Domestic Drug Industries: Some Hard Choices

In the past decade or two, some consumerist leaders have intensified their attack and called for radical changes in the entire drug distribution system. In particular, they are urging Third World countries to depend more on indigenous remedies and to establish their own drug manufacturing and marketing companies. Involved here, however, are at least the threats of retribution by multinational firms and the strong chance that, unless the developing nations first create effective systems to control drug quality, their people will be exposed to low-cost but low-quality and possibly dangerous or lethal products. There will be hard choices, indeed.

For many years some drug industry critics have demanded that all *patents* on drugs must be abolished and *profits* should be drastically reduced or made illegal. We believed in 1982, and still believe, that wiping out patent protection for new drugs would be "a short-term boon for some countries but a long-term disaster for the world."[14] Our feeling is based not on any particular affection for the drug industry but on our strong concern for our children and grandchildren and for children and grandchildren everywhere.

The abolition of drug profits and of the patent system that makes these profits possible would signal the end of most industry investment in drug research and the development of new and better pharmaceuticals. The major multinational firms that conduct the greater portion of drug research and development would quickly recognize that investing hundreds of millions of dollars each year in activities that would yield no profits would be economically insane. (Some have claimed that the research could be transferred easily to universities or government laboratories. But, although the record of such institutions in carrying out basic or fundamental research has been noteworthy, their record in the actual development or creation of important new drugs has been far less impressive. Moreover, few academic or government institutions would show much willingness to gamble enormous sums of money on projects that may or may not pay off.)

Halting drug research and development as it stands today would therefore sentence future generations to lives—or deaths—with no really effective drugs to control AIDS, and only an inadequate supply of products to prevent or control most types of cancer, coronary disease, diarrhea, cirrhosis, malaria, leprosy, trypanosomiasis, filariasis, and a host of other painful, crippling, or fatal diseases.

Various activists have insisted that, at least in the Third World, the drug crisis cannot be satisfactorily solved unless the "profit-hungry, research-oriented" multinational firms are replaced by local or domestic firms, which presumably would have no interest in profits. Where it seemed appropriate, these domestic companies would manufacture and market patented drugs in violation of patent. This approach is already in effect in some countries, and the matter of *patent infringement* has become the center of furious international controversy.

Those in developing nations who have simply ignored drug patents see themselves as pharmaceutical Robin Hoods, taking wealth—in this case, valuable patents—and distributing it to the poor. Such action obviously represents a matter of social justice. The patent infringers were astounded to discover that the multinational companies viewed such activities as piracy, and that, in industrialized nations, stealing intellectual property was considered to be just as criminal as stealing such physical assets as land and money. The infringers were even more astounded to find that, at least in the United States, the multinationals could press their government into punishing the offending Third World country by invoking federal law and raising import taxes on products being shipped to the United States. (See Chapter 12.) This unexpected retaliation, the Robin Hoods insisted in anguish, was outrageous and unjust.

Another hard choice involves the weeding out of spurious, fraudulent, or counterfeit drugs, which may be useless or dangerous or both. Here, too often, the culprit is not some faceless money-grabbing corporation in a capitalist nation half a world away but the friendly neighbor who may live in the house across the street. Another concerns the willingness or unwillingness to purchase a high-quality, low-cost generic product—possibly from one of those remote multinational firms—rather than a high-priced brand-name product that happens to be marketed by friends of powerful government officials or politicians. And always—perhaps the hardest choice of all—there is the need to find an effective means of controlling or minimizing corruption and bribery.

Eternal Vigilance, Unending Consultation

Inferior drugs will undoubtedly continue to come to market. In the past, most of these were detected—sometimes quickly, sometimes only after the passage of much time—in any one of a variety of ways:

- The suspicions of an individual clinician would be aroused when a patient failed to respond to a drug as expected.
- A pharmacologist or a clinical pharmacologist would find that the claims made for a new product or the disclosed risks of an adverse reaction did not conform to the information published in the scientific literature.
- One pharmaceutical manufacturer would note that one of its own products, or perhaps one of its competitor's, did not perform as labeled and promoted.
- An individual consumerist or a consumerist group would collect reports from physicians on the adverse effects of a suspected drug product and then publish the information.
- A drug regulatory agency in one nation would reject a proposed product because tests showed it to be ineffective or needlessly dangerous, and would then pass this information on to other countries where the product had previously been approved or was being considered for approval.

In this surveillance, much credit must go to such knowledgeable and courageous individuals as the late Olle Hansson in Sweden, Sidney

Wolfe in the United States, Andrew Chetley, Andrew Herxheimer, W. H. W. Inman, Charles Medawar, and Dianna Melrose in Great Britain, M. N. Graham Dukes in Denmark, Mike Muller in Mozambique, Mira Shiva in India, Syed Rizwanuddin Ahmad in Pakistan, Peter Mansfield of Australia and his associates, and Hirokuni Beppu in Japan.

Consumer groups have played valuable roles in many parts of the world: notably Anwar Fazal and the International Organization of Consumers Unions (IOCU), Health Action International (HAI), the Public Citizen Health Research Group and the Interfaith Center on Corporate Responsibility in the United States, Social Audit in Great Britain, the Bundeskongress entwicklungspolitischer Aktionsgruppen (BUKO) in Germany, the Werkgroep Medische Ontwikkeling Samenwerking (WEMOS) in the Netherlands, the Bureau Européen des Unions des Consommateurs (BEUC) in Belgium, the Voluntary Health Association of India (VHAI), the International Congress Against Drug-Induced Suffering (ICADIS) in Japan, the Health Action Information Network (HAIN) in the Philippines, and the Medical Lobby for Appropriate Marketing (MaLAM) based in Australia.

Within industry, the International Federation of Pharmaceutical Manufacturing Associations (IFPMA) has gradually stepped up its activities: It is beginning to make stronger efforts to enforce its international drug marketing code; it has stopped much of the unqualified use of the word "safe" in drug promotion; it has apparently ended its irrational and unsuccessful warfare against any use of essential drugs lists. The IFPMA and its national members, however, have yet to demonstrate any significant monitoring or control of drug labeling and promotion by domestic companies in the Third World. In those developing nations, drug promotion may well be at its worst, but IFPMA explains that it cannot control firms that are not even members of IFPMA. It is our strong belief that the pharmaceutical industry as a whole will suffer if the leaders do not lead.

In the industrialized countries IFPMA members—most of them the so-called multinationals—have yet to do an adequate job of monitoring their own promotional activities. Even as recently as 1989, when we demonstrated—in print—the claims made for their products in Third World countries and the failure to disclose known hazards, the presidents or chief executive officers of some multinational firms assured us that "we didn't realize" or that "nobody ever told me that our affiliate was saying *that!*" It is all too evident that the multinational drug firms must give a much higher priority to centralized review of all published labeling, and that far better training and more rigorous supervision must be provided to company representatives or drug detailers. In this case, time is running out for the drug companies. Sooner or later, the people of the Third World will discover liability lawsuits.

But ceaseless vigilance and surveillance are only first steps. There must be, not constant confrontation, but constant consultation. Some of the various participants in the drug crisis seem confident that he, she, or it has "the" solution. The consumerists, the industry, the World Health Organization, the government agencies, and the medical and pharmacy professions all feel certain that there actually is a simple, single solution to the entire problem, and each is equally convinced that it and it alone possesses the secret.

We are convinced that no single solution exists, that there are many different solutions to different parts of the problem, and that the situation will not be improved until the various participants sit down together—not to confront, demand, denounce, or threaten, but to converse and consult. Until only a few years ago, we would have rejected this approach as naive and impractical. We have now modified our thinking. Months of painful involvement in the SMON affair (see Chapter 11) and months of negotiations with top management at Ciba-Geigy and a few other pharmaceutical companies—months of consultation rather than noisy debate—convinced us that the consultative approach can sometimes work.

In such negotiations, there is no room for efforts to cripple or destroy the industry, or to descend to character assassination. The World Health Organization must continue to take an increasingly active leadership role. *The Ethical Criteria for Medicinal Drug Promotion*, drafted by a WHO group and endorsed by the World Health Assembly in 1988,[15] represents a major advance. Consumer groups, industry groups and individual companies, international and national governmental agencies, nongovernmental organizations, major philanthropic groups, medical and pharmacy associations and their professional schools, the media, and dedicated individuals all have a part to play.

Throughout, one crucial point must never be overlooked: To consult, cooperate, and communicate is not to sell out.

Appendix

APPENDIX

Tables of Product Indications, Contraindications, and Warnings

Table 1
Dipyrone

(Analgin, Antalgin, Dipirona, Metamizole, Methampyrone, Sulpyrone, etc; single entities only)

	SPECIFIC WARNING OF SERIOUS OR FATAL AGRANULOCYTOSIS	
	Warning	No warning
United States		
None Listed		
United Kingdom		
None Listed		
Indonesia		
Antalgin—Soho (Indonesia)		✓
Cennoval—Japhar (Indonesia)	(a)	
Conmel—Sterling-Winthrop (U.S.)	(a)	
Fastalgin—Pharos Indonesia (Indonesia)	(a)	
Fastan—New Interbat (Indonesia)	(a)	
Kalpyron—Kalbe Farma (Indonesia)	(a)	
Magnopyrol—Siegfried (Switzerland)	(a)	
Mepron—Meprofarm (Indonesia)	(a)	
Metilon—Daiichi-Otto (Japan)	(a)	
Neomed—Kenrose (Indonesia)	(a)	
Novalgin—Hoechst (West Germany)	(a)	
Pyronal—Tanabe-Abadi (Japan)	(a)	
Rapidon—Mecosin (U.S.)	(a)	
Ronalgin—Dexa Medica (Indonesia)	(a)	
Scanalgin—Scanchemie (Indonesia)	(a)	
Thailand		
Acodon—Thai Nakorn Patana (Thailand)	(a)	
Conmel—Winthrop/Sterling (U.S.)	(a)	
Deparon—Westmont (Philippines)	(a)	
Genergin—General Drugs House (Thailand)		✓
Invogin—Chew Brothers (Thailand)	(a)	
Kno-Paine—Continental Pharm (U.S.)	(a)	
Medalgin—Medical Supply (Thailand)	(a)	
Nalgin-P—P. P. Lab (Thailand)	(a)	
Nominfone—Atlantic (Thailand)	(a)	
Novalgin—Hoechst (West Germany)	(a)	
Unigen—Unison (Thailand)	(a)	
Philippines		
Bipyrine—Pascual (Spain)	(a)	
Gifaril—Wander (Switzerland)	(a)	

Table 1 continued

	SPECIFIC WARNING OF SERIOUS OR FATAL AGRANULOCYTOSIS	
	Warning	No warning
Lagalgin—Lagap (Switzerland)	(a)	
Melubrin—Hoechst (West Germany)	(a)	
Africa		
Conmel—Winthrop (U.S.)	(a), (b)	
Nebagin—IPCA (India)	(a), (b)	
Novalgin—Hoechst (West Germany)	(a), (b)	
West Africa		
Novalgin—Hoechst (West Germany)	√	
Middle East		
Conmel—Winthrop (U.S.)	√, (b)	
Nebagin—IPCA (India)	√, (b)	
Novalgin—Hoechst (West Germany)	√	
Caribbean		
Lagalgin—Lagap (Switzerland)	√, (b)	
Novalgin—Hoechst (West Germany)	√	
Mexico		
Bridanol—Promeco (West Germany)		√
Conmel—Winthrop (U.S.)	√	
Dalmasin—Columbia (Mexico)	(c)	
Exodalina—Quimico Sons (Mexico)	√	
Indigon—IQFA (Mexico)	(c)	
Magnol Atlantis—Atlantis (Mexico)		√
Magnopyrol—Siegfried (Switzerland)	√	
Neo-Melubrina—Hoechst (West Germany)	√	
Pifrol—Arlex (Mexico)		√
Piraken—Kendrick (Mexico)	(c)	
Pirongyl—Arlex (Mexico)		√
Prodolina—Promeco (West Germany)	√	
Utidol—Diba (Mexico)		√
Central America		
Bridanol—Europharma, Promeco (West Germany)		√
Conmel—Winthrop (U.S.)	√	
Neo-Melubrina—Hoechst (West Germany)	√	
Novalgina—Hoechst (West Germany)	√	
Termin—Hessel (El Salvador)		√

Table 1 continued

	SPECIFIC WARNING OF SERIOUS OR FATAL AGRANULOCYTOSIS	
	Warning	No warning
Colombia		
Conmel—Winthrop (U.S.)	✓	
Gifaril—Sandoz/Wander (Switzerland)	✓	
Pediatrics Antipiretico—Pediatrics (Colombia)	✓	
Ecuador		
Conmel—Winthrop (U.S.)	✓	
Peru		
Cortalgina—Farmindustria (Peru)		✓
Novalgina—Hoechst (West Germany)	✓	
Venezuela		
Bral—Palenzona (Venezuela)		✓
Conmel—Winthrop (U.S.)	✓	
Delsal—Meyer (Venezuela)		✓
Dipirona—Proton (Venezuela)		✓
Inquirona—Drovepat (Venezuela)		✓
Klinomel—Klinos (Venezuela)		✓
Magnepyrol—Siegfried (Switzerland)		✓
Novalcina—Hoechst (West Germany)	✓	
Piradro—Fesa (Venezuela)		✓
Piretyl—Pulmobronk (Venezuela)		✓
Brazil		
Febralgin—De Angeli (West Germany)	✓	
Novalgina—Hoechst (West Germany)		✓

(a) Footnote reference to warnings.
(b) Use for pain only where no other alternative is available.
(c) Nonspecific warning.

Table 2 **Phenacetin** *(combination products)*	SPECIFIC WARNING OF SERIOUS OR FATAL KIDNEY DAMAGE	
	Warning	No warning
United States None Listed		
United Kingdom None Listed		
Indonesia Erceefagon—Kimla Farma (Indonesia)		√
Caribbean Apracur—Schering AG (West Germany)		√
Mexico Antiflu-Des—Chinoin (Mexico)		√
Robaxisal—Robins (U.S.)	√	
Central America Antiflu-Des—Chinoin (Mexico)		√
Venezuela Saridon—Roche (Switzerland)		√

Table 3
Benzydamine

(single entities only)

	INDICATIONS			WARNINGS				
	Acute inflammatory conditions, pain	Posttrauma, postsurgery pain, swelling	Caution in pregnancy	Caution with gastrointestinal disturbances	Caution with alcohol use	May cause anxiety, hallucinations, convulsions	May cause palpitations, tachycardia	May cause insomnia
Indonesia								
Tantum—Angelini/Francesco/Soho (Italy)	√	√	√					
Thailand								
Tantum—Organon (Netherlands)	√	√						
Africa								
Tantum—Organon (Netherlands)	√			√	√			
Central America								
Tantum—Industrias Quimicas (El Salvador)	√	√				√	√	
Colombia								
Benzerin—Fixalia (Colombia)	√	√				√		
Ecuador								
Omniflam—Francar (Ecuador)	√	√						
Tantum—Organon (Netherlands)	√	√	√	√	√		√	√
Venezuela								
Tantum—Elmar (Italy)	√							
Peru								
Tantum—Instituto Sanitas (Peru)	√	√						
Brazil								
Benflagin—Labofarma (West Germany)	√	√	√	√		√	√	√
Benzitrat—Searle (U.S.)	√	√	√	√		√	√	√
Tantum—Organon (Netherlands)	√	√						√

Table 4
Glafenine

(single entities only)

	Do not use in severe heart failure	No use in ischemic heart disease	No use in acute liver disease	No use in kidney disease	No use in pregnancy	No use with alcohol	Caution with children	None
WARNINGS								
Indonesia								
Biofenin—Biomedia (Indonesia)								✓
Citofen—Pyridam (Indonesia)			✓	✓	✓			
Fenal—Meprofarm (Indonesia)								✓
Glaphen—Pharos Indonesia (Indonesia)								✓
Glifanan—Hoechst (West Germany)	✓	✓	✓	✓	✓	✓		
Thailand								
Glafine—Siam Bheasach (Thailand)			(a)	(a)	(a)		✓	
Malaysia/Singapore								
Glifanan—Roussel (West Germany)	✓	✓	✓	✓	✓	✓		
Philippines								
Glafen—United American (Philippines)				✓		✓		
Glanin—Terramedic (Philippines)				✓		✓		
Glifanan—Roussel (West Germany)				✓			✓	
Revalan—Biomedia (Philippines)				✓		✓		
Unilab Glafenine—Unilab (Philippines)								✓
Africa								
Glifanan—Roussel (West Germany)	✓	✓	✓	✓	✓	✓	✓	
West Africa								
Glifanan—Roussel (West Germany)	✓	✓	✓	✓	✓	✓	✓	
Middle East								
Glifanan—Roussel (West Germany)	✓	✓	✓	✓	✓	✓	✓	
Caribbean								
Glifanan—Roussel (West Germany)	✓	✓	✓	✓	✓	✓	✓	
Venezuela								
Atoxane—Drovepat (Venezuela)								✓
Benzal—Isern (Venezuela)								✓
Eltafen—Galeno Química (Venezuela)								✓
Glafen—Ronava (Venezuela)								✓
Glafenino—Klinos (Venezuela)			✓	✓				

Table 4 continued

	Do not use in severe heart failure	No use in ischemic heart disease	No use in acute liver disease	No use in kidney disease	No use in pregnancy	No use with alcohol	Caution with children	None
Gliboral—Cofasa (Venezuela)							✓	
Glifanan—Roussel (West Germany)				(a)		(a)		
Niglafen—Valmorca (Venezuela)			✓	✓				
Rosavil—Fleming (U.S.)								✓
Stepron—Medicamente (U.S.)			-	✓				
Brazil								
Glifanan—Sarsa (Brazil)					✓		✓	

(a) Footnote reference to warnings.

Table 5
Phenylbutazone

(single entities only)

	Not drug of first choice	WARNING OF SERIOUS OR FATAL BLOOD DYSCRASIAS	
		Warning	No warning
United States			
Butazolidin—Geigy (Switzerland)	✓	✓	
Phenylbutazone—Barr (U.S.)			✓
United Kingdom			
Butacote—Geigy (Switzerland)		(a)	
Butazolidin—Geigy (Switzerland)		(a)	
Indonesia			
Irgapan—Dexa Medica (Indonesia)		(a)	
Thailand			
Butazolidin—Ciba-Geigy (Switzerland)		(a)	
Dexalin—General Drugs House (Thailand)		(a)	
Malaysia/Singapore			
Baotazone—SPIC (Malaysia/Singapore)		(a)	
Zolandin—Pharmmalaysia (Malaysia)		✓	
Philippines			
Nortaludin—Crovis Philcom (Italy)		(a)	
Pyrazon—United American (Philippines)		(a)	
Africa			
Butacote—Geigy (Switzerland)	✓	✓	
Butazolidin—Geigy (Switzerland)	✓	✓	
West Africa			
Butazolidine—Geigy (Switzerland)		✓	
Middle East			
Butazolidine—Geigy (Switzerland)	✓	✓	
Caribbean			
Butacote—Geigy (Switzerland)	✓	✓	
Butazolidin—Geigy (Switzerland)	✓	✓	
Mexico			
Butazolidina—Ciba-Geigy (Switzerland)	✓	✓	
Fenilidina—Mavi (Mexico)			✓
Tisatin—Labys (Mexico)			✓
Central America			
Fenilbutazona—McKesson (U.S.)			✓

Table 5 continued

	Not drug of first choice	WARNING OF SERIOUS OR FATAL BLOOD DYSCRASIAS	
		Warning	No warning
Colombia			
Fenilbutazona—Genéricos Farmacéuticas (Colombia)			√
Fenilbutazona—McKesson (U.S.)			√
Venezuela			
Armol—Leti (Venezuela)			√
Butavol—Valmorca (Venezuela)			√
Butazolidina—Geigy (Switzerland)	√	(b)	
Promifen—Ergos (Venezuela)			√
Ticinil—Fher (West Germany)			√
Brazil			
Butazolidina—Geigy (Switzerland)	√	√	

(a) Footnote reference to warnings.
(b) Warning in appendix.

Table 6
Oxyphenbutazone

(single entities only)

	WARNING OF SERIOUS OR FATAL BLOOD DYSCRASIAS	
	Warning	No warning
India		
Inflavam—Khandelwal (India)		✓
Phenabid—IDPL (India)		✓
Reparil—FDC (India)		✓
Sioril—Albert David (India)		✓
Suganril—SG Pharmaceuticals (India)		✓
Versalin—Uniloids (India)		✓
Indonesia		
Reozon—Medichem (Philippines)	(a)	
Rheumapax—Ercopharm (Finland)	(a)	
Sponderil—Bernofarm (Indonesia)	(a)	
Malaysia/Singapore		
Mepharil—Mepha (Switzerland)	(a)	
Africa		
Mepharil—Mepha (Switzerland)		✓
Middle East		
Mepharil—Mepha (Switzerland)		✓
Mexico		
Fedezona—IQFA (Mexico)		✓
Colombia		
Oxifenbutazona—McKesson (U.S.)		✓
Ecuador		
Mefaril—Mepha (Switzerland)	✓	
Omnizona—Francor (Ecuador)	✓	
Venezuela		
Butafen—Meyer (Venezuela)		✓
Butoxifen—Spefar (Venezuela)		✓
Peru		
Dolo-Oxifen-N—Atral (Portugal)		✓
Oxifenibutol—Atral (Portugal)		✓
Brazil		
Tandrexin—Sintofarma (West Germany)	✓	

(a) Footnote reference to warnings.

Table 7
Naproxen

(single entities only)

	Serious or fatal gastrointestinal damage	Serious or fatal liver damage	Can cause kidney damage	Caution in heart disease	Caution in liver disease	Caution in kidney disease	Caution in elderly	Caution in children
United States								
Anaprox—Syntex (U.S.)	√	√	√	√	√	√	√	√
Naprosyn—Syntex (U.S.)	√	√	√	√	√	√	√	√
United Kingdom								
Naprosyn—Syntex (U.S.)	√		√	√	√	√	√	√
Synflex—Syntex (U.S.)	√		√		√	√	√	√
India								
Antisvel—Martel Hammer (India)				√		√		√
Artagen—Montori (India)								√
Naprosyn—Searle (U.S.)					√	√	√	
Naxid—CIPLA (India)					√	√	√	
Rumaxen—Alkem (India)								
Indonesia								
Danaprox—Dankos (Indonesia)				(a)				
Naxen—Syntex (U.S.)				(a)		√		
Thailand								
Arthrisil—Silom-Medical (Thailand)				(a)				
Gibixen—Gibipharma (Thailand)				(a)				
Med-Naproxen—Asian Pharm (Thailand)				(a)				
Naprosyn—Syntex (U.S.)				(a)	√	√		
Napxen—Berlin Pharm (Thailand)				(a)				
Roxen—B. L. Hua (Thailand)				(a)				
Soflyn—Biolab (Thailand)				(a)				
Synflex—Syntex (U.S.)				(a)	√	√		
Synogin—Chinta (Thailand)				(a)				
Malaysia/Singapore								
Naprosyn—Syntex (U.S.)				(a)		√		√
Synflex—Syntex (U.S.)				(a)		√		
Philippines								
Naprosyn—Syntex (U.S.)				(a)		√		

Table 7 continued

	Serious or fatal gastrointestinal damage	Serious or fatal liver damage	Can cause kidney damage	Caution in heart disease	Caution in liver disease	Caution in kidney disease	Caution in elderly	Caution in children
WARNINGS								
Africa								
Naprium—Radiumfarma (Italy)								
Naprosyn—Syntex (U.S.)				√	√	√		
Priaxen—Remedica (Cyprus)	√	√	√	√	√	√		
Prodexin—Prodes (Spain)						√		
West Africa								
Apranax—Laroche Navarron (France)	√	√	√	√	√	√	√	√
Napro—Roussel (West Germany)	√	√	√	√	√	√	√	√
Middle East								
Naprium—Radiumfarma (Italy)								
Naprosyn—Syntex (U.S.)	√	√	√	√	√	√		√
Priaxen—Remedica (Cyprus)	√	√	√	√	√	√		
Prodexin—Prodes (Spain)					√	√		
Proxen—Grünenthal (West Germany)	√	√	√					
Caribbean								
Naprosyn—Syntex (U.S.)	√	√	√	√	√	√		√
Priaxen—Remedica (Cyprus)	√	√	√	√	√	√		
Mexico								
Artrixen—Cryopharma (Mexico)	√			√	√	√		√
Darimal—Carnot (Mexico)	√			√	√	√		√
Flanax—Syntex (U.S.)	√	√	√	√	√	√	√	√
Naxen—Syntex (U.S.)	√	√	√	√	√	√	√	√
Pro-Mav—Mavi (Mexico)	√				√	√		√
Central America								
Artrixen—Cryopharma (Mexico)				√	√	√		√
Flanax—Syntex (U.S.)	√	√	√	√	√	√		√
Naprosyn—Syntex (U.S.)	√	√	√	√	√	√	√	√
Prodexin—Prodes (Spain)								√
Colombia								
Apronax—Librapharma (Colombia)				√	√	√		√
Naprosyn—Syntex (U.S.)				√	√	√		√

Table 7 continued

	Serious or fatal gastrointestinal damage	Serious or fatal liver damage	Can cause kidney damage	Caution in heart disease	Caution in liver disease	Caution in kidney disease	Caution in elderly	Caution in children
WARNINGS								
Venezuela								
Apranax—SmithKline & French (U.S.)								√
Synaprosyn—SmithKline & French (U.S.)					√	√		√
Peru								
Naprosyn—Grünenthal (West Germany)	√		√	√	√	√		√
Sinartrin—Sanitas (Peru)								√
Brazil								
Naprosyn—Syntex (U.S.)								

NOTE: Most of the products listed here are contraindicated in pregnancy, in patients sensitive to aspirin and NSAIDs, and in those with a history of GI disorders.
(a) Footnote reference to warnings.

Table 8
Tiaprofenic Acid

(single entities only)

	INDICATIONS				WARNINGS		
	Serious forms of arthritis	Soft-tissue inflammation	Low back pain	Posttraumatic or postsurgical pain	Caution in heart disease	Caution in kidney disease	Caution in liver disease
United Kingdom Surgam—Roussel (West Germany)	√					√	√
Indonesia Surgam—Hoechst (West Germany)	√	√			√	√	√
Thailand Surgam—Roussel (West Germany)	√	√	√	√			
Malaysia/Singapore Surgam—Roussel (West Germany)	√	√					
Philippines Surgam—Roussel (West Germany)	√	√	√	√		√	√
Africa Surgam—Roussel (West Germany)	√	√				√	√
West Africa Surgam—Roussel (West Germany)	√	√		√	√	√	√
Caribbean Surgam—Roussel (West Germany)	√	√				√	√
Mexico Surgam—Roussel (West Germany)	√	√			√	√	√
Central America Surgam—Roussel (West Germany)	√	√		√			
Ecuador Surgam—Roussel (West Germany)	√	√	√		√		
Venezuela Torpas—Roussel (West Germany)				√	√	√	√
Peru Surgam—Roussel (West Germany)	√	√			√		

NOTE: Virtually all products listed here carry warnings against use in pregnancy and lactation, in children, in peptic ulcer, and in any sensitivity to aspirin or NSAIDs.

Table 9
Piroxicam

(single entities only)

	WARNINGS								
	Serious or fatal gastrointestinal damage	Serious or fatal liver damage	Can cause kidney damage	Caution in heart disease	Caution in liver disease	Caution in kidney disease	Caution with use of diuretics	Caution in elderly	Caution in children
United States									
Feldene—Pfizer (U.S.)	√	√	√	√	√	√	√	√	√
United Kingdom									
Feldene—Pfizer (U.S.)					√	√			√
India									
Brexic—Wockhardt (India)				√	√	√			√
Movon—IPCA (India)				√	√	√	√		√
Pirox—CIPLA (India)				√	√	√			√
Toldin—Torrent (India)				√	√	√			√
Indonesia									
Arpyrox—Kenrose (Indonesia)									
Felco—Coronet (Indonesia)									
Feldene—Pfizer (U.S.)									
Indene—Kalbe Farma (Indonesia)									
Infeld—New Interbat (Indonesia)									
Mepirox—Meprofarm (Indonesia)									
Pirodene—Medikon Prima (Indonesia)									
Rexicam—Otto (Indonesia)									
Rheumaden—Pharos Indonesia (Indonesia)									
Rosic—Pharos Indonesia (Indonesia)									
Roxidene—Combiphar (Indonesia)					√	√			
Thailand									
Felcam—Asian Pharm (Thailand)									
Feldene—Pfizer (U.S.)									
Flamic—Siam Bheasach (Thailand)									
Focus—Yung Shin (Thailand)									
Med-Proxicam—Medical Supply (Thailand)									

Table 9 continued

	Serious or fatal gastrointestinal damage	Serious or fatal liver damage	Can cause kidney damage	Caution in heart disease	Caution in liver disease	Caution in kidney disease	Caution with use of diuretics	Caution in elderly	Caution in children
Piram—General Drugs House (Thailand)									
Piroxen—Codal Synto (Thailand)									
Pyroxy—Shiwa (Thailand)									
Riacen—Chiesi (Italy)									
Sotilen—Medochemie (Switzerland)									
Malaysia/Singapore									
Feldene—Pfizer (U.S.)									
Philippines									
Feldene—Pfizer (U.S.)									
Africa									
Feldene—Pfizer (U.S.)									
Piroxim—R & N (Greece)									
Roxitan—Remedica (Cyprus)						√		√	
Sotilen—Medochemie (Cyprus)						√			
West Africa									
Feldene—Pfizer (U.S.)	√			√	√	√	√		√
Middle East									
Feldene—Pfizer (U.S.)									
Piroxim—R & N (Greece)									
Riacen–Chiesi (Italy)				√	√	√			
Roxitan—Remedica (Cyprus)						√		√	
Sotilen—Medochemie (Cyprus)						√			
Caribbean									
Feldene—Pfizer (U.S.)				√	√				
Roxitan—Remedica (Cyprus)						√			√
Sotilen—Medochemie (Cyprus)						√			
Mexico									
Algidol—Carnot (Mexico)	√								√
Dixonal—Medix (Spain)	√		√	√		√			√

Table 9 continued — WARNINGS

	Serious or fatal gastrointestinal damage	Serious or fatal liver damage	Can cause kidney damage	Caution in heart disease	Caution in liver disease	Caution in kidney disease	Caution with use of diuretics	Caution in elderly	Caution in children
Facicam—Senosiain (Mexico)			√		√				√
Osteral—Silanes (Mexico)						√			√
Piroxan—Diba (Mexico)						√			√
Central America									
Arten—Donovan Werke (Guatemala)									√
Dixonal—Medix (Spain)	√			√	√	√			√
Feldene—Pfizer (U.S.)	√	√	√	√	√	√	√		√
Osteral—Silanes (Mexico)						√			√
Vitaxicam—Robert (Spain)	√					√			
Colombia									
Artrimed—Medicalsa (Colombia)			√			√			
Feldene—Pfizer (U.S.)	√	√	√	√	√	√	√		√
Medoptil—Lafrancol (Colombia)									√
Monidem—Kressfor (Colombia)						√			√
Piroxedol—Incobra (Colombia)									√
Piroxicam—Gen-Far (Colombia)						√			√
Piroxicam—McKesson (U.S.)						√			√
Piroxim—Hisubiette (Colombia)						√			√
Proxigel—Procaps (Colombia)									√
Stopen—Biogen (Colombia)									√
Ecuador									
Artronil—Acromax (Ecuador)	√								√
Feldene—Pfizer (U.S.)	√	√	√	√	√	√	√		√
Piroxicam—McKesson (U.S.)						√			√
Piroxim—ECU (Ecuador)	√				√	√			√
Venezuela									
Feldene—Pfizer (U.S.)									√
Lepexal—Palenzona (Venezuela)									
Pelsan—Proton (Venezuela)									
Pirocam—Leti (Venezuela)						√	√		

Table 9 continued

	Serious or fatal gastrointestinal damage	Serious or fatal liver damage	Can cause kidney damage	Caution in heart disease	Caution in liver disease	Caution in kidney disease	Caution with use of diuretics	Caution in elderly	Caution in children
Piroxicam—McKesson (U.S)									
Pixorid—Klinos (Venezuela)						√	√		√
Peru									
Desinflam—Sintyal (Argentina)									
Feldene—Pfizer (U.S.)	√	√	√	√	√	√	√		√
Pirocaps—Magma (Peru)									
Brazil									
Anartrit—Química Intercontinental (Brazil)									
Feldene—Pfizer (U.S.)	√				√	√			√
Inflamene—Farmalab (West Germany)									
Piroxene—Sintofarma (West Germany)									
Piroxiflam—Luitpold (West Germany)	√				√				

NOTE: Virtually all products listed here are contraindicated for use in pregnancy and in patients sensitive to aspirin or NSAIDs.

Table 10
Clioquinol

(includes chloriodohydroxyquinolone and other
halogenated hydroxyquinolones; combinations and
single entities)

	WARNING OF NEUROLOGICAL DAMAGE	
	Warning	No warning
India		
(Listed as "essential drug" by government agency)		
#Aldiamycin—Alkem (India)	√	
#Alliquin Forte—Standard (India)	√	
#Amicline Plus—Franco Indian (India)	√	
#Chlorambin—AFD (India)	√	
#Demigyl—Deepharma (India)		√
Diiodoquin—Searle (U.S.)	√	
Dysenchlor—SG Pharmaceuticals (India)	√	
#Dysfur Plus—Biological E (India)	√	
Entero Quinol—East India (India)	√	
#Entrozyme—Stedmed (India)	√	
Iodomegyl—Indoco (India)		√
#Nivembin—May & Baker (France)		√
#Qugyl—Searle (U.S.)	√	
#Saril—Rallis (India)	√	
Indonesia		
Bintaform—Bintang Toedjoe (Indonesia)	(a)	
#Diarent—Kenrose (Indonesia)	(a)	
#Diarex—Pharmac Apex (Indonesia)	(a)	
#Enterobiotic—New Interbat (Indonesia)	(a)	
#Enterodiastop—Combiphar (Indonesia)	(a)	
Enterosept—Soho (Indonesia)	(a)	
#Enteroviosulfa—Kimla Farma (Indonesia)	(a)	
#Himaform Sulfa—Himajaya (Indonesia)	(a)	
#Koniform—Konimex (Indonesia)	(a)	
#Libroform—Bintang Toedjoe (Indonesia)	(a)	
#Mebinol Complex—Farmitalia Carlo Erba (Italy)	(a)	
#Nifural—Pharos Chemie (Indonesia)	(a)	
Quixalen—Squibb (U.S.)	(a)	
#Sulfa-Plus—Nellco (Indonesia)	(a)	
#Viostreptin—Bernofarm (Indonesia)	(a)	
#Viosulfan—Pharos Indonesia (Indonesia)	(a)	
Thailand		
#Chlorotracin—Chew Brothers (Thailand)	(a)	
#Coccila—Thai Nakorn Patana (Thailand)	(a)	

Table 10 continued

	WARNING OF NEUROLOGICAL DAMAGE	
	Warning	No warning
#Diolin—Chinta (Thailand)	(a)	
Dysetrin—B. L. Hua (Thailand)	(a)	
#Mediocin—Medical Supply (Thailand)	(a)	
#Neomobin—Osoth (Thailand)	(a)	
#Vanoform—Vana (Thailand)	(a)	
Middle East		
#Entox—Wyeth (U.S.)	√	
Egypt		
#Chlodiquine—Misr (Egypt)		√
#Diamycin—Memphis (Egypt)		√
#Dysentrin—Pharco (Egypt)		√
#Enteroguanil—Nile (Egypt)		√
Enteroquin—Adco (Egypt)		√
#Enteroquin Compound—Adco (Egypt)		√
#Entocid—Cid (Egypt)		√
#Entox—Wyeth (U.S.)		√
#Gabion Forte—Kahira (Egypt)		√
#Gabiozol—Kahira (Egypt)		√
#Intestopan—Sandoz (Switzerland)		√
#Mebinol Complex—Carlo Erba Farmitalia (Italy)		√
#Neo-Carbotrina—Adco (Egypt)		√
#Neo-Enterocin—Memphis (Egypt)		√
Paramibe Forte—Cid (Egypt)		√
#Resotrene Compound—Alex/Bayer (Egypt/West Germany)		√
Mexico		
Amoecol—Byk Gulden (West Germany)		√
#Amoecol Plus—Byk Gulden (West Germany)		√
#Anayodil—Willmar (Mexico)	√	
#Antral Pediátrico Suspensión—Carnot (Mexico)		√
Barak—Zerboni (Mexico)	√	
#Barak-Plus—Zerboni (Mexico)		√
#Colfur—Carter-Wallace (U.S.)	√	
Diiodoquin—Searle (U.S.)	√	
#Dipec—Yauquimia de Mexico (Mexico)	√	
Di-Sulkin—Arlex (Mexico)	√	

Table 10 continued

	WARNING OF NEUROLOGICAL DAMAGE	
	Warning	No warning
#Ditayod—Solfran (Mexico)	√	
Diyoleina—Carnot (Mexico)	√	
Entero-Diyod—Serral (West Germany)	√	
#Entero-Diyod Compuesta—Serral (West Germany)		√
Entodiba—Diba (Mexico)	√	
#Farmeban—Farmasa (Mexico)	√	
#Flagenase-400—Liomont (Mexico)	√	
#Mebinol Compuesto—Carlo Erba Farmitalia (Italy)	√	
#Metodine—Searle (U.S.)	√	
#Metrodiyod—Serral (West Germany)	√	
#Metroviform Pharmexakta—Pharmacos Exacta (Mexico)	√	
Oxibeldina—Lagasa (Mexico)	√	
#Prometac—Provit (Mexico)	√	
#Solfurol—Solfran (Mexico)	√	
#Stopen—Berman (Mexico)		√
#Vioftalyl—Andre Bigaux (Mexico)	√	
#Yosul—Rigers (Mexico)		√
#Zetaquin—Kener (Mexico)	√	
Central America		
#Combiase—Luitpold-Werk (West Germany)	√	
#Diaprin—Laprin (Colombia)		√
Diiodoquin—Searle (U.S.)	√	
Diyodo—Bonin (Guatemala)	√	
Diyodomeb—Laprin (Colombia)		√
#Enterogamma—Gamma (Netherlands)		√
#Enterolan—Lancasco (Guatemala)	√	
#Metodine—Searle (U.S.)	√	
#Metro-Van—Donovan (Guatemala)		√
Colombia		
Diiodoquin—Searle (U.S.)	√	
#Metodine—Searle (U.S.)	√	
#Metronidil—Hisubiette (Colombia)	√	
Pediarsan—Pediátrica (Colombia)		√
Ecuador		
#Acromeba—Acromax (Ecuador)		√

Table 10 continued

	WARNING OF NEUROLOGICAL DAMAGE	
	Warning	No warning
Venezuela		
Diiodoquin—Searle (U.S.)		√
Enterquin—Klinos (Venezuela)		√
#Mebinol Complex—Farmitalia Carlo Erba (Italy)		√
#Micyn-2—Meyer (Venezuela)		√
#Vioformol—Vita (Venezuela)		√
#Viotan—Gache (Venezuela)		√
Brazil		
#Adesinter Pedriático Granulado—Opofarm (Brazil)		√
#Atacoly—Profarb (Brazil)		√
#Darm-Sept—Elofar (Brazil)		√
#Diapulgil—Prismut (Brazil)		√
#Diarrepax Comprimidos—U.S. Med (Brazil)		√
#Enterobion—Makros (Brazil)		√
#Enterovital—Vital Brazil (Brazil)		√
#Furacitren—Laborsil (Brazil)		√
#Furazolin—de Mayo (Brazil)		√
#Intestiazin—Endoterápica do Brasil (Brazil)		√
#Neobacter—Osorio de Moraes (Brazil)		√
#Suspensão de Furazolidona—Laborsil (Brazil)		√
#Tratocoli—Ima (Brazil)		√

(#) Combination product.
(a) Footnote reference to warnings of possible neurological damage.

Table 11

Diphenoxylate + Atropine

	Extreme caution with children	Minimum age (years)	No use in intestinal obstruction	No use in obstructive jaundice	No use in diarrhea associated with pseudomembranous colitis	Caution in liver, kidney disease	Caution in acute ulcerative colitis	Caution with use of CNS depressants[1]
					WARNINGS			
United States								
Lomotil—Searle (U.S.)	√	2	√	√	√	√	√	√
United Kingdom								
Lomotil—Gold Cross (U.S.)	√	4	√	√	√		√	√
India								
Lomotil—Searle (U.S.)	√	6		√	√		√	√
Indonesia								
Lomotil—Searle (U.S.)		2	√		√		√	
Thailand								
Dilomil—Siam Bheasach (Thailand)		2	√	√	√			√
Diphensil—Silom Medical (Thailand)		2	√	√	√			√
Ditropine—Asian Pharm (Thailand)		2	√	√	√			√
Katevan—Medica Pharma (Thailand)		2	√		√			√
Lomotil—Searle (U.S.)		2	√		√		√	√
Malaysia/Singapore								
Diarase—Asia Pharm (Thailand)		2	√		√			√
Lomotil—Searle (U.S.)		2	√		√			√
Reasec—Janssen (U.S.)			√				√	
Philippines								
Lomotil—Searle (U.S.)	√	2						√
Africa								
Lomotil—Searle (U.S.)								√
Reasec—Janssen (U.S.)		2				√		
Middle East								
Lomotil—Searle (U.S.)								√
Reasec—Janssen (U.S.)		5						√
Caribbean								
Lomotil—Searle (U.S.)								√

Table 11 continued

	Extreme caution with children	Minimum age (years)	No use in intestinal obstruction	No use in obstructive jaundice	No use in diarrhea associated with pseudomembranous colitis	Caution in liver, kidney disease	Caution in acute ulcerative colitis	Caution with use of CNS depressants[1]
					WARNINGS			
Mexico								
Lomotil—Searle (U.S.)	√	2			√	√	√	√
Tropatil—Cryopharma (Mexico)								√
Central America								
Gastril—Raven (Costa Rica)				√				√
Lomotil—Searle (U.S.)	√	2		√	√	√	√	√
Tropatil—Cryopharma (Mexico)								√
Colombia								
Lomotil—Searle (U.S.)	√	2		√	√	√	√	√
Ecuador								
Lomotil—Searle (U.S.)	√	2			√	√	√	√
Venezuela								
Lomotil—Searle (U.S.)		2			√			
Brazil								
Lomotil—Searle (U.S.)								

[1]Sedatives, tranquilizers, alcohol, MAO inhibitors.

Table 12
Loperamide

(single entities only)

	INDICATIONS			WARNINGS						
	Acute or chronic diarrhea[1]	Diarrhea of any cause	Gastroenteritis, chronic colitis, ulcerative colitis	No use with organisms that perforate intestinal mucosa[2]	Caution in liver disease	Caution in pregnancy, lactation	Caution in ulcerative colitis	Minimum age (years)	No use if peristalsis must be maintained	Stop if no improvement in 48 hours
United States										
Imodium—Janssen (U.S.)	✓			✓	✓	✓	✓	2	✓	✓
United Kingdom										
Imodium—Janssen (U.S.)		✓					✓	4		
India										
Diarlop—Jagson Pal (India)		✓							✓	
Lopamide—Torrent (India)		✓						2	✓	
Lopestal—Sarabhai (India)		✓						2	✓	
Lorico—Raptakos (India)		✓						2	✓	
Tylox-2—Deepharma (India)		✓						2	✓	
Indonesia										
Antida—Bernofarm (Indonesia)	✓					✓		2		✓
Imodium—Janssen (U.S.)	✓			✓		✓		2		✓
Imore—Soho (Indonesia)	✓			✓		✓		2		✓
Lodia—Sanbe (Indonesia)	✓			✓				2	✓	✓
Loremid—Meprofarm (Indonesia)	✓					✓		2		
Mecodiar—Mecosin (Indonesia)		✓		✓		✓		2		✓
Motilex—Dankos (Indonesia)		✓		✓		✓		2		✓
Normudal—Combiphar (Indonesia)		✓		✓		✓		2		
Oramide—Medichem (Philippines)	✓			✓					✓	
Promodium—Ikapharmindo (Israel)	✓							5	✓	
Tanitril—Kenrose (Indonesia)	✓			✓		✓		2		✓
Thailand										
Diarodil—Greater Pharma (Thailand)	✓			✓	✓	✓		1	✓	✓
Imodium—Janssen (U.S.)	✓			✓	✓	✓		6	✓	✓
Lomide—Siam Bheasach (Thailand)	✓			✓		✓		1		✓
Perasian—Asian Pharm (Thailand)	✓			✓		✓		2		✓
Vacontil—Medochemie (Switzerland)	✓			✓		✓		2		✓

Table 12 continued

	INDICATIONS			WARNINGS						
	Acute or chronic diarrhea[1]	Diarrhea of any cause	Gastroenteritis, chronic colitis, ulcerative colitis	No use with organisms that perforate intestinal mucosa[2]	Caution in liver disease	Caution in pregnancy, lactation	Caution in ulcerative colitis	Minimum age (years)	No use if peristalsis must be maintained	Stop if no improvement in 48 hours
Malaysia/Singapore										
Beamodium—Upha (Malaysia/ Singapore)	√			√		√		5		
Imodium—Janssen (U.S.)	√			√		√		5		√
Vacontil—Medochemie (Switzerland)	√							5		
Philippines										
Alomide—Terramedic (Philippines)	√			√	√	√		2	√	√
Imodium—Janssen (U.S.)	√			√		√		2	√	√
Lormide—Medichem (Philippines)	√			√		√		2	√	√
Rodderhea—Roddensers (Philippines)	√			√		√		2	√	√
VCP Loperamide—VCP (Philippines)	√							3	√	
Africa										
Imodium—Janssen (U.S.)		√				√		1	√	
Loperium—Remedica (Cyprus)		√					√	1		
Vacontil—Medochemie (Cyprus)		√						1		
West Africa										
Imodium—Janssen (U.S.)	√									√
Middle East										
Imodium—Janssen (U.S.)		√				√		1	√	
Loperium—Remedica (Cyprus)		√					√	1		
Miraten—Codal Synto (Cyprus)		√					√			
Vacontil—Medochemie (Cyprus)		√						1		
Caribbean										
Imodium—Janssen (U.S.)		√				√		1	√	
Imosec—ICI (U.K.)		√					√	4	√	
Loperium—Remedica (Cyprus)		√					√	1		
Vacontil—Medochemie (Cyprus)		√					√	1		

Table 12 continued

	INDICATIONS				WARNINGS					
	Acute or chronic diarrhea[1]	Diarrhea of any cause	Gastroenteritis, chronic colitis, ulcerative colitis	No use with organisms that perforate intestinal mucosa[2]	Caution in liver disease	Caution in pregnancy, lactation	Caution in ulcerative colitis	Minimum age (years)	No use if peristalsis must be maintained	Stop if no improvement in 48 hours
Mexico										
Acanol—Columbia (Mexico)		√						2	√	
Imodium—Janssen (U.S.)	√				√	√	√	2	√	
Regulene—Searle (U.S.)	√					√		2	√	
Central America										
Imodium—Janssen (U.S.)	√	√	√			√	√	1	√	
Lopediar—Gutis (Costa Rica)	√	√	√			√	√	1	√	
Loperam—Lafsa (El Salvador)		√					√	1		
Prodom—Feltrex (Dominican Republic)	√	√	√					1	√	
Colombia										
Imodium—Janssen (U.S.)	√	√				√	√	2	√	
Loperamida—McKesson (U.S.)	√						√	2		
Novadiar—Chalver (Colombia)		√				√	√	2	√	
Pebisul—Caribe (Colombia)		√					√	2	√	
Plenterox—Incobra (Colombia)		√				√		2	√	
Stomalix—Laboratorios América (Colombia)	√					√	√	2	√	
Ecuador										
Imodium—Janssen (U.S.)	√					√		1	√	
Loriden—Acromax (Ecuador)	√					√		1	√	
Venezuela										
Glucitol—Isern (Venezuela)		√						5		
Imodium—Janssen (U.S.)		√				√	√	1		
Loperam—Bequim (Venezuela)		√				√		1		
Oldan—Adromaco (Spain)		√					√			
Pricilone—SM (Venezuela)		√				√	√	1		
Peru										
Imodium—Janssen (U.S.)	√	√	√			√			√	
Brazil										
Imosec—Janssen (U.S.)	√	√	√	√	√	√	√	2	√	

[1]Control and symptomatic relief of acute nonspecific diarrhea and of chronic diarrhea associated with inflammatory bowel disease.
[2]E.g., *Salmonella, Shigella.*

Table 13
Chloramphenicol
(single entities only)

	No use for trivial infections or prophylaxis, no prolonged use	No such warnings	Comments
United States			
Chloromycetin—Parke-Davis (U.S.)	√		
United Kingdom			
Chloromycetin—Parke-Davis (U.S.)	√		
Kemicetine—Farmitalia Carlo Erba (Italy)		√	
India			
All listed products	(a)		
Southeast Asia (Indonesia, Thailand, Malaysia/Singapore, Philippines)			
All listed products	(a)		
Africa, West Africa, Middle East			
All listed products	√		
Caribbean			
Chloromycetin—Parke-Davis (U.S.)	√		
Paraxin—Boehringer-Mannheim (West Germany)	√		
Suismycetin—Lagap (Switzerland)	√		
Mexico			
Cetina—Infar (Mexico)		√	
Cofarmycin—Zerboni (Mexico)		√	
Chloromycetin—Parke-Davis (U.S.)	√		
Furocloran—Laboratorios A.F. (Mexico)		√	
Italmicin—Italmex (Mexico)	√		
Nicopirinas—Productos Tera-péuticos Méxicanos (Mexico)		√	
Palmiclor—F. Universales (Mexico)		√	
Paraxin—Boehringer-Mannheim (West Germany)		√	
Quemicetena—Farmitalia Carlo Erba (Italy)	√		
Tetrafenicol—Grossman (Mexico)		√	No use in trivial infections
Central America			
Chloromycetin—Parke-Davis (U.S.)	√		
Chloranfenicol—McKesson (U.S.)		√	
Quemicetina—Farmitalia Carlo Erba (Italy)		√	

Table 13 continued

	No use for trivial infections or prophylaxis, no prolonged use	No such warnings	Comments
Colombia			
Chloromycetin—Parke-Davis (U.S.)	√		
Cloranfenicol—Gen-Far (Colombia)		√	No use in trivial infections
Infa Portal—Pediátricas (Colombia)		√	No use for prophylaxis
Quemicetina—Carlo Erba (Italy)		√	
Sintomicetina—Legrand (Colombia)		√	
Ecuador			
Acromaxfenicol—Acromax (Ecuador)		√	No prolonged use
Alfa-Cloromicol—Laboratorios H.G. (Ecuador)		√	
Venezuela			
Chloromycetin—Parke-Davis (U.S.)	√		
Chloramfenicol—McKesson (U.S.)		√	
Chloramfesa—Fesa (Venezuela)		√	
Peru			
Chloromisan—Sanitas (Peru)		√	Caution in prolonged use
Clorosantina—Unidos (Peru)		√	
Farmicetina—Farmindustria (Peru)		√	
Quemicetina—Farmitalia Carlo Erba (Italy)		√	

(a) Footnote reference to warnings.

Table 14
Tetracycline

(single entities only)

	No use in pregnancy, children	No use in kidney disease	Caution in liver disease	No such warnings
United States				
Achromycin V—Lederle (U.S.)	✓	✓	✓	
Sumycin—Squibb (U.S.)	✓	✓	✓	
Tetracycline—Warner-Chilcott (U.S.)	✓	✓	✓	
United Kingdom				
Achromycin—Lederle (U.S.)	✓	✓	✓	
Sustamycin—MCP (U.K.)	✓	✓	✓	
Tetrabid—Organon (Netherlands)	✓	✓	✓	
Tetrechel—Berk (U.S.)	✓	✓	✓	
Tetrex—Bristol-Myers (U.S.)	✓	✓	✓	
India				
Achromycin—Cyanamid (U.S.)	✓	✓	✓	
Alcyclin—Alembic (India)	✓	✓	✓	
Hostacycline—Hoechst (West Germany)	✓	✓	✓	
Lymesal—Walter Bushnell (India)			✓	
Resteclin—Sarabhai (India)		✓	✓	
Threocycline—IDPL (India)		✓	✓	
Southeast Asia (Indonesia, Thailand, Malaysia/Singapore, Philippines)				
All listed products	(a)	(a)	(a)	
Africa				
All listed products	(a)	(a)	(a)	
West Africa				
Hexacycline—Roussel (West Germany)	✓	✓	✓	
Tetracycline Diamant—Roussel (West Germany)	✓	✓	✓	
Middle East				
All listed products	(a)	(a)	(a)	
Caribbean				
All listed products	(a)	(a)	(a)	
Mexico				
Acromicina—Lederle (U.S.)	✓	✓	✓	
Cofarcilina—Zerboni (Mexico)				✓

Table 14 continued

	No use in pregnancy, children	No use in kidney disease	Caution in liver disease	No such warnings
Maviciclina—Mavi (Mexico)	√	√	√	
Quimocyclar—Grossman (Mexico)	√	√	√	
Tetra—Atlantis (Mexico)	√			
Tetrex—Bristol (U.S.)	√	√	√	
Central America				
Quimocyclar—Grossman (Mexico)	√	√	√	
Steclin—Squibb (U.S.)		√		
Tetraciclina MK—McKesson (U.S.)	√			
Tetrasuk—Sukia (Costa Rica)	√	√	√	
Tetrex—Bristol (U.S.)	√	√	√	
Colombia				
Ambramicina 500—Legrand (Colombia)	√	√	√	
Pirocyclina—America (Colombia)		√	√	
Tetraciclina—Gen-Far (Colombia)	√	√	√	
Ecuador				
Tetrabiotica—Laboratorios H.G. (Ecuador)	√			
Tetraciclina—McKesson (U.S.)	√			
Tetracu—Ecu (Ecuador)	√			
Tetrex—Bristol (U.S.)	√	√		
Venezuela				
Acromicina—Lederle (U.S.)				√
Ambramicina—Lepetit (U.S.)				√
Peru				
Tetracina—Pfizer (U.S.)	√	√	√	
Tetranase 500—Rorer (U.S.)	√		√	
Brazil				
Terramicina—Pfizer (U.S.)	√	√	√	

(a) Footnote reference to warnings.

Table 15
Lincomycin
(single entities only)

	WARNINGS			
	Severe or fatal colitis	Colitis	Gastro-intestinal disorder	No colitis warning
United States				
Lincocin—Upjohn (U.S.)	✓			
United Kingdom				
Lincocin—Upjohn (U.S.)		✓		
India				
Lincocin—Wallace (U.S.)	✓			
Indonesia				
Lincocin—Upjohn (U.S.)		✓		
Thailand				
Linco—General Drugs House (Thailand)				✓
Linco-P—P.P. Labs (Thailand)				✓
Lincocin—Upjohn (U.S.)		✓		
Lincolan—Olan (Thailand)				✓
Lingo—Siam Bheasach (Thailand)		✓		
Linmycin—Vana (Thailand)		✓		
Malaysia / Singapore				
Lincocin—Upjohn (U.S.)		✓		
Philippines				
Lincocin—Upjohn (U.S.)			✓	
Africa				
Lincocin—Upjohn (U.S.)				✓
West Africa				
Lincocine—Upjohn (U.S.)	✓			
Middle East				
Lincocin—Upjohn (U.S.)				✓
Caribbean				
Lincocin—Upjohn (U.S.)			✓	
Mexico				
Lincocin—Upjohn (U.S.)	✓			
Princol—Provit (Mexico)	✓			
Colombia				
Clordelin—Chalver (Colombia)	✓			
Lincocin—Upjohn (U.S.)	✓			

Table 15 continued

	WARNINGS			
	Severe or fatal colitis	Colitis	Gastro-intestinal disorder	No colitis warning
Venezuela				
Bekalin—Leti (Venezuela)				✓
Formicine—Fleming (U.S.)				✓
Lincocin—Upjohn (U.S.)			✓	
Peru				
Lincocin—Upjohn (U.S.)	✓			
Brazil				
Frademicina—Upjohn (U.S.)				✓
Lincomicina—Royton (Brazil)				✓

Table 16
Nalidixic Acid

(single entities only)

	Urinary infections	Intestinal infections	Convulsive disorders	Liver disease	Kidney disease	Cerebral arteriosclerosis	Exposure to sunlight	Use in pregnancy	Use in infants
United States									
Neg Gram—Winthrop (U.S.)	✓		✓	✓	✓	✓	✓	✓	✓
United Kingdom									
Negram—Sterling (U.S.)	✓		✓	✓	✓		✓		✓
Uriben—R.P. Drugs (U.K.)	✓		✓	✓	✓		✓		✓
India									
Gramoneg—Ranbaxy (India)	✓		✓	✓	✓		✓	✓	
Negadix—CFL Pharma (India)	✓		✓	✓	✓		✓	✓	
Urodic—Deepharma (India)	✓		✓	✓	✓		✓	✓	
Wintomylon—Win-Medicare (U.S.)	✓		✓	✓	✓		✓	✓	✓
Indonesia									
Negram—Sterling Winthrop (U.S.)	✓	✓	(a)	(a)	(a)	(a)	(a)		✓
Urineg—Conmed (Indonesia)	✓	✓	(a)	(a)	(a)	(a)	(a)		✓
Thailand									
Gramoneg—Ranbaxy (India)	✓	✓	✓	(a)	(a)	(a)	(a)		
Wintomylon—Winthrop-Sterling (U.S.)	✓	✓	(a)	(a)	(a)	(a)	(a)		
Malaysia/Singapore									
Wintomylon—Winthrop (U.S.)	✓	✓	✓	(a)	(a)	(a)	(a)	✓	✓
Philippines									
Wintomylon—Winthrop (U.S.)	✓	✓	✓	(a)	(a)	(a)	✓	✓	
Africa									
Navigramon—Medimpex (Hungary)	✓		✓	✓	✓		✓		
Wintomylon—Winthrop (U.S.)	✓			✓	✓		✓		
Middle East									
Gramoneg—Ranbaxy (India)	✓	✓	✓	✓	✓		✓		
Negram—Winthrop (U.S.)	✓	✓	✓	✓	✓		✓		
Nevigramon—Medimpex (Hungary)	✓		✓	✓	✓		✓		
Mexico									
Acidix—Solfran (Mexico)	✓			✓	✓			✓	✓
Acinal—Tegur (Mexico)	✓			✓				✓	✓

Table 16 continued

	Urinary infections	Intestinal infections	Convulsive disorders	Liver disease	Kidney disease	Cerebral arteriosclerosis	Exposure to sunlight	Use in pregnancy	Use in infants
	INDICATIONS		WARNINGS						
Bonalidix—Zerboni (Mexico)	✓	✓		✓			✓	✓	✓
Dianoc—Carnot (Mexico)	✓	✓	✓	✓	✓		✓	✓	✓
Ditracil—Grossman (Mexico)	✓	✓	✓	✓	✓	✓	✓	✓	✓
Dixik—Welfer (Mexico)	✓		✓	✓	✓			✓	✓
Dixilon—Marcel (Mexico)	✓	✓		✓			✓	✓	✓
Nalidac—Sanofi (France)	✓		✓	✓	✓	✓	✓	✓	✓
Nalidixico—Briter (Mexico)	✓	✓					✓	✓	✓
Nalix—Reuffer (Mexico)	✓						✓	✓	✓
Novaldrin—Mavi (Mexico)	✓		✓				✓	✓	✓
Patixico—IQFA (Mexico)	✓			✓	✓		✓	✓	✓
Patobac—Rudefsa (Mexico)	✓		✓	✓	✓		✓	✓	✓
Quimedix—IQFA (Mexico)	✓	✓					✓	✓	✓
Seltomylon—Diba (Mexico)	✓	✓	✓				✓	✓	
Unidixina—Universales (Mexico)	✓						✓	✓	✓
Wintomylon—Winthrop (U.S.)	✓	✓	✓	✓	✓	✓	✓	✓	✓
Central America									
Nalydixine—Quimifar (Dominican Republic)	✓	✓	✓	✓	✓			✓	✓
Wintomylon—Winthrop (U.S.)	✓	✓	✓	✓	✓	✓	✓	✓	
Colombia									
Negatrate—Winthrop (U.S.)	✓		✓	✓	✓			✓	✓
Wintomylon—Winthrop (U.S.)	✓		✓	✓	✓			✓	✓
Ecuador									
Wintomylon—Winthrop (U.S.)	✓	✓	✓	✓	✓		✓	✓	✓
Venezuela									
Lixi—Palenzona (Venezuela)	✓							✓	✓
Nalix—Copharma (Venezuela)	✓	✓							
Wintomylon—Winthrop (U.S.)	✓	✓	✓	✓	✓	✓	✓	✓	✓
Peru									
Negatrate—Winthrop (U.S.)	✓		✓	✓	✓	✓	✓	✓	✓
Wintomylon—Winthrop (U.S.)	✓	✓	✓	✓	✓	✓	✓	✓	✓

(a) Footnote reference to warnings.

Table 17

Cyproheptadine

(single entities only)

	Allergic conditions	Appetite stimulation	Caution in children	Caution in pregnancy	Caution in elderly	Caution with glaucoma	Caution with urinary retention	Caution with MAO inhibitors	No warnings
	INDICATIONS		WARNINGS						
United States									
Periactin—MSD (U.S.)	√		√	√	√	√	√	√	
United Kingdom									
Periactin—MSD (U.S.)	√	√	√	√	√	√	√	√	
India									
Ciplactin—Cipla (India)	√	√	√	√	√	√	√	(a)	
Peritol—Themis (India)		√	√	√	√	√	√	√	
Practin—Merind (India)	√	√	√	√	√	√	√	√	
Indonesia									
Actinal—Pharmac Apex (Indonesia)	√	√	√	(a)	(a)	√	√	(a)	
Arsipron—Meprofarm (Indonesia)	√	√	(a)	(a)	(a)	(a)	(a)	(a)	
Nelactin—Nellco (Indonesia)	√	√	(a)	(a)	(a)	(a)	(a)	(a)	
Thailand									
Aptide—Siam Bheasach (Thailand)	√	√	(a)	(a)	(a)	(a)	(a)	(a)	
Cyheptine—Greater Pharma (Thailand)	√	√	(a)	(a)	(a)	(a)	(a)	(a)	
Cyprogin—Vana (Thailand)	√	√	(a)	(a)	(a)	(a)	(a)	(a)	
Cyprosian—Asian Pharm (Thailand)	√	√	(a)	(a)	(a)	(a)	(a)	(a)	
Periactin—MSD (U.S.)	√	√	(a)	√	√	(a)	√	√	
Malaysia/Singapore									
Periactin—MSD (U.S.)	√		√	(a)	√	(a)	√	√	
Philippines									
Periactin—MSD (U.S.)	√	√	(a)	(a)	(a)	(a)	(a)	(a)	
Africa									
Periactin—MSD (U.S.)	√	√	√	√	√	√	√	√	
Peritol—Medimpex (Hungary)	√			√	√	√	√	√	
Middle East									
Periactin—MSD (U.S.)	√	√	√	√	√	√	√	√	
Peritol—Medimpex (Hungary)	√			√	√	√	√	√	

Table 17 continued

	Allergic conditions	Appetite stimulation	Caution in children	Caution in pregnancy	Caution in elderly	Caution with glaucoma	Caution with urinary retention	Caution with MAO inhibitors	No warnings
	INDICATIONS		WARNINGS						
Caribbean									
Peritol—Egla/Medimpex (Hungary)	√			√	√	√	√	√	
Central America									
Aperitol—Farmacéuticos (Finland)	√	√	√	√		√	√	√	
Ciprop—Gamma (Netherlands)	√	√		√	√	√	√	√	
Colombia									
Anapeptol—Remo (Colombia)	√	√				√	√		
Ecuador									
Periactin—MSD (U.S.)	√	√	√	√	√	√	√	√	
Venezuela									
Agotex—Beta (Venezuela)	√			√		√	√		
Ciclovetin—Interfarma (Venezuela)	√								√
Cipramin—Meyer (Venezuela)	√								√
Ciprogan—Physia (Venezuela)	√								√
Ceptadin—Copharma (Venezuela)	√								√
Cyprodin—Klinos (Venezuela)	√					√	√		
Eptadina—Galeno/Química (Venezuela)	√								√
Periactin—MSD (U.S.)	√	√	√	√	√				
Rosolio—Schweitzer (Venezuela)	√								√
Peru									
Periactin—Prosalud/MSD (Peru/U.S.)	√	√	√	√	√	√	√	√	

(a) Footnote reference to warnings.

Table 18 **Pizotifen** (*single entity only*)	INDICATIONS			WARNINGS		
	Appetite stimulation	Mood changes in elderly	Prevention of migraine	Caution in children	Caution in urinary retention	Caution in glaucoma
United Kingdom						
Sanomigran—Sandoz (Switzerland)			✓	✓	✓	✓
Indonesia						
Sandomigran—Sandoz (Switzerland)			✓	✓	✓	✓
Thailand						
Anorsia—Asian Pharm (Thailand)	✓		✓			
Mosegor—Wander (Switzerland)	✓	✓			✓	✓
Sandomigran—Sandoz (Switzerland)	✓		✓		✓	✓
Malaysia / Singapore						
Mosegor—Wander (Switzerland)	✓	✓		✓	✓	✓
Sandomigran—Sandoz (Switzerland)			✓	✓	✓	✓
Philippines						
Litec—Sandoz (Switzerland)	✓	✓		✓	✓	✓
Mosegor—Wander (Switzerland)	✓			✓	✓	✓
Africa						
Mosegor—Wander (Switzerland)	✓	✓		✓	✓	✓
Sandomigran—Sandoz (Switzerland)			✓	✓	✓	✓
Middle East						
Mosegor/Litec—Wander (Switzerland)	✓	✓		✓	✓	✓
Sandomigran—Sandoz (Switzerland)			✓	✓	✓	✓
Mexico						
Sandomigran—Sandoz (Switzerland)			✓	✓	✓	✓
Colombia						
Sandomigran—Sandoz (Switzerland)	✓		✓	✓	✓	✓
Venezuela						
Sandomigran—Sandoz (Switzerland)	✓		✓		✓	✓
Brazil						
Sandomigran—Sandoz (Switzerland)			✓	✓	✓	✓

Table 19
Clofibrate

(single entities only)

	INDICATIONS			WARNINGS					
	Hyperlipidemia	Atherosclerosis	Coronary disease	Liver disease	Kidney disease	Use in pregnancy	Use during lactation	Use with anticoagulants	No warnings
United States									
Atromid-S—Wyeth-Ayerst (U.S.)	✓			✓	✓	✓	✓	✓	
United Kingdom									
Atromid-S—ICI (U.K.)	✓			✓	✓	✓		✓	
India									
Atromid-S—IEL (India)	✓			✓	✓	✓	✓	✓	
Lipomid—Cipla (India)	✓	✓		✓	✓	✓	✓	✓	
Indonesia									
Arterol—Pharos Chemie (Indonesia)	✓	✓	✓	✓	✓	✓	✓	✓	
Atromid-S—ICI (U.K.)	✓			✓	✓	✓	✓	✓	
Liposol—E. Merck (West Germany)	✓	✓							✓
Thailand									
Atromid-S—ICI (U.K.)	✓			✓	✓	✓	✓	✓	
Clof—Siegfried (Switzerland)	✓	✓		✓	✓	✓		✓	
Coles—Labatec (Thailand)	✓			✓	✓	✓		✓	
Malaysia/Singapore									
Atromid-S—ICI (U.K.)	✓			✓	✓	✓	✓	✓	
Philippines									
Atromid-S—ICI (U.K.)	✓			✓	✓	✓	✓	✓	
Africa									
Atromid-S—ICI (U.K.)	✓			✓	✓	✓	✓	✓	
Skleromexe—Mepha (Switzerland)	✓			✓	✓	✓	✓	✓	
Middle East									
Atromid-S—ICI (U.K.)	✓			✓	✓	✓	✓	✓	
Caribbean									
Atromid-S—ICI (U.K.)	✓			✓	✓	✓	✓	✓	
Mexico									
Atromid-S—ICI (U.K.)	✓	✓		✓	✓	✓	✓	✓	
Central America									
Atromid-S—ICI (U.K.)	✓	✓		✓	✓	✓	✓	✓	

Table 19 continued

	INDICATIONS			WARNINGS					
	Hyperlipidemia	Atherosclerosis	Coronary disease	Liver disease	Kidney disease	Use in pregnancy	Use during lactation	Use with anticoagulants	No warnings
Colombia									
Clofibrato—Procaps (Colombia)	√			√	√	√		√	
Ecuador									
Atromid-S—Life/ICI (U.S./U.K.)	√	√	√	√	√	√		√	
Duolip—Mepha (Switzerland)	√			√	√	√	√	√	
Venezuela									
Plasmosin—North Medicaments (Venezuela)	√	√	√	√	√	√		√	
Reliveran—Schweitzer (Venezuela)	√	√	√			√		√	

Table 20
Prazosin

(single entities only)

	RISK OF SYNCOPE, SUDDEN LOSS OF CONSCIOUSNESS	
	Warning	No warning
United States Minipress—Pfizer (U.S.)	✓	
United Kingdom Hypovasc—Pfizer (U.S.)	✓	
Indonesia Minipress—Pfizer (U.S.)	✓	
Thailand Minipress—Pfizer (U.S.)	✓	
Malaysia/Singapore Minipress—Pfizer (U.S.)	✓	
Philippines Minipress—Pfizer (U.S.)	✓	
Africa Minipress—Pfizer (U.S.)		✓
Middle East Minipress—Pfizer (U.S.)	✓	
Caribbean Minipress—Pfizer (U.S.)		✓
Mexico Minipress—Pfizer (U.S.)	✓	
Central America Minipress—Pfizer (U.S.)	✓	
Colombia Minipres—Pfizer (U.S.)	✓	
Ecuador Minipres—Pfizer (U.S.)	✓	
Venezuela Minpres—Pfizer (U.S.)		✓
Peru Minipress—Pfizer (U.S.)	✓	
Brazil Minipress—Pfizer (U.S.)	✓	

Table 21

Piracetam

(single entities only)

	Peripheral vascular disturbances	Cerebral vascular disturbances	Lack of concentration	Loss of memory	Personality changes	Vertigo, dizziness	Fatigue	Sleep disturbances	Intellectual deterioration
India									
Normabrain—Torrent (India)	√								
Piratam—Biddle Sawyer (India)				√					
Thailand									
Nootropil—UCB (Belgium)	√			√					
Normabrain—Torrent (India)	√					√			
Malaysia / Singapore									
Nootropil—UCB (Belgium)	√			√					
Middle East									
Nootropil—UCB (Belgium)	√								
Mexico									
Dinagen—Hormona (Mexico)	√			√		√			√
Nootropil—Riker (U.S.)	√								
Colombia									
Anoxon—Kressfor (Colombia)	√								
Gabot—California (Colombia)	√								
Neurobasal—Incobra (Colombia)	√	√							
Neurobifan—Bifan (Colombia)	√	√							
Piracetam—McKesson (U.S.)	√								
Reasten-P—Synthesis (Colombia)	√								
Venezuela									
Breinax—Dysfa (Venezuela)	√	√	√				√		
Dinacel—Meyer (Venezuela)		√				√			√
Nootropil—UCB/Searle (Belgium/U.S.)	√								
Tonum—North Medicamenta (Venezuela)									√
Peru									
Nootropil—Hoechst (West Germany)	√			√		√			
Brazil									
Nootron—Biosintética (Brazil)			√	√	√				√
Nootropil—Rhodia (Brazil)	√	√		√	√	√			

Table 22
Bencyclane
(single entities only)

	Peripheral vascular disturbances	Cerebral vascular disturbances	Lack of concentration	Loss of memory	Personality changes	Vertigo, dizziness	Fatigue	Sleep disturbances	Intellectual deterioration
Indonesia									
Fludilat—Organon (Netherlands)	✓	✓							
Thailand									
Fludilat—Organon (Netherlands)	✓	✓	✓	✓		✓		✓	✓
Malaysia/Singapore									
Fludilat—Organon (Netherlands)	✓	✓	✓	✓		✓			
Mexico									
Fludilat—Organon (Netherlands)	✓	✓							
Central America									
Fludilat—Asta Pharma AG (West Germany)	✓	✓						✓	✓
Ecuador									
Fludilat—Organon (Netherlands)	✓	✓							
Venezuela									
Fludilat—Organon (Netherlands)	✓	✓	✓			✓		✓	✓
Peru									
Fludilat—Organon (Netherlands)	✓	✓	✓	✓					
Brazil									
Fludilat Retard—Organon (Netherlands)	✓	✓	✓			✓	✓	✓	

INDICATIONS

Table 23
Buflomedil

(single entities only)

	Peripheral vascular disturbances	Cerebral vascular disturbances	Lack of concentration	Loss of memory	Personality changes	Vertigo, dizziness	Fatigue	Sleep disturbances	Intellectual deterioration
Indonesia									
Loftyl—Abbott (U.S.)	✓	✓		✓		✓			
Thailand									
Irrodan—Biomedica Foscama (Thailand)	✓	✓							
Malaysia/Singapore									
Loftyl—Abbott (U.S.)	✓	✓		✓	✓	✓		✓	✓
Philippines									
Loftyl—Abbott (U.S.)	✓	✓		✓	✓	✓		✓	✓
Middle East									
Loftyl—Abbott (U.S.)	✓	✓							
Mexico									
Loftyl—Abbott (U.S.)	✓	✓	✓	✓		✓	✓	✓	✓
Central America									
Loftyl—Abbott (U.S.)	✓	✓			✓	✓		✓	✓
Colombia									
Fluzer—Lafrancol (Colombia)	✓	✓		✓		✓		✓	✓
Loftyl—Abbott (U.S.)	✓	✓							
Microcir—Incobra (Colombia)	✓	✓							
Ecuador									
Givotan—Roemmers (Ecuador)	✓	✓							
Venezuela									
Loftyl—Abbott (U.S.)	✓	✓	✓	✓	✓				✓
Peru									
Loftyl—Abbott (U.S.)	✓	✓		✓	✓	✓		✓	✓
Brazil									
Bufedil—Abbott (U.S.)	✓	✓							

Table 24
Cinnarzine

(single entities only)

	Peripheral vascular disturbances	Cerebral vascular disturbances	Lack of concentration	Loss of memory	Personality changes	Vertigo, dizziness	Fatigue	Sleep disturbances	Intellectual deterioration
United Kingdom									
Stugeron—Janssen (U.S.)	✓								
India									
Stugeron—Ethnor (India)				✓					
Indonesia									
Cinnipirine—Kimla Farma (Indonesia)	✓	✓	✓						
Stugeron—Janssen (U.S.)	✓	✓	✓			✓			
Vertizine—Bernofarm (Indonesia)	✓	✓				✓			
Thailand									
Celenid—Biolab (Thailand)	✓	✓				✓			
Cerebroad—Chinta (Thailand)	✓	✓				✓			
Cinnar—Atlantic (Thailand)	✓	✓				✓			
Cinnaza—Pharmaland (Thailand)	✓	✓				✓			
Cinrizine—Medifive (Thailand)	✓	✓				✓			
Linazine—Asian Pharm (Thailand)	✓	✓				✓			
Med-Circuron—Medical Supply (Thailand)	✓	✓				✓			
Olamin—Siegfried (Switzerland)	✓	✓				✓			
Sorebral—Condrugs (Thailand)	✓	✓				✓			
Stugeron—Janssen (U.S.)	✓	✓				✓			
Malaysia/Singapore									
Celenid—Biolab (Thailand)	✓	✓				✓			
Cerepar—Mepha (Switzerland)	✓	✓							
Cinnar—Malaysia Chemist (Malaysia)	✓					✓			
Cinnarzine—Green Cross (Japan)		✓							
Stugeron—Janssen (U.S.)	✓	✓				✓			
Philippines									
Stugeron—Janssen (U.S.)	✓	✓			✓	✓	✓	✓	
Africa									
Cinnaron—Remedica (Cyprus)						✓			
Stugeron—Janssen (U.S.)	✓					✓			

Table 24 continued

	Peripheral vascular disturbances	Cerebral vascular disturbances	Lack of concentration	Loss of memory	Personality changes	Vertigo, dizziness	Fatigue	Sleep disturbances	Intellectual deterioration
Middle East									
Stugeron—Janssen (U.S.)						✓			
Caribbean									
Stugeron—Janssen (U.S.)						✓			
Mexico									
Stugeron—Janssen (U.S.)		✓	✓	✓	✓	✓		✓	
Central America									
Cerepar—Mepha (Switzerland)	✓	✓	✓			✓			
Stugeron—Janssen (U.S.)	✓	✓	✓	✓	✓	✓	✓	✓	
Colombia									
Ectasil—Anglopharma (Colombia)	✓	✓		✓	✓	✓			
Stugeron—Janssen (U.S.)	✓					✓			
Ecuador									
Cerepar—Mepha (Switzerland)	✓	✓	✓			✓			
Stugeron Forte—Janssen (U.S.)	✓	✓	✓	✓		✓		✓	
Venezuela									
Cinnax—York (Venezuela)	✓	✓	✓	✓	✓	✓	✓	✓	
Stugeron—Janssen (U.S.)	✓	✓	✓	✓	✓	✓		✓	
Trigeron—Muskus (Venezuela)	✓	✓		✓	✓	✓	✓	✓	
Peru									
Endoxin—Laboratoires OM (Peru)	✓	✓	✓	✓	✓	✓		✓	
Stugeron—Janssen (U.S.)	✓	✓				✓			✓
Brazil									
Antigeron—Farmasa (Brazil)	✓	✓		✓	✓	✓			
Stugeron—Janssen (U.S.)	✓	✓	✓	✓	✓	✓	✓	✓	

Table 25
Ergoloid Mesylates

(codergocrine mesylates; single entities only)

	Peripheral vascular disturbances	Cerebral vascular disturbances	Lack of concentration	Loss of memory	Personality changes	Vertigo, dizziness	Fatigue	Sleep disturbances	Intellectual deterioration
United States									
Hydergine—Sandoz (Switzerland)				√	√		√		√
United Kingdom									
Hydergine—Sandoz (Switzerland)									√
Indonesia									
Ergotika—Ikapharmindo (Indonesia)				√	√	√			√
Hydergin—Sandoz (Switzerland)	√			√	√		√		√
Thailand									
Cebralest—Pharmachemie BV (Thailand)	√	√							
Codergine—Shiwa (Thailand)	√	√							
Hydergine—Sandoz (Switzerland)	√	√	√	√	√	√			√
Hymed—Medifive (Thailand)		√							√
Trigogine—Atlantic (Thailand)	√	√							√
Vasculin—Gedeon Richter (Hungary)		√							√
Vasian—Asian Pharm (Thailand)		√							√
Malaysia/Singapore									
Hydergine—Sandoz (Switzerland)	√	√							√
Vasculin—Biolab (Thailand)		√							√
Philippines									
USA Codergocrine—USA Generics (Philippines)			√	√	√	√			
Africa									
Hydergine—Sandoz (Switzerland)	√	√							√
Middle East									
Hydergine—Sandoz (Switzerland)	√	√							√
Mexico									
Hydergina—Sandoz (Switzerland)	√	√	√	√	√	√			√
Central America									
Hydergina—Sandoz (Switzerland)	√	√	√	√	√	√			√

Table 25 continued

	INDICATIONS								
	Peripheral vascular disturbances	Cerebral vascular disturbances	Lack of concentration	Loss of memory	Personality changes	Vertigo, dizziness	Fatigue	Sleep disturbances	Intellectual deterioration
Colombia									
Hydergina—Sandoz (Switzerland)	√	√							√
Venezuela									
Hydergina—Sandoz (Switzerland)	√	√							
Brazil									
Hydergine—Sandoz (Switzerland)									

Table 26
Flunarizine

(single entities only)

INDICATIONS

	Peripheral vascular disturbances	Cerebral vascular disturbances	Lack of concentration	Loss of memory	Personality changes	Vertigo, dizziness	Fatigue	Sleep disturbances	Intellectual deterioration
Indonesia									
Sibelium—Janssen (U.S.)	✓					✓			
Thailand									
Fluden—Biolab (Thailand)		✓	✓	✓		✓		✓	
Liberal—Asian Pharm (Thailand)		✓	✓	✓		✓			
Medilium—Medifive (Thailand)		✓		✓					
Sibelium—Janssen (U.S.)		✓	✓	✓	✓	✓		✓	
Malaysia/Singapore									
Sibelium—Janssen (U.S.)		✓	✓	✓	✓	✓			
Philippines									
Sibelium—Janssen (U.S.)	✓	✓							
Africa									
Sibelium—Janssen (U.S.)		✓							
Middle East									
Sibelium—Janssen (U.S.)		✓							
Caribbean									
Sibelium—Janssen (U.S.)		✓							
Mexico									
Sibelium—Janssen (U.S.)	✓								
Central America									
Sibelium—Janssen (U.S.)	✓	✓	✓	✓	✓	✓		✓	
Colombia									
Dinegal—Lafrancol (Colombia)	✓	✓			✓	✓			
Fluzina—Bussie (Colombia)	✓	✓		✓		✓		✓	✓
Sibelium—Janssen (U.S.)	✓								
Venezuela									
Sibelium—Janssen (U.S.)	✓	✓							
Peru									
Sibelium—Janssen (U.S.)	✓	✓	✓			✓		✓	
Brazil									
Flunarin—Labofarma (West Germany)	✓	✓			✓	✓		✓	✓

Table 27

Pentoxifylline

(single entities only)

	Peripheral vascular disturbances	Cerebral vascular disturbances	Confusional states	Loss of social contact	Sleep disturbances	Vertigo, dizziness	Forgetfulness; loss of memory	Lack of concentration
				INDICATIONS				
United States Trental—Hoechst-Roussel (West Germany)	√							
United Kingdom Trental—Hoechst (West Germany)	√							
India Trental-400—Hoechst (West Germany)	√	√						
Indonesia Trental—Hoechst (West Germany)		√					√	√
Thailand Trental—Hoechst (West Germany)	√	√						
Malaysia/Singapore Trental—Hoechst (West Germany)	√	√						
Philippines Trental—Hoechst (West Germany)	√	√	√	√	√	√		
Africa Trental—Hoechst (West Germany)	√	√						
Middle East Trental—Hoechst (West Germany)	√	√						
Caribbean Trental—Hoechst (West Germany)	√	√						
Mexico Trental—Hoechst (West Germany)	√	√			√	√	√	√
Central America Trental—Hoechst (West Germany)	√	√			√	√	√	√
Venezuela Trental—Hoechst (West Germany)	√	√			√	√	√	√
Peru Trental—Hoechst (West Germany)	√	√			√	√	√	√

Table 28
Pyritinol

(Pyrithioxine; single entities only)

INDICATIONS

	For treatment after brain injury, apoplectic attack, intoxication, encephalitis, etc.	Lack of concentration	Mental retardation in children	Loss of memory	Organic psychoneurosis	Cerebral degeneration	Senile, presenile involution	Mental fatigue
India								
Encephabol—E. Merck (West Germany)			√		√			
Indonesia								
Cerebron—Kalbe Farma (Indonesia)						√		
Encebolin—Phapros (Indonesia)					√		√	
Encepan—New Interbat (Indonesia)			√			√		
Encephabol—E. Merck (West Germany)			√			√		
Encidin—Bernofarm (Indonesia)	√							
Thailand								
Encephabol—E. Merck (West Germany)			√			√		
Enerbol—Ciech-Polfa (Poland)			√			√		√
Pyritil—Biolab (Thailand)	√							
Malaysia/Singapore								
Encephabol—E. Merck (West Germany)			√			√		
Pyritil—Biolab (Thailand)	√		√			√		
Philippines								
Encephabol—E. Merck (West Germany)			√			√		
Mexico								
Encephabol—E. Merck (West Germany)	√	√	√					
Central America								
Encefabol—E. Merck (West Germany)							√	
Colombia								
Acticer—Higea (Colombia)						√		
Biotrefon—Italmex (Mexico)						√		
Encefabol—E. Merck (West Germany)						√		
Ecuador								
Encefabol—E. Merck (West Germany)		√			√	√		√

Table 28 continued

	For treatment after brain injury, apoplectic attack, intoxication, encephalitis, etc.	Lack of concentration	Mental retardation in children	Loss of memory	Organic psychoneurosis	Cerebral degeneration	Senile, presenile involution	Mental fatigue
Venezuela								
Acon—Proton (Venezuela)			✓				✓	✓
Bonifen—E. Merck (West Germany)	✓		✓				✓	
Garan—Interfarma (Venezuela)			✓				✓	
Mezol—Galeno (Venezuela)			✓				✓	
Nauril—Bequim (Venezuela)							✓	
Tioxal—Isern (Venezuela)			✓				✓	✓
Brazil								
Encetam—E. Merck (West Germany)		✓		✓			✓	

Table 29

Chlorpromazine

(single entities only)

WARNINGS

	May cause tardive dyskinesia, extrapyramidal symptoms	Caution in chronic respiratory disease	Caution in cardiovascular disease	Caution in liver disease	Caution with alcohol, CNS depressants	Caution in epilepsy	Caution in pregnancy	Caution in children
United States								
Thorazine—SmithKline (U.S.)	√	√	√	√	√	√	√	√
United Kingdom								
Largactil—May & Baker (France)			√	√		√	√	√
India								
Largactil—May & Baker (France)			√	√		√	√	
Sunprazin—Sun Pharma (India)			√	√		√	√	
Indonesia								
Ethibernal—Ethica (Indonesia)	(a)	(a)	(a)	(a)	(a)	(a)		
Largactil—Rhône-Poulenc (France)	(a)	(a)	(a)	(a)	(a)	(a)	√	
Meprosefil—Meprofarm (Indonesia)	(a)	(a)	(a)	(a)	(a)	(a)		
Promactil—Combiphar (Indonesia)	(a)	(a)	√	(a)	√	(a)		
Thailand								
Chlorpromed—Medifive (Thailand)	(a)	(a)	(a)	(a)	(a)	(a)		
Largactil—May & Baker (France)	(a)	(a)	(a)	(a)	√	(a)	√	
Matcine—Atlantic (Thailand)	(a)	(a)	(a)	(a)	√	(a)	√	
Malaysia/Singapore								
Chlorpromazine—Pharmmalaysia (Malaysia)	(a)	(a)	(a)	(a)	(a)	(a)		
Largactil—May & Baker (France)	(a)	(a)	(a)	(a)	√	(a)	√	
Protran—Protea (U.K.)	(a)	(a)	√	(a)	√	√	√	
Philippines								
Dormazine—Crovis Philcom (Italy)	(a)	(a)	(a)	(a)	√	(a)		
Romazine—Radachem (Philippines)	(a)	(a)	(a)	(a)	(a)	(a)		
Thorazine—SmithKline (U.S.)	(a)	(a)	(a)	(a)	√	(a)		
Africa								
Largactil—May & Baker (France)					√			
Middle East								
Largactil—May & Baker (France)			√		√			√
Plegomazine—Medimpex (Hungary)		√						

Table 29 continued

	May cause tardive dyskinesia, extrapyramidal symptoms	Caution in chronic respiratory disease	Caution in cardiovascular disease	Caution in liver disease	Caution with alcohol, CNS depressants	Caution in epilepsy	Caution in pregnancy	Caution in children
Caribbean								
Largactil—May & Baker (France)					√			√
Mexico								
Largactil—Rhône-Poulenc (France)			√	√	√		√	√
Central America								
Clorpromazina—Productos Farmacéuticos (Ecuador)	√			√			√	√
Largactil—Rhône-Poulenc (France)								
Colombia								
Largactil—Specia (France)			√	√	√	√		
Ecuador								
Largactil—Rhône-Poulenc (France) (Only contraindication: "Do not administer in case of alcohol or barbiturate coma")								
Venezuela								
Largactil—Rhône-Poulenc (France)								
Peru								
Largactil—Rhône-Poulenc (France)	√							

(a) Footnote reference to warnings.

Table 30
Sulpiride

(single entities only)

	Schizophrenia	Other mental disorders	Duodenal, gastric ulcer	No use in phaeochromocytoma	Caution in hypertension	Caution in kidney disease	May cause gastric ulcer	Caution in epilepsy	Caution in pregnancy	Caution in children
United Kingdom										
Dolmatil—Squibb (U.S.)	✓			✓	✓	✓		✓	✓	✓
Sulpitil—Tillotts (U.K.)	✓			✓	✓	✓		✓	✓	✓
Indonesia										
Dogmatil—Delagrange (France)	✓	✓	✓	✓	✓					
Thailand										
Dogmatyl—Fujisawa (Japan)				✓	✓	✓				
Malaysia/Singapore										
Dogmatil—Delagrange (France)		✓	✓	✓	✓					
Philippines										
Dogmatyl—Fujisawa/Pascual (Japan/Spain)				✓		✓			✓	
West Africa										
Dogmatil—Delagrange (France)	✓	✓		✓			✓			
Middle East										
Devōdil—Remedica (Cyprus)		✓	✓	✓		✓		✓	✓	
Dogmatil—Delagrange (France)	✓	✓	✓	✓	✓		✓	✓		
Meresa—Dolorgiet (West Germany)	✓	✓				✓		✓	✓	
Mexico										
Dogmatil Carnotpirid—Carnot (Mexico)		✓	✓	✓		✓				
Ekilid—Lepetit (U.S.)		✓		✓		✓		✓	✓	
Pontiride—Psicofarma (Mexico)	✓	✓							✓	✓
Central America										
Dogmatil—Delagrange (France)		✓	✓						✓	
Ekilid—Lepetit (U.S.)		✓		✓	✓	✓		✓	✓	
Colombia										
Dogmatil—Vitafarma (Colombia)		✓	✓	✓	✓			✓	✓	✓
Equilid—Legrand (Colombia)		✓			✓	✓		✓	✓	✓

Table 30 continued

	INDICATIONS			WARNINGS						
	Schizophrenia	Other mental disorders	Duodenal, gastric ulcer	No use in phaeochromocytoma	Caution in hypertension	Caution in kidney disease	May cause gastric ulcer	Caution in epilepsy	Caution in pregnancy	Caution in children
Venezuela										
Guven—Leti (Venezuela)		√								
Megotyl—Vargas (Venezuela)			√							
Suride—North Medicamente (Venezuela)			√							
Peru										
Finul—Pavil (Peru)	√	√								
Brazil										
Dogmatil—Espasil (France)	√	√	√	√	√				√	√
Equilid—Merrell/Lepetit (U.S.)	√	√	√						√	
Sulpan—Espasil (France)		√	√						√	√

Table 31
Chlordiazepoxide

(selected countries; single entities only)

WARNINGS

	No use in narrow angle glaucoma	No use in hazardous occupations	No abrupt withdrawal	No use with alcohol, CNS depressants	Caution in pregnancy	Caution in elderly	Possible habituation	Caution in liver, kidney, lung disease	No use in myasthenia gravis
United States									
Librium—Roche (Switzerland)		√	√	√	√	√	√	√	
Africa									
Librium—Roche (Switzerland)		√		√	√				
Caribbean									
Librium—Roche (Switzerland)			(a)	(a)	(a)	(a)	(a)	(a)	(a)
Mexico									
Librium—Roche (Switzerland)	√			√	√	√			√
Central America									
Kalmocaps—Medix (Spain)	√								√
Librium—Roche (Switzerland)		√		√		√			
Tensin—Infasa (Guatemala)	√	√		√	√				√
Venezuela									
Florema—Palenzona (Venezuela)									

(a) Footnote reference to warnings.

Table 32
Diazepam

(selected countries; single entities only)

	No use in psychosis	No use in narrow angle glaucoma	No use in hazardous occupations	No abrupt withdrawal	No use with alcohol, CNS depressants	Caution in pregnancy	Caution in elderly	Possible habituation	Caution in liver, kidney, lung disease	No use in myasthenia gravis
United States										
Diazepam—Warner-Chilcott (U.S.)	✓	✓	✓	✓	✓	✓	✓	✓	✓	✓
Valium—Roche (Switzerland)	✓	✓	✓	✓	✓	✓	✓	✓	✓	✓
India										
Calmod—IDPL (India)	✓	✓				✓			✓	✓
Calmpose—Ranbaxy (India)	✓	✓				✓			✓	✓
Elcion CR—Ranbaxy (India)	✓				✓	✓			✓	✓
Paci-Quil—Stadmed (India)	✓				✓	✓			✓	✓
Paxum—East India (India)	✓					✓			✓	✓
Somatin—Khandelwal (India)	✓				✓	✓			✓	✓
Valium—Roche (Switzerland)	✓					✓			✓	✓
Mexico										
Alboral—Silanes (Mexico)	✓	✓			✓					✓
Arzepam—Solfran (Mexico)	✓	✓				✓			✓	✓
Britazepam—Briter (Mexico)	✓	✓			✓	✓	✓			
Nerozen—Welfer (Mexico)		✓			✓	✓		✓		
Ortopsique—Psicofarma (Mexico)	✓	✓			✓	✓			✓	✓
Pacitran—Grossman (Mexico)	✓	✓	✓		✓	✓	✓			✓
Valium—Roche (Switzerland)		✓			✓	✓			✓	
Central America										
Alboral—Silanes (Mexico)	✓		✓			✓	✓	✓		
Diazepam—McKesson (U.S.)	✓				✓	✓			✓	✓
Diazepan—Feltrex (Dominican Republic)	✓				✓		✓		✓	✓
Paranten—Bonin (Guatemala)		✓				✓			✓	✓
Paxium—Vijosa (El Salvador)	✓	✓				✓			✓	✓
Valium—Roche (Switzerland)		✓				✓				✓

Table 32 continued

	No use in psychosis	No use in narrow angle glaucoma	No use in hazardous occupations	No abrupt withdrawal	No use with alcohol, CNS depressants	Caution in pregnancy	Caution in elderly	Possible habituation	Caution in liver, kidney, lung disease	No use in myasthenia gravis
Colombia										
Diazepam—Ecar (Colombia)	✓									✓
Valium—Roche (Switzerland)					✓					✓
Ecuador										
Consilium—Rocnarf-Francor (Ecuador)	✓				✓					✓
Dipaz—ECU (Ecuador)					✓	✓				✓
Paxate—Mead-Johnson (U.S.)	✓	✓	✓		✓		✓			
Venezuela										
Diazepam—McKesson (U.S.)										
Diazum—Klinos (Venezuela)	✓						✓			✓
Elinar—Beta (Venezuela)	✓						✓			✓
Pacitran—U.S. Vitamin (U.S.)										✓
Rendin—Interfarma (Venezuela)										
Talema—Palenzona (Venezuela)										✓
Taximel—Physia (Venezuela)								✓		
Valium—Roche (Switzerland)			✓		✓					✓
Peru										
Pacitran—Peikard (Peru)							✓			
Reposepan—Unidos (Peru)		✓			✓	✓	✓			✓
Vazen—Farmindustria (Venezuela)							✓			
Brazil										
Dienpax—Sanofi (France)					✓	✓				✓
Dualid—Labofarma (West Germany)	✓					✓	✓		✓	✓
Kiatrium—Gross (Brazil)					✓	✓				✓
Valium—Roche (Switzerland)					✓	✓				✓

Table 33

Lorazepam

(selected countries; single entities only)

	No use in psychosis	No use in narrow angle glaucoma	No use in hazardous occupations	No abrupt withdrawal	No use with alcohol, CNS depressants	Caution in pregnancy	Caution in elderly	Possible habituation	Caution in liver, kidney, lung disease	No use in myasthenia gravis
United States										
Ativan—Wyeth (U.S.)	✓	✓	✓	✓	✓	✓	✓	✓		
India										
Ativan—Wyeth (U.S.)	✓					✓			✓	
Larpose—Cipla (India)	✓				✓	✓			✓	
Trapex—Sun Pharm (India)	✓				✓	✓			✓	
Mexico										
Ativan—Wyeth Ayerst (U.S.)	✓	✓	✓	✓	✓	✓	✓	✓	✓	✓
Sinestron—Medix (Spain)	✓		✓		✓	✓				✓
Central America										
Ativan—Wyeth (U.S.)						✓				
Enerpax—Raven (Costa Rica)			✓		✓					
Lorazepam—McKesson (U.S.)			✓	✓		✓				✓
Sinestron—Medix (Spain)	✓		✓		✓	✓				✓
Colombia										
Ativan—Wyeth (U.S.)	✓	✓	✓		✓	✓	✓	✓	✓	✓
Ecuador										
Ativan—Wyeth (U.S.)						✓				
Venezuela										
Ativan—Wyeth (U.S.)			✓	✓	✓	✓		✓		
Lorazepam—Klinos (Venezuela)			✓	✓		✓		✓		
Brazil										
Lorax—Fontoura-Wyeth (U.S.)			✓		✓		✓	✓	✓	

Table 34
Bromazepam
(single entities only)

	No use in narrow angle glaucoma	No use in hazardous occupations	No abrupt withdrawal	No use with alcohol, CNS depressants	Caution in pregnancy	Caution in elderly	Possible habituation	Caution in liver, kidney, lung disease	No use in myasthenia gravis
United Kingdom									
Lexotan—Roche (Switzerland)		(a)	(a)	(a)	(a)	(a)	(a)	(a)	
Indonesia									
Lexotan—Roche (Switzerland)	(a)		(a)	√	(a)	(a)	(a)	(a)	(a)
Thailand									
Lexotan—Roche (Switzerland)	(a)		(a)	√	√	(a)	√	(a)	(a)
Malaysia/Singapore									
Lexotan—Roche (Switzerland)	(a)		(a)	√	√	(a)	√	(a)	(a)
Philippines									
Lexotan—Roche (Switzerland)	(a)		(a)	(a)	(a)	(a)	(a)	(a)	(a)
Africa									
Akamon—Medochemie (Cyprus)			(a)	(a)	(a)	(a)	(a)	(a)	(a)
Lexotanil—Roche (Switzerland)			(a)	(a)	(a)	(a)	(a)	(a)	(a)
West Africa									
Lexomil—Roche (Switzerland)		√	√	√	√			√	√
Middle East									
Akamon—Medochemie (Cyprus)			(a)	(a)	(a)	(a)	(a)	(a)	(a)
Lexilium—Remedica (Cyprus)			(a)	(a)	(a)	√	(a)	(a)	(a)
Caribbean									
Akamon—Medochemie (Cyprus)			(a)	(a)	(a)	(a)	(a)	(a)	(a)
Lexotan—Roche (Switzerland)			(a)	(a)	(a)	(a)	(a)	(a)	(a)
Mexico									
Lexotan—Roche (Switzerland)		√		√	√				√
Central America									
Bromazepam—Raven (Costa Rica)		√		√		√			√
Lexotan—Roche (Switzerland)		√	√	√		√		√	√
Colombia									
Lexotan—Roche (Switzerland)		√	√	√	√	√			√
Venezuela									
Lexotanil—Roche (Switzerland)				√			√		√

Table 34 continued

	No use in narrow angle glaucoma	No use in hazardous occupations	No abrupt withdrawal	No use with alcohol, CNS depressants	Caution in pregnancy	Caution in elderly	Possible habituation	Caution in liver, kidney, lung disease	No use in myasthenia gravis
Peru									
Lexotan—Roche (Switzerland)		√	√	√		√			√
Brazil									
Deptran—Beecham (U.K.)	√			√	√				√
Lexotan—Roche (Switzerland)		√		√	√				√

(a) Footnote reference to warnings.

Table 35
Buspirone

(single entities only)

WARNINGS

	No use for psychoses	No use with MAO inhibitors	No use with alcohol	Caution with hazardous occupations	Caution in pregnancy	Caution in children	Caution in kidney, liver disease	May cause dizziness	May cause nervousness	May cause nausea	May cause headache
United States											
Buspar—Mead Johnson (U.S.)	√	√	√	√	√	√	√	√	√	√	√
United Kingdom											
Buspar—Bristol-Myers (U.S.)					√	√	√	√	√		√
Malaysia/Singapore											
Buspar—Bristol (U.S.)			√	√	√	√					
Mexico											
Buspar—Mead Johnson (U.S.)	√	√	√	√	√	√	√	√	√	√	√
Peru											
Buspar—Mead Johnson (U.S.)			√		√	√	√		√	√	√
Brazil											
Buspar—Bristol (U.S.)	√		√	√	√	√	√		√	√	√

Table 36 **Imipramine** *(single entities only)*	WARNINGS	
	No use with MAO inhibitor	Caution in cardiovascular disease
United States		
Tofranil—Geigy (Switzerland)	√	√
United Kingdom		
Tofranil—Geigy (Switzerland)	(a)	(a)
India		
Antidep—Torrent (India)	√	√
Depsol—Intas (India)	√	√
Depsonil—SG Pharmaceuticals (India)	√	√
Impramine—Sun Pharma (India)	√	√
Indonesia		
Tofranil—Geigy (Switzerland)	(a)	(a)
Thailand		
Antidep—Torrent (India)	(a)	(a)
Tofranil—Ciba-Geigy (Switzerland)	(a)	(a)
Topramine—Condrugs (Thailand)	(a)	(a)
Malaysia/Singapore		
Imprin—Protea (U.K.)	(a)	(a)
Tofranil—Geigy (Switzerland)	(a)	√
Philippines		
Tofranil—Geigy (Switzerland)	(a)	√
Africa		
Melipramine—Medimpex (Hungary)	(a)	(a)
Surmontil—May & Baker (France)	(a)	(a)
Tofranil—Geigy (Switzerland)	(a)	(a)
West Africa		
Tofranil—Geigy (Switzerland)	√	√
Middle East		
Imiprex—Dumex (Denmark)	(a)	(a)
Pryleugan—Germed (West Germany)	(a)	(a)
Surmontil—May & Baker (France)	(a)	(a)
Tofranil—Geigy (Switzerland)	(a)	(a)
Caribbean		
Melipramine—Egis/Medimpex (Hungary)	(a)	(a)
Surmontil—May & Baker (France)	(a)	(a)
Tofranil—Geigy (Switzerland)	(a)	(a)

Table 36 continued

	WARNINGS	
	No use with MAO inhibitor	Caution in cardiovascular disease
Mexico		
Talpramin—Psicofarma (Mexico)		
Tofranil—Geigy (Switzerland)		√
Central America		
Imipramina—Profacasa (Guatemala)	√	√
Venezuela		
Surmontil—Rhône-Poulenc (France)	√	
Tofranil—Geigy (Switzerland)	√	√
Brazil		
Tofranil—Geigy (Switzerland)		

(a) Footnote reference to warnings.

| *Table 37* | | WARNINGS | |
| **Stanozolol** | Growth stunting in children | Masculinization of girls, women | No use to enhance athletic ability |
(single entities only)			
United States			
Winstrol—Winthrop (U.S.)	√	√	√
United Kingdom			
Stromba—Sterling Research Labs (U.S.)		√	
India			
Menabol—CFL Pharma (India)	√	√	√
Stromba—Win-Medicare (U.S.)	√	√	√
Africa			
Winstrol—Winthrop (U.S.)	(a)	(a)	(a)
Middle East			
Winstrol—Winthrop (U.S.)	(a)	(a)	(a)

(a) Footnote reference to warnings.

Table 38
Allyl Estranol

(single entities only)

	INDICA-TIONS			WARNINGS							
	Threatened or habitual abortion	Threatened premature labor	Premenstrual tension	No use in pregnancy	No use with history of thromboembolic disease	No use with breast or genital cancer	Caution in kidney disease	Caution in liver disease	Caution in heart disease	Caution in epilepsy	Caution in asthma
United Kingdom											
Gestanin—Organon (Netherlands)	√				√	√		√		√	
India											
Fetugard—Biddle-Sawyer (India)	√		√		√	√		√		√	
Gestanin—Infar (Netherlands)	√	√			√	√		√		√	
Indonesia											
Gestanon—Organon (Netherlands)	√	√		(a)	(a)	(a)	(a)	(a)	(a)	(a)	(a)
Thailand											
Gestanon—Organon (Netherlands)	√	√		(a)	(a)	(a)	(a)	(a)	(a)	(a)	(a)
Malaysia/Singapore											
Gestanin—Organon (Netherlands)	√	√									
Turinal—Gedeon Richter (Hungary)	√	√		(a)	(a)	(a)	(a)	(a)	(a)	(a)	(a)
Philippines											
Gestanon—Organon (Netherlands)	√	√		(a)	(a)	(a)	(a)	(a)	(a)	(a)	(a)
West Africa											
Gestanon—Organon (Netherlands)	√	√									
Middle East											
Gestanon—Organon (Netherlands)	√	√									
Turinal—Medimpex (Hungary)	√										
Mexico											
Gestanon—Organon (Netherlands)	√	√									
Central America											
Gestanon—Organon (Netherlands)	√	√									
Ecuador											
Gestanon—Organon (Netherlands)	√	√									
Peru											
Gestanon—Organon (Netherlands)	√	√									

(a) Footnote reference to warnings.

Table 39

Ethyl Estranol

(single entities only)

	WARNINGS								
	No use in prostate or breast cancer in men	No use in liver disease	No use in pregnancy	Caution in kidney disease	Caution in heart disease	Caution in hypertension	Caution in epilepsy	Caution in children	May cause virilism in females
India									
Orabolin–Infar (Netherlands)	√	√	√						
Thailand									
Orgabolin—Organon (Netherlands)	(a)	(a)	(a)	(a)	(a)	(a)	(a)	(a)	(a)
Philippines									
Orgabolin—Organon (Netherlands)	(a)	(a)	(a)	(a)	(a)	(a)	(a)	(a)	(a)

(a) Footnote reference to warnings.

Table 40

"Sex Tonics"	Components	Indications
Indonesia		
Kalvitop—Kalbe Farma (Indonesia)	Methyl testosterone, ethinyl estradiol, lysine, glutamic acid, vitamins, and minerals	Climacteric, premature senility
Padibu—Kimla Farma (Indonesia)	Methyl testosterone, yohimbine, strychnine, vitamin E, caffeine	Fatigue, sexual weakness in men
Vixtron-Ginseng— Samphindo (Indonesia)	Methyl testosterone, ginseng, ethinyl estradiol, vitamins A, B_1, B_2, B_{12}, D, E, K, niacinamide, pantothenate, rutin, methionine, choline, inositol, phosphate	Male climacteric, impotence, menopausal symptoms
Malaysia/Singapore		
Asparten—Euro-Labor (Malaysia)	Arginine aspartate	Physical, sexual, psychic fatigue
Philippines		
Mysgen—Medichem (Philippines)	Methyl testosterone, ginseng, yohimbine, vitamin E, nicotinate	"To improve physical and mental work capacity, and prolong endurance in athletic activities . . . intensify male image or profile, and enhance sexual fulfillment"
Mexico		
Restauvit—Ind. Farm. Remir (Mexico)	Metandrostenolone, vitamins A, B_1, B_2, B_6, B_{12}, C, D_2, iron, copper, calcium, etc.	Male climacteric, etc.
Central America		
Bio-Star—Ferrer (Spain)	Ginseng	Climacteric, etc.
Juniormen—Menarini (Spain)	Ginseng, pyridoxine, choline, rutin, vitamins A, B_1, E	Male and female climacteric, etc.
Lipogeron H3—Natterman (West Germany)	Methyl testosterone, phospholipids, ethinyl estradiol, procaine, vitamins A, B_1, B_2, B_6, nicotinamide, E, K	Climacteric, etc.

References

REFERENCES

Chapter 1

1. *Health for All* (Geneva: World Health Organization, 1983).

2. Halfdan Mahler, address to the 11th assembly of the International Federation of Pharmaceutical Manufacturing Associations, Washington, D.C., June 1982.

3. Charles Medawar, *Drugs and World Health* (The Hague: International Organization of Consumers Unions, 1984), pp. 27–30.

4. Willy Brandt and Anthony Sampson, eds., *North-South: A Programme for Survival* (The Brandt Report) (London: Pan Books, 1981).

5. Editor's note on Charles Medawar, "International Regulation of the Supply and Use of Pharmaceuticals," *Development Dialogue* 2 (1985): 15.

6. Commission on Health Research for Development, *Health Research: Essential Link to Equity in Development* (Oxford: Oxford University Press, 1990).

7. Larry Minear, "Balancing Politics, Ethics in Foreign Policy," *San Francisco Chronicle*, Feb. 1, 1989.

8. Lester Brown, Sandra Postel, and Christopher Flavin, "Bleak Outlook for Global Food Production," *San Francisco Chronicle*, Mar. 8, 1989.

9. James Grant, cited in Madeleine J. Goodman and Lenn E. Goodman, "Medicalization and Its Discontents," *Social Science and Medicine* 25 (1987): 733–40.

10. "Essential Drugs: A Concept in Action," *HAI News*, Apr. 1988.

11. *HAI News*, Dec. 1987.

12. "The Bamako Initiative," *Lancet* 2 (1988): 1177; UNICEF, *The State of the World's Children 1989* (Oxford: Oxford University Press, 1989), p. 50; Philip R. Lee, Peter Lurie, Milton Silverman, and Mia Lydecker, "Drug Promotion and Labeling in Developing Countries: An Update," *Journal of Clinical Epidemiology* 44, Supp. II (1991): 49S–55S.

13. "U.N. Agency Says Half a Billion Have Tropical Diseases," *San Francisco Chronicle*, Mar. 28, 1990.

14. "1.5 Billion People Without Clean Water," *Indonesian Observer* (Jakarta), May 25, 1988.

15. Jesse Kagimba, *The Problem of Drug Supply in Primary Health Care in Developing Countries* (Nairobi, Kenya: African Medical, Research, and Education Foundation, 1983), pp. 6, 7; Klaus M. Leisinger, *International Development: The Ideal and the Reality* (Basel: Ciba-Geigy, 1988), pp. 23, 24.

16. "The Most Vicious Circle," *Newsweek*, Dec. 1, 1986.

17. Jessica Tuchman Mathews, "Africa's Struggle to Improve Human Welfare," *San Francisco Chronicle*, May 24, 1989.

18. Leisinger, *International Development*, pp. 76–79.

19. Desmond Tutu, cited in George B. N. Ayittey, "Holding Black Africa to Democracy's Account," *San Francisco Chronicle*, Jan. 18, 1989.

20. Andrew Chetley, *A Healthy Business? World Health and the Pharmaceutical Industry* (London: Zed Books, 1990), pp. 129, 130, 169.

21. David W. Dunlop and A. Mead Over, "Determinants of Drug Imports to Poor Countries: Preliminary Findings and Implications for Financing Primary Health Care," paper prepared for Joint U.K. and Nordic Health Economics Study Group meeting in Vadstena, Sweden, July 3–5, 1985.

22. James P. Grant, *The State of the World's Children 1984*. United Nations Children's Fund and Oxford University Press, 1983; J. D. Snyder and M. H. Merson, "The Magnitude of the Global Problem of Acute Diarrhoeal Disease: A Review of Active Surveillance Data," *Bulletin of the World Health Organization* 60 (1982): 605.

23. Calvin M. Kunin et al., "Social, Behavioral, and Practical Factors Affecting Antibiotic Use Worldwide: Report of Task Force 4," *Reviews of Infectious Diseases* 9 (supp. 3) (1987): s270–80.

24. Leisinger, *International Development*, pp. 20, 21.

Chapter 2

1. *Physicians' Desk Reference* (Oradell, N.J.: Medical Economics, 1988).

2. Colin Duncan, ed., *MIMS* (London: MIMS, 1988).

3. Chandra Gulhati, ed., *MIMS India* (New Delhi: A. E. Morgan Publications, 1988).

4. Jenny Oo, ed., *IIMS* (Hong Kong: IMS Pacific, 1988).

5. Jenny Oo, ed., *TIMS* (Singapore: TIMS, 1987).

6. Jenny Oo, ed., *DIMS* (Hong Kong: IMS Pacific, 1988).

7. Jenny Oo, ed., *PIMS* (Hong Kong: IMS Pacific, 1987).

8. Frances Wilson, ed., *MIMS Africa* (Epsom, Surrey, England: A. E. Morgan Publications, 1988).

9. *Guide Thérapeutique d'Afrique* (Dakar, Senegal: Medicafrique, 1987).

10. Frances Wilson, ed., *MIMS Middle East* (Epsom, Surrey, England: A. E. Morgan Publications, 1988).

11. Frances Wilson, ed., *MIMS Caribbean* (Epsom, Surrey, England: A. E. Morgan Publications, 1988).

12. Emilio Rosenstein, ed., *Diccionario de Especialidades Farmacéuticas* (Mexico City: Ediciones P.L.M., 1988).

13. Emilio Rosenstein, ed., *Diccionario de Especialidades Farmacéuticas—Edición C.A.D.* (Panama: Panamericana de Libros de Medicina, 1988).

14. Emilio Rosenstein, ed., *Diccionario de Especialidades Farmacéuticas—Edición Ecuador* (Bogotá: Editorial Para Los Médicos, 1988).

15. Emilio Rosenstein, ed., *Diccionario de Especialidades Farmacéuticas—Edición Colombia* (Bogotá: Editorial Para Los Médicos, 1988).

16. Emilio Rosenstein, ed., *Diccionario de Especialidades Farmacéuticas—Edición Peru* (Lima, Peru: Editorial Para Los Médicos, 1988).

17. Manuel Velasco et al., eds., *INTERCON 87-88—Indice de Especialidades Farmacéuticas* (Caracas: Tribuna Médica Venezolana, 1987).

18. Austra Spilva de Lehr, *Guía de las Especialidades Farmacéuticas en Venezuela* (Caracas: Servicios Educativos Alfa Omega, 1986–87).

19. J. M. S. Melo, ed., *DEF 87/88—Dicionário de Especialidades Farmacêuticas* (São Paulo: Publicações Médicas, 1987–88).

20. Egyptian Drug Organization, *Egyptian Index of Medical Specialities* (Cairo: Egyptian Ministry of Health, 1986–87).

21. Milton Silverman, *The Drugging of the Americas* (Berkeley: University of California Press, 1976).

22. Milton Silverman, Philip R. Lee, and Mia Lydecker, *Prescriptions for Death: The Drugging of the Third World* (Berkeley: University of California Press, 1982).

23. Milton Silverman, Philip R. Lee, and Mia Lydecker, "Drug Promotion: The Third World Revisited," *International Journal of Health Services* 16 (1986): 659–67.

24. William H. W. Inman, "Prescription-Event Monitoring: Its Strategic Role in Post-Marketing Surveillance for Drug Safety," *PEM News*, no. 4 (1987): 24–28.

25. Lincoln C. Chen, Mizanur Rahman, and A. M. Sarder, "Epidemiology and Cause of Death Among Children in a Rural Area of Bangladesh," *International Journal of Epidemiology* 9 (1980): 25–33.

26. Arnfield A. Kielman and Colin McCord, "Home Treatment of Childhood Diarrhoea in a Punjab Village," *Journal of Tropical Pediatrics and Environmental Child Health* 23 (1977): 197–201.

27. Hamilton H. Anderson and Dorothy A. Koch, "Iodochloroxyquinoline (Vioform N.N.R.) as an Amebecide in Macaques," *Proceedings of the Society for Experimental Biology and Medicine* 28 (1931): 838–41; Norman A. David, Herbert C. Johnstone, A. C. Reed, and Chauncey D. Leake, "The Treatment of Amebiasis with Iodochlorhydroxyquinoline (Vioform N.N.R.)," *Journal of the American Medical Association* 100 (1933): 1658–61.

28. E. Riklis and J. H. Quastel, "Effects of Cations on Sugar Absorption by Isolated Surviving Guinea Pig Intestine," *Canadian Journal of Biochemistry and Physiology* 36 (1958): 347–62.

29. Peter F. Curran, "Na, Cl, and Water Transport by Rat Ileum *in vitro*," *Journal of General Physiology* 43 (1960): 1137–48.

30. Harold P. Schedl and James Clifton, "Solute and Water Absorption by the Human Small Intestine," *Nature* 199 (1963): 1264–67.

31. R. A. Phillips, "Water and Electrolyte Losses in Children," *Proceedings, Federation of American Societies for Experimental Medicine* 23 (1964): 705–12.

32. Norbert Hirschhorn, Richard A. Cash, William E. Woodward, and Gary H. Spivey, "Oral Fluid Therapy of Apache Children with Infectious Diarrhoea," *Lancet* 2 (1972): 15–18.

33. Editorial, "Water with Sugar and Salts," *Lancet* 2 (1978): 300.

34. WHO/UNICEF, *The Management of Diarrhoea and Use of Oral Rehydration Therapy*, 2nd ed. (Geneva: World Health Organization, 1985), p. 6; Michael L. Merson, "Oral Rehydration Therapy: From Theory to Practice," *WHO Chronicle* 40 (1986): 417–19; Madeleine J. Goodman and Lenn E. Goodman, "Medicalization and Its Discontents," *Social Science and Medicine* 25 (1987): 733–40.

35. David Werner, "Egypt: Another Approaching Storm on the Desert," Newsletter from the Sierra Madre, no. 24 (Palo Alto, Calif.: Hesperian Foundation, June 1991).

36. Colin Forbes, personal communication, 1988.

37. James P. Grant, *The State of the World's Children* (New York: UNICEF, 1987), pp. 4, 33, 37, 44.

38. *Drugs and the Third World: Lincomycin and Clindamycin (Antibiotics), Unnecessary Health Hazards* (Penang, Malaysia: Consumers' Association of Penang, 1988).

39. John G. Bartlett, "Antibiotic-Associated Pseudomembranous Colitis," *Hospital Practice*, Dec. 1981, p. 85.

40. *MaLAM Newsletter*, Nov. 1989.

41. J. L. T. Birley, "Drug Advertisements in Developing Countries," *Lancet* 1 (1989): 220.

42. "MaLAM," *HAI News*, Dec. 1987.

43. Gwilym Hosking, "Drug Marketing in the Third World," *Lancet* 2 (1986): 164.

44. D. N. Bateman and S. Chaplin, "New Drugs: Centrally Acting Drugs," *British Medical Journal* 296 (1988): 417–19.

45. *Le médicament au Maghreb et en Afrique Noire francophone* (Grenoble: Presses universitaires de Grenoble, 1989); "'Misleading Promotion' in Africa Attacked," *Scrip*, Jan. 26, 1990; Andrew Herxheimer, "Medicines in Francophone Africa," *Lancet* 335 (1990): 1449–50.

Chapter 3

1. Klaus von Grebmer, paper presented before a symposium on international drug pricing, University of California, San Francisco, Feb. 2, 1990.

2. Ahmed Aly Abul-Enein, personal communication, 1987.

3. Faisal K. Hamad, personal communication, 1987.

4. Hassanein Rifat and Wasif I. Wasif, personal communications, 1987.

5. U.S. Senate, Committee on the Judiciary, Subcommittee on Antitrust and Monopoly, *Administered Prices in the Drug Industry* (Washington, D.C.: U.S. Government Printing Office, 1959–62) (the Kefauver hearings); U.S. Senate, Select Committee on Small Business, Subcommittee on Monopoly, *Present Status of Competition in the Pharmaceutical Industry* (Washington, D.C.: U.S. Government Printing Office, 1967–76) (the Nelson hearings); Milton Silverman and Philip R. Lee, *Pills, Profits, and Politics* (Berkeley: University of California Press, 1974).

6. Robert J. Ledogar, *Hungry for Profits* (New York: IDOC/North America, 1975); Milton Silverman, *The Drugging of the Americas* (Berkeley: University of California Press, 1976); Milton Silverman, Philip R. Lee, and Mia Lydecker,

Prescriptions for Death: The Drugging of the Third World (Berkeley: University of California Press, 1982); Dianna Melrose, *Bitter Pills: Medicines and the Third World Poor* (Oxford, England: OXFAM, 1982); Mike Muller, *The Health of Nations* (London: Faber and Faber, 1982).

7. Steven N. Wiggins, *The Cost of Developing a New Drug*, (Washington, D.C.: Pharmaceutical Manufacturers Association, 1987); "Developing a New Drug Costs $231 Million, Tufts Center Study Finds," *PMA Newsletter*, Apr. 23, 1990.

8. Karl Heusler, *Health through Research: Pharmaceutical Research and the Challenge of Disease* (Basel: Information Service of Ciba-Geigy, Roche and Sandoz, 1988).

9. *New Drug Approvals in 1990* (Washington, D.C.: Pharmaceutical Manufacturers Association, 1990).

10. William Rhode, personal communication, 1991.

11. Mario Lieberman, personal communication, 1987.

12. Sylvestre Frenk, personal communication, 1987.

13. *The Selection of Essential Drugs*, Technical Report Series, No. 615 (Geneva: World Health Organization, 1977).

14. Silverman, Lee, and Lydecker, *Prescriptions for Death,* pp. 141–42.

15. Pharmaceutical Manufacturers Association, *The Health Consequences of a Restricted Drug List* (Washington, D.C.: Pharmaceutical Manufacturers Association, 1985).

16. Joseph K. Wang'ombe and Germano M. Mwabu, "Economics of Essential Drugs Schemes: The Perspectives of the Developing Countries," *Social Science and Medicine* 25 (1987): 625–30.

17. E. Lauridsen, "Essential Drugs: A Concept in Action," *HAI News*, Apr. 1988.

18. George Teeling Smith, "The Economics of Essential Drug Programmes," *Social Science and Medicine* 25 (1987): 621–24.

19. "WHA Applauds Essential Drug Report," *Scrip*, May 25, 1990.

20. Milton Silverman, Philip R. Lee, and Mia Lydecker, *Pills and the Public Purse* (Berkeley: University of California Press, 1981).

21. Richard J. Barnet and Ronald E. Müller, *Global Reach: The Power of the Multinational Corporations* (New York: Simon & Schuster, 1974).

22. Sanjoy Hazarika, "India Does an About-Face and Courts the Drug Industry," *New York Times*, June 20, 1988.

23. Jay Kingham, personal communication, 1988.

24. *PMA Newsletter*, Sept. 16, 1985.

25. *PMA Newsletter*, July 27, 1987.

26. *PMA Newsletter*, Apr. 25, 1988.

27. *PMA Newsletter*, July 25, 1988.

28. *PMA Newsletter*, Oct. 24, 1988.

29. *HAI News*, Dec. 1988.

30. A. Boots, "American Chamber of Commerce Pharmaceuticals Committee: Achieve Industry Goals," *China Post*, July 4, 1990.

31. *PMA Newsletter*, Mar. 6, 1989.

32. Charles Medawar, "Failings of the Pharmaceutical Industry," *Pharmaceutical Medicine* 2 (1987): 259.

33. Harry Schwartz, "A World Apart: Physician Attitudes Here and Abroad," *Pharmaceutical Executive*, Sept. 1987.

34. D. M. Burley, "Seeks Reasoned Discussion" (letter to the editor), *Pharmaceutical Executive*, Dec. 1987.

35. Klaus M. Leisinger, "Sell Solutions, Not Just Products," *New York Times*, Feb. 21, 1988.

36. Klaus M. Leisinger, *International Development: The Ideal and the Reality* (Basel: Ciba-Geigy, 1988), pp. 20–28, 61, 67, 78, 90, 94.

37. Klaus M. Leisinger, *Poverty, Sickness and Medicines: An Unholy Alliance* (Geneva: International Federation of Pharmaceutical Manufacturers Associations, 1989), p. 42.

38. Hans-Christian Röglin and Klaus von Grebmer, *The Pharmaceutical Industry and the Public: An Approach to a New Communication Concept* (Richmond, Surrey, England: *Scrip*, PJB Publications, 1990).

Chapter 4

1. Milton Silverman and Philip R. Lee, *Pills, Profits, and Politics* (Berkeley: University of California Press, 1974), p. 144.

2. *Pills, Profits, and Politics*, pp. 96–97, 110–18, 144, 237, 286.

3. *Pills, Profits, and Politics*, pp. 154, 155.

4. U.S. Department of Health, Education, and Welfare, Office of the Secretary, Task Force on Prescription Drugs, *The Drug Users* (Washington, D.C.: U.S. Government Printing Office, 1968), pp. 36, 37.

5. *Pills, Profits, and Politics*, p. 168.

6. "The Big Lie About Generic Drugs," *Consumer Reports*, 1987, pp. 480–85.

7. Michael Waldholz, "Drug Battle Heats Up Between Brand-Name and Generic Makers," *Wall Street Journal*, Aug. 13, 1984.

8. "The Big Lie About Generic Drugs."

9. Bernard S. Bloom, David J. Wierz, and Mark V. Pauly, "Cost and Price of Comparable Branded and Generic Pharmaceuticals," *Journal of the American Medical Association* 256 (1986): 2523–30.

10. "Ayerst's Line in Dirt: Generics War Looms," *Dickinson's FDA* 2, Feb. 1, 1986, p. 1.

11. *HAI News*, Oct. 1987.

12. *Pills, Profits, and Politics*, pp. 155–59.

13. Winston Williams, "Glory Days End for Pharmaceuticals," *New York Times*, Feb. 24, 1985.

14. Brian L. Strom, "Generic Drug Substitution Revisited," *New England Journal of Medicine* 316 (1987): 1456–62.

15. J. V. Tapster, "Generic Substitution," *Pharmaceutical Journal* 230 (1983): 150.

16. Kumariah Balasubramaniam, personal communications, 1985–90.

17. Gerald A. Faich, James Morrison, Edwin V. Dutra, Jr., Donald B. Hare,

and Peter H. Rheinstein, "Reassurance About Generic Drugs," *Journal of the American Medical Association* 316 (1987): 1473–75.

18. Issa Diop, personal communication, 1987.

19. Frans Tshai, personal communication, 1988.

20. FDA News Release, Sept. 21, 1988.

21. Roy McKnight, statement before House Subcommittee on Oversight and Investigations, May 11, 1989.

22. Gregory Stricharchuk, "Drug Firm's Probe of the FDA Threatens Major Agency Scandal: Mylan Charges Corruption in Granting of Approvals, Sues 4 Competitors Too," *Wall Street Journal*, June 9, 1989.

23. Ibid.

24. "Generics Division 'Irregularities Were Widespread,' Dingell Says," *PMA Newsletter*, May 8, 1989.

25. Ibid.

26. United States Attorney for the District of Maryland, Press Release, May 9, 1989; Affidavit of Charles Y. Chang, Baltimore, May 9, 1989.

27. Marvin Seife, Director, Division of Generic Drugs, Center for Drug Evaluation and Research, Food and Drug Administration, testimony before hearings on "FDA's Generic Drug Approval Process," Subcommittee on Oversight and Investigations of the Committee on Energy and Commerce, U.S. House of Representatives (hereafter referred to as Dingell Subcommittee), May 3, 1989.

28. "Firm Admits Submitting Another's Drug for Federal Test," *Washington Post*, July 2, 1989.

29. Frank E. Young, Commissioner, Food and Drug Administration, testimony before Dingell Subcommittee, July 11, 1989.

30. James C. Hyatt, "Par Pharmaceutical Will Plead Guilty in U.S. Probe of Generic Drug Industry," *Wall Street Journal*, July 17, 1989.

31. "FDA Drug-Scandal Figure Gets Prison Sentence, Fine," *Wall Street Journal*, July 14, 1989; Paul W. Valentine, "Former Drug Firm Chief Gets 60 Days," *Washington Post*, Sept. 15, 1989.

32. Malcolm Gladwell, "Top Generic Drug Loses FDA Approval: Hypertension Drug Not Proved to Be Equivalent to Dyazide," *Washington Post*, Aug. 29, 1989; Bruce Ingersoll and Gregory Stricharchuk, "Bolar to Lose FDA Approval of Its Dyazide," *Wall Street Journal*, Aug. 29, 1989.

33. Malcolm Gladwell, "Maker of Generic Diazide May Have Lied, Letter Says: Documents Likely False, Bolar Attorneys Tell FDA," *Washington Post*, Jan. 24, 1990.

34. "Bolar Destroyed Documents and Fabricated Others," *Health News Daily*, Aug. 22, 1990; "Bolar Destroyed Some Documents, Fabricated Others, Rep. Dingell Tells Justice Aug. 16; Firm Authorizes Outside Counsel to Reveal Generic Dyazide Coverups," *F-D-C Reports*, Aug. 27, 1990.

35. Malcolm Gladwell, "Generic Drug Firm Allegedly Tried to Cheat on Tests," *Washington Post*, Sept. 1, 1989.

36. Malcolm Gladwell, "Generic Firm Told to Withdraw Generic Anti-

biotic," *Washington Post*, Oct. 7, 1989; Malcolm Gladwell, "FDA Seeking Legal Action in Drug Recall," *Washington Post*, Oct. 14, 1989.

37. John D. Dingell and Thomas J. Bliley, Jr., letter to Eugene M. Pfeiffer, King & Spalding, Washington, D.C., Jan. 23, 1990.

38. Gregory Stricharchuk, "Bolar's Shulman Resigns as President, Sources Say, as Mylan Seeks to Buy Drug," *Wall Street Journal*, Feb. 13, 1990.

39. Frank E. Young, statement before hearing of the Dingell Subcommittee, Nov. 17, 1989; Bruce Ingersoll, "FDA Says Tests of Generic Drugs Find Only 1.1% Deficient in Safety, Quality," *Wall Street Journal*, Nov. 20, 1989.

40. "Young Moves from FDA Commissioner to Deputy ASH/Science & Environment . . . ," *PMA Newsletter*, Nov. 20, 1989.

41. "SmithKline Will Produce a Generic of Its Dyazide," *New York Times*, Aug. 24, 1990.

42. Gregory Stricharchuk, "American Home Generic Drug Lines Halted," *Wall Street Journal*, Sept. 22, 1989.

43. Jeffrey M. Levine, statement before hearing of the Dingell Subcommittee, Sept. 11, 1989.

44. *PMA Newsletter*, Oct. 22, 1990.

45. "Fraud & Obstruction of Justice—How Bolar Passed Its Bio Tests," *PMA Newsletter*, Oct. 29, 1990.

46. *PMA Newsletter*, Nov. 5, 1990.

47. "Generic Mess Not Cleaned Up; Investigation Not Over: Dingell Staffer," *PMA Newsletter*, Nov. 19, 1990.

48. "Employees Won't Use Generic Drugs; FDA Testimony Explains Why," *PMA Newsletter*, Jan. 7, 1991.

49. "Generics Most Corrupt Industry They've Seen; Dingell & US Attorney," *PMA Newsletter*, Jan. 7, 1991.

50. "Dingell Slams Generic Enforcement," *PMA Newsletter*, Mar. 11, 1991.

51. "Generic Drug Maker Fined a Record $10 Million," *San Francisco Chronicle*, Mar. 23, 1991.

52. "Subcommittee Documented Thai Abuse of Pharmaceutical Patents in 1986," *PMA Newsletter*, Feb. 18, 1991.

53. "Dingell, Waxman, et al. Introduce Generic Drug Enforcement Act This Week," *PMA Newsletter*, May 20, 1991.

54. Malcolm Gladwell, "Burdened With New Duties, FDA Is Seen Handicapped by Reagan-Era Cuts," *Washington Post*, Sept. 6, 1989; Bruce Ingersoll and Gregory Stricharchuk, "Generic-Drug Scandal at the FDA Is Linked to Deregulation Drive," *Wall Street Journal*, Sept. 13, 1989; Michael Specter, "Leaderless FDA's Daunting Task," *Washington Post*, Nov. 22, 1989.

55. "Philippines: Generics Act 1988 Takes Effect," *HAI News*, Apr. 1989; "Philippines: Action on Generic Labeling," *HAI News*, Dec. 1989.

56. "Philippine Health Secretary Wins Prestigious Olle Hansson Award," *HAI News*, June 1989.

57. "Uphold the Generics Law: A Call to Action," *HAI News*, Oct. 1989; "Generics Act Under Siege," *Drug Monitor* (Quezon City, Philippines), Aug. 1989; "Philippines: PDAN Meet," *HAI News*, Dec. 1989.

58. "Generics Act Under Seige."

59. Ibid.

60. "Philippines: Generics Update," *HAI News*, Aug. 1990.

61. Jean Hizon, personal communication, 1991.

62. "IFPMA Briefing Papers; World Health Assembly" (Geneva: International Federation of Pharmaceutical Manufacturers, 1990), unpublished, pp. 10, 12, 13.

Chapter 5

1. Milton Silverman, *Magic in a Bottle* (New York: Macmillan, 1941).

2. Maurice L. Tainter, "Pain," *Annals of the New York Academy of Science* 51 (1948): 3–11.

3. J. B. Spooner and J. G. Harvey, "The History and Usage of Paracetamol," *Journal of Internal Medicine Research* 4 (Supplement 4) (1976): 1–6.

4. Kay Brune, "Knorr and Filehne in Erlangen," in K. Brune, ed., *100 Years of Pyrazolone Drugs: An Update* (Basel: Birkhäuser Verlag, 1986), pp. 19–29.

5. Milton Silverman, Philip R. Lee, and Mia Lydecker, "Drug Promotion: The Third World Revisited," *International Journal of Health Services* 16 (1986): 659–66.

6. Spooner and Harvey.

7. Barbara Ameer and David J. Greenblatt, "Acetaminophen," *Annals of Internal Medicine* 87 (1977): 202–9.

8. "Brand Names of Acetaminophen-Containing Products," *Pediatrics* 52 (1973): 85–90.

9. Timothy J. Meredith, John Allister Vale, and Roy Goulding, "The Epidemiology of Acute Acetaminophen Poisoning in England and Wales," *Archives of Internal Medicine* 141 (1981): 397–400; L. F. Prescott, "Paracetamol Overdosage: Pharmacological Considerations and Clinical Management," *Drugs* 25 (1983): 290–314.

10. Frederick W. Madison and Theodore L. Squier, "Etiology of Primary Granulocytopenia (Agranulocytic Angina)," *Journal of the American Medical Association* 102 (1934): 755–59.

11. J. L. T. Birley, "Drug Advertising in Developing Countries," *Lancet* 1 (1989): 220.

12. American Medical Association, Department of Drugs, *AMA Drug Evaluations* (Chicago: American Medical Association, 1973), pp. 262, 267.

13. Ainley Wade, ed., *Martindale: The Extra Pharmacopoeia*, ed. 27 (London: Pharmaceutical Press, 1977).

14. L. E. Böttiger and B. Westerholm, "Drug-Induced Blood Dyscrasias in Sweden," *British Medical Journal* 3 (1973): 339–43; L. Offerhaus, "Metamizol: een honderdjarige treurnis," *Nederlands Tijdschrift voor Geneeskunde* 131 (1987): 479–81.

15. Issy Levy, "The Saga of Dipyrone," *Modern Medicine of South Africa*, Nov. 1986, pp. 52–54.

16. "Risks of Agranulocytosis and Aplastic Anemia: A First Report of Their

Relation to Drug Use with Special Reference to Analgesics" (The International Agranulocytosis and Aplastic Anemia Study), *Journal of the American Medical Association* 256 (1986): 1749–57.

17. Gerald A. Faich, "Analgesic Risks and Pharmacoepidemiology," *Journal of the American Medical Association* 256 (1986): 1788.

18. "Analgesics, Agranulocytosis, and Aplastic Anemia: A Major Case-Control Study," *Lancet* 2 (1986): 102.

19. L. Offerhaus, "Metamizol: een honderdjarige treurnis."

20. L. Offerhaus, Letter to the Editor, *Nederlands Tijdschrift voor Geneeskunde* 131 (1987): 1681–83.

21. C. P. H. van Dijke, "Analgesic Use, Agranulocytosis, and Aplastic Anemia," Letter to the Editor, *Journal of the American Medical Association* 257 (1987): 2590.

22. A. del Favero, "Anti-Inflammatory Analgesics," in *Meyler's Side Effects of Drugs Annual*, ed. M. N. G. Dukes, 11 (1987): 89–91.

23. Michael S. Kramer, David A. Lane, and Tom A. Hutchinson, "Analgesic Use, Blood Dyscrasias, and Case-Control Pharmacoepidemiology: A Critique of the International Agranulocytosis and Aplastic Anemia Study," *Journal of Chronic Diseases* 40 (1987): 1073–81.

24. R. Timmers, "Practical Handguide to the 'Boston Study'" (Frankfurt, Germany: Hoechst-Roussel, Nov. 3, 1987. Unpublished).

25. "Hoechst's First Application Rejected," *Scrip*, no. 1197, Apr. 17, 1987.

26. William Jenkins, letter to Suntaree Vitayanatpaisan, Drug Study Group, Bangkok, Thailand, Dec. 8, 1987.

27. Diane F. Walker, letter to Suntaree Vitayanatpaisan, Drug Study Group, Bangkok, Thailand, Mar. 21, 1988.

28. W. H. W. Inman, personal communication, Mar. 15, 1989.

29. *HAI News*, Feb. 1986; Francesca Lyman, "Testing, Testing, Testing," *New Internationalist*, Nov. 1986, pp. 21–24.

30. "Hoechst Withdraws Nomifensine," *Scrip*, no. 1072, Jan. 29, 1986; "Withdrawal of Nomifensine," *Lancet* 1 (1986): 281.

31. "Senator Questioning Lack of Publicity on a Drug," *New York Times*, Feb. 6, 1986.

32. L. Offerhaus, Letter to the Editor, *Nederlands Tijdschrift voor Geneeskunde* 131 (1987): 1681.

33. Phornvit Phacharintanakul, personal communication, 1991.

34. Walter Rummel, "Metamizol: Kommentar zu Berichten über lebensbedrohliche Kreislauferkrankungen," *Deutsche Ärzteblatt* 84 (1987): 2408–12.

35. "West Germany: Federal Health Office Decides on Dipyrone," *Lancet* 2 (1986): 1450–51; "West Germany: Dipyrone Put on Prescription After All," *Lancet* 1 (1987): 95.

36. "Ban of Dipyrone Combinations," *HAI News*, Apr. 1990.

37. "Bonpyrine to Be Withdrawn," *HAI News*, Aug. 1987.

38. "Dipyrone Combinations Banned," *HAI News*, Dec. 1987.

39. *Time Seems to Stop . . . When You're Suffering from Gastro-Intestinal Colic* (Bangkok: Hoechst, 1987).

40. "German MP Blasts Hoechst Over Baralgan Sales," *The Nation* (Bangkok), Oct. 21, 1987.

41. Thanong Khanathong, "Hoechst Asserts Its Drug Not Harmful," *The Nation* (Bangkok), Oct. 22, 1987.

42. Judith Richter, personal communications, 1988–90.

43. Translation of original letter, dated Nov. 24, 1987, supplied by Drug Information for Action Centre/Drug Study Group, Bangkok, 1988.

44. Phornvit Phacharintanakul, personal communication, 1991.

45. *The True Data About Spasmolytic Painkiller Combination Drugs* (Bangkok: Hoechst, 1987).

46. *Junkyard Thailand: The Fight Against Drug Dumping* (Bangkok: Drug Action for Information Centre/Drug Study Group, Sept. 1988).

47. *Dipyrone: A Drug No One Needs* (Bielefeld, Federal Republic of Germany: BUKO Pharma-Campaign, and Amsterdam: HAI-Europe, 1989).

48. Micha Levy and Samuel Shapiro, "Reply to Offerhaus," *Nederlands Tijdschrift voor Geneeskunde* 131 (1987): 1680–81; Micha Levy et al., "Analgesic Use, Agranulocytosis, and Aplastic Anemia," Letter to the Editor, *Journal of the American Medical Association* 257 (1987): 2591–92.

49. Samuel Shapiro, statement for the Philippine drug authorities concerning the risk of agranulocytosis in relation to the use of dipyrone. Aug. 15, 1989. Unpublished.

50. Hassan Nour-Eldin, personal communications, 1990–91.

Chapter 6

1. Githa Hariharan, "The Hazards of Pregnancy Tests," *Indian Express* (Bombay), July 11, 1982; Mira Shiva, personal communications, 1988–90.

2. Padma Prakash, "Dangers to the Unborn," *Indian Express* (Bombay), Jan. 25, 1987.

3. Mira Shiva, personal communications.

4. *Delhi Statesman*, May 5, 1988.

5. Mira Shiva, personal communications.

6. *A Rational Drug Policy* (New Delhi: All India Drug Action Network, 1986), pp. 113–25; Trisha Greenhalgh, "Drug Prescriptions and Self-Medication in India," *Social Science and Medicine* 25 (1987): 307.

7. *Rational Drugs Policy: Facts and Figures* (New Delhi: All India Drug Action Network, 1980), p. 58.

8. Mira Shiva, personal communications.

9. B. Palaniappan and V. Poorva Devi, "Hormones for Withdrawal Bleeding," *Journal of the Indian Medical Association* 74 (1980): 67–70.

10. D. Vengadasalam, T. H. Lean, Gary S. Berger, and Eva R. Miller, "Estrogen-Progesterone Withdrawal Bleeding in Diagnosis of Early Pregnancy," *International Journal of Gynaecology and Obstetrics* 14 (1976): 348–52.

11. "Pregnancy Drugs Can Deform Babies—Ban Them," *Onlooker* (Bombay), Apr. 1979.

12. Isabel Gal, Brian Kirman, and Jan Stern, "Hormonal Pregnancy Tests

and Congenital Malformation," *Nature* 216 (1967): 83; Isabel Gal, "Risks and Benefits of the Use of Hormonal Test Tablets," *Nature* 246 (1972): 24.

13. Edith P. Levy, Avrahm Cohen, and F. Clarke Fraser, "Hormone Treatment During Pregnancy and Congenital Heart Defects," *Lancet* 1 (1973): 611.

14. James J. Nora and Audrey H. Nora, "Birth Defects and Oral Contraceptives," *Lancet* 1 (1973): 941–42. Audrey H. Nora and James J. Nora, "A Syndrome of Multiple Congenital Anomalies Associated With Teratogenic Exposure," *Archives of Environmental Health* 30 (1975): 17–21; James J. Nora and Audrey H. Nora, "Editorial—Can the Pill Cause Birth Defects?" *New England Journal of Medicine* 291 (1974): 731–32; James J. Nora et al., "Exogenous Progestogen and Estrogen Implicated in Birth Defects," *Journal of the American Medical Association* 240 (1978): 837–43.

15. Dwight T. Janerich, Joyce M. Piper, and Donna M. Glebatis, "Oral Contraceptives and Congenital Limb-Reduction Effects," *New England Journal of Medicine* 291 (1974): 697–700; Dwight T. Janerich, Joyce Piper, and Donna M. Glebatis, "Oral Contraceptives and Birth Defects," *American Journal of Epidemiology* 112 (1980): 73–79.

16. Olli P. Heinonen, Dennis Slone, Richard R. Monson, Ernest Hook, and Samuel Shapiro, "Cardiovascular Birth Defects and Antenatal Exposure to Female Sex Hormones," *New England Journal of Medicine* 296 (1977): 67–70.

17. Pravin Kasan and Joan Andrews, "Oral Contraception and Congenital Abnormalities," *British Journal of Obstetrics and Gynaecology* 87 (1980): 545–51.

18. Nora et al., *Journal of the American Medical Association*.

19. Mira Shiva, personal communications.

20. Minister of Health and Family Welfare (India), DO No. 12-48/79-DC, Delhi, June 21, 1982; *Drug Action Network* (New Delhi: Voluntary Health Association of India, 1982); *HAI News*, Aug. 1988.

21. Marius Tausk, *Organon: The Story of an Unusual Pharmaceutical Enterprise* (Oss, the Netherlands: AKZO Pharma, 1984), pp. 16–17, 29, 32–38.

22. "Why Ban High Dose EP Drugs?" *Economic and Political Weekly*, Aug. 1, 1987.

23. *HAI News*, Oct. 1987.

24. Rita Manchando, "Public Hearings on E.P. Drugs," *Indian Post* (Bombay), June 27, 1987.

25. Mira Shiva, personal communications.

26. P. K. Bhattacharjee (Infar), letter to Drugs Controller (India), July 7, 1987.

27. Minu Jain, "EP Battle Draws to a Close," *Times of India* (New Delhi), July 9, 1987.

28. Mira Shiva, personal communications.

29. K. Klijn (Organon), letter to Peter Mansfield (MaLAM, Australia), July 13, 1988.

30. Mira Shiva, testimony, New Delhi hearing, Apr. 10, 1987.

31. Mira Shiva, personal communications.

32. *HAI News*, Oct. 1987.

33. Mira Shiva, testimony, New Delhi hearing, Apr. 10, 1987.

34. H. S. Jacobs, letter to Mira Shiva, Apr. 3, 1987.

35. Stephen Franks, letter to Mira Shiva, Apr. 3, 1987.

36. M. D. Rawlins, letter to Mira Shiva, Apr. 2, 1987.

37. Manchando, "Public Hearings on E.P. Drugs."

38. Trisha Greenhalgh, "Drug Marketing in the Third World: Beneath the Cosmetic Reforms," *Lancet* 1 (1986): 1318–20; Trisha Greenhalgh, personal communication, 1986.

39. Trisha Greenhalgh, "Drug Prescriptions and Self-Medication in India."

40. Mira Shiva, personal communications.

41. "Doctors Come to Blows," *Amrita Bazar Patrika* (Calcutta), July 11, 1987.

42. "Plea for Total Ban of EP Drugs," *Indian Post* (Bombay), July 16, 1987.

43. Menka Shivdasani, "Fast and Furious Debate on EP Drugs," *Afternoon Despatch & Courier* (Bombay), July 17/20, 1987.

44. "Industry Arguments on EP Drugs . . . Arguments Put Forward by Unichem, Organon et al.," July 2, 1987. Unpublished.

45. Mira Shiva, letter to Drugs Controller (India), July 12, 1987; Mira Shiva, testimony, Bombay hearing, July 15, 1987.

46. Pieter van Keep, personal communication, 1990.

47. *Facts About E.P. Combinations,* Unichem Laboratories, July 1987.

48. Mira Shiva, letter to Prem K. Gupta (Drugs Controller, India), June 11, 1987.

49. Pieter van Keep, personal communication.

50. Mira Shiva, letter to Drugs Controller (India), June 1, 1988.

51. Prem K. Gupta, letter to Mira Shiva, June 29, 1988.

52. Mira Shiva, letter to Milton Silverman and Mia Lydecker, Oct. 17, 1988.

53. Pieter van Keep, personal communication.

Chapter 7

1. Francis Rolt, *Pills, Policies, and Profits* (London: War on Want, 1985), pp. 53–57.

2. Rolt, p. 54.

3. Rolt, p. 19.

4. Rolt, p. 24.

5. *Bangladesh: Finding the Right Prescription* (London: War on Want, 1982).

6. Ibid.

7. "Pharmaceuticals: Merchants of Health," *Dhaka Courier*, Apr. 31, 1984.

8. Zafrullah Chowdhury, personal communication, 1988.

9. Nurum Islam, "On a National Drug Policy for Bangladesh," *Tropical Doctor* 14 (1984): 3.

10. D. C. Jayasuriya, *The Public Health and Economic Dimensions of the New Drug Policy of Bangladesh* (Washington, D.C.: Pharmaceutical Manufacturers Association, 1985).

11. *Bangladesh: Finding the Right Prescription.*

12. Andrew Veitch, "The Great Drugs Raid," *Guardian* (London), July 15, 1982.

13. Penny Chorlton, "U.S. Is Aiding Drug Companies in Bangladesh," *Washington Post*, Aug. 19, 1982.

14. S. E. Smith, "Editorial," *Tropical Doctor* 14 (1984): 1.

15. Jayasuriya, p. 2.

16. Jayasuriya, p. 2.

17. Chowdhury, personal communication.

18. Chorlton, *Washington Post*.

19. *Bangladesh: Finding the Right Prescription.*

20. Rolt, p. 42.

21. Sidney Wolfe, cited in Chorlton, *Washington Post*.

22. *Bangladesh: Finding the Right Prescription.*

23. Rolt, p. 74.

24. *Bangladesh: Finding the Right Prescription.*

25. "Drug Giants Sell On," *New Statesman*, Oct. 29, 1982.

26. Jayasuriya, p. 17.

27. S. M. Peretz, Letter to the Editor, *Tropical Doctor* 14 (1984): 7.

28. Jayasuriya, p. 17.

29. Rolt, p. 27.

30. Rolt, p. 38.

31. Jayasuriya, pp. 48–51.

32. Rolt, p. 39.

33. D. J. Tiranti, *The Bangladesh Example: Four Years On—1982–1986* (Penang, Malaysia: International Organization of Consumers Unions; Oxford: New Internationalist Publications; and London: War on Want, 1986), p. 21; *Bangladesh: Finding the Right Prescription.*

34. Rolt, p. 48.

35. Tiranti, p. 14.

36. Jayasuriya, p. 26.

37. Jayasuriya, p. 27.

38. Jayasuriya, p. 38.

39. Jayasuriya, p. 39.

40. Jayasuriya, p. 28.

41. Chowdhury, personal communication.

42. Susanne Chowdhury and Zafrullah Chowdhury, "Tubectomy by Paraprofessional Surgeons in Rural Bangladesh," *Lancet* 1 (1975): 567.

43. Chowdhury, personal communication.

44. "GPL: The Factory with a Difference," *Essential Drugs Monitor* (Geneva: World Health Organization, 1986).

45. Chowdhury, personal communication.

46. Milton Silverman and Philip R. Lee, *Pills, Profits, and Politics* (Berkeley: University of California Press, 1974).

47. Jayasuriya, p. 29.

48. Jayasuriya, p. 27.

49. Jayasuriya, p. 17.

50. Jayasuriya, pp. 12, 37.

51. Jayasuriya, p. 43.

52. Jayasuriya, pp. 2, 44.
53. Rolt, pp. 79–81; Tiranti, p. 6.
54. Rolt, pp. 83–86; Tiranti, p. 14.
55. Tiranti, p. 8.
56. Tiranti, pp. 8, 9.
57. Rolt, p. 87.
58. Michael Bennish, "The Bangladesh Drug Policy; the Next Step: Using Good Drugs 'Goodly,'" *Bangladesh Journal of Child Health* 11 (1987): 63; Bennish, personal communication, 1990.

Chapter 8

1. Raymond Bonner, "A Reporter at Large: The New Order," *New Yorker*, June 6 and June 13, 1988.
2. Stephen Jones and Raphael Pura, "All in the Family: Indonesian Decrees Help Suharto's Friends and Relations Prosper," *Asian Wall Street Journal*, Nov. 24, 1986.
3. Iwan Darmansjah, personal communication, 1988.
4. "Membongkar Skandal Obat Palsu" ("Exposing the Scandal of Counterfeit Drugs"), *Tempo* (Jakarta), May 21, 1988.
5. Kartono Mohamad, personal communication, 1988.
6. B. Lentin, *Report of the Commission of Inquiry (Re. Deaths of Patients in J. J. Hospital at Bombay in January–February 1986 Due to Alleged Reaction of Drugs* (Bombay: Government Central Press, 1988).
7. Lentin, *Report*; "Health Ministers Indicted by Probe into J. J. Hospital Tragedy," *India-West* (Emeryville, Calif.), Apr. 8, 1988; Sunil K. Pandya, "Letter from Bombay: An Unmitigated Tragedy," *British Medical Journal* 297 (1988): 117–19.
8. Antonio Carlos Zanini, personal communications, 1987–91.
9. Luiz Gonçalves Paulo, personal communication, 1987.
10. Nelson Proença, personal communication, 1987.
11. Marcio Falci, personal communication, 1987.
12. Leonardo Peach, personal communication, July 1987.
13. Antonio Carlos Zanini, personal communication.
14. Elizaldo Luiz Carlini, personal communication, 1987.
15. Antonio Carlos Zanini, personal communication; Luiz Gonçalves Paulo, personal communication.
16. Milton Silverman, Mia Lydecker, and Philip R. Lee, "The Drug Swindlers," *International Journal of Health Services* 20 (1990): 561–72.
17. "Third-World Drug Swindlers," *PMA Newsletter*, Nov. 12, 1990.
18. Tom Masland and Ruth Marshall, "The Pill Pirates," *Newsweek*, Nov. 5, 1990.

Chapter 9

1. Klaus M. Leisinger, *International Development: The Ideal and the Reality* (Basel: Ciba-Geigy, 1988), pp. 20, 61, 95.
2. Milton Silverman, Philip R. Lee, and Mia Lydecker, *Prescriptions for Death:*

The Drugging of the Third World (Berkeley: University of California Press, 1982), pp. 97–99.

3. Pharmaceutical Manufacturers Association, "Research Against Tropical Diseases Triples," *PMA Newsletter*, July 16, 1984.

4. *Progress Against Tropical Diseases: A Report from the Pharmaceutical Industry* (Washington, D.C.: Pharmaceutical Manufacturers Association, undated).

5. Leisinger, pp. 76, 77.

6. *A Program for Improved Management and Distribution of Pharmaceuticals in The Gambia: Final Report to Donors* (Washington, D.C.: Africare, 1984).

7. Alan Alemian and Gabriel Daniel, personal communications, 1988.

8. *Project Update—1986—Improved Management and Distribution of Pharmaceuticals, Sierra Leone* (Washington, D.C.: Africare, 1986).

9. *The Selection of Essential Drugs. Report of a WHO Expert Committee.* WHO Technical Report Series 615 (Geneva: World Health Organization, 1977).

10. International Federation of Pharmaceutical Manufacturers Associations, cited in Anil Agarwal, *Drugs and the Third World.* Briefing Document No. 10 (London: Earthscan Press, 1978), p. 23.

11. *Prescriptions for Death*, p. 142.

12. Agarwal, p. 34.

13. "Drugs You Can Trust at Prices You Can Afford," *Ciba-Geigy Journal*, Mar. 1983.

14. *Ciba-Geigy and the Third World: Policy, Facts, and Examples* (Basel: Ciba-Geigy, undated).

15. "Drug Firms Head Off International Restrictions with Ideas of Their Own," *Business International*, Mar. 26, 1982.

16. *The WHO and the Pharmaceutical Industry* (Penang, Malaysia: Health Action International, 1982).

17. Fritz Schneiter, personal communications, 1988–90.

18. Ibid.

19. Pharmaceutical Manufacturers Association, news release, Feb. 26, 1985.

20. *Tropicare: Three Years of Progress* (Morris Plains, N.J.: Warner-Lambert Co., undated).

21. Christian Chatelard, personal communication, 1987.

22. Mounirou Ciss, Adrian Diop, Issa Diop, and Issa Lo, personal communications, 1987.

23. Aracelia Vila, personal communications, 1987–88.

24. *Ten Years of Onchocerciasis Control in West Africa* (Geneva: World Health Organization, 1985).

25. Ibid.

26. Merck Sharp & Dohme, press release, Oct. 21, 1987.

27. W. C. Campbell, M. H. Fisher, E. O. Stapley, G. Albers-Schoenberg, T. A. Jacob, "Ivermectin: A Potent New Antiparasitic Agent," *Science* 221 (1983): 823–28.

28. Mohammed A. Aziz, Samba Diallo, Iba M. Diop, Michel Lariviere, and Mauro Porto, "Efficacy and Tolerance of Ivermectin in Human Onchocerciasis," *Lancet* 2 (1982): 171–73.

29. Mohammed A. Aziz, "Chemotherapeutic Approach to Control of Onchocerciasis," *Review of Infectious Diseases* 8 (1986): 500; S. Diallo, M. A. Aziz, M. Lariviere, J. S. Diallo, et al., "A Double-Blind Comparison of the Efficacy of Ivermectin and Diethylcarbamazine in a Placebo-Controlled Study of Senegalese Patients with Onchocerciasis," *Transactions of the Royal Society of Tropical Medicine and Hygiene* 80 (1986): 92; Samba Diallo, personal communication, 1987.

30. P. Roy Vagelos, remarks at Mectizan press briefing, Oct. 21, 1987.

Chapter 10

1. Graham Dukes, "Risk Management and Good Medicine," *International Journal of Risk and Safety in Medicine* 1 (1990): 1–3.

2. U.S. Department of Health, Education, and Welfare, Office of the Secretary, Task Force on Prescription Drugs (Washington, D.C.: U.S. Government Printing Office): *The Drug Users* (1968); *The Drug Makers and the Drug Distributors* (1968); *The Drug Prescribers* (1968); *Current American and Foreign Programs* (1968); *Approaches to Drug Insurance Design* (1969); *Final Report* (1969).

3. Milton Silverman and Philip R. Lee. *Pills, Profits, and Politics* (Berkeley: University of California Press, 1974).

4. Milton Silverman, *The Drugging of the Americas* (Berkeley: University of California Press, 1976).

5. Kurt Langbein, Hans-Peter Martin, and Hans Weiss, *Bittere Pillen* (Cologne: Verlag Kiepenheuer & Witsch, 1986).

6. Charles Medawar, statement before 10th World Congress, International Organization of Consumers Unions, The Hague, the Netherlands, June 23, 1981.

7. Milton Silverman, Philip R. Lee, and Mia Lydecker, *Prescriptions for Death: The Drugging of the Third World* (Berkeley: University of California Press, 1982).

8. Mahmoud Hussein, personal communication, 1988.

9. Sylvestre Frenk and Jorge Olarte (Mexico City); Enrique Segovia (Mérida); Raul Fernandez Barbosa, Jacinto Convit, and Honorio Silva (Caracas); and Nelson Proença (São Paulo), personal communications, 1988.

10. Jorge Olarte, personal communication, 1988.

11. Iwan Darmansjah, personal communication, 1988.

12. Colin Forbes, personal communication, 1988.

13. "MaLAM's Origins," *MaLAM Newsletter*, Dec. 1988.

14. V. A. Wade, P. R. Mansfield, and P. J. McDonald, "Drug Companies' Evidence to Justify Advertising," *Lancet* 2 (1989): 1261.

15. "Breast-Milk Substitutes: Violations of WHO Code of Marketing," *Lancet* 2 (1987): 1349.

16. K. Balasubramaniam, *The Pharmaceutical Sector in the Third World: A Strategy for Collective Self-Reliance* (Penang, Malaysia: Consumers' Association of Penang, 1984); Kumariah Balasubramaniam, personal communications, 1984–90.

17. "Attack on Pharmaceutical Companies Part of Larger Plan, Kirkpatrick Says," *PMA Newsletter*, Apr. 14, 1986.

18. Jill Turner, "Antibiotic Conference Cancelled for Second Time," *Lancet* 1 (1986): 333.

Chapter 11

1. Lennart Berggren and Olle Hansson, "Treating Acrodermatitis Enteropathica," *Lancet* 1 (1966): 52.

2. Milton Silverman, Philip R. Lee, and Mia Lydecker, *Prescriptions for Death: The Drugging of the Third World* (Berkeley: University of California Press, 1982), pp. 48–50.

3. Paul Erni, *The Basel Marriage: History of the Ciba-Geigy Merger* (Zurich: Neue Zürcher Zeitung, 1979), p. 73.

4. Lennart Berggren and Olle Hansson, "Absorption of Intestinal Antiseptics Derived from 8-Hydroxyquinolines," *Journal of Clinical Pharmacology and Therapeutics* 9 (1968): 67.

5. Olle Hansson, personal communications, 1979–85, notably Dec. 19–24, 1984.

6. Hamilton H. Anderson and Dorothy A. Koch, "Iodochloroxyquinoline (Vioform N.N.R.) as an Amebecide in Macaques," *Proceedings of the Society for Experimental Biology and Medicine* 28 (1931): 828–41.

7. Norman A. David, Herbert C. Johnstone, A. C. Reed, and Chauncey D. Leake, "The Treatment of Amebiasis with Iodochlorhydroxyquinoline (Vioform N.N.R.)," *Journal of the American Medical Association* 100 (1933): 1658–61.

8. P. Busse Grawitz, "Nuevas orientaciones en la terapéutica de la amebiasis," *Semana Médica* 42 (1935): 525–29; Enrique Barros, "Amebas, y mas amebas," *Semana Médica* 42 (1935): 907–908.

9. Paul Hangartner, "Troubles nerveux observés chez le chien après absorption d'Entero-Vioforme Ciba," *Schweizer Archiv für Tierheilkunde* 107 (1965): 43.

10. Olle Hansson, "Oxyquinoline Intoxication Outside Japan, Its Recognition and the Scope of the Problem," in *Drug-Induced Sufferings: Medical, Pharmaceutical and Legal Aspects. Proceedings of the Kyoto International Conference Against Drug-Induced Sufferings, 14–18 April 1979, Kyoto*, ed. T. Soda (Amsterdam: Excerpta Medica, 1980), pp. 429–32.

11. Oliver Gillie, "How Safe Is This Holiday-Tummy Pill?" *Sunday Times* (London), May 22, 1977.

12. Tadao Tsubaki, Yasuo Toyokura, and Hiroshi Tsukagoshi, "Subacute Myelo-Optico-Neuropathy Following Abdominal Symptoms. A Clinical and Pathological Study," *Japanese Journal of Medicine* 4 (1965): 181–84.

13. Olle Hansson, *Arzneimittel-Multis und der SMON Skandal: Die Hintergründe einer Arzneimittelkatastrophe* (Berlin: Arzneimittel-Informations-Dienst, 1979), pp. 22–24.

14. Kiyohiko Katahira, Kugahisa Teshima, Hidehiro Sugisawa, Shigeki Kuzuhara, and Reisako Kono, "An International Survey on the Recent Reports Concerning Intoxication with Halogenated Oxyquinoline Derivatives and the Regulations Against Their Use," in *Drug-Induced Sufferings*, pp. 441–55.

15. Toshio Higashida, "The Characteristics and Prevention of Drug-Induced Suffering in Japan," in *Drug-Induced Sufferings*, pp. 401–3.

16. Norman A. David, N. M. Phatak, and F. B. Zener, "Iodochlorhydroxyquinoline and Diiodohydroxyquinoline: Animal Toxicity and Absorption in Man," *American Journal of Tropical Diseases* 24 (1944): 29–33; Norman A. David,

"Uncontrolled Use of Oral Amebecides," *Journal of the American Medical Association* 129 (1945): 572.

17. B. H. Kean and Somerset R. Waters, "The Diarrhea of Travelers. III. Drug Prophylaxis in Mexico," *New England Journal of Medicine* 261 (1959): 71–74.

18. Tadao Tsubaki, Yoshiaki Honma, and Makato Hoshi, "Neurological Syndrome Associated with Clioquinol," *Lancet* 1 (1971): 696–97; Tadao Tsubaki, "Etiology of SMON: An Early Study and Its Development," in *Drug-Induced Sufferings*, pp. 423–28.

19. Olle Hansson, tape-recorded interview, Dec. 19–24, 1984.

20. *Drug-Induced Sufferings*.

21. Ichiro Matsubara, statement before Tokyo District Court, May 16, 1979.

22. Hiroshi Izumi and Etsuro Totsuka, personal communications, 1980–91; Walter Wenger, personal communications, 1985–88.

23. "Apology to SMON Plaintiffs by Ciba-Geigy (Japan) Ltd." *Proceedings, Geneva Press Conference on SMON, April 28, 1980* (Tokyo: Organizing Committee of Geneva Press Conference on SMON, 1980), Appendix IV, p. 36.

24. Walter Wenger, personal communication, June 17, 1985.

25. Milton Silverman, *The Drugging of the Americas* (Berkeley: University of California Press, 1976); Silverman, Lee, and Lydecker, *Prescriptions for Death*.

26. Dianna Melrose, *Bitter Pills: Medicines and the Third World Poor* (Oxford: OXFAM, 1982).

27. Mike Muller, *The Health of Nations: A North-South Investigation* (London: Faber and Faber, 1982).

28. Olle Hansson, letter to Louis von Planta, Aug. 22, 1983.

29. Olle Hansson, *Inside Ciba-Geigy* (Penang, Malaysia: International Organization of Consumers Unions, 1989), p. 63.

30. Walter von Wartburg, personal communication, Apr. 3, 1985.

31. Ulrich Moebius, personal communication, 1985.

32. Klaus von Grebmer, personal communications, 1985–91; Walter Wenger, personal communication, June 17, 1985.

33. Walter von Wartburg, personal communication, Apr. 3, 1985.

34. Olle Hansson, letter to Louis von Planta, Dec. 8, 1984.

35. Walter Wenger, personal communication, June 17, 1985.

36. Olle Hansson, *Inside Ciba-Geigy.*

Chapter 12

1. Milton Silverman and Philip R. Lee, *Pills, Profits, and Politics* (Berkeley: University of California Press, 1974), pp. 83, 84.

2. Ibid., pp. 86, 87.

3. Ibid., pp. 94–96.

4. Ibid., pp. 38, 39.

5. B. Cromie, "Present Problems: The Effects of British Regulations," *Medicines for the Year 2000* (London: Office of Health Economics, 1979).

6. Graham Dukes, *The Effects of Drug Regulation* (Lancaster, England: MTP Press, 1985), pp. 22, 23.

7. Philip R. Lee and Jessica Herzstein, "International Drug Regulation," *Annual Review of Public Health* 7 (1986): 217–35.

8. Dukes, p. 106.

9. Dukes, p. 104.

10. Lee and Herzstein, p. 226.

11. Lee and Herzstein, p. 225.

12. Dukes, pp. 29, 30; Olav M. Bakke, William M. Wardell, and Louis Lasagna, "Drug Discontinuations in the United Kingdom and the United States, 1964 to 1983: Issues of Safety," *Clinical Pharmacology and Therapeutics* 35 (1984): 559–67.

13. *Pills, Profits, and Politics*, p. 237.

14. Ibid., pp. 64, 105, 106, 238.

15. Ibid., pp. 119, 238.

16. Siegbert and Elly Holz, personal communication, 1987.

17. Raul J. Fernandez Barboza, personal communication, 1987.

18. "Rational Use of Drugs: Cooperation Prevails at WHO Conference in 'Spirit of Nairobi,'" WHO press release, Geneva, Dec. 3, 1985.

19. "WHO Conference of Experts on the Rational Use of Drugs," *HAI News*, Feb. 1986.

20. Gerald J. Mossinghoff, letter to Pharmaceutical Manufacturers Association Board of Directors, Dec. 1, 1985.

21. "Right Under the Wire: Carter Signs Hazardous Substance Export Policy," *PMA Newsletter*, Jan. 18, 1981.

22. "Reagan Revokes Hazardous Substances Export Policy," *PMA Newsletter*, Feb. 23, 1981.

23. "Don't Export Unapproved Drugs," editorial, *New York Times*, Sept. 12, 1984.

24. Gerald Mossinghoff, "Drug Exports Ban Costing U.S. Jobs and Investment, PMA Tells Senate Committee," *PMA Newsletter*, June 10, 1985.

25. "Administration Supports Revisions," *PMA Newsletter*, June 10, 1985.

26. "Drug Exports, Vaccine Compensation in Omnibus Bill Passed by Congress," *PMA Newsletter*, Oct. 27, 1986; "Controversial Drug Export Bill Enacted at Last Moment," *Lancet* 2 (1986): 1389.

27. Joost van der Meer, "Exports of Medicines from the EEC: HAI Time for Action," *HAI News*, Feb. 1989.

28. Health Program, Office of Technology Assessment, U.S. Congress, *Drug Labeling in Developing and Newly-Industrialized Countries* (Washington, D.C.: U.S. Government Printing Office, in preparation).

Chapter 13

1. Milton Silverman, *The Drugging of the Americas* (Berkeley: University of California Press, 1976), p. 106.

2. Ibid., pp. 132, 133.

3. Milton Silverman, Philip R. Lee, and Mia Lydecker, *Prescriptions for Death: The Drugging of the Third World* (Berkeley: University of California Press, 1982), p. 148.

4. *Prescriptions for Death*; Milton Silverman, Philip R. Lee, and Mia Lydecker, "Drug Promotion: The Third World Revisited," *International Journal of Health Services* 16 (1986): 659–67; Milton Silverman, Mia Lydecker, and Philip R. Lee, "The Drug Swindlers," *International Journal of Health Services* 20 (1990): 561–72.

5. World Health Organization, *Guidelines for Developing National Drug Policies* (Geneva: World Health Organization, 1988); U.S. Congress, Office of Technology Assessment, Health Program, *Drug Labeling in Developing and Newly-Industrialized Countries.* Interim Report, Appendix C (Washington, D.C.: Office of Technology Assessment, 1988).

6. *Drug Labeling in Developing and Newly Industrialized Countries*, Interim Report, pp. 14, 15; Calvin M. Kunin, ed., "Proceedings of the Conference: Pharmacoepidemiology in Developing Countries," *Journal of Clinical Epidemiology* 44, Supp. II (1991): 1S–4S.

7. "WHA Applauds Essential Drug Report," *Scrip*, May 25, 1990.

8. Ibid.; Stuart L. Nightingale, statement before 43rd World Health Assembly, May 7–8, 1990, Geneva.

9. "Commerce Chief Sees Need for 'Little Bribes,'" *San Francisco Chronicle*, Mar. 24, 1981; Norman C. Miller, "U.S. Business Overseas: Back to Bribery?" *Wall Street Journal*, Apr. 30, 1981.

10. *Prescriptions for Death*, p. 133.

11. "Wages of Singapore," *Wall Street Journal*, Aug. 16, 1990.

12. Kurt Langbein, Hans Peter Martin, Hans Weiss, and Roland Werner, *Gesunde Geschäfte: Die Praktiken der Pharma-Industrie* (Cologne: Kiepenheuer and Witsch, 1981).

13. Charles van der Horst, Mark Grayson, and Sidney Wolfe, cited in Carla Atkinson and John Geiger, "Just Say No?" *Public Citizen*, Mar.–Apr. 1991, pp. 12–14.

14. *Prescriptions for Death*, p. 139.

15. *Drug Labeling in Developing and Newly-Industrialized Countries*, Interim Report, Appendix B.

INDEX

In this index an "f" after a number indicates a separate reference on the next page, and an "ff" indicates separate references on the next two pages. A continuous discussion over two or more pages is indicated by a span of page numbers, e.g., "57–59." *Passim* is used for a cluster of references in close but not consecutive sequence. Subentries are listed in page number order rather than alphabetical order.

Library of Congress Cataloging-in-Publication Data

Silverman, Milton, 1910–
    Bad medicine: the prescription drug industry in the Third World /
    Milton Silverman, Mia Lydecker, and Philip R. Lee.
        p.   cm.
    Includes bibliographical references and index.
    ISBN 0-8047-1669-2 (cloth: alk. paper)
    1. Pharmaceutical industry—Developing countries—Corrupt
    practices.   2. Pharmaceutical policy—Developing countries.
    I. Lydecker, Mia, 1926—   .   II. Lee, Philip R. (Philip Randolph).
    1924–   .   III. Title.
    [DNLM: 1. —Developing Countries.   2. Drug Industry—standards.
    QV 736vs587b]
    HD9674.D44S54   1992
    338.4'76151'091724—dc20
    DNLM/DLC   91-5085
    for Library of Congress   CIP

⊗   This book is printed on acid-free paper.